AWS for System Administrators
Second Edition

Build, automate, and operate scalable cloud infrastructure on AWS

Marcel Neidinger

Prashant Lakhera

AWS for System Administrators
Second Edition

Portfolio Director: Kartikey Pandey
Relationship Lead: Deepak Kumar
Project Manager: Sonam Pandey
Content Engineer: Arun Nadar
Proofreader: Arun Nadar
Technical Editor: Simran Ali
Copy Editor: Safis Editing
Indexer: Manju Arasan
Production Designer: Ganesh Bhadwalkar
Growth Lead: Amit Ramadas

First published: February 2021
Second edition: May 2025

Production reference: 3071125

Published by Packt Publishing Ltd.
Grosvenor House
11 St Paul's Square
Birmingham
B3 1RB, UK.

ISBN 978-1-83546-366-6
www.packtpub.com

To my mom and dad – the most important writers in my life.

*And to my (former) colleagues Julio, Andy, and Michał – I wouldn't be where
I am today professionally without you.*

Contributors

About the authors

Marcel Neidinger is a developer turned solutions architect with a focus on cloud networking. He holds four AWS certifications, including SysOps Associate and Advanced Networking Specialty. Marcel has a passion for automation and previously wrote a book about network automation in Python.

I want to thank my manager Philipp Knecht for supporting me in writing this book. Michael, Frederic, Sven, Simon, Bernhard, Nikola, Christian, and Malte – thank you for your friendship and for bearing with me during this time.

Prashant Lakhera (lakhera2015 on Twitter) is an X-RHCA (Red Hat Certified Architect) and a seasoned Linux and open source specialist with over 15 years of enterprise open source experience.

Having a positive impact on the world is important to him, which is why he shares his knowledge with others through his website, blog posts, and YouTube channel, which also helps him to dig deep into topics and build on his expertise.

About the reviewer

Saurabh Dhawan is an AWS and GenAI certified enterprise architect with over 20 years of IT experience. He has first-hand knowledge of building cloud-native solutions and a number of years of consulting experience.

Saurabh has worked in a number of companies across the world in various roles and is currently part of the Enterprise Architecture team in a New Zealand government department. He also reviewed the previous edition of this book.

I am grateful to Packt Publishing for the opportunity to review this book. I also want to extend my thanks to everyone who contributes to my learning and growth every day—whether at home, at work, through YouTube videos, web publishers, and more.

Table of Contents

Part 2: Building Infrastructure   49

3

Creating a Data Center in the Cloud Using a VPC   51

4

Scalable Compute Capacity in the Cloud via EC2   81

Part 3: Scalability and Elasticity of our Cloud Infrastructure   103

5

Increasing Application Fault Tolerance and Efficiency with Elastic Load Balancing   105

6

Increasing Application Performance Using AWS Auto Scaling   125

7

Scaling a Relational Database in the Cloud Using Amazon Relational Database Service (RDS)   147

8

Managing Secrets and Encryption Keys with AWS Secrets Manager and KMS   167

Part 4: Monitoring, Metrics, and the Backup Layer   195

9

Centralized Logging and Monitoring with Amazon CloudWatch   197

10

Centralizing Cloud Backup Solutions   233

Part 5: Deployments at Scale   281

Preface

Welcome to the fascinating world of **systems operations** – or **SysOps** – in AWS. *AWS for System Administrators, Second Edition* is your introduction to deploying, automating, and operating workloads in AWS. Over its 17 chapters, this book introduces you to the tools and techniques required to operate workloads in the cloud.

After finishing this book, you'll have explored the world of scalable compute, learned how to automate the deployment of relational databases, set up a multi-account organization, and much more.

Throughout the book, you'll see hands-on examples of automating the deployment of these infrastructure components through the use of Infrastructure-as-Code tools such as Terraform or CloudFormation. You'll get architectural guidance and explanations for the central concepts of operating workloads within AWS.

Who this book is for

This book is designed for technology professionals with some basic cloud experience who aim to understand how to automate and operate software systems and their underlying infrastructure on AWS.

Whether you are a systems administrator, DevOps engineer, or solutions architect looking into getting the most out of AWS, this book will enable you to better understand the challenges and the solutions involved when running applications on AWS.

A basic understanding of cloud concepts and services within AWS as well as some familiarity with IT tools such as Git and Terraform and a programming language such as Python is recommended. But if you don't have these prerequisites, the book offers explanations to bring you up to speed on these concepts.

Use this book to get started on your journey to becoming a systems operator on AWS!

What this book covers

Chapter 1, Setting Up the AWS Environment, introduces you to the basics of setting up an account on AWS as well as the **Infrastructure-as-Code (IaC)** tools we'll use throughout this book: Terraform, CloudFormation, and AWS **Cloud Development Kit (CDK)**.

Chapter 2, Protecting Your AWS Account Using IAM, explains the concepts of the **Identity and Access Management (IAM)** service that is used throughout AWS for authentication and authorization.

Chapter 3, Creating a Data Center in the Cloud Using a VPC, covers the basic networking concepts of the **virtual private cloud** (**VPC**) – your *data center* in AWS.

Chapter 4, Scalable Compute Capacity in the Cloud via EC2, looks at concepts of **Elastic Compute Cloud** (**EC2**) – the AWS service to provision virtual machines within AWS.

Chapter 5, Increasing Application Fault-Tolerance and Efficiency with Elastic Load Balancing, explains how we can use **Elastic Load Balancing** (**ELB**) to route traffic between multiple instances to increase fault-tolerance and efficiency.

Chapter 6, Increasing Application Performance Using AWS Auto Scaling, covers how we can use Auto Scaling Groups in AWS to automatically scale our compute up or down.

Chapter 7, Scaling a Relational Database in the Cloud Using Amazon Relational Database Service (RDS), explains how to deploy an open source Postgres database using the Amazon **Relational Database Service** (**RDS**) and explores the concept of managed services.

Chapter 8, Managing Secrets and Encryption Keys with AWS Secrets Manager and KMS, teaches you how to handle secrets such as passwords or access tokens as well as the basic concepts of encryption in the cloud.

Chapter 9, Centralized Logging and Monitoring with Amazon CloudWatch, explains how you can use CloudWatch and SNS for centralized logging, metrics, and alerting on AWS.

Chapter 10, Centralizing Cloud Backup Solutions, explains AWS Backup and how you can use this service to implement backup plans.

Chapter 11, Disaster Recovery Options with AWS, explores the different options available to architect resilient applications on AWS. The chapter also explains the key concepts of **Recovery Time Objective** (**RTO**) and **Recovery Point Objective** (**RPO**).

Chapter 12, Testing the Resilience of Your Infrastructure and Architecture with AWS Fault Injection Service, introduces you to chaos engineering and AWS **Fault Injection Service** (**FIS**) – a service that lets you inject failures into your AWS-deployed applications to test their ability to withstand such failures when they happen in production.

Chapter 13, Deploying Infrastructure Using CI/CD Pipelines, covers the topic of automated infrastructure rollout based on IaC code that is stored in the version control system git.

Chapter 14, Building Reusable Infrastructure-as-Code Components, covers patterns and best practices when building reusable components for your teams to scale IaC usage.

Chapter 15, Ensuring Compliance Using AWS Config and SCPs, introduces two different methods, a proactive and reactive way, to block or detect the creation of infrastructure that is non-compliant with your set of rules and requirements.

Chapter 16, Operating in a Multi-Account Environment, introduces AWS Organizations as a way to set up the multiple AWS accounts usually required when operating a real-world application in the cloud.

Chapter 17, End-to-End Deployment of an Application, uses the tools, techniques, and concepts learned throughout the book to cover the end-to-end deployment of an application. From account setup to deployment pipeline and fault testing, this chapter shows how all the concepts introduced throughout this book fit together.

To get the most out of this book

To make full use of this book, you should have a working knowledge of cloud computing concepts, AWS services, and a basic understanding of computer networking concepts such as subnets, IP addresses, and CIDR ranges.

Throughout this book, we'll use IaC tools such as CloudFormation, Terraform, and CDK to automate the creation of our infrastructure and its maintenance. A working knowledge of at least one of these tools as well as a working knowledge of the Python programming language is beneficial.

You'll also need an AWS account to which you can test the hands-on learning parts of this book. Be advised that the examples in this book will incur a charge for the provisioned infrastructure.

An internet connection is required to interact with AWS and to download and install the required tools (see the following table).

Software/hardware covered in the book	OS requirement
AWS CLI	Windows, Linux, or macOS
Git	Windows, Linux, or macOS
Visual Studio Code (or similar code editor)	Windows, Linux, or macOS
Docker / Docker Desktop	Windows, Linux, or macOS
Python	Windows, Linux, or macOS
Node.js	Windows, Linux, or macOS (optional)
Web browser	Windows, Linux, or macOS
Terraform	Windows, Linux, or macOS

The required software is listed in the *Technical requirements* section of the applicable chapter.

Download the example code files

You can download the example code files for this book from GitHub at `https://github.com/PacktPublishing/AWS-for-System-Administrators-Second-Edition`. If there's an update to the code, it will be updated on the existing GitHub repository.

We also have other code bundles from our rich catalog of books and videos available at https://github.com/PacktPublishing/. Check them out!

Code in Action

The Code in Action videos for this book can be viewed at https://packt.link/vQuEI

Conventions used

There are a number of text conventions used throughout this book.

Code in text: Indicates code words in text, database table names, folder names, filenames, file extensions, pathnames, dummy URLs, user input, and Twitter handles. Here is an example: "We'll modify the previously created setup.tf file in order to create our ALB."

A block of code is set as follows:

```
tags = {
  Name = "Main ALB"
  }
}
```

When we wish to draw your attention to a particular part of a code block, the relevant lines or items are set in bold:

```
def lambda_handler(event, context):
    url = SLACK_HOOK
    msg = {
        "channel": SLACK_CHANNEL,
        "username": "WEBHOOK_USERNAME",
        "text": event["Records"][0]["Sns"]["Message"],
        "icon_emoji": "",
    }
```

Any command-line input or output is written as follows:

```
sudo /opt/aws/amazon-cloudwatch-agent/bin/amazon-cloudwatch-agent-ctl
-a fetch-config -m ec2 -c file:/opt/aws/amazon-cloudwatch-agent/bin/
config.json -s
```

Bold: Indicates a new term, an important word, or words that you see onscreen. For instance, words in menus or dialog boxes appear in **bold**. Here is an example: "Click the **Configuration** tab and then select **Environment variables** in the left navigation."

> **Tips or important notes**
> Appear like this.

Get in touch

Feedback from our readers is always welcome.

General feedback: If you have questions about any aspect of this book, email us at customercare@ packtpub.com and mention the book title in the subject of your message.

Errata: Although we have taken every care to ensure the accuracy of our content, mistakes do happen. If you have found a mistake in this book, we would be grateful if you would report this to us. Please visit www.packtpub.com/support/errata and fill in the form.

Piracy: If you come across any illegal copies of our works in any form on the internet, we would be grateful if you would provide us with the location address or website name. Please contact us at copyright@packt.com with a link to the material.

If you are interested in becoming an author: If there is a topic that you have expertise in and you are interested in either writing or contributing to a book, please visit authors.packtpub.com.

Reviews

Please leave a review. Once you have read and used this book, why not leave a review on the site that you purchased it from? Potential readers can then see and use your unbiased opinion to make purchase decisions, we at Packt can understand what you think about our products, and our authors can see your feedback on their book. Thank you!

For more information about Packt, please visit packt.com.

Free Benefits with Your Book

This book comes with free benefits to support your learning. Activate them now for instant access (see the "*How to Unlock*" section for instructions).

Here's a quick overview of what you can instantly unlock with your purchase:

PDF and ePub Copies   **Next-Gen Web-Based Reader**

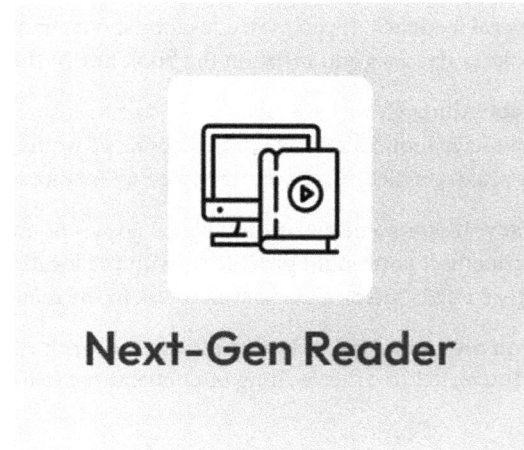

Access a DRM-free PDF copy of this book to read anywhere, on any device.

Use a DRM-free ePub version with your favorite e-reader.

Multi-device progress sync: Pick up where you left off, on any device.

Highlighting and notetaking: Capture ideas and turn reading into lasting knowledge.

Bookmarking: Save and revisit key sections whenever you need them.

Dark mode: Reduce eye strain by switching to dark or sepia themes

How to Unlock

UNLOCK NOW

Scan the QR code (or go to `packtpub.com/unlock`). Search for this book by name, confirm the edition, and then follow the steps on the page.

Note: Keep your invoice handly. Purchase made directly from packt don't require one.

Share Your Thoughts

Once you've read *AWS for System Administrators, Second Edition* we'd love to hear your thoughts! Scan the QR code below to go straight to the Amazon review page for this book and share your feedback.

https://packt.link/r/1835463665

Your review is important to us and the tech community and will help us make sure we're delivering excellent quality content.

Stay Sharp in Cloud and DevOps – Join 44,000+ Subscribers of CloudPro

CloudPro is a weekly newsletter for cloud professionals who want to stay current on the fast-evolving world of cloud computing, DevOps, and infrastructure engineering.

Every issue delivers focused, high-signal content on topics like:

- AWS, GCP & multi-cloud architecture

- Containers, Kubernetes & orchestration

- Infrastructure as Code (IaC) with Terraform, Pulumi, etc.

- Platform engineering & automation workflows

- Observability, performance tuning, and reliability best practices

Whether you're a cloud engineer, SRE, DevOps practitioner, or platform lead, CloudPro helps you stay on top of what matters, without the noise.

Scan the QR code to join for free and get weekly insights straight to your inbox:

https://packt.link/cloudpro

Part 1:
AWS Services and Tools

In this part, we'll look into the initial setup of your AWS environment and the installation of tools such as Terraform, CDK, CloudFormation, and the AWS CLI that will be used throughout the book to automate the deployment of your infrastructure. We'll then see how authorization and authentication are handled within AWS through IAM.

This part contains the following chapters:

- *Chapter 1, Setting Up the AWS Environment*
- *Chapter 2, Protecting Your AWS Account Using IAM*

1

Setting Up the AWS Environment

AWS and the cloud have fundamentally changed the way we operate infrastructure. Before the cloud, most companies would operate data centers, where they would buy compute and network resources such as servers, routers, and switches. All this hardware would then be set up, maintained, and operated.

In contrast, the cloud has not only changed the way we procure infrastructure (shifting from a model with large capital expenditures for buying hardware to a *pay-as-you-go* model) but also changed the way we operate this infrastructure. Instead of cabling servers and switches, everything in the cloud is software-defined and just one **application programming interface** (**API**) call away.

This chapter starts off the journey to cloud-based systems operations by installing the tools that will be used throughout the book. We begin by installing the AWS **command-line interface** (**CLI**), a versatile tool that allows us to interact with resources in the AWS Cloud from our terminal.

Next, we'll set up Boto3, the **software development kit** (**SDK**) for the Python programming language that will be used throughout the book to write automation scripts. And finally, we'll set up three different **infrastructure-as-code** (**IaC**) tools. IaC allows us to specify our infrastructure (such as a compute instance in Amazon EC2 or a bucket in Amazon S3) in code and thus treat our infrastructure configuration as we would treat software.

First, we'll set up CloudFormation, the AWS-native tool for the declarative definition of our infrastructure. Next, we'll set up the AWS **Cloud Development Kit** (**CDK**), which allows us to define our infrastructure in a high-level programming language such as Python and then have it automatically translated into CloudFormation. Lastly, we'll install Terraform from HashiCorp. Terraform is a declarative IaC tool that, besides AWS, can also be used for other cloud providers such as Microsoft Azure or **Google Cloud Platform** (**GCP**) as well as on-premises infrastructure.

In this chapter, we're going to cover the following main topics:

- Setting up the environment
- Introducing Boto3 for Python
- What is CloudFormation?
- Exploring the AWS CDK
- Introducing Terraform

Free Benefits with Your Book

Your purchase includes a free PDF copy of this book along with other exclusive benefits. Check the *Free Benefits with Your Book* section in the Preface to unlock them instantly and maximize your learning experience.

Technical requirements

Before following this section, please create an AWS account for yourself. You can sign up at `https://aws.amazon.com`. A basic understanding of AWS – for example, what a service is – will be beneficial to the understanding of this chapter.

A fundamental understanding of Python will help with the programming-based sections of this chapter. A basic understanding of IaC tools such as Terraform and the Linux command line will help you with following along in this chapter.

The commands in this chapter assume that you are using a Linux-based operating system. We will point out the Windows version where needed and possible.

You'll also need the following software installed on your system:

- Python version 3.8 or later
- Node.js version 14.15.0 or later

Both of these version requirements are at the time of writing in May 2024. You can check the following links for the required versions:

- For Python: `https://boto3.amazonaws.com/v1/documentation/api/latest/guide/quickstart.html#install-or-update-python`
- For Node.js: `https://docs.aws.amazon.com/cdk/v2/guide/getting_started.html#getting_started_prerequisites`

All scripts from this chapter can be found at the following GitHub link:

`https://github.com/PacktPublishing/AWS-for-System-Administrators-Second-Edition.`

The CiA video for this chapter can be found at `https://packt.link/vi5WB`

Setting up the environment

AWS offers two ways of interacting with its services. One is the web interface, and the other is the API. The API is used by tools such as the AWS CLI or Terraform for programmatic interactions, while the web interface allows us to configure resources by clicking. Throughout this book, we'll refer to the web interface (the **AWS Management Console**, which you can find at `https://console.aws.amazon.com`) as the *AWS Console* and will refer to the tool that you can use on the terminal as the *AWS CLI*.

The AWS CLI, Terraform, CloudFormation, and CDK all interact with the AWS services via the API and need to authenticate themselves against the API with an AWS access key and a secret access key.

For our initial setup, we'll create an **Identity and Access Management** (**IAM**) user using the AWS Console. We can then use the access key ID and secret access key from our newly created IAM user to authenticate ourselves in the AWS CLI.

> **Important note**
>
> For our first steps, we'll be using a simple IAM user with long-lived credentials and a broad access policy that operates in the root account. Throughout the book, we'll tighten the security to adhere to AWS best practices by tightening the policy to least-privilege access, using short-lived credentials, and an AWS organization.

Don't worry if these words don't mean too much to you right now. After finishing the book, you'll understand all these concepts. For now, let's start the setup:

1. Navigate to `https://console.aws.amazon.com` and log in with your username, password, and **multi-factor authentication (MFA)** details. Once you are logged in, search for `IAM` and open up the **Identity and Access Management (IAM)** service. In **IAM Dashboard**, click on **Users** in the left-hand navigation.

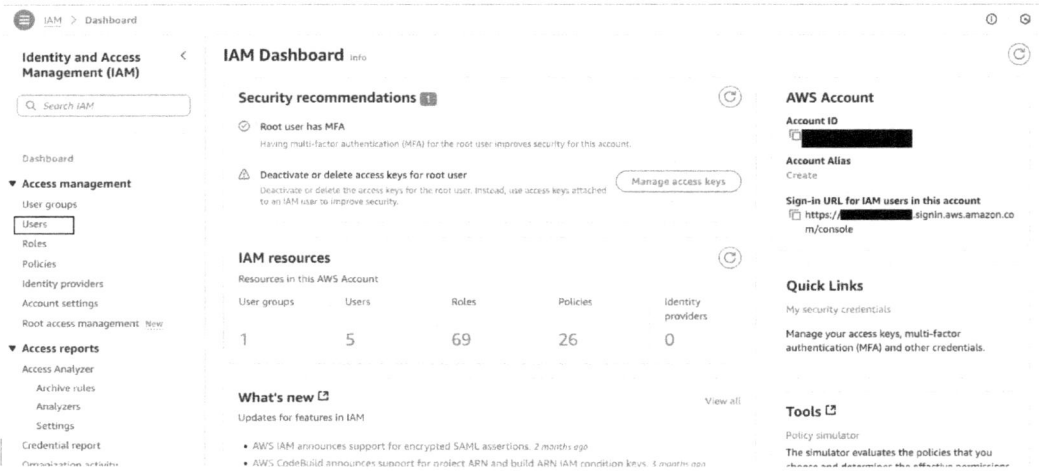

Figure 1.1 – Interface of the AWS IAM service in the AWS console

2. Click on **Create User** to create a new user. In the next window, specify a username (i.e., `packt`) and click **Next**.

3. On the **Set permissions** screen (see the following figure), select **Attach policies directly**. Then, search for and select an **AWS managed - job function** policy called **AdminstratorAccess**.

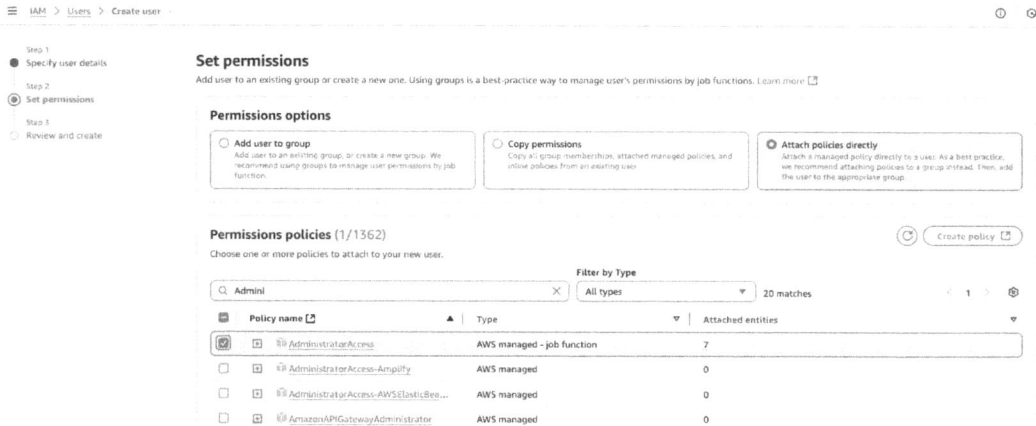

Figure 1.2 – Interface to set permissions in the AWS console

> **Important note**
>
> It is a best practice to assign the least privileges required to a user. You should thus rarely need to assign *Administrator* access directly to a user. In the following chapters, we'll tighten this security to adhere to this principle.

4.   On the review page, click **Create user** to create the new user. You'll be taken back to the overview of IAM users in your account.

5.   To retrieve your credentials, click on the username you just created.

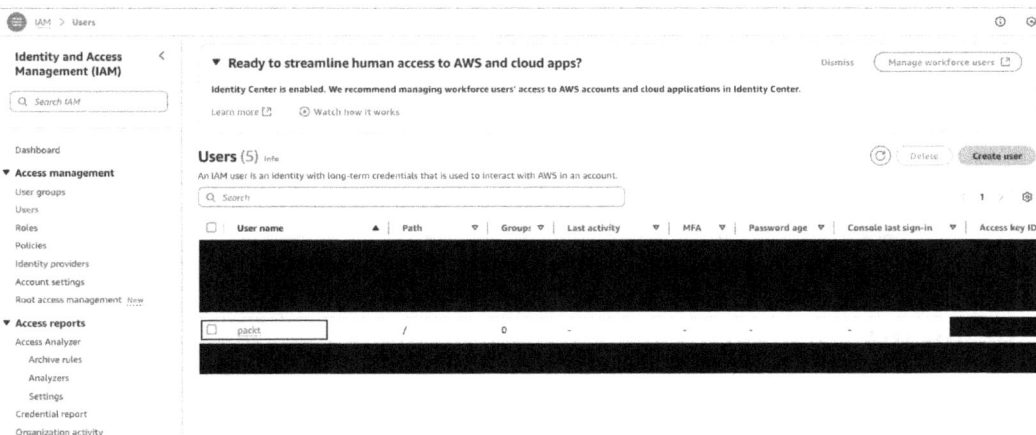

Figure 1.3 – Overview of users in IAM

6. On the user details page, click on the **Create access key** link to create your access key. The link is highlighted in red in the following figure.

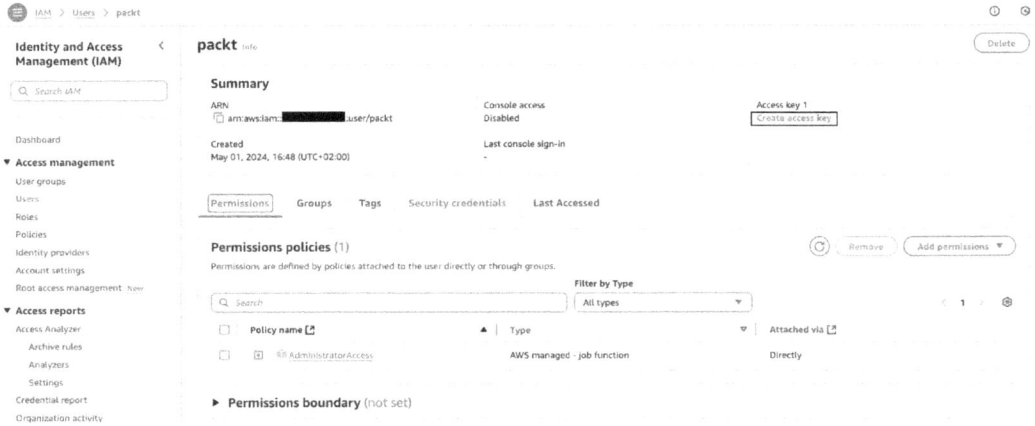

Figure 1.4 – Details view of your newly created user

7. On the **Access key best practices & alternatives** page, select the **Command Line Interface (CLI)** use case and check the checkbox saying **I understand the above recommendations and want to proceed to create an access key**.

Note that we'll be following the recommendations provided by AWS in the following chapters and setting up short-lived tokens.

8. On the next page, click **Create access key**. You'll be shown an access key and a secret access key. Copy both.

> **Important note**
>
> Note down your access key and secret access key. The secret access key can't be retrieved again after you leave this page.
>
> Also, *never* commit these into a source code repository. Otherwise, people with access to your source code repository could extract these credentials and use them to gain access to the AWS user.

Installing the AWS CLI

The AWS CLI is written in Python and you'll thus need Python installed on your system:

1. If you are on an X86 machine on a Linux-based operating system, run the following command to download the latest version of the CLI:

```
curl "https://awscli.amazonaws.com/awscli-exe-linux-x86_64.zip"
-o "awscliv2.zip"
```

If you are on a Windows machine, use the following command:

```
msiexec.exe /i https://awscli.amazonaws.com/AWSCLIV2.msi
```

If you are on an ARM-based system on a Linux-based operating system, run the following command:

```
curl "https://awscli.amazonaws.com/awscli-exe-linux-aarch64.zip"
-o "awscliv2.zip"
```

2. Next, unzip the package:

```
unzip awscliv2.zip
```

3. Then, run the installer:

```
sudo ./aws/install
```

You can verify the installation by running this command:

```
aws --version
```

With the AWS CLI now installed on our system, we can use the `aws configure` command to set up our user by using the credentials we retrieved from the AWS console in the previous steps.

To do this, run the following command that will ask you for some information such as the previously retrieved AWS access and secret access keys. For the default region, use `us-east-1` for now:

```
aws configure
AWS Access Key ID [None]: XXXXXXXXXXXX
AWS Secret Access Key [None]: XXXXXXXXXXXX
Default region name [None]: us-east-1
Default output format [None]: json
```

In this step, we defined the following information:

- **AWS access key ID/AWS secret access key**: These are the credentials used to authenticate the API requests that the AWS CLI will make against the AWS services.

- **AWS Region**: This is the AWS region where our infrastructure is being deployed. We'll expand more on the region concept in *Part 2: Building Infrastructure*, specifically, *Chapter 3, Creating a Data Center in the Cloud Using a VPC*. For now, we set this value to `us-east-1`.

- **Output format**: This specifies how the CLI will format its output. We chose **JavaScript Object Notation (JSON)**.

To verify that all has worked correctly, you can run the following command. This will return your user information to you:

```
aws sts get-caller-identity
```

The output of this command should look similar to the following:

```
{
    "UserId": "<redacted>",
    "Account": "<redacted>",
    "Arn": "arn:aws:iam::<redacted>:<username>"
}
```

Understanding the structure of AWS CLI commands

The AWS CLI commands follow a set pattern that is split up into three or four parts:

- The command has this syntax:

```
aws command subcommand [options and parameters]
```

- All AWS CLI commands start with aws.

- Next is the command or service. Usually, the command is the name of an AWS service. In our previous example, this was sts, short for **Secure Token Service**. Other examples would be the IAM service we previously used in the AWS Console.

- Next comes the subcommand or action. These actions map to API actions available for that specific service. In our previous example, we used the get-caller-identity command, which maps to the GetCallerIdentity API action documented on this page: https://docs.aws. amazon.com/STS/latest/APIReference/API_GetCallerIdentity.html.

If you need help with any actions/subcommands or want to get a list of all available actions, you can use the help command, which gives you a list of all available services and global configuration options:

```
aws help
```

To get all available options for a service (i.e., STS), type the following:

```
aws sts help
```

To get help on a subcommand/action (i.e., the get-caller-identity subcommand), type the following:

```
aws sts get-caller-identity help
```

This will return all information for this subcommand such as the required parameters or the attributes that are returned to you (under OUTPUT).

> **Important note**
>
> Some frequently used services (such as Amazon S3) have specific shorthands (such as `aws s3 ls` to list all S3 buckets). Other services might have multiple commands. For example, Amazon SageMaker, a service used for machine learning projects, has `aws sagemaker` for managing resources and `aws sagemaker-runtime` to interact with them.

While the AWS CLI offers us a powerful way to interact with the AWS services from our terminal and can easily be used to carry out a sequence of commands that would take many clicks in the AWS Console, it is not the best choice for programmatic interaction when dealing with more complex tasks. While we can use the AWS CLI in Bash scripts, these can get harder to read, write, and maintain once we move from a script that runs one or two simple commands to more complex workflows that potentially contain nestings and conditionals. In this case, our script would profit from being written in a higher-level programming language such as Python.

In this section, we learned how to set up the AWS CLI environment and also understood the basic structure of the commands. Next, let's look at how to set up the Boto3 SDK for Python for cases where we require more complex scripts.

Introducing the Boto3 SDK for Python

In this section, we'll be installing and setting up the AWS SDK for Python, called Boto3. Boto3 is a powerful abstraction that allows us to interact with the AWS APIs from our Python code. This allows us to write automation scripts for complex operations.

Installing Boto3

We can use the `pip` package manager to install the Python package. To do so, run the following command:

```
python3 -m pip install boto3
```

If you are using Windows as your operating system, you might have to use the following command instead:

```
python -m pip install boto3
```

> **Trivia**
>
> You might be wondering why this SDK is called `boto` and not something like `aws-python-sdk`. The library is named after a breed of dolphins (called boto) that are native to the Amazon River. The creator of the original `boto` library, Mitch Garnaat, wanted a name that was *"short, unusual, and with at least some kind of connection to Amazon."* You can read more details – including an explanation from Mitch Garnaat himself – in the following GitHub issue from which the preceding quote is taken: `https://github.com/boto/boto3/issues/1023.`

We can verify that the installation worked properly by writing a short Python script that uses `boto3` to call the previously used `sts` service and the previously used `GetCallerIdentity` action.

Open up a file called `test_sts.py` in a text editor of your choice (i.e., Visual Studio Code) and copy the following lines of Python code:

```python
import boto3
client = boto3.client("sts")
resp = client.get_caller_identity()
print(resp)
```

Run this script by using the following command in your terminal:

```
python3 test_sts.py
```

The result will contain the same information (`UserId`, `Account`, and `Arn`) as the CLI command (`aws sts get- caller-identity`) we have seen before. In addition, `boto3` adds some metadata around the request such as the HTTP status code, `RequestId`, and HTTP headers under the `ResponseMetadata` field. We can ignore this additional information for now.

You might be wondering how `boto3` has authenticated itself since nowhere in the script have we passed any credentials. It can read the credentials written by the AWS CLI when you run the `aws configure` command and use them.

Also, notice the similarity between the syntax in `boto3` and the AWS CLI. In line two, we create a `client` object to interact with the `sts` service. This is similar to how, in the AWS CLI, we specified the `sts` service as our command. On the `client` object, we then call the `get_caller_identity()` function that maps to the `GetCallerIdentity` API action of the AWS STS service. In the AWS CLI, this action was mapped to the `get-caller-identity` command. You can see how, coming from the API action (i.e., `GetCallerIdentity` of the STS service), we can translate this into the corresponding AWS CLI command (`aws sts get-caller-identity`) or corresponding `boto3` function call (`get_caller_identity()` on the `sts` client).

The difference between clients and resources

Boto3 gives you two different abstraction levels to interact with an AWS service. A **resource**, created using the `boto3.resource("<name of resource>")` code line and the **client** created using the `boto3.client("<name of client>")` code line.

A `boto3` client is a low-level interface that maps closely to the API actions of the corresponding AWS services. Resources, on the other hand, provide an object-oriented abstraction to some commonly used AWS services. Not all AWS services have resources and the "*AWS Python SDK team does not intend to add new features to the resources interface in boto3*" (see the documentation at this link: `https://boto3.amazonaws.com/v1/documentation/api/latest/guide/resources.html#`). We will thus primarily use clients throughout this book.

In this chapter, we have installed `boto3` and written our first script that interacts with the AWS APIs. Throughout this book, we will use `boto3` whenever we have the need to write automation scripts. Next, we will see how we can use CloudFormation to set up infrastructure programmatically.

What is CloudFormation?

While we could use the previously introduced AWS CLI or custom scripts using Python and Boto3 to create our infrastructure – at scale – we would like a tool that takes care of things such as abstracting the AWS API and keeping track of the state (maybe we want to modify an existing resource instead of creating a new one). This is where an IaC tool such as CloudFormation comes into play.

CloudFormation allows us to *declaratively* define how we want our infrastructure to look (i.e., that we want an S3 bucket named `marcel-this-is-my-test-bucket`) instead of having to *imperatively* write a script that contains all the API actions needed to create an S3 bucket with that name.

CloudFormation templates are written in either YAML or JSON. Throughout this book, we'll use the YAML version due to its brevity and readability.

With CloudFormation being a fundamental AWS service, we don't need to install anything. It can be used with the previously installed AWS CLI or from the AWS Console.

Writing your first CloudFormation template

Let's write our first CloudFormation template that will create an S3 bucket for us:

1. Open up a file called `s3-bucket.yml` in an editor of your choice, such as Visual Studio Code, Notepad++, or Vim.

2. First, define the version of the template to use:

    ```
    AWSTemplateFormatVersion: "2010-09-09"
    ```

3. Next, define a description for our stack:

    ```
    Description: "Simple stack to create an S3 Bucket"
    ```

4. We can next define the list of resources (for example, an S3 bucket or an EC2 instance) that should be associated with this stack. Pay attention to the indention. Each resource has an identifier (OurS3Bucket, in the following sample), Type, and Properties. We can choose the identifier ourselves while Type and Properties are defined by the resource:

```
Resources:
  OurS3Bucket:
    Type: AWS::S3::Bucket
    Properties:
      BucketName: <insert_unique_bucket_name>
```

The entire CloudFormation template should look like this:

```
AWSTemplateFormatVersion: "2010-09-09"
Description: "Simple stack to create an S3 Bucket"
Resources:
  OurS3Bucket:
    Type: AWS::S3::Bucket
    Properties:
      BucketName: <insert_unique_bucket_name>
```

Notice that the name of your bucket needs to be globally unique. This is because all S3 accounts share the same namespace for their S3 bucket names. An easy way to achieve uniqueness is by prefixing it with your name or by prefixing or postfixing random numbers.

> **Note**
>
> AWS has published conventions for naming buckets that you can find at the following link: https://docs.aws.amazon.com/AmazonS3/latest/userguide/bucketnamingrules.html.

Deploying the template

With our first template ready, we can use the AWS CLI to first verify and then deploy the template. To verify it, make sure that you are in the same folder as the template, and then run the following:

```
aws cloudformation validate-template --template-body file://s3-bucket.yml
```

The output should be an empty JSON with the description that you provided:

```
{
    "Parameters": [],
    "Description": "Simple stack to create an S3 Bucket"
}
```

With the validation done, we can next start the deployment of our template into a new stack by using the following command:

```
aws cloudformation create-stack --stack-name first-stack --template-
body file://s3-bucket.yml
```

CloudFormation organizes resources into a **stack**. In this example, we used the previously created CloudFormation **template** and created a stack based on it called `first-stack`. This stack contains a **resource** of the `S3 bucket` type with the name and other properties we defined inside of the CloudFormation stack. The resources are associated with this stack and any changes we want to make to the resources (such as deleting the S3 bucket, creating another bucket, or changing its properties) will result in a change to the stack.

To see the details, including the deployment status of a stack, we can use the AWS CLI and the `DescribeStacks` API action. Run the following command to check whether your stack has successfully deployed:

```
aws cloudformation describe-stacks --stack-name first-stack
```

Inside the output, you'll find, among other information about your stack, the `StackStatus` property. While your deployment is in progress, this status will be `CREATE_IN_PROGRESS`. Upon completion, the status changes to `CREATE_COMPLETE`, which means that all resources in the stack have been created successfully.

You can also check this by running a CLI command to list all S3 buckets in your account. Run the following command, where you should find the bucket we just created via CloudFormation:

```
aws s3 ls
```

One benefit of the IaC approach is that we can easily delete resources. In the case of CloudFormation, we just delete the stack, which then deletes all resources associated with it. To do so, run the following:

```
aws cloudformation delete-stack --stack-name first-stack
```

> **Important note**
>
> Some resources, such as S3 buckets, have deletion policies that prevent them from being deleted unless certain conditions (such as the bucket being empty in the case of an S3 bucket) are met. You can configure these when creating the resource. Only set the deletion policy of a bucket to be deleted, even when objects are in it, if you are 100% sure that you won't need the data in that bucket.

In this section, we have seen how we can use CloudFormation and its templates – written in either YAML or JSON – to declare the infrastructure we want. While these templates can be short and easy to understand for simple infrastructure, such as creating a single S3 bucket, large-scale infrastructure can become cumbersome in CloudFormation due to its low-level nature. You can think of CloudFormation as a low-level programming language. While it is possible to write all our code in such a language, it gets verbose and error-prone. Similar to how modern high-level programming languages abstract a lot of the underlying mechanisms of a computer (such as memory allocation), we can use the AWS CDK to do the same with CloudFormation.

Exploring the AWS CDK

With the CDK, we describe our infrastructure using constructs in a high-level programming language such as Python, Java, or TypeScript. This then gets *compiled* into CloudFormation templates for us.

Installing the AWS CDK

In order to use the CDK – regardless of which of the offered programming languages you want to use – you'll need Node.js installed. We can then use the node package manager (npm) to install the latest version of the CDK.

The following command will install cdk as a global package:

```
npm install -g aws-cdk
```

You can check that cdk is installed properly by running the following command:

```
cdk version
```

> **Important note**
> Regardless of the fact that we'll be using Python to describe our CDK project, we still need to have Node.js installed since the core of CDK is written in JavaScript.

At the time of writing (May 2024), the CDK supports the following programming languages:

- TypeScript
- JavaScript
- Python
- Java
- C#
- Go

To limit the number of languages used in this book, we'll use Python.

> **How can CDK support different languages?**
>
> You might be wondering how CDK is able to support different languages. To do this, CDK leverages an open source project called **jsii** (see `https://github.com/aws/jsii`). With this, you can write code (such as the underlying components of the CDK) in JavaScript and then generate language-specific bindings in different languages (such as Python) for it. Language-specific here refers to the fact that the bindings generated by `jsii` take language-specific patterns (such as keyword arguments in Python or the builder pattern in Java) into account.

If you're curious to know how this works exactly, you can have a look at the official documentation of `jsii` at `https://aws.github.io/jsii/`.

Writing and deploying your first CDK project

With the CDK installed, we can start our first CDK project:

1. Create a new folder called `first-cdk-stack` and navigate into it by running the following command:

   ```
   mkdir first-cdk-stack && cd first-cdk-stack
   ```

2. Initiate a new CDK project (using Python as our language of choice):

   ```
   cdk init app --language python
   ```

3. A virtual environment is a lightweight abstraction that lets us create isolated environments for Python. Each of these environments has its own Python interpreter and packages. This way, we can install different versions of the same Python package for different projects and avoid version conflicts or version incompatibilities. To activate the Python virtual environment that the CDK has created for you, run the following command:

   ```
   source .venv/bin/activate
   ```

4. If you are on Windows, run the following command:

   ```
   .\.venv\Scripts\activate.bat
   ```

5. After activating the virtual environment, install the packages required by the project. You can do this by running the following:

   ```
   python3 -m pip install -r requirements.txt
   ```

> **Note**
>
> If you want to take a look at the packages that will be installed, you can open up the `requirements.txt` file. In it, you will find an entry for each package that is being installed – for example, `aws-cdk-lib==2.14.0`. Each entry has two components. The first is the name of the package, and the second, after the two = signs, is the version of the package that is being installed.

Now, we can get started on defining our infrastructure. Inside the `first_cdk_stack` folder, you'll find a file called `first_cdk_stack_stack.py`. Open this file in a code editor of your choice (i.e., Visual Studio Code).

The file should look like this:

```
from aws_cdk import (
    # Duration,
    Stack,
    # aws_sqs as sqs,
)
from constructs import Construct
class FirstCdkStackStack(Stack):
    def __init__(self, scope: Construct, construct_id: str, **kwargs)
-> None:
        super().__init__(scope, construct_id, **kwargs)
        # The code that defines your stack goes here
        # example resource
        # queue = sqs.Queue(
        #     self, "FirstCdkStackQueue",
        #     visibility_timeout=Duration.seconds(300),
        # )
```

As you can see, the concept of a stack we have previously seen in CloudFormation is also present in the CDK. In Python, a stack is a class that inherits from the `aws_cdk.Stack` class (the `FirstCdkStackStack` class on line 8 in the preceding example). Inside of the constructor of the class (line 10 in the example), we can then define our stack by using constructs.

Let's first recreate our bucket example from CloudFormation in the CDK before diving into an explanation of what a construct in CDK is:

1. The AWS CDK splits its constructs into different modules that we need to import. Modify the import on the first line to look like the following:

   ```
   from aws_cdk import (
       Stack,
       aws_s3 as s3
   )
   from constructs import Construct
   ```

2. With the s3 module imported, we can now create our bucket. Inside the __init__ method, define a new bucket:

```
bucket = s3. Bucket(self, "my-first-bucket", bucket_
name="<insert-unique-bucket-name>")
```

Your entire code should look like this:

```
from aws_cdk import (
    Stack,
    aws_s3 as s3
)
from constructs import Construct
class FirstCdkStackStack(Stack):
    def __init__(self, scope: Construct, construct_id: str, **kwargs)
-> None:
        super().__init__(scope, construct_id, **kwargs)
        # The code that defines your stack goes here
        bucket = s3.Bucket(self, "my-first-bucket", bucket_
name="<insert-unique-bucket-name>")
```

The first argument passed to the Bucket constructor is the scope that this resource should be associated with. In this instance, we are associating the newly created bucket with the FirstCdkStackStack stack and thus using the self keyword in Python. Next, we pass an id string that, together with some random numbers and letters, will be used as the resource identifier in our rendered cloud formation template.

Following these required arguments, we can use Python keyword arguments to set the properties, such as the bucket name, which we would normally set inside the Properties section in CloudFormation.

In order to deploy our previously created application, we need to bootstrap our environment. This needs to be done once per account and region. The bootstrapping deploys some basic resources needed by the CDK into your account. Inside your project folder, run the following:

cdk bootstrap

As mentioned previously, the CDK provides an abstraction over CloudFormation and ultimately translates into CloudFormation. We can use the synth command to show the CloudFormation template that will be rendered from our CDK code.

Run the following command and scroll through the generated template:

cdk synth

Among other things, you should find a resource of the AWS::S3::Bucket type with the name you specified in your CDK code (line 15 in the complete code).

We can now go ahead and start deploying the stack we just created by running the `deploy` command, as follows:

```
cdk deploy
```

Similar to what we just did manually, CDK now synthesizes (or translates) the CDK code into a CloudFormation template and then deploys this CloudFormation template.

During the deployment, you can see the progress of your deployment in the output of the `cdk deploy` command, as shown in the following figure.

```
FirstCdkStackStack: deploying... [1/1]
FirstCdkStackStack: creating CloudFormation changeset...
[                                        ] (3/3)

7:32:42 PM | CREATE_IN_PROGRESS    | AWS::CDK::Metadata | CDKMetadata/Default

[]
```

Figure 1.5 – Progress of the CDK deployment shown on the command line

Once the command is done, it'll show the **Amazon Resource Name** (**ARN**) of the CloudFormation stack that was just deployed as well as the total time this took.

You can check that the bucket was created by running the `aws s3 ls` command again.

If you want to remove all resources created by the CDK, you can use the `cdk destroy` command. This command will trigger a deletion of all the resources associated with your stack.

Additional information

Many CDK constructs will let you set a removal policy. Removal policies govern how resources are handled if a user runs the `cdk destroy` command mentioned previously. To be more precise, the removal policy governs how a resource is treated when it is no longer managed by CloudFormation. Remember that the CDK just generates CloudFormation code.

There are three reasons why a resource might no longer be under the management of CloudFormation: if the resource is removed from the template, if the resource requires a change that cannot be handled in place and thus the resource is deleted and recreated, or if the entire stack that the resource was part of is deleted.

Especially for resources such as S3 buckets, which might potentially contain irreplaceable data, we might want to control whether the bucket is truly removed in order to prevent accidents where a wrongly configured script triggers the deletion of a bucket.

There are four different removal policies:

- DESTROY will trigger the deletion of the resource once it is no longer managed by CloudFormation.

- RETAIN means that the resource will be kept in the account. This is the default policy for S3 buckets created with the L2 construct we used previously.

- RETAIN_ON_UPDATE_OR_DELETE means that resources that were in use will be retained while unused resources will be deleted.

- SNAPSHOT is a removal policy that is only available for some resources (such as databases) where – before deletion – a snapshot is taken so that the data can be restored.

What is a construct in the CDK?

In the previous section, we used the S3 Bucket construct to create a new bucket. But what exactly is a **construct**?

Constructs are the way that the CDK uses to abstract resources. They can be separated into three different levels called layer 1, layer 2, and layer 3 – or shorter, L1, L2, and L3.

Let's learn more about these:

- **Layer 1 construct**: This is a one-to-one mapping to a resource inside of CloudFormation. Every resource in CloudFormation (i.e., the previously used AWS::S3::Bucket resource in CloudFormation) has a corresponding L1 construct in CDK. These L1 constructs are prefixed with Cfn to indicate their L1 status. So there is a CfnBucket construct.

- **Layer 2 construct**: However, we didn't use the CfnBucket construct to create our bucket in the previous example. Instead, we used a layer 2 construct called Bucket. While L1 constructs are automatically generated based on CloudFormation, L2 constructs are hand-crafted by humans. They still map to a resource (such as a bucket) but offer more abstraction and functions for typical operations.

  Let's say I want to grant a different IAM user called marcel read access to the bucket. With CloudFormation or L1 constructs, this is an involved piece of code (you can see an example of the CDK and CloudFormation required in the repository here: https://github.com/PacktPublishing/AWS-for-System-Administrators-Second-Edition). With the CDK, we can do it in two lines of code:

  ```
  user = iam.User.from_user_name("marcel")
  bucket.grant_read(user)
  ```

  Underneath, the grant_read() function defines a least-privilege policy that grants read access to the user identified by the name marcel.

- **Layer 3 construct**: While a layer 2 construct already offers a lot of useful abstraction, it is still usually mapped to a resource (such as a bucket) in AWS. Layer 3 constructs build on top of layer 2 and layer 1 constructs to deploy patterns. A layer 3 construct might implement a pattern such as a load-balanced application running on Amazon **Elastic Container Service** (**ECS**). Such a pattern might combine tens or even a hundred different resources.

> **Note**
> The preceding example mentioned does exist in the CDK. Have a look at the `ApplicationLoadBalancedFargateService` construct if you are curious. The docs are available here: `https://docs.aws.amazon.com/cdk/api/v2/python/aws_cdk.aws_ecs_patterns/ApplicationLoadBalancedFargateService.html#applicationloadbalancedfargateservice`.

We will talk more about how we can use these concepts to design reusable components in *Chapter 15*.

In the previous sections, we have seen how we can leverage tools such as the AWS-native CloudFormation to declare the infrastructure we want. However, one of the drawbacks of using such a tool is that it is native to AWS. This can have its drawbacks when operating in a multi-cloud environment. This is where the IaC tool Terraform by HashiCorp comes into play.

Introducing Terraform

Terraform is declarative. This means that we declare a resource (such as our S3 bucket) and Terraform then figures out the required API actions to create this resource. To describe the resources, Terraform uses its own language called **HashiCorp Configuration Language** (**HCL**) or, optionally, JSON. We'll be using HCL throughout this book as it offers a more concise way to write our Terraform code as well as additional abilities such as adding comments to our code.

Terraform uses providers (usually written in Go) to translate the resources and changes defined in your Terraform code into API calls to AWS. The benefit of Terraform is that there are providers not only for AWS but also for other hyperscalers such as Microsoft Azure and GCP, as well as other providers.

This means that you can use the same language (HCL) and the same technology (Terraform) to describe your resources in different cloud providers.

Installing Terraform

To install Terraform, find the appropriate package for your system on the download page (`https://developer.hashicorp.com/terraform/install`). Either use your systems package manager (as described on the page) to install Terraform or download the appropriate `.zip` file for your operating system and processor.

Verify that your installation was successful by running the following command:

```
terraform version
```

Creating resources in Terraform

To create our first resource, we need to create a `.tf` file that contains the definitions of our resources. Create a new folder called `my-first-tf` and navigate into it. Inside the folder, create a new file called `s3-bucket.tf` and write the following code:

```
provider "aws" {
  region = "us-east-1"
}
resource "aws_s3_bucket" "example" {
  bucket = "<insert-unique-bucket-name>"
}
```

Inside this file, we have two fundamental concepts of Terraform – the provider and the resource:

- **Provider**: The `provider` block (lines 1 to 3) defines that we want to use the `aws` provider. We additionally pass information about what region (`us-east-1`, in the example) we want to use.

- **Resource**: Next, we define an `aws_s3_bucket` resource using a `resource` block. Resources that are provided by the `aws` provider are prefixed with `aws_`. In the example, we use this to create a bucket. You can see that we also define a *logical name*, in this case, `example`.

In order to create the bucket from this simple example, we'll need to first initiate `terraform`. This is done by running the `init` command:

```
terraform init
```

This downloads the latest AWS provider and initiates our project.

Next, we can use the `plan` command to show what actions Terraform would like to perform:

```
terraform plan -out tfplan
```

At the bottom of the output, you'll see a summary of the resources Terraform plans to add, change, or destroy:

```
Plan: 1 to add, 0 to change, 0 to destroy.
```

At the top, you can see a list of all the actions Terraform plans to take:

- A + sign indicates a resource or property being created

- A - sign indicates a resource or property being deleted

- A ~ sign indicates a resource or property being modified

By using the -out tfplan flag, we have written the plan into a file called tfplan. We can use this file to now apply the changes. This is done using the aptly named apply command in Terraform. Run the following command:

```
terraform apply tfplan
```

Terraform will show you a log of resources (in this case, only the one s3 bucket resource) that are being created, as well as, after completion, a summary of the number of resources that were added, changed, or deleted.

> **Note**
>
> Naming the file containing your plan tfplan has become a typical convention but is not a must. This convention is mentioned in the documentation from HashiCorp. You can find more information at https://developer.hashicorp.com/terraform/cli/commands/plan under **Other options**.

You can once again verify that the bucket was created using the aws s3 ls command:

```
aws s3 ls
```

Terraform also offers a way to delete all resources associated with it. To do so, we can use the destroy command:

```
terraform destroy
```

This command first prints a summary of all resources that are being destroyed and then asks for your confirmation. When prompted, enter yes to destroy the previously created resources.

> **Note**
>
> An important aspect of IaC tools such as Terraform that we have so far omitted is state management. We have the configuration in this chapter; the state is saved in the same folder as the Terraform code itself. This is fine for exploration but won't scale. We'll talk about strategies and patterns to handle state management across teams in *Chapter 14*.

In this section, we successfully installed Terraform and created our first small piece of code in HCL that created an S3 bucket in AWS. Terraform is a widely used tool for implementing IaC, and we will use it throughout this book together with CloudFormation and CDK.

Summary

In this chapter, we installed and set up the required tools such as the AWS CLI, the boto3 SDK for Python, the AWS CDK, and Terraform. Using these tools, we wrote some simple scripts, templates, or programs to create infrastructure following the IaC paradigm. We will use these tools in the coming chapters to build our infrastructure.

In the next chapter, we'll see how the IAM service works and how we can use it to tighten security.

Get This Book's PDF Version and Exclusive Extras

UNLOCK NOW

Scan the QR code (or go to `packtpub.com/unlock`). Search for this book by name, confirm the edition, and then follow the steps on the page.

Note: Keep your invoice handly. Purchase made directly from packt don't require one.

2

Protecting Your AWS Account Using IAM

One of the biggest benefits of the cloud is its software-defined nature. In the previous chapter, we saw how different tools such as Terraform or CloudFormation allow us to programmatically interact with resources, such as an S3 bucket in AWS.

Another benefit of this software-defined nature is the fine-grained controls we can use for resources. Since every interaction, from creating to modifying or deleting a resource, is an API call to AWS, we can put fine-grained policies in place for what actions can be carried out by what user.

In this chapter, we're going to cover the following main topics:

- What is AWS IAM?
- Understanding IAM users, policies, and roles
- Programmatically interacting with IAM using Boto3

Let's get started!

Technical requirements

Before beginning this chapter, please create an AWS account for yourself. You can sign up at `https://aws.amazon.com`. You should also have basic knowledge as well as a working installation of both Terraform and Boto3. We covered both of these in *Chapter 1*.

A basic understanding of Python will help with the programming-based sections of this chapter.

All scripts from this section can be found at the following GitHub link:

`https://github.com/PacktPublishing/AWS-for-System-Administrators-Second-Edition`

The CiA video for this chapter can be found at `https://packt.link/fVqvE`

What is AWS IAM?

Before we go deeper into creating users, groups, and policies, we'll start by introducing some basic concepts of the **Identity and Access Management (IAM)** service. IAM provides two crucial security components: authentication and authorization. Let's learn more about them:

- **Authentication**: This identifies a user; it is the login, be it via a password or via an API token, that gives the system the information that whoever is sending a request is the identity that they are claiming to be. This chapter will show you how authentication is handled by IAM in the context of AWS.

- **Authorization**: This defines what action a user is allowed to perform. In this chapter, we'll see how AWS handles authorization using the IAM service.

> **Note**
>
> In this chapter, we'll be using IAM users in a single-account scenario. *Chapter 17* will cover scenarios that involve multiple AWS accounts as well as using federated access from another identity provider to allow logging in to AWS.

What are IAM users?

An IAM user, as the name suggests, is a *user* that has access to your AWS account. Contrary to how your personal GitHub account has a one-to-one relation between the user and the account (i.e., only you are using your account), an AWS account can have many different users accessing it. You might have an *admin* user who is allowed to perform all actions, a *developer* user who is allowed to start new infrastructure, and an audit user who is only allowed to view but not create new resources within your AWS account.

IAM users are a global resource. But what exactly does it mean for a resource or service to be *global*? Before creating a new IAM user, let's dive a bit deeper into different types of AWS services and pick up some information on the way the AWS infrastructure is built along the way.

Types of AWS services and its global infrastructure

When dealing with the 200+ services, at the time of writing, that AWS offers, it is only natural for us to think in categories. However, there are multiple ways to categorize them. When we look in the AWS Console, we most often see them organized by categories such as *Compute*, *Storage*, or *Machine Learning*.

While this is a great separation for identifying a service that might be useful for solving a problem we have, there is also a categorization based on *service types*. AWS has three different service types: *zonal*, *regional*, and *global services*.

To understand the different types of services, let's take a step back and look into the way AWS organizes its infrastructure. The basic building block of the AWS cloud is an **Availability Zone**, commonly abbreviated to **AZ**. An AZ is made up of one or more data centers that have independent and redundant networking and power.

Multiple AZs are then grouped together into a **Region**. Regions carry names that give an indication of where, geographically speaking, the AZs of that region are located. For example, the central European region is called eu-central-1 (*Frankfurt*). The AZs within a region then carry letters. Within the *Frankfurt* region, which, at the time of writing, has three AZs, you have the eu-central-1a, eu-central-1b, and eu-central-1c AZs. The AZs within a region are geographically separated by up to 100 kilometers. This allows for fault isolation in case of natural disasters such as flooding or earthquakes while being close enough in terms of latency. The AZs of a region are connected to the internet as well as the AWS backbone network via two **transit centers**. *Figure 2.1* shows the schematics of what an AWS Region looks like.

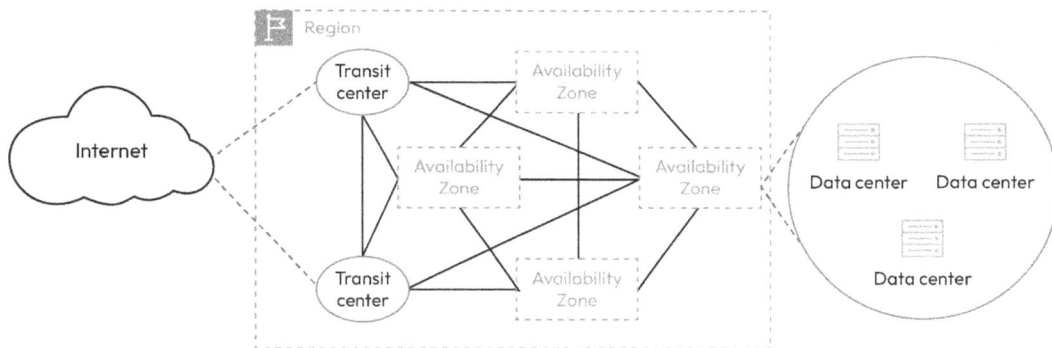

Figure 2.1 – Schematic of a Region with four AZs (source: https://docs.aws.amazon.com/whitepapers/latest/aws-fault-isolation-boundaries/availability-zones.html)

One or more regions then make up a **partition**. The most common partition is the partition containing all the commercial regions (such as us-east-1, eu-central-1, etc.). This partition is the aws partition. Partitions are separated and have their own IAM. This means that a user that was created in a commercial region within the aws partition (assuming it is allowed by a policy) can create resources in all regions within that partition. This user can't interact with resources in regions of a different partition, such as the AWS GovCloud regions (the aws-us-gov partition).

One final concept is the separation between **control planes** and **data planes**. A control plane provides the APIs to administer (create, read, update, or delete) a resource while the data plane provides the primary function of the service. Taking our previous example of creating a bucket in S3: The action of creating the bucket is handled by the control plane while the operation of putting an object into the bucket is handled by the data plane.

> **Note**
>
> We have deliberately left out AWS Local Zones and AWS Outposts as well as **Points of Presence (PoPs)**. You can find more information on these in the AWS whitepaper on fault isolation boundaries (`https://docs.aws.amazon.com/whitepapers/latest/aws-fault-isolation-boundaries/availability-zones.html`).

Now that we have an understanding of how AWS infrastructure is built up, we can come back to the topic of service types. As previously mentioned, there are three service types that map into the infrastructure concepts.

A **zonal service** operates independently inside the AZs. This means that every AZ has its own data plane as well as an AZ-specific control plane. In addition to the AZ-specific control plane, we have a regional control plane to control actions that need to be coordinated between multiple AZs. An example of a zonal service is EC2. When launching a new instance, we can specify which AZ to launch into. We'll talk more about the implications of this when it comes to disaster recovery and resiliency in *Chapter 12*.

A **regional service** operates within a region. A service such as Amazon DynamoDB abstracts the underlying zonal concepts and provides a region-specific endpoint. The control and data planes are specific to a region.

And finally, a **global service** has a control and data plane that isn't specific to a region. These services have a control plane in one region and a data plane that is spread across regions. The most common examples of a global service are IAM and Route 53. When selecting one of these services in the AWS Console, the region indicator at the top right will show **Global**.

Creating a new IAM user using the AWS CLI

To create a new user in IAM from the CLI, we can use the `create-user` command. Type the following command to create a new user with the name `packt-user`:

```
aws iam create-user --user-name packt-user
{
    "User": {
        "Path": "/",
        "UserName": "packt-user",
        "UserId": "<redacted>",
```

```
            "Arn": "arn:aws:iam::<redacted>:user/packt-user",
            "CreateDate": "2024-06-01T15:08:14+00:00"
      }
  }
```

The output of the command has the following components:

- `Path` is the path of the username, defaulting to `/`.

- `UserName` is the name of the user we have provided.

- `UserId` is a generated user ID that lets us identify the user.

- `Arn` is the **Amazon Resource Name (ARN)** of our user. The `redacted` part will show your account ID.

- `CreateDate` indicates when the user was created.

What are ARNs?

In the previous section, we saw that an IAM user has an ARN that can be used to uniquely identify the resource. ARNs play a central part in IAM policies, and their format follows a general form. The exact format depends on the resource:

```
arn:<partition>:<service>:<region>:<account-id>:<resource-id>
```

or

```
arn:<partition>:<service>:<region>:<account-id>:<resource-
type>/<resource-id>
```

or

```
arn:<partition>:<service>:<region>:<account-id>:<resource-
type>:<resource-id>
```

Let's have a look at the different components:

- `partition` is the previously mentioned group of AWS regions. In the case of the IAM ARN we see in the previous code, this is `aws`.

- `service` is the AWS service, such as IAM or S3.

- `region` is the AWS Region, for example, `us-east-1`.

- `account-id` identifies the account that owns this resource.

- `resource-type` is the type of resource that is identified by this ARN. In our example, this is the user.

- `resource-id` is a unique identifier. The form of this identifier depends on the service and resource. In the case of the IAM user, it is the user name. Other services might use numbered IDs or UUIDs here.

You might be wondering how the ARN squares with the previously introduced concepts of global services. The resources of these services are not region-specific and thus we can't specify a region within the ARN. The ARN simply doesn't have a region within it. As you can see in the ARN of your previously created IAM user, there are two columns after the service identifier.

Notably, ARNs support wildcards. Let's say we wanted to have an ARN that specifies all users within an account, we could do this by using the * wildcard. So the ARN for all users in an account (with the exemplary `account-id` value of `12345678910`) would be the following:

```
arn:aws:iam::12345678910:user/*
```

This can become useful when assigning policies to a collection of resources.

IAM groups

We previously talked about how you might want to have an admin user, a developer user, and an audit user with different sets of permissions. The idea of separating by user might be fine for a very small account but what if your team is growing? You'd either have to share the credentials of your developer account with all developers in the team or attach the same policies, thus giving the same rights, manually. This becomes cumbersome when a user changes teams (for example, a DevOps engineer becoming a developer) and we need to rearrange all permissions.

Instead of sharing credentials or manual assignment, we can use IAM groups to group users by their function. Instead of then assigning a policy, and thus rights, to the user, we assign the policy to the group. If a user is in the group, they have all the rights from all the policies attached to the group. If we move a user out of the group, they no longer have that access.

> **Note**
>
> IAM groups are not real identities that can be mentioned in a permission policy. It's an administrative vehicle that allows us to attach the same policy to a group of IAM users.

Creating a new IAM group

We can use the `create-group` command to create a new IAM group called Ops:

```
aws iam create-group --group-name Ops
```

This command will output the following JSON:

```
{
    "Group": {
        "Path": "/",
        "GroupName": "Ops",
        "GroupId": "<redacted>",
        "Arn": "arn:aws:iam::<redacted>:group/Ops",
        "CreateDate": "2024-06-01T15:33:49+00:00"
    }
}
```

The output is similar to what we saw when creating a new user. It contains the information (such as our provided name) of the newly created group resource as well as some meta information such as creation date and time.

Adding a user to a group

We can now also add the previously created IAM user, packt-user, to the Ops group. To do this, we use the add-user-to-group command:

```
aws iam add-user-to-group --user-name packt-user --group-name Ops
```

This command has no output.

So far, we have learned how to create new users and how we can categorize them into groups. However, these newly created users do not have the right to do anything so far. In order to allow them to perform actions within our AWS account, we need to attach a policy that allows them to perform this action. Before we can attach policies, we need to understand them. Let's do that next!

Understanding IAM policies

An **IAM policy** is a JSON-formatted document that specifies the actions on what resources and under what conditions a user or role can perform. On every request to the AWS API, the IAM policy engine evaluates whether the caller has the required permissions to carry out the operation. Thinking back to the *What is AWS IAM?* section, this is the *authorization* of the request.

> **Note**
> By default, all requests are implicitly denied and an IAM identity (user, role, or group) has no permissions or policies attached to it.

AWS has four types of policies:

- **Identity-based policies**: These grant permission to an IAM identity (a user, group, or role).

- **Resource-based policies**: These grant permission to access a resource, such as an S3 bucket or a role, to a principal (i.e., another AWS service).

- **Permission boundaries**: These define the maximum permissions (i.e., the boundaries) that can be granted with an identity-based policy.

- **Organizational SCPs**: Short for **service control policies**, these can be used to restrict what kind of permissions can be granted in AWS Organizations. We will learn more about these concepts in detail in *Chapter 15*.

Now that we are acquainted with the basics of IAM policies, let's move on to understanding their core aspects.

Structure of IAM policies

Each statement of an IAM policy follows the same structure and, in turn, has four main parts, as follows:

- **Effect**: This is either `Allow` or `Deny` and specifies whether the following actions should be allowed or denied.

- **Action**: This is the list of actions that can be carried out. Each API operation within AWS is defined by a string that follows the same format. It is the service name, for example, `s3`, followed by a column and the name of the API action, for example, `GetObject`. So, the string identifying the action to get an object from S3 is `s3:GetObject`.

- **Resource**: This defines what resources the previously mentioned actions are allowed or denied. To stay within the example of S3, this could be the ARN of a single object within a bucket (`arn:aws:s3:::examplebucket/myobject`) or we can use a wildcard to allow access to all objects in a bucket (`arn:aws:s3:::examplebucket/*`).

- **Condition**: This is an optional construct that lets us specify conditions under which the access should be denied. For example, we can use this to allow access to an object in S3 only from a specified set of source IPs:

```
"Condition": {
"NotIpAddress": {
"aws:SourceIp": [
    "192.0.2.0/24",
    "203.0.113.0/24"
  ]
 }
}
```

Combining all of this, our IAM policy will look like the following example:

```
{
    "Statement":[{
      "Effect":"effect",
      "Action":"action",
      "Resource":["arn"],
      "Condition":{
        "condition":{
          "key":"value"
        }
      }
    }]
}
```

The following is a real example of a policy that blocks traffic to an S3 bucket unless the traffic is coming from a specific IP. To achieve this, we use the `Condition` construct together with the `aws:SourceIp` condition:

```
{
    "Version": "2012-10-17",
    "Statement": [
      {
        "Sid": "Stmt1604259864802",
        "Action": "s3:*",
        "Effect": "Deny",
        "Resource": "arn:aws:s3:::myexamplebucket/*",
        "Condition": [{
          "NotIpAddress": {
            "aws:SourceIp": "192.168.1.10/24"
          }
        }],
      }
    ]
}
```

As you can see in the example, we also need to specify a `Version` number. This is not the version of your policy but rather the version of the AWS policy language. As of the time of writing, the current version of the policy language is `2012-10-17` and it is the one that should be used for writing your policies. In very old code bases or very old blog posts, you might still see the previous version (`2008-10-17`), which should not be used for writing new policies.

You can also see `Sid`, or **statement ID**, in the statement. This is an optional identity that can be added to each statement.

We have seen that we can write a policy document to grant a user permission to carry out certain actions. But do we always have to reinvent the wheel? The answer is no. Besides the *customer-managed* policies that we can create on our own, AWS offers a set of *common managed* policies that AWS maintains.

Introduction to AWS managed policies

AWS managed policies are standard policies from AWS that follow best practices such as *least privilege*. There are two different subtypes of AWS managed policies:

- **AWS managed**: The AWS managed type, such as the `AmazonS3FullAccess` policy, grants access to all actions on all buckets in an account, while the `AmazonS3ReadOnlyAccess` policy allows only the read operations. These kinds of policies exist for typical separations (such as full access or read-only access) for many of the services.

- **AWS managed for job functions**: The second type is AWS managed policies for job functions. Instead of being service-specific, these policies allow the actions commonly associated with a job function, such as the `SecurityAudit` policy that grants the required permissions a security auditor might need.

Figure 2.2 shows the overview of available managed policies in the AWS Console. Clicking on the + button in front of a policy lets us view the detailed definition (in JSON format) of what rights this policy grants.

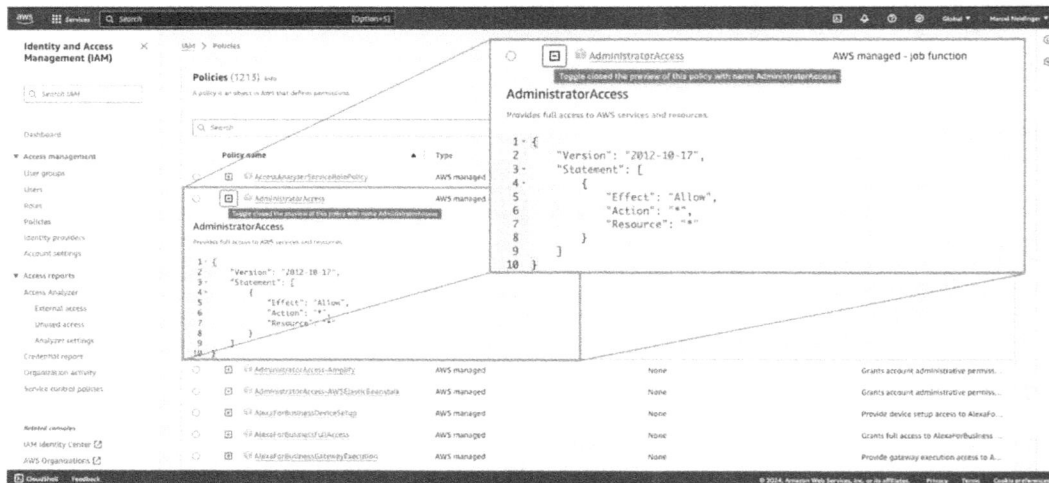

Figure 2.2 – View of the different managed policies in the IAM console

Now that we have seen how to write our own policies in theory and have also seen how the managed policies from AWS work, it's time for one last piece of theory. With IAM policies being such a central and important concept, it makes sense to get a deeper understanding of how they are evaluated.

IAM policy evaluation

When evaluating whether a request should be allowed, AWS performs the following four steps in order:

1. **Authentication**: The actor that is sending the request is authenticated.

2. **Processing the request context**: In this step, the information around the request (such as the actions, resources, environment data, and so on) is gathered. This is all the information that is needed during the policy evaluation to determine whether the request should be denied or allowed.

3. **Evaluating policies within a single account**: Here, the policies of the different types (identity-based policies, resource-based policies, etc.) within the account are gathered and put in order of evaluation.

4. **Determining whether a request is allowed or denied**: In this step, the request context is evaluated against the policies and a decision as to whether it should be denied or allowed is made.

The following diagram shows a simplified version of the evaluation process.

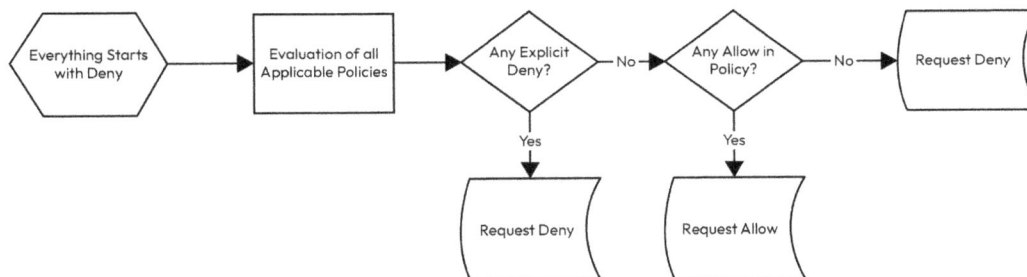

Figure 2.3 – Simplified flow of the evaluation of a policy

> **Note**
>
> You can find a more detailed version of the preceding flow chart in the AWS documentation at this link: https://docs.aws.amazon.com/IAM/latest/UserGuide/reference_policies_evaluation-logic.html#policy-eval-denyallow.

When talking about policy evaluation, we have two different modes for an effect. An effect can either be **implicit** or **explicit**. As an example, by default, all actions are *implicitly denied*. This means that we need to add an *explicit allow* (i.e., a policy statement that allows the given action) to override this default. This *explicit allow* can be overridden by an *implicit deny* in a different policy such as a *permission boundary*. Also, an *explicit deny* will always override any allows.

To illustrate, have a look at the following policy. This policy has two different statements. The first gives an explicit allow for all actions on an S3 bucket (s3:*) while the second one does an explicit deny on the s3:GetObject action:

```
{
    "Version": "2012-10-17",
    "Statement": [
      {
        "Sid": "GrantS3FullAccess",
        "Effect": "Allow",
        "Action": [
          "s3:*"
        ],
        "Resource": [
          "arn:aws:s3:::mytest-bucket/*"
        ]
      },
      {
        "Sid": "RevokeS3GetObjectAccess",
        "Effect": "Deny",
        "Action": [
          "s3:GetObject"
        ],
        "Resource": [
          "arn:aws:s3:::mytest-bucket/*"
        ]
      }
    ]
}
```

A user with this policy attached would not have the ability to perform the s3:GetObject operation on the bucket. Even though the Allow effect of the first statement explicitly allows this, the explicit Deny in the second statement supersedes this.

> **Note**
>
> This is not an example of a good policy and is just here to showcase the ranking of the different explicit allows and denies.

With the theory out of the way, let's give our previously created user the right to access files in an S3 bucket using a policy.

Creating an IAM policy using the AWS CLI

Let's create a new IAM policy that allows our user to perform all actions on an S3 bucket. First, create an S3 bucket. You can use the example from the previous chapter for this. After that, follow these steps:

1. Create a new file called `s3-policy-wide-priviledges.json` and paste the following code. Before jumping to the explanation, try reading through the policy and formulate what API operations are allowed on what resources by this policy (you'll find the answer at the end of this subsection):

```
{
    "Version": "2012-10-17",
    "Statement": [
        {
            "Sid": "AllowS3Access",
            "Effect": "Allow",
            "Action": [
                "s3:*"
            ],
            "Resource": [
                "*"
            ]
        }
    ]
}
```

2. To attach this policy to a previously created user, we can use the `put-user-policy` command:

```
aws iam put-user-policy --user-name packt-user --policy-name
s3_unrestricted --policy-document file:// s3-policy-wide-
priviledges.json
```

3. We can then retrieve the policy via the `get-user-policy` command:

```
aws iam get-user-policy --user-name packt-user --policy-name
s3_unrestricted
{
    "UserName": "packt-user",
    "PolicyName": "s3_unrestricted",
    "PolicyDocument": {
        "Version": "2012-10-17",
        "Statement": [
            {
                "Sid": "AllowS3Access",
                "Effect": "Allow",
                "Action": [
```

```
                              "s3:*"
                    ],
                    "Resource": [
                        "*"
                    ]
                }
            ]
        }
    }
```

Now what does this policy allow the user to do? It grants the ability to execute all S3 API operations (s3:*) on all S3 resources in the account (via "*" in the Resource section). While this is a syntactically correct policy and there *might* be use cases where this kind of unrestricted access is the correct way to go, in general, we want to provide the least amount of privileges that are required to perform the actions. This is the principle of least privilege, and in the next section, we'll rewrite the policy to follow the principle.

Before progressing to the next section, however, let's delete this wide policy from our IAM user using the delete-user-policy command:

```
aws iam delete-user-policy --user-name packt-user --policy-name s3_
unrestricted
```

The command does not show any output when the deletion is successful.

Rewriting our policy as least privilege

To rewrite our policy as least privilege, we first need a scenario. Let's say we want to write a policy that allows read access to objects in an S3 bucket while restricting the write access to a prefix. We can craft this with two different IAM statements.

Open up a code editor and create a new file called s3-restricted.json. Paste the following policy document into it:

```
{
    "Version": "2012-10-17",
    "Statement": [
        {
            "Sid": "AllowS3ReadAccessToBucket",
            "Effect": "Allow",
            "Action": [
                "s3:Get*",
                "s3:List*",
                "s3:Describe*"
            ],
```

```
        "Resource": [
            "arn:aws:s3:::<your-bucket-name>",
            "arn:aws:s3:::<your-bucket-name>/*"
        ]
    },
    {
        "Sid": "AllowS3WriteAccessToBucketPrefix",
        "Effect": "Allow",
        "Action": [
            "s3:PutObject",
            "s3:GetObject",
            "s3:GetObjectTagging",
            "s3:DeleteObject",
            "s3:DeleteObjectVersion",
            "s3:GetObjectVersion",
            "s3:GetObjectVersionTagging",
            "s3:GetObjectACL",
            "s3:PutObjectACL"
        ],
        "Resource": [
            "arn:aws:s3:::<your-bucket-name>/my-writable-prefix",
            "arn:aws:s3:::<your-bucket-name>/my-writable-prefix/*"
        ]
    }

    ]
}
```

As you can see, the policy got a lot longer but also a lot more specific. In the first statement, we grant access to all read operations (`Get*`, `List*`, and `Describe*`) on the bucket and all of its objects. In the second statement, we specify the write operations we want to allow.

So, this policy now specifies the actions that can be taken as well as restricts the resources on which these actions can take place.

You can use the previous commands to apply this policy if you want to.

Note

A question you might have is, *How do I find the permissions that are needed?* A good starting point is the AWS managed permissions. You can find them in the AWS Console in IAM.

Introduction to IAM roles

So far, we have dealt with IAM users and these make sense when thinking about humans interacting with the AWS API. But what about programmatic access such as from an EC2 instance? This is where **IAM roles** come into play. IAM roles are similar to a user wherein we can attach policies to grant access to certain API actions to that role. We can also specify who can *assume* an IAM role. This can be an application but also a user.

Creating an IAM role with Terraform

In this example, we'll be attaching an IAM role to an EC2 instance. This means that we will allow the EC2 instance to assume the role (and thus be granted the permissions by the associated role policy) and access an S3 bucket.

Create a file called `iam_role.tf` and copy and paste the code from the GitHub folder into it.

Let's go through this example and examine what we are doing here:

```
resource "aws_iam_role" "my-test-iam-role" {
    name = "my-test-iam-role"
    assume_role_policy = <<EOF
    {
            "Version": "2012-10-17",
            "Statement": [
            {
                    "Action": "sts:AssumeRole",
                    "Principal": {
                    "Service": "ec2.amazonaws.com"
            },
            "Effect": "Allow"
    }
    ]
    }
    EOF
}
```

First, in the `my-test-iam-role` resource, we grant the EC2 service (via its service principal, `ec2.amazonaws.com`) the right to perform the `sts:AssumeRole` action. This is the API action that the EC2 instance can use to assume the role.

As you can see, we are just writing the same JSON policy format we did previously by hand.

This Terraform code has created the role, but it is not yet attached to our instance. To do this, we need to create an EC2 instance profile:

```
resource "aws_iam_instance_profile" "my-test-iam-
instance-profile" {
  name = "my-test-iam-instance-profile"
  role = "${aws_iam_role.my-test-iam-role.name}"
}
```

With `instance_profile` done, we can create an IAM policy that restricts the instance profile to carry out only a few actions on one bucket:

```
resource "aws_iam_role_policy" "my-test-policy" {
  name = "my-test-iam-policy"
  role = "${aws_iam_role.my-test-iam-role.id}"
  policy = <<EOF
{
  "Version": "2012-10-17",
  "Statement": [
    {
      "Sid": "GrantS3Access",
      "Effect": "Allow",
      "Action": [
        "s3:ListBucket",
        "s3:PutObject",
        "s3:GetObject"
      ],
      "Resource": [
        "<insert-bucket-arn>",
        "<insert-bucket-arn>/*"
      ]
    }
  ]
}
EOF
}
```

Finally, we create an EC2 instance with the previously created instance profile. Before that, please read the following note.

> **Important note**
>
> Make sure to create a public/private key pair called `packtpub` in the EC2 console or via the CLI. You can use the following command to create a key pair with the correct name and save it as `packtpub.pem`:
>
> ```
> aws ec2 create-key-pair --key-name packtpub --key-type rsa --key-
> format pem --query "KeyMaterial" --output text > packtpub.pem
> ```
>
> Remember that if you want to use this key to SSH into your machine on Linux, you'll have to change the access rights to read-only permissions for the user. The command to do this is `chmod 400 packtpub.pem`.

Here is the EC2 instance:

```
resource "aws_instance" "test_ec2_role" {
  ami = "ami-0d5fad86866a3a449"
  instance_type = "t2.micro"
  iam_instance_profile = "${aws_iam_instance_profile.my -test-iam-
instance-profile.name}"
  key_name = "packtpub"
}
```

To create the infrastructure using the Terraform code, we first need to initialize the Terraform working directory. This downloads the required providers and creates a state file:

```
terraform init
```

Next, we can apply the changes:

```
terraform apply
```

To verify that the IAM role was properly attached, you can log in to your EC2 instance (using SSH). Make sure to have the private key you previously created handy:

```
ssh -I <path-to-key> ec2-user@<instance-ip>
```

You can then query the `instance` metadata to see the `arn` value of the attached instance profile:

```
curl http://169.254.169.254/latest/meta-data/iam/info
{
    "Code" : "Success",
    "LastUpdated" : "2020-06-28T05:18:17Z",
    "InstanceProfileArn" : "arn:aws:iam::XXXXXXX:instance-
profile/test-iam-profile1",
    "InstanceProfileId" : "XXXXXXX"
}
```

In the previous example, we saw how **Security Token Service (STS)** is used to allow the EC2 service principal to assume a role. But what is STS?

Short introduction to AWS STS

AWS STS is a service that allows you to request temporary, limited privilege credentials that can last from 15 minutes to 36 hours. The benefit of short-lived credentials is that, in the event of a leak of these keys, they remain active only for a limited amount of time.

Let's say you commit the credentials retrieved from STS to GitHub by accident. At most, these would be valid for 36 hours, thus limiting the time an attacker could use the credentials. Paired with only attaching the least privileges required to those credentials, this is a great way to limit the surface and blast radius of an attack.

To use AWS STS, an application needs to make a request for credentials to STS. STS then generates dynamic credentials. Upon expiration of the credentials, the application can request new credentials from STS. Upon requesting new credentials, STS will check whether the requestor still has the required permissions to request these credentials.

To illustrate this further, let's see how an IAM user would get permission to retrieve credentials from STS.

First, we have an IAM user. This user has a policy attached to it that allows this user to assume an IAM role called S3ReadOnlyAccessRole. You have seen such a policy (allowing the sts:AssumeRole action on a role) with the instance in the previous example. The authenticated IAM user then calls the assume-role operation, which returns new (and temporary) AWS credentials, namely, an access key ID and a secret access key.

S3ReadOnlyAccessRole has a policy attached to it that allows access to an S3 bucket. Using the new credentials returned from the AssumeRole call, the user/application can carry out actions that are permitted by S3ReadOnlyAccessRole.

The advantages of using STS are the following:

- Provides temporary security credentials
- Uses short-term credentials
- No need to rotate/revoke passwords or access keys manually
- Allows for identity federation (we will cover this in depth in *Chapter 17*)

STS is the preferred way to retrieve credentials but what if we still have a few secret keys? In the following chapter, we will use the AWS API and Boto3 to create a script that can check for credentials with an age over a user-specified threshold and deactivate them.

Rotating IAM credentials using Boto3

As we have previously discussed, AWS strongly recommends the usage of STS. But what if, for legacy reasons, our application requires a permanent access key and security key? We still want to rotate them regularly. In this section, we'll write a script using Python3 and Boto3 to check for outdated keys. If our key is older than the threshold, our script will print a message to warn us about the keys that exceed the threshold.

Prerequisites

The user running this script needs the `iam:ListUsers` and `iam:ListAccessKeys` permissions. Make sure that you have followed the setup instructions in *Chapter 1* to have Boto3 and Python3 set up.

Creating a script to detect keys that should be rotated

To identify keys that are older than the threshold, we will use Boto3 to list all IAM users in our account. Then, for each of the users, we will retrieve all of their active access keys and check whether they are over our rotation threshold.

Follow these steps to create the script:

1. In a code editor, create a file called `check_rotation.py` and open it.

2. We first import the `boto3` library and the `datetime` module:

   ```
   import boto3
   import datetime
   ```

3. Next, we define our key age threshold. In this example, this is set to 7 days:

   ```
   MAX_AGE_DAYS = 7
   ```

4. Since we need access to the IAM service, we'll create a Boto3 client (more details on what a client is can be found in the Boto3 introduction in *Chapter 1*):

   ```
   iam = boto3.client("iam")
   ```

5. Next, we create a function that, given the response of the AWS API for a key, will calculate the current age of a key in days and return it:

   ```
   def get_key_age(access_key):
       create_date = access_key['CreateDate']
       current_date = datetime.datetime.now(tz=datetime.timezone.
   utc)

       age = current_date - create_date
       return age.days
   ```

6. Next, we need a `main` function to string our workflow together. First, we will retrieve all users from IAM and we will also create an empty list to which we will add all the keys that need rotation:

```python
def main():
    all_users = iam.list_users()['Users']
    keys_for_rotation = []
```

7. Next (and still in the `main` function – mind the indentation), we'll iterate over all users and list all of their access keys:

```python
for user in all_users:
    user_name = user['UserName']
    key_response = iam.list_access_keys(UserName=user_name)

    print(f"User: {user_name}")
```

8. Now, we can iterate over each access key, calculate the age, check whether the age is over the threshold, and print out some debug information:

```python
for access_key in key_response['AccessKeyMetadata']:
    key_id = access_key['AccessKeyId']
    age = get_key_age(access_key)
    print(f"- {key_id}: {age}")

    if age > MAX_AGE_DAYS:
        keys_for_rotation.append((user_name, key_id))
```

9. Finally, we want to print out all the keys that have been identified as outdated and run our `main` method. Mind the indentation:

```python
print()
print("Keys for rotation")
for user, key_id in keys_for_rotation:
    print(f"{key_id} from {user}")

if __name__ == "__main__":
    main()
```

10. Run the script by using the `python3` command:

    `python3 check_rotation.py`

The output of such a script can look like this. Your specific output will vary based on the names of the names and number of users you have in your account:

```
python3 check_keys.py
User: packt-user
```

```
- AKI<redacted>: 9
- AKI<redacted>: 8
User: user2
- AKI<redacted>: 290

Keys for rotation:
AKI<redacted> from user user2
```

As you can see in this example output (yours will differ!), we have two users with three active keys. Two of them have an age that is under the threshold, so only `user2` with an access key that has been active for `290` days is identified as a candidate for rotation.

> **Note**
>
> You could automatically invalidate the keys that exceed the threshold. To do this, the user running the script needs the `iam:UpdateAccessKey` permission, and the corresponding function call in Boto3 is as follows: `Iam.update_access_key(UserName=<user_name>, AccessKeyId=<access_key_id>, Status='Inactive')`

In this section, we had a brief introduction to IAM policies. We saw how these policies can be used to handle the authorization of actions within the AWS cloud. We also saw how to write small administrative scripts that can automate common reporting tasks like checking for outdated access keys.

Summary

In this chapter, we explored the different core components that make up the IAM service in AWS. We saw how users and groups can be granted permission to carry out actions on resources within the platform using IAM policies. We also had a first look into STS and wrote a short script using Boto3 to identify access keys that are ready for rotation.

In the next chapter, we'll get started with the first component of infrastructure within AWS, Amazon **Virtual Private Cloud** – or **VPC**.

Get This Book's PDF Version and Exclusive Extras

UNLOCK NOW

Scan the QR code (or go to `packtpub.com/unlock`). Search for this book by name, confirm the edition, and then follow the steps on the page.

Note: Keep your invoice handly. Purchase made directly from packt don't require one.

Part 2:
Building Infrastructure

In this part, we'll introduce the basic blocks of infrastructure within AWS – the **Virtual Private Cloud (VPC)** that defines your network within AWS and **Elastic Compute Cloud (EC2)**. EC2 provides you with the ability to launch virtual machines – called instances – into your VPC. This part explores the concepts of VPCs and EC2 and introduces you to the code required to automate the deployment of the infrastructure.

This part contains the following chapters:

- *Chapter 3, Creating a Data Center in the Cloud Using a VPC*
- *Chapter 4, Scalable Compute Capacity in the Cloud via EC2*

3

Creating a Data Center in the Cloud Using a VPC

In the previous chapter, we had a look at the IAM service and how we can use its roles and policies to allow or deny access to a resource.

But where do we deploy these resources into? This is where **Virtual Private Clouds** (**VPCs**) come into play. You can think of a VPC as your data center in the cloud. It resembles a separate environment in which you can set up your own network topology and later deploy resources.

In this chapter, we're going to cover the following main topics:

- Setting up VPCs in the console and via infrastructure as code
- Cloud networking concepts and their components
- Connecting two VPCs
- Verifying the status of a VPC via Boto3

Let's get started!

Technical requirements

Before following along with this chapter, please create an AWS account for yourself. You can sign up at https://aws.amazon.com. You should also have basic knowledge, as well as a working installation, of both Terraform and Boto3. We covered both of these in *Chapter 1*.

A basic understanding of Python will help with the programming-based sections of this chapter.

Basic knowledge of networking concepts such as subnets, routing, **Classless Inter-Domain Routing** (**CIDR**), and IP addresses will help you get the most out of this chapter.

All scripts from this section can be found with the following GitHub link:

`https://github.com/PacktPublishing/AWS-for-System-Administrators-Second-Edition`

The CiA video for this chapter can be found at `https://packt.link/jCwAi`

A VPC and its components

A VPC functions as a virtual network and thus we will find many concepts from traditional networks reproduced in AWS and within a VPC. When setting up your account, AWS will create a VPC in each of the Regions. This VPC is known as the **default VPC**.

VPCs are Region-specific but you are not limited to one VPC per Region. This means that a VPC can't span multiple Regions, but you can create multiple VPCs in the same Region. The following figure shows an architectural depiction of two VPCs within a Region that has three **Availability Zones (AZs)**.

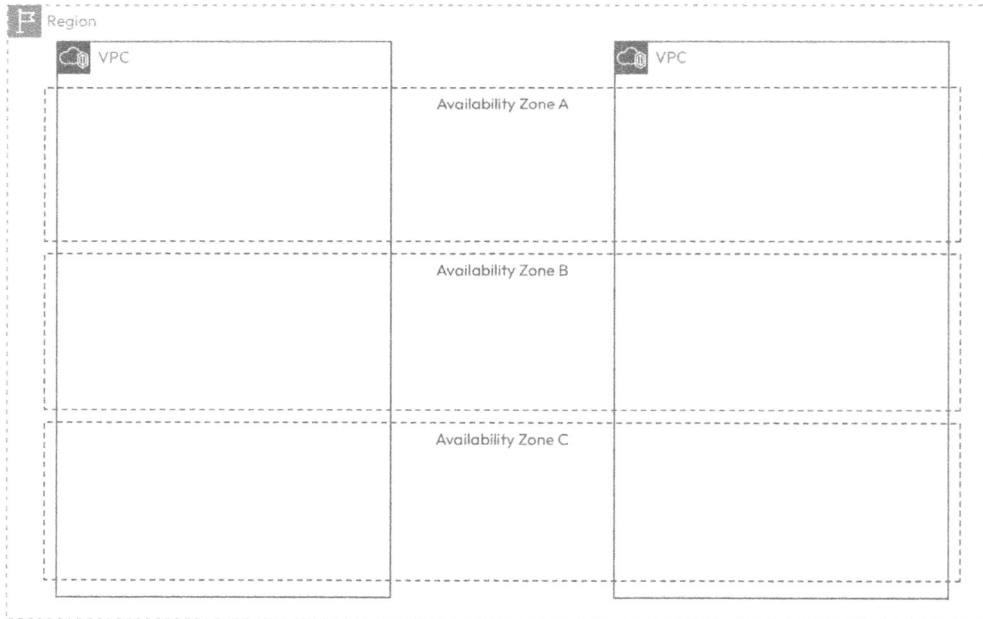

Figure 3.1 – Multiple VPCs within a Region that has three AZs

In the previous chapter, we had a quick introduction to the way the AWS infrastructure is built and saw the concept of AZs. VPCs span all AZs of a Region. When creating a VPC, we assign a range of IP addresses by defining a CIDR block that is associated with this VPC. Resources deployed within the VPC will then be assigned IP addresses out of that CIDR block.

> **Note**
> Be careful when choosing your CIDR block. While many decisions within the cloud can be reworked later, redoing your IPs can be difficult. It is thus advisable to use non-overlapping IP ranges.

To further subdivide our VPC, we use subnets. We can have multiple subnets within a VPC. Subnets always span one AZ, and when creating them, you'll define the subnet to use a CIDR range of IP addresses. The type of your subnet is determined by how you configure your routing. A few common types are the following:

- **Public subnets**: These are for subnets that have direct routes to the public internet
- **Private subnets**: These are for subnets that do not have direct routes to the public internet and thus need a route to a NAT device to make requests to the public internet
- **Isolated subnets**: These are for subnets that can't route to any destinations outside of the VPC

The following figure shows two VPCs within a Region with three AZs. The VPCs contain a private and a public subnet for each of the three AZs.

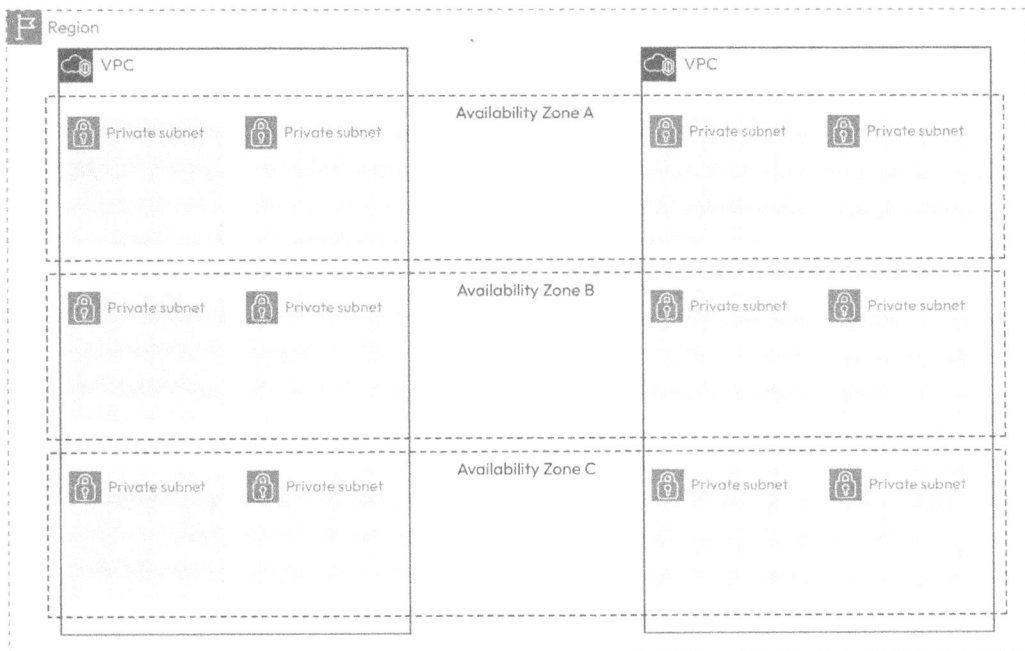

Figure 3.2 – Two VPCs with a public and a private subnet in each AZ

But how do we determine the routing of a subnet? By associating it with a route table. By default, a subnet will be associated with the route table of the VPC that it is part of. We can either change the route table of the VPC or associate the subnet with its own route table.

One piece of information that is missing here is our access to the public internet. To allow communication from and to the public internet, we need another component, called an **internet gateway**. These are commonly abbreviated to **IGW**. A subnet is known as a **public subnet** if it is associated with a route table that has a route to an IGW. Note that you can provide outbound-only access to the internet for a private subnet using a NAT gateway. We'll be covering these in the next chapter.

With this theory at the back of our minds, let's create a VPC as well as a public subnet and an IGW.

Creating a VPC using the AWS console

For this first walk-through, we will use the AWS console and create our VPC and associated subnets. Before creating the VPC and associated subnets, we need to define a few properties:

- The name of our VPC will be vpc-a.
- The CIDR range of our subnet will be 10.0.0.0/16. This is a very large block of 65,536 IP addresses, and you can choose a smaller block if you want to. If you do so, make sure to adjust your subnet ranges.

In the AWS console, follow these steps to create our first VPC:

1. In the AWS console, make sure that you are in the **North Virginia** (**us-east-1**) Region by checking in the Region dropdown in the top-right corner.

2. Search for VPC and select **Your VPCs** in the left navigation. You'll see a **Create VPC** button in the top-right corner, as shown in *Figure 3.3*:

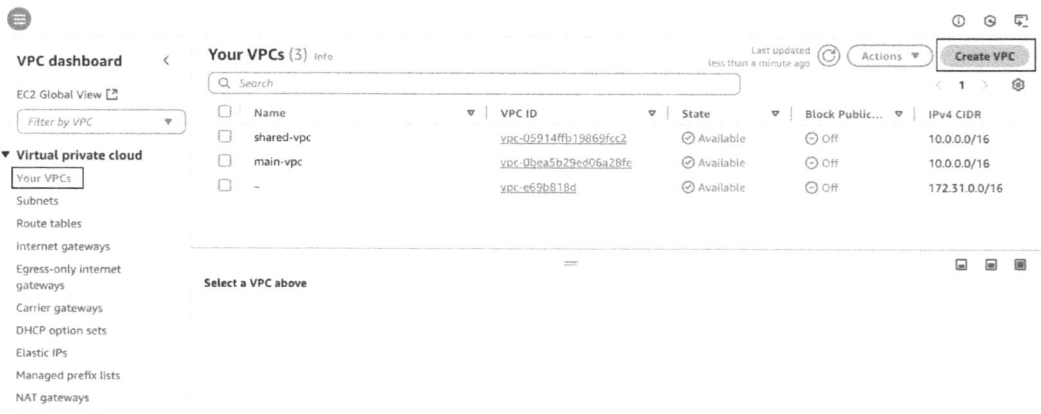

Figure 3.3 – The VPC dashboard with the list of your current VPCs

3. Click the **Create VPC** button. Next, fill out the following details:

    *   **Resources to create**: Select **VPC only** since we'll be creating our subnets, route tables, and so on by hand.

    *   **Name tag**: Type vpc-a.

    *   **IPv4 CIDR block**: Select **IPv4 CIDR manual input** and then type the CIDR block you have chosen. In this example, it is 10.0.0.0/16.

    *   **IPv6 CIDR block**: Select **No IPv6 CIDR block**.

    *   **Tenancy**: Select **Default**. Here, you have the choice between **Default**, which will run instances deployed into this VPC on shared hardware, and **Dedicated**, which, with a fee, will run all instances in this VPC on single-tenant, dedicated hardware. We'll choose the **Default** option since we don't need the single tenancy and want to avoid extra costs.

4. Click **Create VPC** on the bottom right to create the VPC.

Once you have created your VPC, you'll see a few default resources, such as a main route table (number **1** in the following figure) and a main network ACL (number **2** in the following figure).

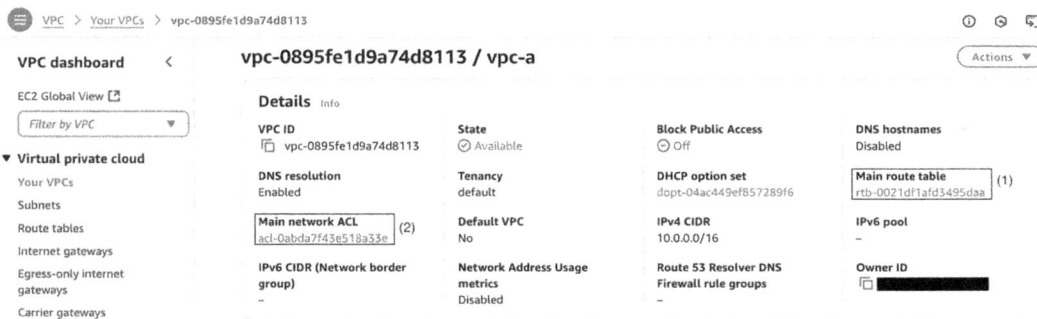

Figure 3.4 – Overview of the newly created VPC with associated default resources

Creating subnets in our VPC

Before having a deeper look into the route table, let's create subnets inside of our VPC.

For this example, we are going to create two subnets, one in AZ A and one in AZ B. For the subnet in AZ A, we'll be using the 10.0.1.0/24 range, and for the subnet in AZ B, we'll be using the 10.0.2.0/24 range. Let's start:

1. Inside the AWS console, choose the **Subnets** entry in the left-hand navigation pane and, on the top right, click on **Create Subnet**.

2. In the dropdown, select the previously created VPC to be able to specify the following subnet settings.

3. Fill in the following details under **Subnet settings**, as shown in *Figure 3.5*:

    -   **Subnet name**: We'll choose `us-east-1-vpc-a-public-a` in this example

    -   **Availability Zone**: We'll set this to **us-east-1a**

    -   **IPv4 subnet CIDR block**: This will be set to **10.0.1.0/24** as we discussed previously

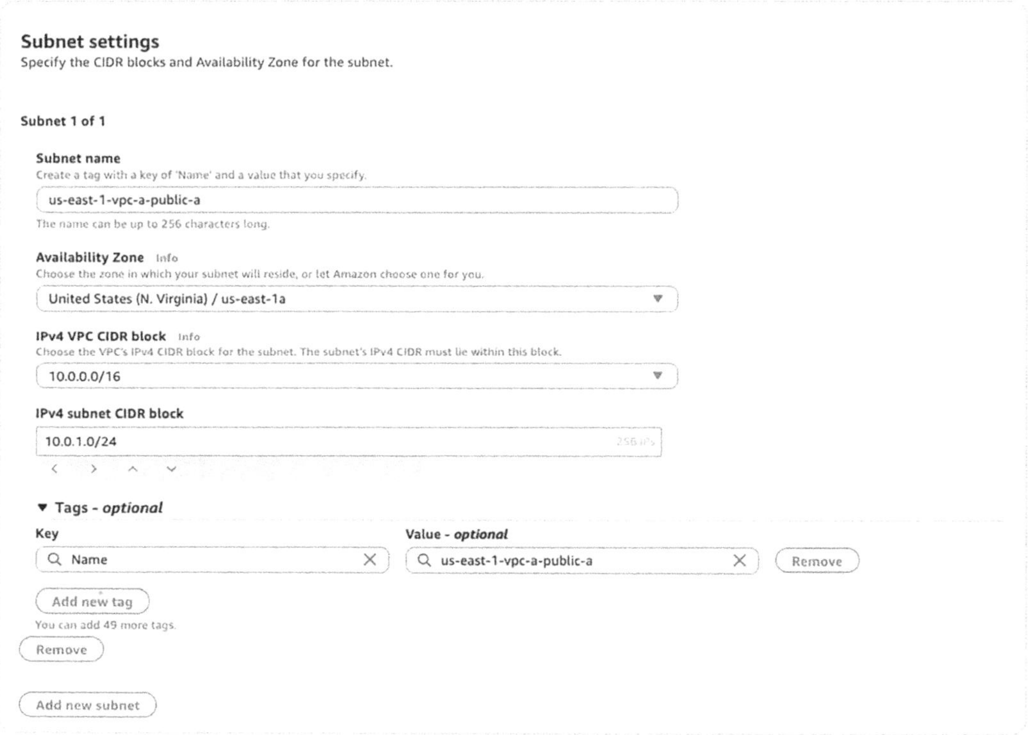

Subnet settings
Specify the CIDR blocks and Availability Zone for the subnet.

Subnet 1 of 1

Subnet name
Create a tag with a key of 'Name' and a value that you specify.

> us-east-1-vpc-a-public-a

The name can be up to 256 characters long.

Availability Zone   Info
Choose the zone in which your subnet will reside, or let Amazon choose one for you.

> United States (N. Virginia) / us-east-1a   ▼

IPv4 VPC CIDR block   Info
Choose the VPC's IPv4 CIDR block for the subnet. The subnet's IPv4 CIDR must lie within this block.

> 10.0.0.0/16   ▼

IPv4 subnet CIDR block

> 10.0.1.0/24   256 IPs

< > ∧ ∨

▼ Tags - *optional*

Key	Value - *optional*	
Q Name ✕	Q us-east-1-vpc-a-public-a ✕	Remove

Add new tag
You can add 49 more tags.

Remove

Add new subnet

Figure 3.5 – Settings for our first subnet

4. Click **Create Subnet** to create the new subnet.

There are two things to note here. In this example, we have used a simple naming convention of `<region>-<vpc-name>-<subnet_type>-<availability_zone>` to come up with the name of `us-east-1-vpc-a-public-a`. While you don't have to follow this exact naming convention, you should come up with your own naming convention to make it easier to identify and associate resources. As you have seen previously, you'd normally have at least one subnet per AZ. In

Regions such as us-east-1, where, at the time of writing, there are six AZs, it can become difficult to identify the subnet you are searching for.

Another thing you might notice is that the number of available IP addresses in the overview doesn't include all the IP addresses in your selected range. Regardless of the CIDR range you chose, you won't be able to use the first four and the last IP address.

Let's take the 10.0.1.0/24 CIDR range as an example:

- 10.0.1.0 is the network address
- 10.0.1.1 is reserved for the AWS VPC router
- 10.0.1.2 is reserved for the AWS DNS server
- 10.0.1.3 is reserved for future use by AWS
- 10.0.1.255 is the network's broadcast address

We need to repeat the steps outlined in this chapter for all subnets we want to add to our VPC. The following figure shows the settings for the second subnet.

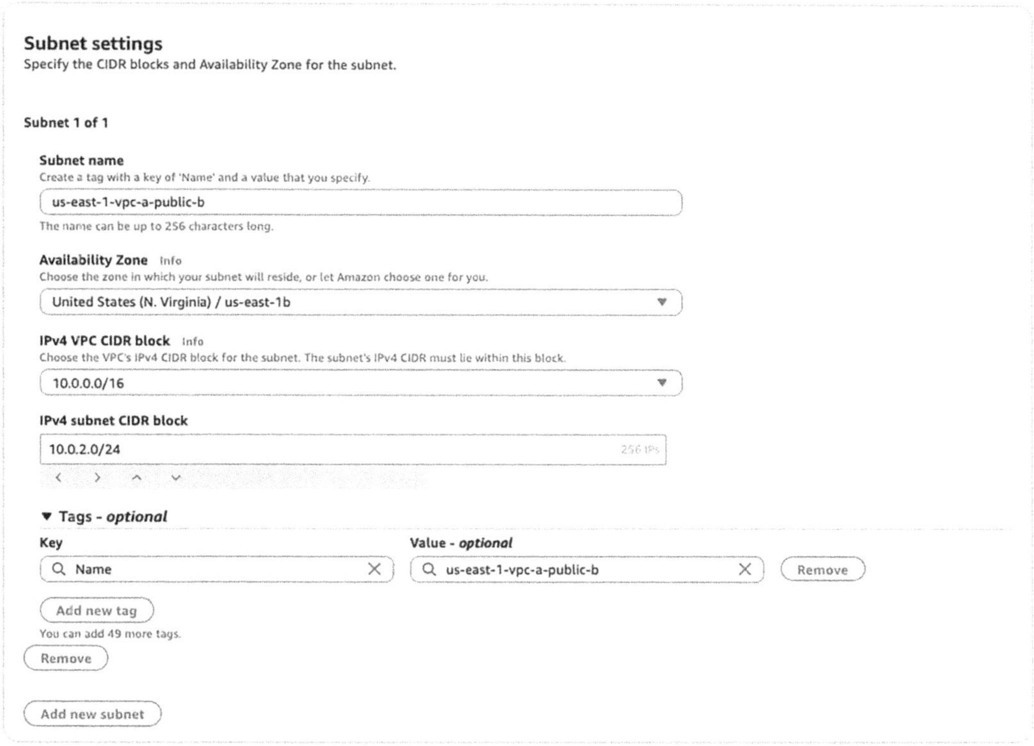

Figure 3.6 – Settings for the second subnet in AZ B

A nice way to get an overview of all the networking-related resources within our VPC is with **Resource map**. The **Resource map** section in the following figure shows an overview of subnets and their association with the specific VPC.

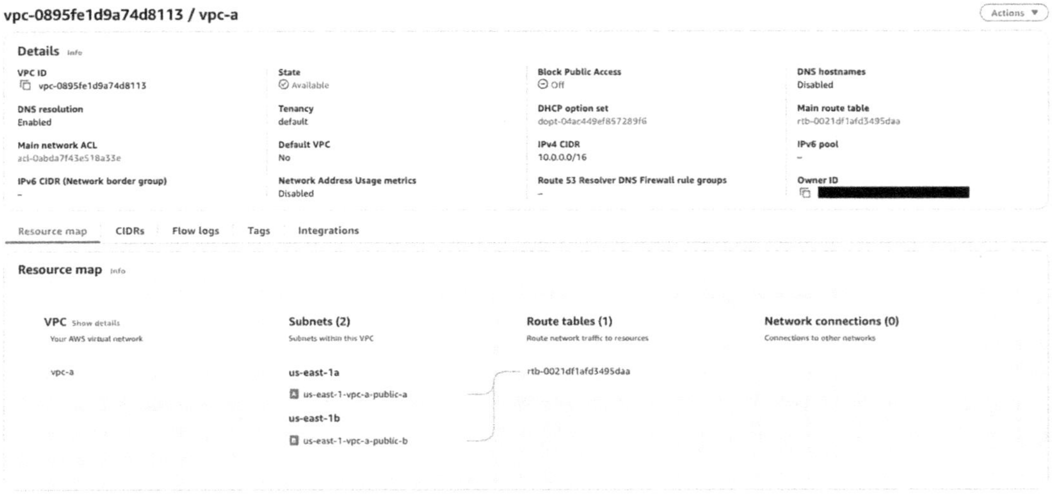

Figure 3.7 – The resource map of our VPC so far

Follow these steps to get to your VPC resource map:

1.   In the left-hand navigation, click **Your VPCs**.

2.   In the list of VPCs, select our previously created vpc-a.

3.   On the details page, click on **Resource Map** on the lower tab menu.

In the map, we can see that we have our two subnets that are associated with this VPC, as well as the default route table. We can also see that both subnets, because we haven't associated a subnet-specific route table with them, have been associated with the VPC's main route table. This is indicated by the gray lines leading from the subnet to the route table.

Technically, our subnets are not *public*, as their naming would suggest, yet. As we have previously discussed, a public subnet is a subnet that has an IGW associated with it. So, let's create one!

Creating an IGW in our VPC

In order for resources in our subnet to be able to reach and be reachable from the internet, we need an IGW.

Follow these steps to create an IGW:

1. Navigate to the **VPC** menu in the AWS console.

2. In the left-hand navigation, select the **Internet Gateways** menu item.

3. On the top right, select the **Create Internet Gateway** button.

Create internet gateway Info
An internet gateway is a virtual router that connects a VPC to the internet. To create a new internet gateway specify the name for the gateway below.

Internet gateway settings

Name tag
Creates a tag with a key of 'Name' and a value that you specify.

| vpc-a-igw |

Tags - optional
A tag is a label that you assign to an AWS resource. Each tag consists of a key and an optional value. You can use tags to search and filter your resources or track your AWS costs.

Key   Value - optional
| Q Name   × | | Q vpc-a-igw   × | (Remove)

(Add new tag)
You can add 49 more tags.

Cancel   **Create internet gateway**

Figure 3.8 – Values for the creation of our IGW

4. In the **Creation** dialog, type a name for your IGW. This can be anything, but for this example, we'll be using a name that makes the association between this IGW and our VPC (vpc-a) clear.

   In the **Name tag** field, type in the name. In this example, you can see it's vpc-a-igw.

5. Click **Create internet gateway**.

   After the IGW has been created, you'll be taken to an overview page for this gateway. Notice that the state says **Detached**. By default, the previously created IGW won't be associated with a VPC. In order to create this association, we need to *attach* it.

6. In the top-right corner, select **Actions**, and in the dropdown, select **Attach to VPC**.

7. In the dialog, choose the previously created VPC from the dropdown and click **Attach internet gateway**.

igw-0ff805e6ff4de2fa9 / vpc-a-igw   (Actions ▲)

                                                                                            | Attach to VPC |
Details Info | Detach from VPC |
Internet gateway ID   State   VPC ID   Owner | Manage tags |
☐ igw-0ff805e6ff4de2fa9   ⊖ Detached   –   ☐ ▮▮▮▮▮▮ | Delete |

Tags   (Manage tags)

| Q Search tags | ‹ 1 › ⚙

Key | Value
Name | vpc-a-igw

Figure 3.9 – Menu item to attach the IGW to a VPC

When navigating back to the resource map of our VPC, we can now see the newly created and attached IGW under **Network connections**.

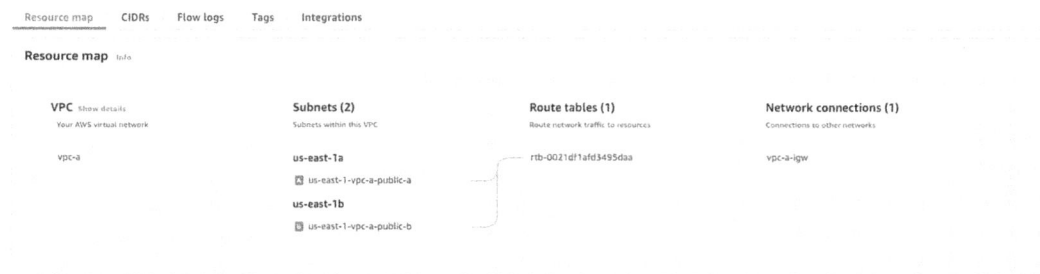

Figure 3.10 – Resource map showing the newly created IGW

Now, there is one last thing missing in order to make these subnets public. We previously stated that we also need the subnets to route their traffic to the IGW. We do this by creating a route table, creating a routing rule to send all traffic to the IGW, and then associating our subnet with the newly created route table.

Creating a route table

Before creating a route table, you might wonder why we can't modify the main route table of our VPC. The answer to this question is that we can. However, one consideration we should take into account when doing this is the fact that subnets that have not been explicitly associated with a route table will be associated with the main route table of our VPC.

This opens us up to a scenario where the default route table has a route to an IGW and thus allows all resources in the associated subnets to route to the internet. This means that if someone creates a subnet in this VPC without associating another route table, the subnet will be public. This can be desired behavior, but we need to be aware of this.

In order to create a new route table, follow these steps:

1. Navigate to the **VPC** menu in the AWS console.

2. On the left navigation menu, click **Route tables**.

3. In the top-right corner, click the **Create route table** button.

4. You'll be asked to fill in the information of your new route table:

   - **Name:** Select something that makes it clear what this route table is about, for example, `vpc-a-public`

   - **VPC:** Select the previously created VPC to associate this route table with the VPC

5.   Click the **Create route table** button, as shown in the following figure:

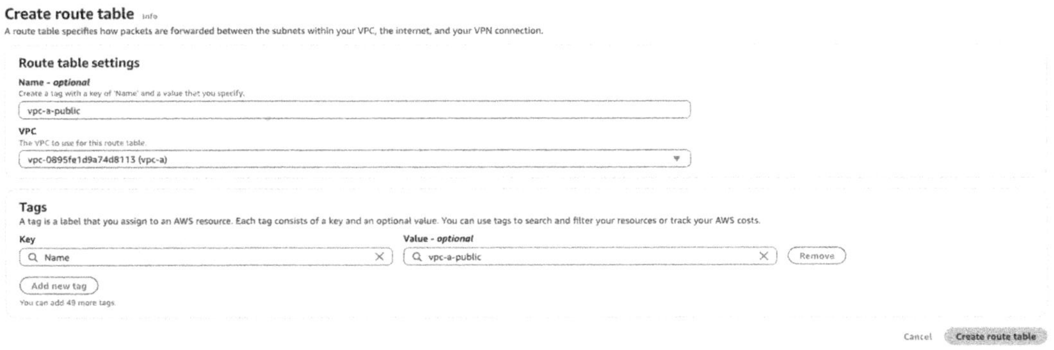

Figure 3.11 – Inputs for our new route table

So far, we have created a new route table and have associated it with our VPC, but we haven't associated the IGW with it yet. To do this, we need to create a route.

As you can see in the overview (*Figure 3.12*), by default, we have a rule that routes the entire range of the VPC (10.0.0.0/16 in this example) to the local targets.

To create a new route, follow these steps:

1.   On the overview page of your route table, click the **Edit routes** button in the lower-right corner.

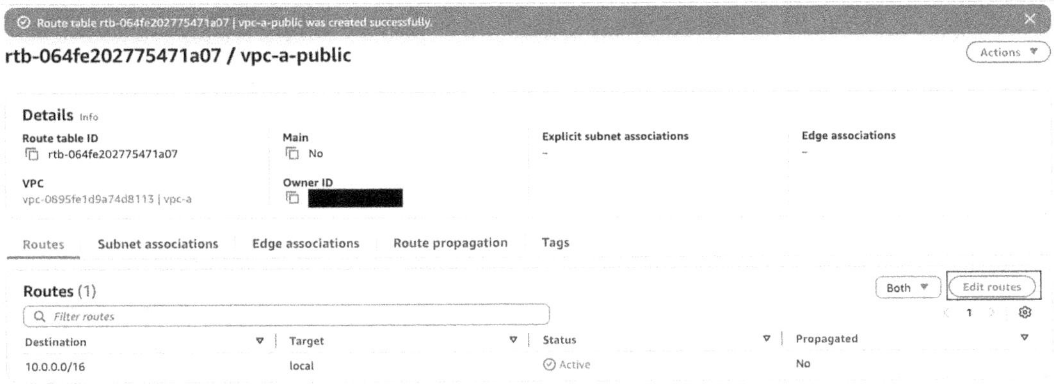

Figure 3.12 – Overview of the route table including the list of currently published routes

2. Inside the **Edit routes** menu, click the **Add route** button on the lower left. For **Destination**, select the 0 . 0 . 0 . 0 / 0 CIDR range. This is the range of all IP addresses. For **Target**, select **Internet Gateway** as the target type and then select our previously created IGW.

Edit routes

Destination	Target	Status	Propagated	
10.0.0.0/16	local ▾	⊘ Active	No	
	Q local ✕			
Q 0.0.0.0/0 ✕	Internet Gateway ▾	–	No	Remove
	Q igw-06bfb4b6506946a1c ✕			

Add route

Cancel Preview Save changes

Figure 3.13 – Route configuration for our IGW in the newly created route table

3. Click **Save changes**.

We now have a route table within our VPC that allows traffic to the internet via the IGW. The last step is to associate the previously created subnets with this route table. Follow these steps to do this:

1. Navigate to the overview of our previously created route table and find the **Subnet associations** tab.

2. In the tab, there are two sections: **Explicit subnet associations**, which indicates all subnets that have been explicitly associated with this routing table, and **Subnets without explicit association**. These are all the subnets that don't have an explicit association and are thus associated with the main route table.

3. Click the **Edit subnet associations** button next to the **Explicit subnet associations** section.

4. On the new page, select the two public subnets we created before and click **Save associations**.

Edit subnet associations
Change which subnets are associated with this route table.

Available subnets (2/2)

	Name	Subnet ID	IPv4 CIDR	IPv6 CIDR	Route table ID
☑	us-east-1-vpc-a-public-b	subnet-0bba1df82603875d6	10.0.2.0/24	–	Main (rtb-0021df1afd3495daa)
☑	us-east-1-vpc-a-public-a	subnet-0daccc6c569a219a1	10.0.1.0/24	–	Main (rtb-0021df1afd3495daa)

Selected subnets

subnet-0bba1df82603875d6 / us-east-1-vpc-a-public-b ✕   subnet-0daccc6c569a219a1 / us-east-1-vpc-a-public-a ✕

Cancel Save associations

Figure 3.14 – Association of subnets with our routing table

We can now navigate back to our resource map in the VPC and notice two changes.

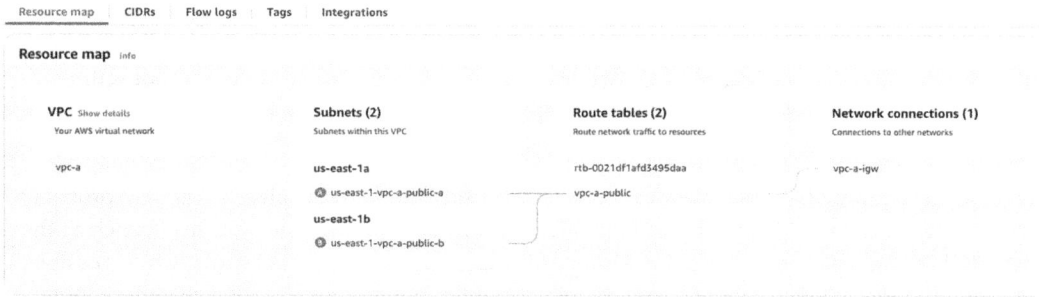

Figure 3.15 – Resource map after all associations

As seen in the preceding figure, the changes are as follows:

- The subnets now have a gray line connecting them to the previously created IGW via the newly created route table
- The little icon next to the subnets has changed from blue (indicating private) to green, indicating a public subnet

This means that we have now successfully associated the public subnets to our IGW via the route table.

Exploring network access control lists

One feature of networking in the VPC that we have seen but haven't had a closer look at yet is **network access control lists**, or **NACLs**.

NACLs allow us to, on a VPC or subnet level, allow or deny traffic based on protocol or port. By default, a VPC will have a main NACL associated with it. NACLs are made up of rules that are divided into **inbound** and **outbound** rules. **Inbound rules** control what traffic is allowed to come into our network and **outbound rules** determine what traffic is allowed to leave our network. The following figure shows the inbound rules for our default NACL. It shows that this rule allows all inbound traffic from any source IP.

Figure 3.16 – Overview of inbound rules of our default NACL

As you can see in the preceding figure, we have a rule that *allows* all traffic, from all protocols, on all ports from all source IP addresses.

While NACLs can be used as an additional layer of security, we generally use **Security Groups (SGs)** when restricting access to our resources. We'll learn more about SGs when we talk about setting up EC2 instances in the next chapter. Once we have introduced SGs in *Chapter 4*, we'll have a discussion about when it would make sense to augment SGs with NACLs.

In this chapter so far, we have seen how to create a VPC using the web console. As you have probably realized, there are many different things to create and configure besides the VPC itself, such as the subnets, IGWs, and custom route tables. Doing this manually in the AWS console, while possible, is not very reproducible and is prone to human error. In the next section, we'll thus automate this process using CloudFormation.

Creating a second VPC using CloudFormation

In this section, we'll create another VPC. But instead of creating the VPC in the console via clicking - often referred to as *ClickOps*, we'll be doing it in a CloudFormation template.

> **Note**
>
> While this example is in CloudFormation, there is a commented version of the same workflow in CDK and Terraform that is available in the GitHub repository for this book.

Setting up the VPC and subnets

Let's begin setting up our CloudFormation stack:

1. Create a file called `vpc.yml` and open it in a code editor of your choice.

2. Add the following AWS template version and description boilerplate:

   ```
   AWSTemplateFormatVersion: "2010-09-09"
   Description: "CloudFormation template to create a VPC"
   ```

3. Next, we specify the parameters that we want to have. **Parameters** are values that we can pass into the CloudFormation template at creation time. In our example, there will be two parameters:

   - VpcCidrPrefix: This is the CIDR prefix for our VPC (i.e., 10.0)

   - VpcName: This is the name of our VPC

   ```
   Parameters:
     VpcCidrPrefix:
       Type: "String"
       AllowedPattern: "(\\d{1,3})\\.(\\d{1,3})"
   ```

```
VpcName:
  Type: "String"
```

Notice how we use a regex to allow only parameters where there are two one- to three-digit numbers that are separated by a dot. Both parameters are of type `String`.

4. Next, we need to create the actual resources. We use the **intrinsic function** of `Join` to combine our CIDR prefix that we defined as a parameter with the hardcoded `0.0/16` postfix. Intrinsic functions are built-in functions that help us with tasks such as combining multiple strings or referencing a variable. We use the `Ref` function to reference the VpcName parameter when setting the name of our VPC. Intrinsic functions such as `Join` and `Ref` are called using an exclamation point followed by the name of the function and the arguments.

Within the definition of the VPC properties, we enable DNS support using the `EnableDnsSupport` property set to `True`. This means that DNS resolution within the VPC on the AWS-provided DNS server is enabled. We then also set `EnableDnsHostnames` to `True`, which tells AWS to assign a hostname to each instance that is launched into this VPC:

```
Resources:
  Vpc:
    Type: "AWS::EC2::VPC"
    Properties:
      CidrBlock: !Join [ "", [!Ref VpcCidrPrefix, ".0.0/16"]]
      EnableDnsSupport: True
      EnableDnsHostnames: True
      Tags:
      - Key: Name
        Value: !Ref VpcName
```

Additional information

In the previous step, we saw how DNS resolution is enabled – but where is the DNS server? When we create a new VPC within AWS and assign it a CIDR range, AWS will reserve five IP addresses (the first four and the last) that are within the CIDR range. These reserved addresses can't be assigned to instances within the VPC.

Let's take the `10.0.0.0/24` range as an example. Within this range, the following IPs are reserved:

- `10.0.0.0`: The network address.
- `10.0.0.1`: The "first" address. This is reserved for the VPC router.
- `10.0.0.2`: The "second" address. This is the address used by the VPC DNS server.
- `10.0.0.3`: The "third" address. This is reserved by AWS for future use.
- `10.0.0.255`: The "last" address, also known as the "broadcast" address. AWS does not support the networking concept of broadcasting and thus this address is also reserved.

5. Next, we'll create a public subnet. In this block, you'll find two new intrinsic CloudFormation functions: `Select` and `GetAZs`.

    `Select` allows us to select an element out of a list, while `GetAZs` returns the list of AZs inside of the Region that this stack is being deployed into. For a Region such as us-east-1 with its (at the time of writing) six AZs, this list would look like this: `["us-east-1a"`, `"us-east-1b"`, `"us-east-1c"`, `"us-east-1d"`, `"us-east-1e"` , `"us-east-1f"]`. So, the `!Select [0, !GetAZs ""]` function call would return us-east-1a.

    Notice that the index for the `Select` function starts at 0. By using `Select` and `GetAZs`, we do not need to hardcode this information. Notice also how we reference the previously created VPC using the `!Ref Vpc` function. Since instances in a public subnet should also receive a public IP address, we set the `MapPublicIpOnLaunch` property to `True`:

    ```
    PublicSubnetA:
      Type: "AWS::EC2::Subnet"
      Properties:
        AvailabilityZone: !Select [0, !GetAZs ""]
        CidrBlock: !Join [ "", [!Ref VpcCidrPrefix, ".1.0/24"]]
        MapPublicIpOnLaunch: True
        VpcId: !Ref Vpc
        Tags:
        - Key: Name
          Value: !Join [ "", [!Ref VpcName, "-public"]]
    ```

6. Now that we have our public subnet created, we can create two more private subnets that will be in the second and third AZs. We indicate that we do not want to assign a public IP address to instances assigned to this subnet by setting the `MapPublicIpOnLaunch` property to `False`. We also use indexes 1 and 2 for our `!Select` function call to retrieve the second and third AZs (`us-east-1b` and `us-east-1c` for the previously seen example of the us-east-1 Region):

    ```
    PrivateSubnetB:
      Type: "AWS::EC2::Subnet"
      Properties:
        AvailabilityZone: !Select [1, !GetAZs ""]
        CidrBlock: !Join [ "", [!Ref VpcCidrPrefix, ".2.0/24"]]
        MapPublicIpOnLaunch: False
        VpcId: !Ref Vpc
        Tags:
        - Key: Name
          Value: !Join [ "", [!Ref VpcName, "-private-1"]]
    PrivateSubnetC:
      Type: "AWS::EC2::Subnet"
      Properties:
    ```

```
        AvailabilityZone: !Select [2, !GetAZs ""]
        CidrBlock: !Join [ "", [!Ref VpcCidrPrefix, ".3.0/24"]]
        MapPublicIpOnLaunch: False
        VpcId: !Ref Vpc
        Tags:
        - Key: Name
          Value: !Join [ "", [!Ref VpcName, "-private-2"]]
```

7. Finally, we need to return some outputs. By defining outputs in one stack, we can reference these outputs in another stack. Outputs contain a logical ID (such as VpcCidr), a description, a value, and an export name. The value is usually determined by referencing a resource (such as the VPC or a subnet) that was defined in this stack. If we want to use the values of these outputs in another stack – this is called cross-stack referencing – we need to define an export name. This is done using the export directive that follows. To define the export name, we use another intrinsic function, called Sub – short for "substitute." Sub allows us to define a template where – during the creation of the stack – placeholders can be substituted for a value that is only known during or after the creation of the stack. Placeholders, also known as variables, are defined using the ${my-variable} syntax.

AWS defines some variables, also called pseudo parameters, such as the name of the stack (AWS::StackName) or the ID of the account that this stack is being deployed into (AWS::AccountId). All of these AWS-provided pseudo parameters start with AWS::. You can find a complete list of them all here: https://docs.aws.amazon.com/AWSCloudFormation/latest/UserGuide/pseudo-parameter-reference.html.

Let's assume that we will deploy this CloudFormation template under the stack name vpc-b. In our example, below the output that, as a value, contains the ID of our newly created VPC, would have the vpc-b-VpcId export name:

```
Outputs:
  VpcId:
    Description : "VPC ID"
    Value: !Ref Vpc
    Export:
      Name: !Sub ${AWS::StackName}-VpcId
  VpcCidr:
    Description : "VPC CIDR"
    Value: !GetAtt Vpc.CidrBlock
    Export:
      Name: !Sub ${AWS::StackName}-VpcCidr
  PublicSubnetA:
    Description : "Public A Subnet ID"
    Value: !Ref PublicSubnetA
    Export:
```

```
      Name: !Sub ${AWS::StackName}-PublicSubnetA
  PrivateSubnetB:
    Description : "Private B Subnet ID"
    Value: !Ref PrivateSubnetB
    Export:
      Name: !Sub ${AWS::StackName}-PrivateSubnetB
  PrivateSubnetC:
    Description : "Private C Subnet ID"
    Value: !Ref PrivateSubnetC
    Export:
      Name: !Sub ${AWS::StackName}-PrivateSubnetC
```

8. With our CloudFormation template done, we can set the Region we want to deploy it into by setting the AWS_DEFAULT_REGION environment variable:

    ```
    export AWS_DEFAULT_REGION=us-east-1
    ```

9. Next, we validate the template to check that there are no syntax errors:

    ```
    aws cloudformation validate-template --template-body file://vpc.
    yml
    ```

10. Finally, we can create a new stack from this command. Notice how we are passing the two parameters we previously defined at the top of our template into CloudFormation. Mind the space separating the two Parameter definitions:

    ```
    aws cloudformation create-stack --stack-name
    vpc-b --template-body file://vpc.yml --parameters
    ParameterKey=VpcCidrPrefix,ParameterValue=10.0
    ParameterKey=VpcName,ParameterValue=vpc-b
    ```

The preceding command will return a StackId, and after the stack has been created successfully, we should be able to see our newly created VPC in the console, as shown in the following figure.

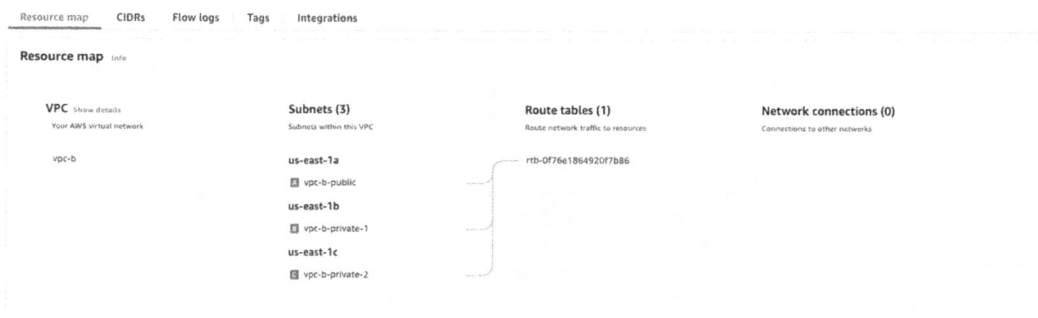

Figure 3.17 – Resource map of the VPC that we have created with CloudFormation

So far, in our CloudFormation stack, we have only recreated a part of the actions we had previously done in the AWS console. We are still missing the route table, IGW, and route table association. So, let's create them in CloudFormation.

Creating an IGW, route table, and subnet association

In this section, we'll complete our CloudFormation-based setup to create the IGW and associate it with our public subnet via the route table.

To do this, follow these steps:

1. Create a file called `attachments.yml` in which we will create our CloudFormation template.

2. Define the default header and a parameter section. We'll create a parameter called `NetworkingStack` that will allow us to pass in the name of our previously created stack. This way, we can reference the outputs from that stack, such as the VPC or subnet ID:

    ```
    AWSTemplateFormatVersion: "2010-09-09"
    Description: "CloudFormation template to create and associate an
    IGW"
    Parameters:
      NetworkStack:
        Type: "String"
    ```

3. Define a new `InternetGateway` resource:

    ```
    Resources:
      InternetGateway:
        Type: AWS::EC2::InternetGateway
        Properties:
          Tags:
            - Key: Name
              Value: !Sub ${NetworkStack}-igw
    ```

4. Next, we define a gateway attachment that will be used to attach our IGW to our VPC. Here, we are using the `Fn::ImportValue` function to import the ID of the VPC we created in the previous stack. Recall that, in the previous stack, we defined an output that had an export name of `<stack-name>-VpcId` (for example, `vpc-b-VpcId`). This is the name we are piecing together here using the `!Sub` function and the parameter we defined for this stack. The `ImportValue` function lets us reference exported values from other stacks as if they were defined in the current stack:

    ```
    InternetGatewayAttachment:
      Type: AWS::EC2::VPCGatewayAttachment
      Properties:
        InternetGatewayId: !Ref InternetGateway
    ```

```
VpcId:
  Fn::ImportValue:
    !Sub ${NetworkStack}-VpcId
```

5. We can then create a public route table:

```
PublicRouteTable:
  Type: AWS::EC2::RouteTable
  Properties:
    VpcId:
      Fn::ImportValue:
        !Sub ${NetworkStack}-VpcId
    Tags:
      - Key: Name
        Value: !Sub ${NetworkStack}-public-rtb
```

6. So far, our route table is empty. So, we'll need to create a route and attach it to the route table. Notice how we use the DependsOn property to make sure that CloudFormation finishes the creation of our IGW attachment (and thus also our IGW) before creating this route entry. We provide the destination CIDR range (0.0.0.0/0 in this example) using the DestinationCidrBlock property and also reference the gateway ID and route table ID using the Ref function to reference the previously created resources:

```
RouteToInternet:
  Type: AWS::EC2::Route
  DependsOn: InternetGatewayAttachment
  Properties:
    DestinationCidrBlock: 0.0.0.0/0
    GatewayId: !Ref InternetGateway
    RouteTableId: !Ref PublicRouteTable
```

7. Finally, we associate our route table with our previously created public subnet by importing the subnet ID from our previous stack:

```
PublicRouteTableAssociation:
  Type: AWS::EC2::SubnetRouteTableAssociation
  Properties:
    RouteTableId: !Ref PublicRouteTable
    SubnetId:
      Fn::ImportValue:
        !Sub ${NetworkStack}-PublicSubnetA
```

8. With our CloudFormation template done, we can set the Region we want to deploy it into by setting the `AWS_DEFAULT_REGION` environment variable. Make sure to use the same Region you used for the previous stack:

    ```
    export AWS_DEFAULT_REGION=us-east-1
    ```

9. Next, we validate the template to check that there are no syntax errors:

    ```
    aws cloudformation validate-template --template-body file://
    attachments.yml
    ```

10. Finally, we can create a new stack from this command. Notice that we are passing the previous stack name (`vpc-b` in this example) as a parameter to the template:

    ```
    aws cloudformation create-stack --stack-name vpc-b-attachments
    --template-body file://attachments.yml --parameters
    ParameterKey=NetworkStack,ParameterValue=vpc-b
    ```

Once the stack has finished completing, we can have a look at the resource map of our VPC and see how the public subnet is now associated with the newly created routing table and that routing table is associated with the newly created IGW.

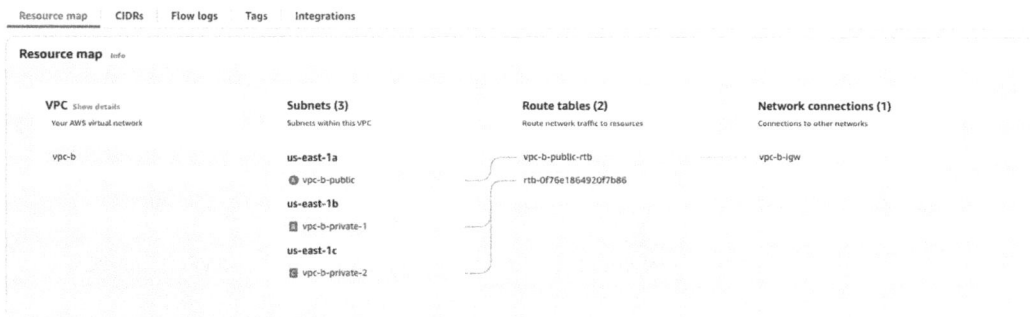

Figure 3.18 – Final resource map of our CloudFormation-created VPC

So far, we have talked a lot about routing traffic from a VPC to the outside internet, but not a lot about routing *between* VPCs. So, in the next section, we will discuss how to interconnect VPCs.

Interconnecting VPCs via peering and Transit Gateway

When dealing with multiple VPCs, there might come a time when we want to enable traffic to flow between these two isolated networks. This is where **VPC peering** comes into play.

VPC peering allows us to interconnect two VPCs and give resources within them to route to resources in the other VPC as if they were in the same network. *Figure 3.19* demonstrates this flow:

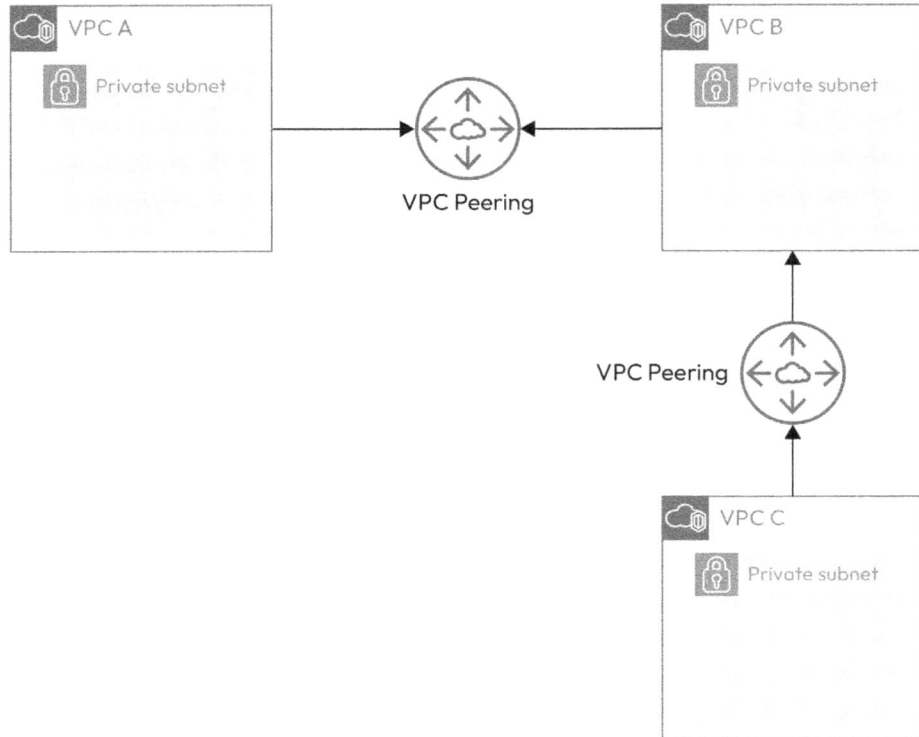

Figure 3.19 – Three VPCs and their two peering connections – VPC A to VPC B and VPC B to VPC C

In the preceding figure, we have a peering between three VPCs. **VPC A** is peered to **VPC B** and **VPC B** is peered to **VPC C**. The peering of two VPCs is always bidirectional. This means that if **VPC A** requests a peering with **VPC B**, then **VPC A** can route traffic into **VPC B** and **VPC B** can route traffic into **VPC A**.

Because of this routing behavior, the VPCs that we want to peer need to have non-overlapping CIDR ranges since we otherwise could not route between them.

Creating a peering between two VPCs

For this section, we'll need two VPCs with non-overlapping CIDR ranges. Luckily, we spent the previous chapter automating the process of creating such VPCs. Let's use the CloudFormation template from the previous chapter to create a new VPC with a non-overlapping CIDR range.

> **Note**
>
> If you haven't followed the previous section, you can download the CloudFormation template from the GitHub repo for this book.

Follow these steps to create the second VPC – we will call it `vpc-c` – with non-overlapping CIDR ranges. Note that we assume that you used the example CIDR range of `10.0.0.0/16` in the previous section to create the first VPC, `vpc-b`. If you used a different CIDR range, please adjust accordingly:

1. Create a new VPC using the template. We'll use the `10.1.0.0/16` CIDR range (which is non-overlapping with the `10.0.0.0/16` CIDR range previously used) and call the `vpc-c` VPC:

    ```
    aws cloudformation create-stack --stack-name
    vpc-c --template-body file://vpc.yml --parameters
    ParameterKey=VpcCidrPrefix,ParameterValue=10.1
    ParameterKey=VpcName,ParameterValue=vpc-c
    ```

2. Next, create the attachments using our second CloudFormation template:

    ```
    aws cloudformation create-stack --stack-name vpc-c-attachments
    --template-body file://attachments.yml --parameters
    ParameterKey=NetworkStackName,ParameterValue=vpc-c
    ```

    With this done, we now have two VPCs (`vpc-b` and `vpc-c`) that have two non-overlapping CIDR ranges (`10.0.0.0/16` and `10.1.0.0/16`). We can now go ahead and initiate a peering connection in the AWS console.

3. Navigate to the VPC dashboard and, in the left-hand navigation, find **Peering connections**. On the top right, you can see a **Create peering connection** button that you can click on to open the dialog to create a new peering.

4. In the **Create peering connection** dialog, type the following details into the form:

    *   **Name:** This is the name of your peering connection. You can use `vpc-b-vpc-c-peering` as an example.

    *   **VPC ID (Requester):** Select the requester VPC. Here, I chose `vpc-b`.

    *   Under **Select another VPC to peer with**, select **My account**, and under **Region**, select **This Region (us-east-1)**.

- **VPC ID (Accepter)**: Select the accepter VPC. Here, I chose `vpc-c`.

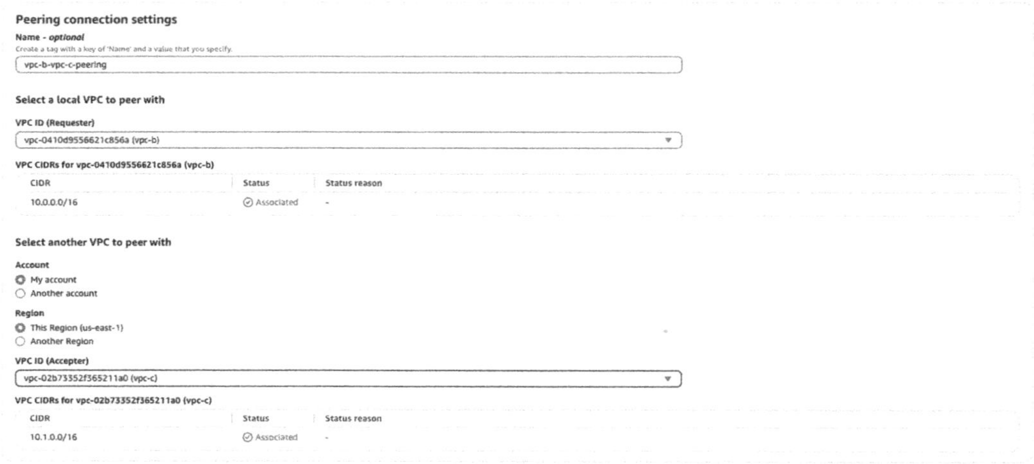

Figure 3.20 – Values for the peering connection

Since peerings are powerful, you can't just create a peering connection – the connection needs to be accepted by the account owning the accepter VPC. In this example, both VPCs belong to our one account.

After the peering connection has been created, you are redirected to a peering overview page. On the top right, you'll see an **Actions** dropdown.

5. Select **Accept request** to accept the peering connection.

In the modal, confirm that you want to peer these two VPCs by clicking **Accept request**.

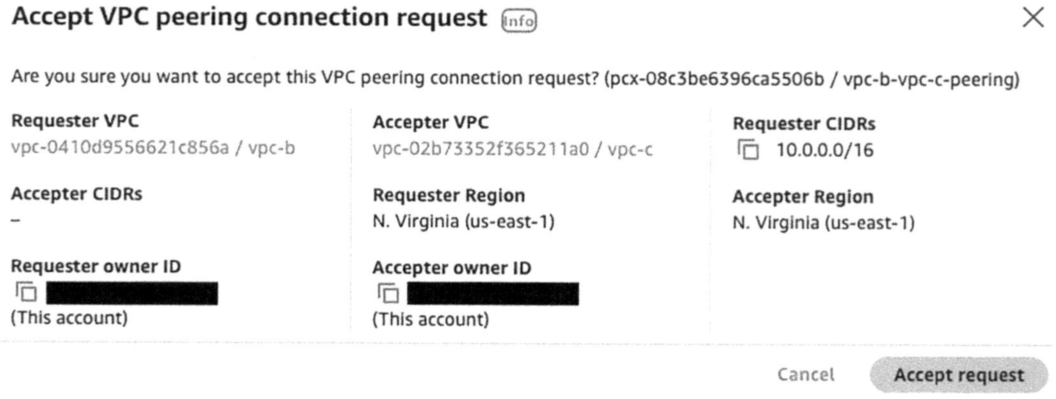

Figure 3.21 – Accept peering request modal

The two VPCs are successfully peered, but we can't route traffic between them since there are no routes allowing traffic to pass from **VPC B** to **VPC C**. To change this, let's modify the routing table of **VPC C**.

6. Find **VPC C** under **Your VPCs** and, on the resource map, click the main route table to modify the routes in it.

7. In the route table overview, click **Edit routes** and **Add route** to create a new route.

8. We want to route all traffic for `10.0.0.0/16` (the CIDR range for **VPC B**) to the peering connection. To do this, fill in the following values:

    - **Destination**: The destination IP range. Use `10.0.0.0/16`.

    - **Target**: The target for all traffic from this IP range. Use **Peering Connection** for **Type** and select the previously created peering in the dropdown.

9. Next, click **Save changes**.

We have just created a route for traffic to flow from **VPC C** to **VPC B**. We'll use this peering in the next chapter, once we have set up EC2 machines, to send traffic from one VPC to the other.

VPC peering offers a convenient way to allow traffic to flow between two VPCs. However, there are a few limitations and caveats. Look back at *Figure 3.19* where we have three VPCs. **VPC A** is paired to **VPC B** and **VPC B** is paired to **VPC C**. One major downside of VPC Peering is that the connectivity is not *transitive*. This means that just because **VPC A** is paired with **VPC B** and **VPC B** is paired with **VPC C**, we *can't* send traffic from **VPC A** to **VPC C**.

In order to achieve traffic flow from **VPC A** to **VPC C**, we'd have to pair the two of them. This results in a **mesh architecture** where every VPC needs to be peered with all other VPCs it should be allowed to route traffic to. This can become too big in terms of peering connections very fast. Assuming you have 50 VPCs that you want to peer with each other (full mesh), you'd need 1,225 peering connections. That's a lot of work, even if automated, and also exceeds the limit of 125 active peerings per VPC.

This is where AWS **Transit Gateway** (**TGW**) comes into play.

What is AWS Transit Gateway?

In this section, you'll get a quick introduction to AWS TGW. We'll have a closer look into TGWs, including the setup of one that is shared between multiple accounts that we will use later in the book in *Chapter 16*.

With AWS TGW, we introduce a centralized **hub-and-spoke** architecture into our cloud network. With TGW, instead of peering all our VPCs together, we attach them to our TGW, as shown in the following figure:

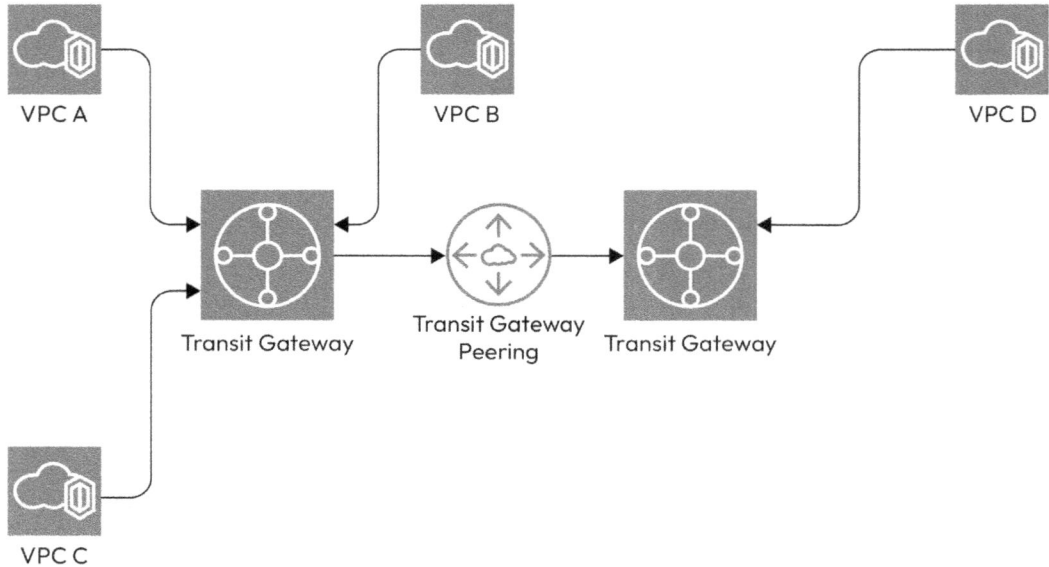

Figure 3.22 – Architecture of two TGWs paired together with multiple VPCs

Besides VPCs, we can also connect TGWs to TGWs, allowing us to build complex cloud networks. The benefit of having the TGW in the middle is that we have a central place to manage a route table that determines how traffic is routed among our spoke VPCs.

This type of setup makes sense in a more complex multi-account environment, and we'll thus revisit it later in the book in *Chapter 16*.

So far, we have set up our VPC infrastructure, first in the AWS console and then via CloudFormation. In this last part of this chapter, let's programmatically check that our VPC has flow logs enabled via Python and Boto3.

Programmatically verifying that VPC flow logs are enabled

VPC flow logs are a form of logs that capture metadata, such as the network interface, source IP address, port, protocol, and whether the traffic was accepted or rejected. This can be useful when diagnosing low-level network issues within our VPC.

Flow logs aren't enabled by default, and in this section, we'll write a script in Python that, using the Boto3 SDK, checks a VPC with a provided ID if flow logs are enabled. If they are not enabled, it'll create a log group and enable them.

Download the `trustpolicy.json` and `flow_log_policy.json` files from the GitHub repository. These two files define the trust policy and IAM policy document for the role that is needed to push logs flow logs into CloudWatch.

Follow these steps to create the script:

1. Firstly, we need to create the role. Use the AWS CLI to first create the role with the attached trust policy. Note down the ARN of the newly created role:

    ```
    aws iam create-role --role-name VpcFlowLogRole --assume-role-
    policy-document file://trustpolicy.json
    ```

2. Add the policy document, allowing this role to push logs, to the role we just created:

    ```
    aws iam put-role-policy --role-name VpcFlowLogRole --policy-name
    VpcFlowLogPolicy --policy-document file://flow_log_policy.json
    ```

3. Create a file called `flow_logs.py` and open it in a code editor of your choice.

4. We'll first import the Boto3 python SDK and the client exception that will be used later to catch errors when log groups already exist:

    ```
    import boto3
    from botocore.exceptions import ClientError
    ```

5. Next, we define the required Boto3 clients (namely one for `ec2` to interact with the VPC and one for `logs` to interact with CloudWatch Logs). We also define a variable with the ARN of the previously created role that will be used for log delivery:

    ```
    ec2_client = boto3.client("ec2")
    logs_client = boto3.client("logs")
    ROLE_ARN = "<Insert role arn here>"
    ```

6. Next, we create a function that checks whether a log group exists by listing all available log groups via the name prefix:

    ```
    def log_group_exists(log_group_name):
        resp = logs_client.describe_log_
    groups(logGroupNamePrefix=log_group_name)
        return len(resp["logGroups"]) > 0
    ```

7. Now that we can check whether a log group exists, we need the corresponding function to create a new log group:

```python
def create_log_group(log_group_name):
    try:
        resp = logs_client.create_log_group(logGroupName=log_
group_name)
    except ClientError:
        raise Exception("Unable to create log group")
```

8. Similarly, we'll use the `DescribeFlowLogs` operation to check whether a VPC has flow logs enabled. We will also create a function to create flow logs for a VPC:

```python
def create_flow_logs(vpc_id, log_group_name):
    resp = ec2_client.create_flow_logs(ResourceIds=[vpc_id],
                                       ResourceType="VPC",
                                       TrafficType="ALL",
                                       LogGroupName=log_group_
name,
                                       DeliverLogsPermissionArn
=ROLE_ARN)
def flow_logs_enabled(vpc_id):
    resp = ec2_client.describe_flow_logs(
        Filter=[
            {
                "Name": "resource-id",
                "Values": [
                    vpc_id,
                ]
            },
        ]
    )
    return len(resp["FlowLogs"]) > 0
```

9. In our main function, we'll ask the user for their VPC ID to check and then go through the process of checking whether flow logs are enabled, enabling them with a new log group if they are not already enabled:

```python
def main():
    vpc_id = input("VpcId: ")
    vpc_has_flow_logs = flow_logs_enabled(vpc_id)
    if not vpc_has_flow_logs:
        print("Enabling flow logs")
        log_group_name = f"{vpc_id}-flow-logs"
        if not log_group_exists(log_group_name):
            print("Creating new log group")
```

```
                create_log_group(log_group_name)
            create_flow_logs(vpc_id, log_group_name)
        else:
            print("Flow logs already enabled")

    if __name__ == "__main__":
        main()
```

10. Using the VPC ID of one of the previously created VPCs, run the Python script by running the following command in your console:

```
python3 flow_logs.py
```

With this script, we can now check whether flow logs are enabled and automatically enable them for a specific VPC. We'll go deeper into CloudWatch Logs and log analysis in *Chapter 10*.

Summary

In this chapter, you've seen an introduction to a vital component of AWS: VPC. We have set up VPCs and their components, such as subnets, route tables, and gateways, both using the AWS console and via infrastructure as code in CloudFormation. We then got a quick overview of how we can allow inter-VPC traffic via VPC peering and got insights into scaling the peering of VPCs via TGW. In the last section, we wrote a small script to interact with our VPCs to check whether flow logs were enabled.

In this chapter, we have seen two approaches to automating infrastructure. One is the declarative approach of CloudFormation, where we defined our infrastructure, such as VPCs, subnets, and IGWs, and the other is the imperative approach with Boto3. Here, we explicitly wrote a Python script that checked whether flow logs were enabled and, if not, enabled them for us.

Both of these approaches can exist together. The declarative approach is great for defining how our infrastructure should look, while a tool such as Boto3 could be used to write automation scripts for common workflows. Imagine you are getting a new compliance directive that all teams need to enable flow logs on their VPCs.

You could then update your CloudFormation template to enable flow logs for a VPC and then – for example, after the deadline for all teams to update their infrastructure has passed – use a script such as the one seen previously to check that all teams have actually enabled flow logs.

With this understanding of VPCs and the infrastructure, we can get started with setting up some machines in the next chapter, where we'll look into the **Elastic Cloud Compute**, or **EC2**, service.

Get This Book's PDF Version and Exclusive Extras

UNLOCK NOW

Scan the QR code (or go to packtpub.com/unlock). Search for this book by name, confirm the edition, and then follow the steps on the page.

Note: Keep your invoice handly. Purchase made directly from packt don't require one.

Join the CloudPro Newsletter with 44000+ Subscribers

Want to know what's happening in cloud computing, DevOps, IT administration, networking, and more? Scan the QR code to subscribe to **CloudPro**, our weekly newsletter for 44,000+ tech professionals who want to stay informed and ahead of the curve.

https://packt.link/cloudpro

4

Scalable Compute Capacity in the Cloud via EC2

In the previous chapters, we set up our network in the cloud. But, so far, this **virtual private cloud** (**VPC**) is pretty empty. In this chapter, we will fill our *data center in the cloud* with virtual machines, called *instances* in AWS terminology, by using the **Elastic Compute Cloud** (**EC2**) service.

Amazon EC2 was one of the first AWS services to be introduced. In a nutshell, it offers the ability to deploy compute capacity in the form of virtual machines, called instances, in the cloud. The keyword in the service description is *elastic*. Instead of requiring you to rent a virtual machine for a set term, such as one year, EC2 lets you spin up and down new instances as you need them. This enables your application to handle changes in demand smoothly and only pay for the amount of compute you have consumed. This *pay-as-you-go* model is the basis of the cloud. This elasticity not only extends to the number of instances (the horizontal scaling) but also to the size of the instance. We can easily spin up an instance that has 4 CPUs and 32 GB of RAM. But if we need (and have the money to pay for) it, AWS will also give us an instance with 192 CPUs and 1.5 TB of memory (the r7i.48xlarge instance). With 600+ (at the time of writing) instance types, EC2 allows us to select the right combination of CPUs, memory, and storage for our use case.

In this chapter, we'll first set up an EC2 instance in the AWS Console before automating the process using CloudFormation. Next, we'll look into cost management by enabling a billing alarm. Finally, we'll write automation scripts to take care of common administrative tasks like shutting off instances.

We will cover the following topics in this chapter:

- Setting up EC2 instances in the AWS Console as well as with Infrastructure-as-Code
- Creating an AWS billing alert to keep informed about our budget
- Writing administrative scripts for common tasks like shutting down all instances or removing unattached EBS volumes

Technical requirements

To get the most out of this chapter, you should have a basic knowledge of the Amazon EC2 service. An understanding of broader terms, such as virtual machines, hypervisor, and block storage, are helpful as well.

You should also have CloudFormation setup according to the instructions in *Chapter 1*.

The solution scripts for this chapter can be found at the following link:

`https://github.com/PacktPublishing/AWS-for-System-Administrators-Second-Edition`

The CiA video for this chapter can be found at `https://packt.link/chK2n`

Setting up EC2 instances

In this section, we are going to set up an EC2 instance. First, we are going to use the AWS Console before doing the same via Infrastructure-as-Code in Terraform. Before getting started with the provisioning of instances, we'll cover some basic vocabulary and concepts for the EC2 service.

A few EC2 concepts

In EC2, there are a few concepts and names that you'll come across regardless of whether you are dealing with the provisioning of instances in the AWS Console or via Infrastructure-as-Code tools.

Here are a few acronyms/names and their definitions:

- **Amazon Machine Image (AMI)**: This is an image, similar to an ISO image, that contains the required information, including the operating system, applications, and application configuration, that is required to launch an instance. You can either use Amazon-provided AMIs or create your own AMIs.

- **Instance type**: This defines the type of instance you are launching. As mentioned earlier, AWS has 600+ different types of instances that differ in memory, CPU, or other performance metrics such as the availability of a high-bandwidth network interface.

- **EBS volume**: This is a type of block storage that can be attached to an instance. This is similar to a hard disk on a physical server. **EBS** stands for **Elastic Block Storage**.

Using the AWS Console to create an EC2 instance

The easiest way to set up an EC2 instance is by using the AWS Console.

> **Note**
>
> Be careful! You are launching actual compute resources that will be billed to you by AWS.

To launch an instance, follow these steps:

1. Navigate to the EC2 console by either searching for EC2 in the search bar or navigating to `https://us-east-1.console.aws.amazon.com/ecs/v2/home`.

2. In the left-hand navigation, select **Instance** and then select **Launch Instance** in the top right.

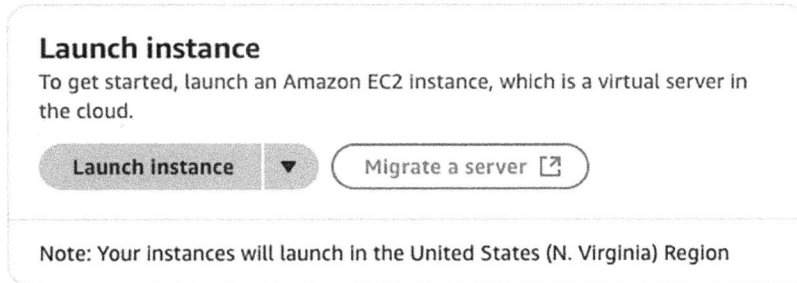

Launch instance

To get started, launch an Amazon EC2 instance, which is a virtual server in the cloud.

    Launch instance   ▼   Migrate a server ↗

Note: Your instances will launch in the United States (N. Virginia) Region

Figure 4.1 – Start the dialog to launch an instance

3. You'll be presented with a configuration dialog. First, set a name for your instance such as `packt-sample`.

4. In the next interface, you'll have to select the AMI to use for your instance. In the interface, you can see a variety of operating systems, from **Amazon Linux**, an Amazon-provided Linux distribution, to **Ubuntu** and **Red Hat Linux**. Besides Linux, you can also choose Windows or Mac OS X. Notice that not all operating systems are available on all instance types. Mac OS with an x86 processor is only available on **mac1.metal** instance types, for example.

> **Note**
>
> The suffix **.metal** on an instance type means that this is the entire bare metal server and is not a virtualized part of an underlying bare metal server.

The following figure shows the operating system selection dialog in the wizard. Here, we can select the type of AMI we want to use and then select the processor architecture as well as the specific version of the OS.

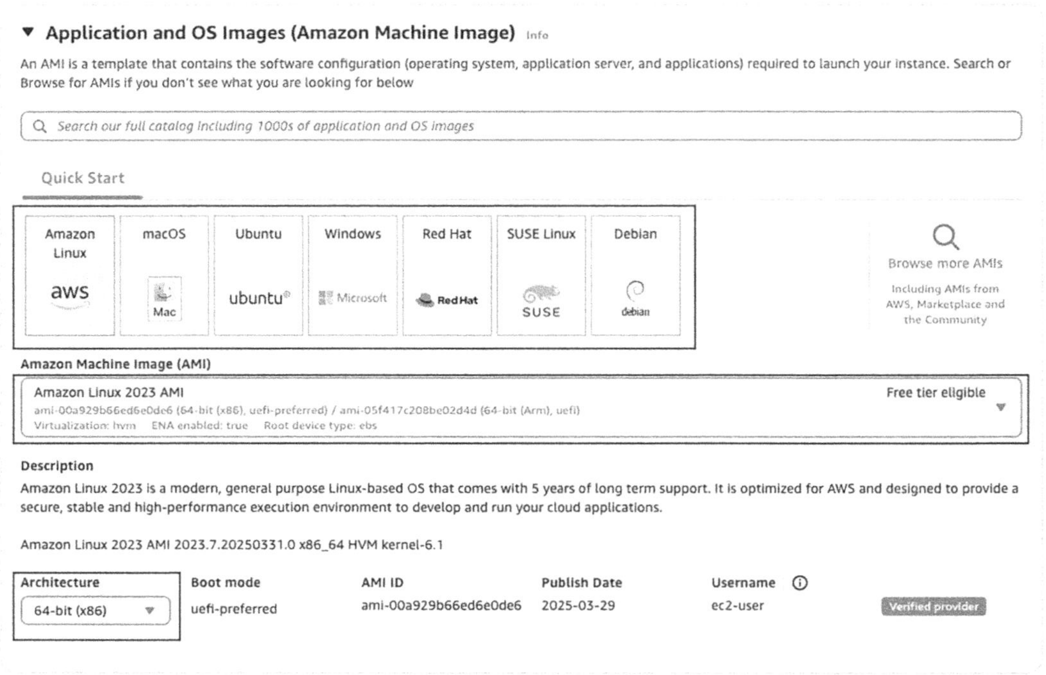

Figure 4.2 – Selecting the correct operating system, AMI, and CPU architecture

As you can see in the preceding figure, you can also select a processor architecture. The choice of processor architecture will also influence the selection of instances. For this first example, we'll go with the **64-bit (x86)** architecture.

Copy the AMI ID that is shown on your screen and save it for later since we'll need it when provisioning the same instance via Infrastructure-as-Code.

> **Note**
>
> AWS has its own ARM-based processor family called **Graviton**. It's an energy-efficient chip that offers great price performance. If you are running an application that can run on ARM—for example, Java applications can often be run easily and without rewrites on ARM—the Graviton instances may be cheaper than Intel or AMD-based instances. You can identify the Graviton instance families by the **g** in their name, for example, r8g.

5. Next, select the instance type. For this example, we are going to go with the inexpensive **t2.micro** instance, which provides **1 vCPU** and **1 GiB** of memory.

▼ Instance type Info | Get advice

Instance type

t2.micro   Free tier eligible
Family: t2   1 vCPU   1 GiB Memory   Current generation: true
On-Demand Windows base pricing: 0.0162 USD per Hour   On-Demand Ubuntu Pro base pricing: 0.0134 USD per Hour
On-Demand SUSE base pricing: 0.0116 USD t2.micro   On-Demand RHEL base pricing: 0.026 USD per Hour
On-Demand Linux base pricing: 0.0116 USD per Hour

⬤ All generations

Compare instance types

Additional costs apply for AMIs with pre-installed software

Figure 4.3 – Selected instance type

6. In order to be able to SSH into our instance, we need to provide a key pair. If you already have
    a key pair, you can select it from the dropdown. Otherwise, click the **Create new key pair**
    link, as shown in *Figure 4.4*. This will open up a dialog to create a new key pair. If you are on
    a Windows machine and use *PuTTy* to establish SSH connections, select the **.ppk** format for
    the **Private key file format**. If you are on a Unix-like operating system such as Mac OS X or
    Linux, select **.pem**. Notice that you'll be prompted to download your private key. Make sure
    to keep that file since you won't be able to download the private key again and we'll use it to
    connect to the machine.

Create key pair   ✕

Key pair name
Key pairs allow you to connect to your instance securely.

packt-key

The name can include up to 255 ASCII characters. It can't include leading or trailing spaces.

Key pair type

◉ RSA
RSA encrypted private and public key
pair

○ ED25519
ED25519 encrypted private and public
key pair

Private key file format

◉ .pem
For use with OpenSSH

○ .ppk
For use with PuTTY

⚠ When prompted, store the private key in a secure and accessible location on
your computer. **You will need it later to connect to your instance.** Learn
more [↗]

Cancel   **Create key pair**

Figure 4.4 – Dialog to create a new key pair

7.   Speaking of SSH, we next need to define the network settings for our instance. An instance is always deployed into a subnet of a VPC. By default, AWS will deploy the instance into the default VPC and will use a random subnet. For now, we'll leave these default settings.

We'll also choose **Enable** for the **Auto-assign public IP** setting. This means that AWS will allocate a public IPv4 address for our instance that we can then use to connect to the instance via SSH.

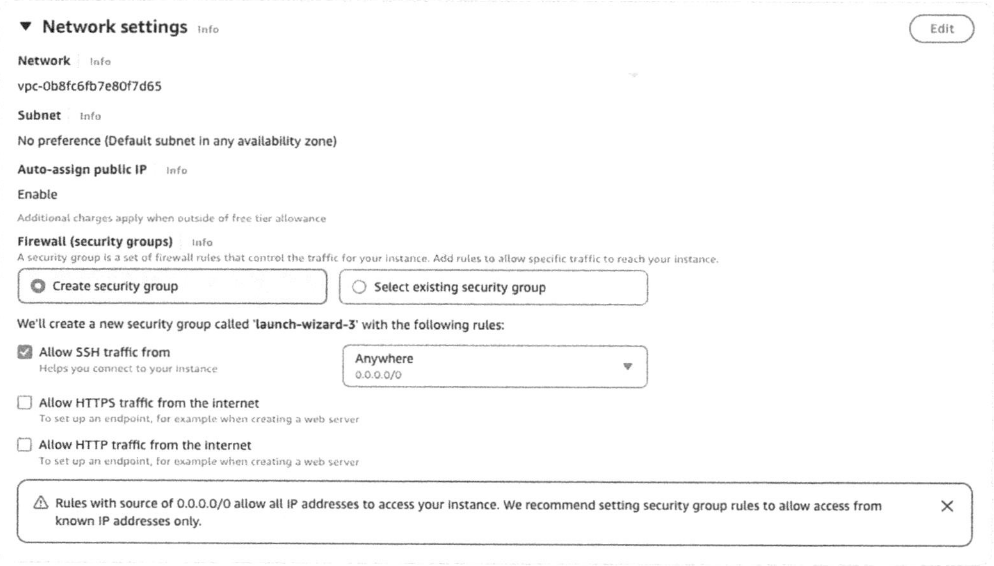

Figure 4.5 – Values for the network settings

In the network settings, we are also creating a **security group**. Security groups are virtual firewalls that we can use to control the inbound and outbound traffic of our instance. You can either add an instance to an existing security group or have the wizard create a new security group for you. The following figure shows a security group in the AWS Console with its inbound rules selected.

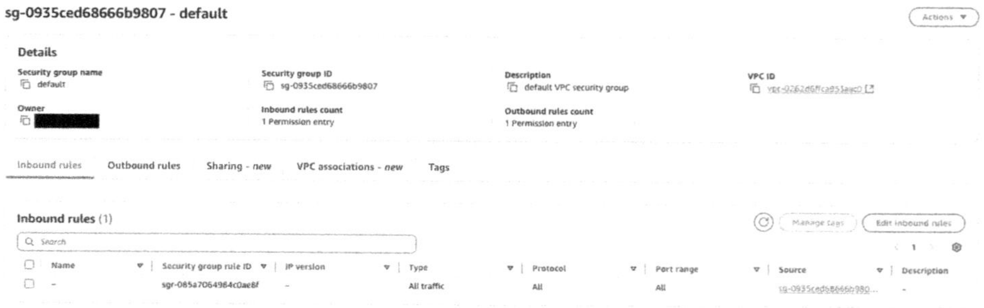

Figure 4.6 – Picture of a security group within the AWS Console

A security group is made up of **inbound rules** and **outbound rules**. Inbound rules specify what type of traffic—for example, all TCP or all UDP—on what port range and from what source is allowed to enter instances that are attached to this security group. By default, all protocols that are not explicitly allowed in a security group are implicitly denied.

Similar to how inbound rules control all traffic coming into the instance, outbound rules define what traffic can leave the instance. Instead of a source, they define the destination of the traffic.

The launch wizard for our instance gives you options to attach common rules, such as allowing SSH traffic (on port 22) to our instance.

8. With our network configured, we next need to configure our block storage. An instance requires an unencrypted root volume. In the **Configure storage** section, you can see the default root volume with 8 GiB of gp3 storage (*Figure 4.7*).

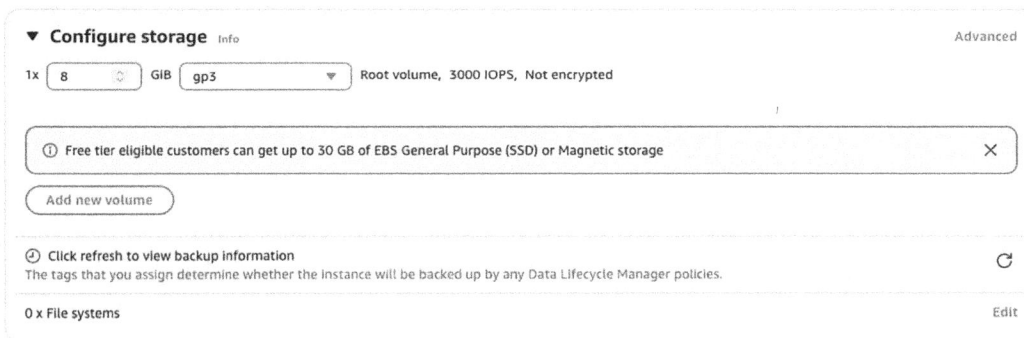

Figure 4.7 – Storage configuration

EBS offers a variety of different options when creating storage devices. The most common types of storage are the **General Purpose SSD 2** and **General Purpose SSD 3**, or **gp2** and **gp3**. These are cost-effective when used for typical applications.

Provisioned IOPS SSDs (**io1** and **io2**) are volume types best suited for I/O-intensive workloads. A classic example is databases.

Both the provisioned IOPS SSDs and General-Purpose SSDs support a configuration option called IOPS. IOPS defines the number of input/output operations that the volume should be able to support every second. For I/O-intensive workloads, tweaking this number can become crucial.

Besides SSD-based storage, you can also select HDD-based storage with **Throughput Optimized HDD (st1)** and **Cold HDD (sc1)**. These are inexpensive magnetic storage volumes that provide storage with lower throughput and are thus a good fit for applications that might need to store a large amount of data but that do not require fast access to that data.

For our root volume, we'll leave it at *8 GiB* of gp3 storage.

9. With our volume configured, we can now go over the **Summary** screen. Here, we can select the number of instances that we want to launch based on our configuration. Leave the number of instances at **1** since we only want to launch one instance in this scenario to keep the cost down.

    In the AWS Console, you'll then find a summary of all our selections as well as the **Launch instance** button. The following figure shows that summary based on the selections we have made.

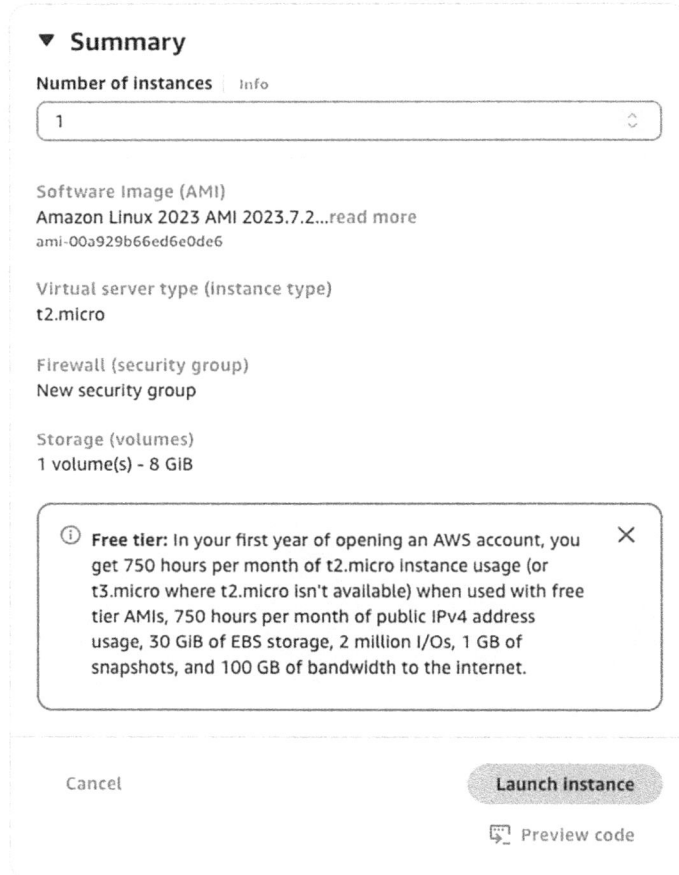

Figure 4.8 – Summary of our instance launch

10. After launching your instance, you'll be presented with a green dialog box indicating the instance ID.

Figure 4.9 – Banner indicating the successful launch of the instance

You'll be presented with an overview of all the instance details. In the top right are your actions and toggles to change the instance state. The instance state dropdown allows you to stop, reboot, or terminate the instance.

11. In the overview, you can also see the **Auto-assigned public IP address**. Copy this address as we are going to use it to SSH into the instance.

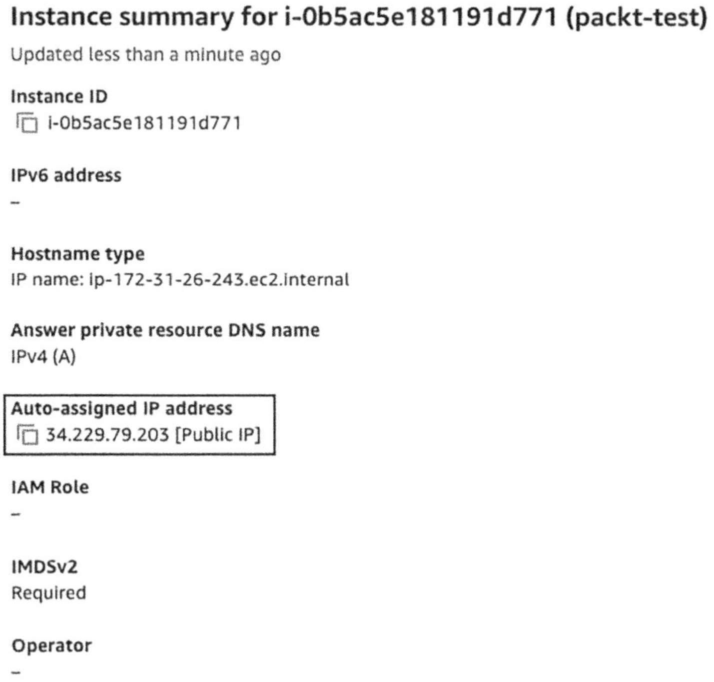

Instance summary for i-0b5ac5e181191d771 (packt-test)

Updated less than a minute ago

Instance ID
☐ i-0b5ac5e181191d771

IPv6 address
–

Hostname type
IP name: ip-172-31-26-243.ec2.internal

Answer private resource DNS name
IPv4 (A)

Auto-assigned IP address
☐ 34.229.79.203 [Public IP]

IAM Role
–

IMDSv2
Required

Operator
–

Figure 4.10 – Details of our instance, including the public IPv4 address

12. In your terminal, first change the file permissions of your previously downloaded key to 400 (which allows only the user to read it):

```
chmod 400 <path_to_key>
```

13. To log into your instance, you'll need the username. This is specific to AMI and can be found on the documentation page for the AMI you chose. For Amazon Linux, the username is ec2-user. Use the SSH key and the public IP address of your instance to connect:

```
ssh -i <path_to_key> ec2-user@<public-ip>
```

14. After you have connected to your instance and played around with it, we need to terminate the instance. To do so, navigate back to the details page for your instance and, in the top-right corner in the **Instance State** dropdown, choose **Stop Instance**. This will put the instance into a stopped state. You can terminate the instance. This will delete the instance and, by default, also the attached EBS volumes. Any data stored on that volume will be lost.

So far, you have seen how to create an instance in the AWS Console, and while this process is easy, it is hard to reproduce, and if you need to launch a bunch of instances, it can be cumbersome.

This is why, in the next section, we are going to learn how to create instances using CloudFormation.

Using CloudFormation to create an EC2 instance

In this section, we'll be creating an EC2 instance and putting it into the VPC that was created via CloudFormation in the previous chapter.

> **Note**
>
> If you haven't followed the previous chapter's instructions, please run the CloudFormation template available at:
>
> `https://github.com/PacktPublishing/AWS-for-System-Administrators-Second-Edition/blob/main/ch03/vpc.yml`

Throughout the book, we switch between Terraform and CloudFormation to showcase these two different tools. The concepts and resources you have to create are the same.

> **Note**
>
> This example uses CloudFormation. If you are up for a challenge, try reading through the following CloudFormation template and then recreate it using Terraform instead of CloudFormation.
>
> The documentation for the AWS Terraform Provider (which you can find at `https://registry.terraform.io/providers/hashicorp/aws/latest/docs`) will be useful for identifying the names of the Terraform resources to use.
>
> Whether you have taken the challenge to implement a version in Terraform or not, the GitHub repository of this book contains a Terraform script that deploys the same infrastructure as this CloudFormation template. You can compare the two if you want.

Let's go step by step and write the CloudFormation required to start and instance into the public subnet of our VPC:

1. Create a file called `instance.yml` that will contain our CloudFormation template.

2. Start by defining the CloudFormation-required properties, such as the template version and the description of the stack:

```
AWSTemplateFormatVersion: "2010-09-09"
Description: "CloudFormation template to create an EC2 instance
in a VPC"
```

3. Next, we define a parameter: `NetworkStack`. This will be the name of the stack in which we ran the provisioning of our VPC in the previous chapter:

```
Parameters:
  NetworkStack:
    Type: "String"
    Description: "Name of the networking stack that created our
VPC"
```

4. Now, we are ready to define some resources. We'll start by defining our security group that allows SSH traffic from anywhere in the internet:

```
SecurityGroupSSHAllow:
  Type: AWS::EC2::SecurityGroup
  Properties:
    GroupName: instance-sg
    GroupDescription: "Instance SG from CloudFormation"
    SecurityGroupIngress:
    - IpProtocol: tcp
      FromPort: 22
      ToPort: 22
      CidrIp: 0.0.0.0/0
      Description: "Allow SSH traffic into our instance"
    VpcId:
      Fn::ImportValue:
        !Sub ${NetworkStack}-VpcId
```

We first define some informational properties, such as the `GroupName` and `GroupDescription`. Next, we define the list of inbound (or *Ingress*) rules via the `SecurityGroupIngress` property. We define that all TCP traffic directed to port 22 from the CIDR range `0.0.0.0/0` (which is all IPv4 addresses) is allowed.

Like our example in the console, this security group does not have any outbound (or *egress*) rules attached.

5. With the security group ready, we can provision our instance. We first need to define the Availability Zone we want to deploy the instance into. Since our public subnet is provisioned in the Availability Zone A, we'll use `us-east-1a` here:

```
Instance:
```

```
Type: AWS::EC2::Instance
Properties:
  AvailabilityZone: "us-east-1a"
```

6. Next, we define our block device. This will be our EBS volume that is mapped into /dev/sda1. We define an EBS volume with 8 GiB of size and of volume type gp2. We also specify that, upon termination of the instance that this EBS volume is attached to, the volume should be deleted:

```
BlockDeviceMappings:
- DeviceName: "/dev/sda1"
  Ebs:
    DeleteOnTermination: true
    VolumeSize: 8
    VolumeType: gp2
```

7. Next, we define the AMI that we want to use. Use the AMI ID you copied previously:

```
ImageId: "ami-01b799c439fd5516a"
```

8. Next, we can select the instance type. In this example, we are going to use the same t2.micro type that we also used in the console:

```
InstanceType: "t2.micro"
```

9. Finally, we need to define a network interface that is attached to this instance. We assign it to the public subnet that this instance will also be deployed into and attach the previously created security group to it:

```
NetworkInterfaces:
- Description: "Primary ENI"
  DeviceIndex: 0
  SubnetId:
    Fn::ImportValue:
      !Sub ${NetworkStack}-PublicSubnetA
  GroupSet:
  - Ref: SecurityGroupSSHAllow
```

Network interfaces in AWS are also called **Elastic Network Interfaces (ENIs)**.

10. Make sure that you are in the same region as your previously created VPC by setting the corresponding environment variable:

```
export AWS_DEFAULT_REGION=us-east-1
```

11. Validate the template to verify that there are no syntax errors. To do this, we can use the validate-template sub-command of the CloudFormation command in the AWS CLI:

```
aws cloudformation validate-template --template-body file://
instance.yml
{
    "Parameters": [
        {
            "ParameterKey": "NetworkStack",
            "NoEcho": false,
            "Description": "Name of the networking stack that
created our VPC"
        }
    ],
    "Description": "CloudFormation template to create an EC2
instance in a VPC"
}
```

12. Finally, create the stack using the create-stack command. Pass the name of your previously created networking stack (in this case, vpc-c) in as a parameter:

```
aws cloudformation create-stack --stack-name instance
--template-body file://instance.yml --parameters
ParameterKey=NetworkStack,ParameterValue=vpc-c
```

You can now navigate to the overview of instances (https://us-east-1.console.aws.amazon.com/ec2/v2/home?region=us-east-1#Instances:sort=instanceId) and follow the creation of your newly launched instance.

We have now created instances both in the AWS Console and from CloudFormation. As you can see, it is quite easy to create instances, and we have learned that you'll be billed for every instance that is running. In the next section, we'll see how you can create an alert that triggers when a cost threshold is passed. This can help you recognize that unneeded infrastructure, such as an unused instance, is running in your account.

Creating a cost alert using budgets

Due to the dynamic nature of pricing in AWS, it can be beneficial to set up alerts that send you a notification whenever your billing crosses a certain threshold. This can be useful to detect unusual spending in your production account or to make sure that you don't accidentally get a huge bill when playing around with AWS in your private account.

Follow these steps to set up a billing alert:

1. Log into the AWS Console and, in the top-right menu, click on your name. In the drop-down, you should see a menu item called **Billing and Cost Management**. Select this service.

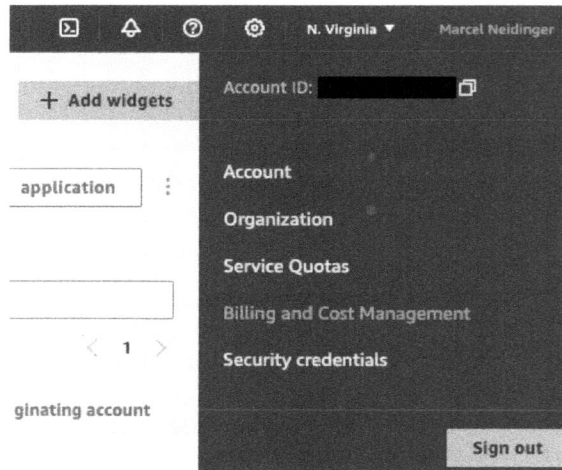

Figure 4.11 – Billing and Cost Management in the User dropdown

2. In the left-hand menu, under **Budgets and Planning**, select the **Budgets** menu item. In the top-right, click the orange **Create budget** button.

3. Under **Budget Setup**, select **Use a template (simplified)**.

4. Under **Templates**, you have a selection of budget templates. Select **Monthly cost budget** here.

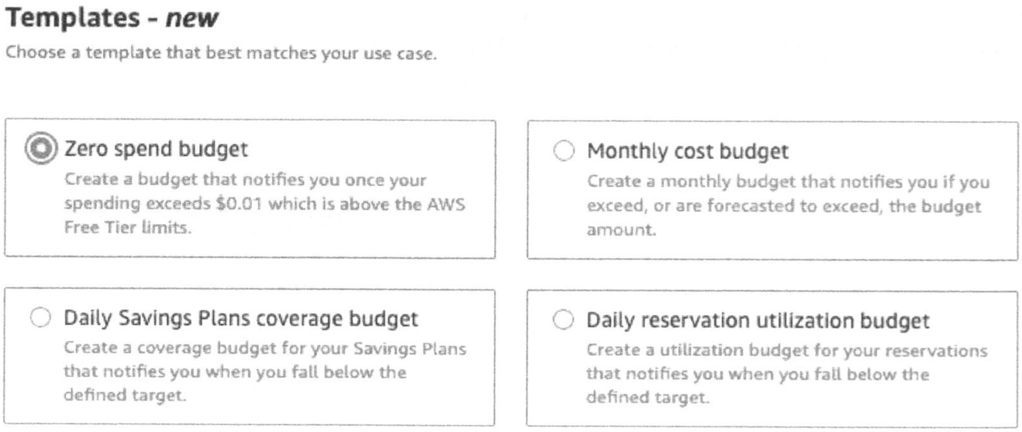

Figure 4.12 – Selection of budget templates

Let's learn about all the options:

- **Zero spend budget**: This will alert you as soon as you exceed the AWS Free Tier. This alert will trigger when your account bills more than $0.00 and is useful if you want to stay within the free tier.

- **Monthly cost budget**: This will let you specify a set dollar amount and, when either your bill or your forecasted month-end bill exceeds this threshold, you'll be notified.

- The **Daily Savings Plans coverage budget** and **Daily reservation utilization budget** are two types of budgets that act on two different pricing models available in AWS.

> **Note**
>
> In order to encourage hands-on experience with the services, AWS offers a Free Tier on many of them. Visit `https://aws.amazon.com/free/` to get an overview of what is available for free in AWS.

Before continuing with setting up our budget, let's take a quick excursion into pricing models and find out what Savings Plans are.

So far, we have seen the on-demand nature of AWS. When choosing, for example, a compute instance, we used the pay-as-you-go pricing and were billed for the amount of time we used the instance. This is a great billing model when we are experimenting or for very spiky workloads, but what if you *know* that for a set period of time you'll require this number of instances? This is where **Reserved Instances** and **Savings Plan** come into play.

Reserved Instances allow you to enter into a contract with AWS where, for a period of one or three years, you commit to using an instance family. You'll pay the price for that instance regardless of whether you use it or not. In exchange, you'll get a discount (up to 72% compared to the on-demand price). So, for steady, predictable load, Reserved Instances offer a way to optimize your spending.

Instead of committing to a **Reserved Instance** (or **RI**) you can also use a **Compute Savings Plan**. The setup is similar to reserved instances where, in exchange for committing to pay for a certain amount of compute power, you'll get discounted rates. In comparison to Reserved Instances, Compute Savings Plans are not specific to an instance/instance family but rather count all types of compute (such as EC2 instances, AWS Fargate, or AWS Lambda). In essence, with a Compute Savings Plan, you commit to buying a certain amount of compute from AWS (measured in $/hour) and get a discounted rate on that compute in exchange.

Let's go back to our setup now:

1. Enter a name for your budget under **Budget name**. Next, enter your threshold, such as 5 dollars, under **Enter your budgeted amount ($)**. AWS will show you your last month's spend to give you an idea of what a suitable threshold might be.

2.   Next, specify the list of e-mail addresses you want to send this budget alert to:

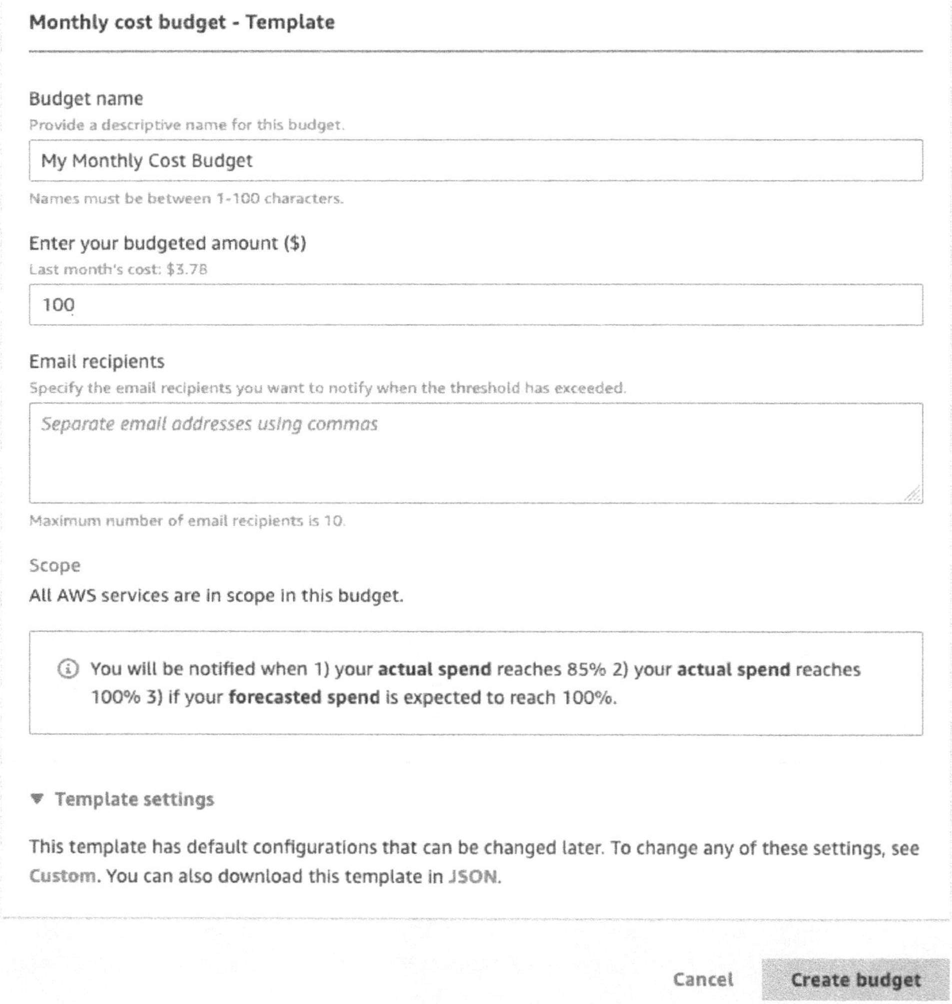

Monthly cost budget - Template

Budget name
Provide a descriptive name for this budget.

My Monthly Cost Budget

Names must be between 1-100 characters.

Enter your budgeted amount ($)
Last month's cost: $3.78

100

Email recipients
Specify the email recipients you want to notify when the threshold has exceeded.

Separate email addresses using commas

Maximum number of email recipients is 10.

Scope
All AWS services are in scope in this budget.

ⓘ You will be notified when 1) your **actual spend** reaches 85% 2) your **actual spend** reaches 100% 3) if your **forecasted spend** is expected to reach 100%.

▼ Template settings

This template has default configurations that can be changed later. To change any of these settings, see Custom. You can also download this template in JSON.

Cancel   **Create budget**

Figure 4.13 – Details for the billing alert

3.   Once you have filled in all the information, click **Create Budget** to create your new budget. AWS will then send three tiers of emails:

- The first e-mail is sent when your actual spend reaches 85% of your budget

- The second e-mail is sent when your actual spend reaches 100% of your budget

- The third e-mail is sent when your forecasted spend reaches 100% of your budget

Reacting to the e-mail for when your budget exceeds 85% should leave you with enough time to shut down resources causing unwanted costs. Notice that this is purely a notification. Even if you exceed your threshold, there won't be any automated measures taken to shut down instances or reduce costs on your behalf.

Automatically shutting down instances

One effective method to cut your AWS bill is to shut down unused instances during times of low usage. We'll see how you can automatically scale your compute capacity up and down based on load in the next chapter, but there are examples where we can completely stop instances.

A classic example is testing and integration environments. During the workday, the development teams need these environments to test their changes, but after hours and on the weekend it can be a great cost-saver to shut them down.

In this section, we'll write a script that checks for running instances in all regions and stops them. However, we do not want to just stop all of our instances. Instead, we want to be able to specify whether or not an instance should be shut down upon this script running or not.

To do this, we'll use a **tag**. Tags are key-value pairs that are used all over AWS to provide user-defined metadata.

Follow these steps to create an automated shutdown script:

1. Inside the AWS Console, find a running instance and navigate to the detail page. On the detail page, you'll find the **Tags** tab (see *Figure 4.14*).

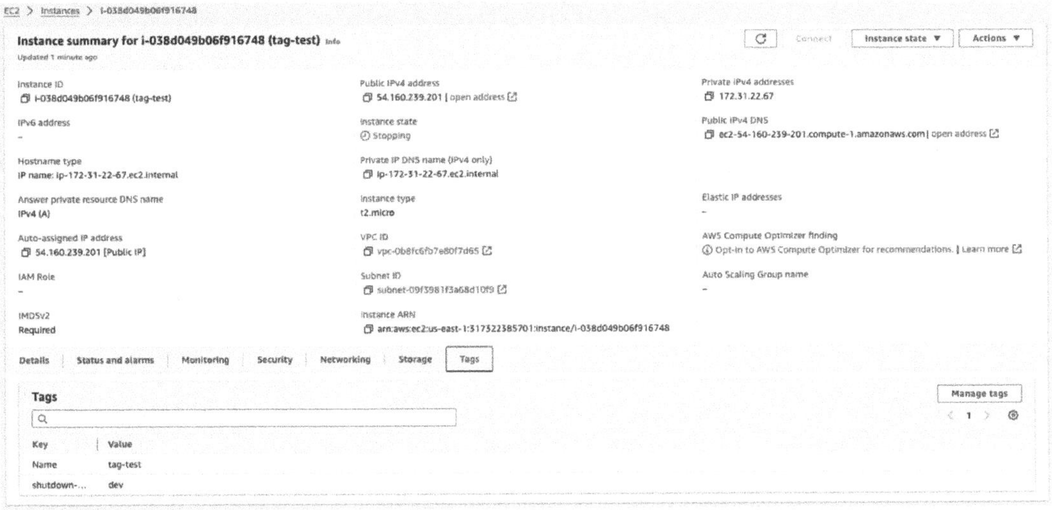

Figure 4.14 – Tags overview in the instance details

2. Select **Manage tags** and click **Add new tag** in the **Manage tags** dialog.

3. You can give your tag any **Key** you want. For this example, I have chosen **shutdown-group**. For the value, you could—for example—define two different groups. All resources with a **shutdown-group** value of **dev** will be shut down every evening. Resources with a **shutdown-group** value of **prod** won't be touched.

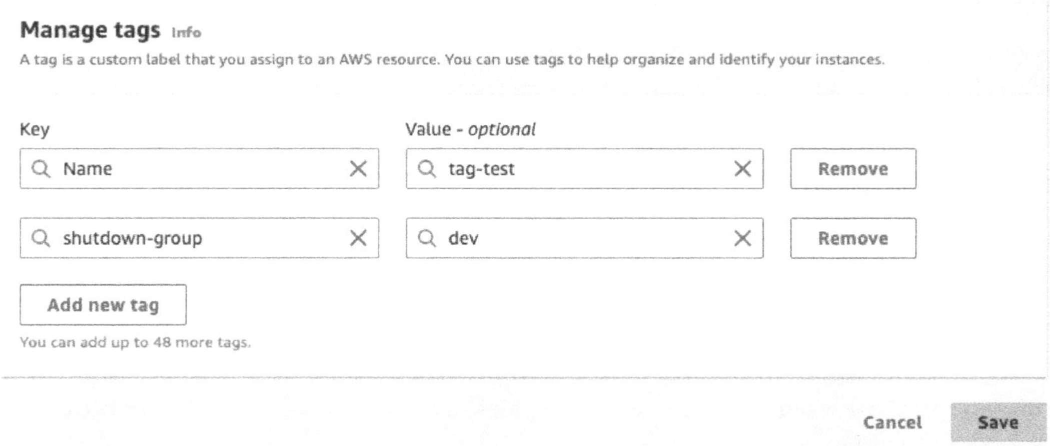

Manage tags Info

A tag is a custom label that you assign to an AWS resource. You can use tags to help organize and identify your instances.

Key	Value - *optional*	
🔍 Name ✕	🔍 tag-test ✕	Remove
🔍 shutdown-group ✕	🔍 dev ✕	Remove

Add new tag

You can add up to 48 more tags.

Cancel   **Save**

Figure 4.15 – Shutdown tags settings

4. With our instance tagged, we can get started on the script. Create a new file called `check_instances.py`.

5. First, we need to import boto3, the AWS SDK for Python, and then we need to create an EC2 client. We'll use this client to get the names of all the regions that our account has access to:

```
import boto3
ec2_client = boto3.client("ec2")
```

6. Next, we iterate over the names of all regions and print out the region we are currently checking for debug purposes:

```
for region in ec2_client.describe_regions()["Regions"]:
    region_name = region["RegionName"]
    print(f"Checking instances in {region_name}")
```

7. For each of the regions, we'll then create an `ec2` resource. Remember that resources are a higher-level abstraction than the previously used `ec2` client:

```
ec2_resource = boto3.resource("ec2", region_name=region_name)
```

8. We want to filter all running instances. We can use a filter on the `instance-state-name` property to do this:

```
running = ec2_resource.instances.filter(Filters=[{
        "Name": "instance-state-name",
        "Values": ["running"]
    }])
```

9. Next, we iterate over all of the running instances:

```
for i in running:
```

10. With the instance object, we also get the tags so finally we can iterate over all tags that are attached to this instance and check whether they have the `shutdown-group` tag with a value of `dev` attached to it. If this is the case, we stop the instance:

```
for tag in i.tags:
            if tag["Key"] == "shutdown-group" and tag["Value"]
== "dev":
                print(f"Stopping instance with id {i.id}")
                i.stop()
```

11. We can now execute this script by running the following command. Your output will differ based on the region your instance is deployed into and the ID of your instance:

```
python3 check_instances.py
Checking instances in us-east-1
Stopping instance with id i-038d049b06f916748
```

In this example, you have seen how to handle a common admin task, the automated shutdown of instances, based on tags with a Python script. In the next section, you'll see another such cleanup task where we detect unattached EBS volumes. We'll revisit these topics when talking about managing multi-account environments for larger organizations.

Identifying unattached EBS Volumes with boto3

When it comes to EC2 a sometimes overlooked cost driver are EBS volumes. An EBS volume is usually attached to an instance; however, it doesn't have to be. This means that the life cycle of an EBS volume is independent of the instance it was created for.

In the CloudFormation example, when we created the instance, we saw a flag called **DeleteOnTermination** in the EBS section. This flag indicates that the EBS volume should be deleted whenever the instance is terminated. However, what if this flag was not properly set? In that case, unattached EBS volumes will continue to bill despite the instance they were originally attached to being long gone.

In this final section, we'll write a script to identify any detached EBS volumes. Once we have detected a detached volume, we'll create a *snapshot* of that volume before deleting it.

A **snapshot** of a volume represents the state of the EBS volume at the time the snapshot was taken. It's effectively a copy of the volume that is stored in Amazon S3. When creating a new EBS volume, we can create it from a snapshot. This means that if the script deletes an unattached resource that was needed after all, we can still restore it.

Before we write the script, we need to create an unattached EBS volume to work with:

1. In order for our script to return anything, we'll need an unattached EBS volume. To create one, open the AWS Console and navigate to the EC2 service. In the left menu, find the **Volumes** entry under **Elastic Block Store**.

2. You should see a bunch of volumes that all have the **Volume State** of **In-Use**. In the top right, click the **Create volume** button.

3. Choose any **Volume type** that you want (**gp3** in this example), a **Size** of your liking (**10 GiB** in this example), and suitable **IOPS**, **Throughput**, and **Availability Zone**.

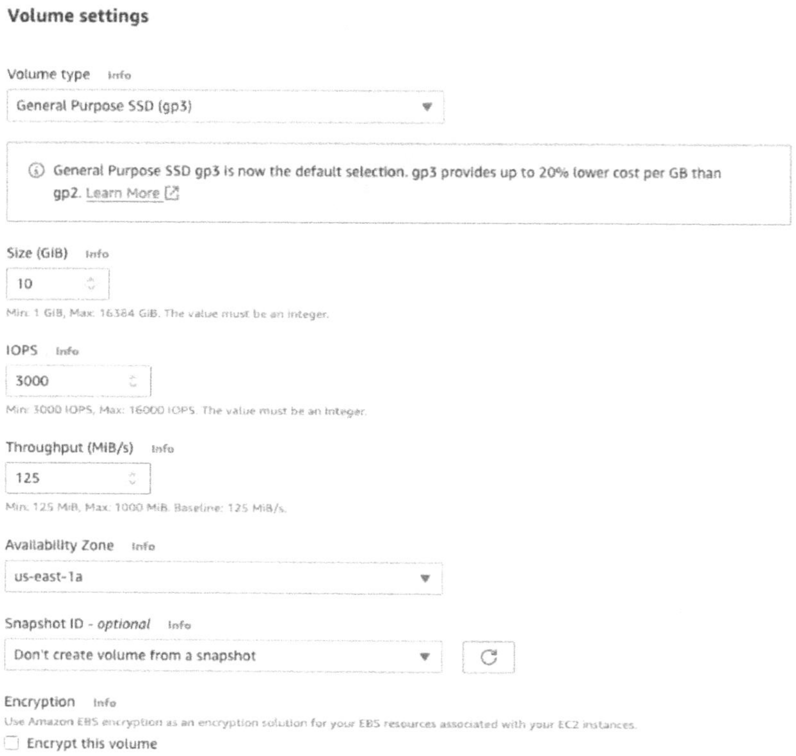

Volume settings

Volume type   Info

General Purpose SSD (gp3)   ▼

ⓘ General Purpose SSD gp3 is now the default selection. gp3 provides up to 20% lower cost per GB than gp2. Learn More ⬈

Size (GiB)   Info

10   ↕

Min: 1 GiB, Max: 16384 GiB. The value must be an integer.

IOPS   Info

3000   ↕

Min: 3000 IOPS, Max: 16000 IOPS. The value must be an integer.

Throughput (MiB/s)   Info

125   ↕

Min: 125 MiB, Max: 1000 MiB. Baseline: 125 MiB/s.

Availability Zone   Info

us-east-1a   ▼

Snapshot ID - *optional*   Info

Don't create volume from a snapshot   ▼   ↻

Encryption   Info
Use Amazon EBS encryption as an encryption solution for your EBS resources associated with your EC2 instances.
☐ Encrypt this volume

Figure 4.16 – Options for the newly created EBS volume

4. Click **Create Volume** in the bottom right. You should now see a new volume with a **Volume state** of **Available**.

5. Create a new script called `check_ebs.py` and open it.

6. First, we need to import boto3, the AWS SDK for Python, and then create an EC2 client and get all the regions our account has access to:

```
import boto3
ec2_client = boto3.client("ec2")
```

7. Next, we iterate over all regions and print the current region out:

```
for region in ec2_client.describe_regions()["Regions"]:
    region_name = region["RegionName"]
    print(f"Checking volumes in {region_name}")
```

8. For each of the regions, we'll then create an `ec2` resource:

```
ec2_resource = boto3.resource("ec2", region_name=region_name)
```

9. Similar to our EC2 instance filtering before, we'll filter for all unattached volumes by checking that their status is `available`:

```
unattached = ec2_resource.volumes.filter(Filters=[{
        "Name": "status",
        "Values": ["available"]
    }])
```

10. Next, we iterate over all `unattached` volumes and get an object representation of that volume:

```
for vol in unattached:
        v = ec2_resource.Volume(vol.id)
```

11. We can then use the `create_snapshot()` method of our volume to create the snapshot:

```
snap = v.create_snapshot()
```

12. With the snapshot taken, we can delete the volume:

```
print(f"Snapshot of {v.id} taken as {snap.id}. Deleting the
volume.")
        v.delete()
```

13. You can run this script by typing the following command:

```
python3 check_ebs.py
Checking volumes in us-east-1
Snapshot of vol-089a056fea2e2b799 taken as snap-
049df9f282a6795a6. Deleting the volume.
Snapshot of vol-0692c27eaa7527ad3 taken as snap-
0e178f965f23d6efd. Deleting the volume.
```

In this section, you have seen how to safely delete unused EBS volumes after taking a snapshot in case you still require the data after all. This is an example of a common admin task that can easily be automated by using the AWS APIs and Python.

Summary

In this chapter, we have covered the basics of EC2. We have seen how to create instances in the AWS Console and via Infrastructure-as-Code by writing and then deploying a CloudFormation template. Finally, we looked into setting up a budget alert as well as writing scripts to handle common administrative tasks such as shutting down instances automatically or deleting unused volumes after taking a snapshot.

In the next two chapters, we'll see how the elasticity of EC2 can be used automatically. Adding more servers as the demand on our application increased and then automatically scaling down the number of servers as the load decreases while evenly distributing, or load balancing, between our available instances.

As you can see, EC2 is the basis for many of the benefits that come with the cloud, and in the next chapters, we'll put that to use to deploy a scalable application.

Part 3: Scalability and Elasticity of our Cloud Infrastructure

In this part, we'll introduce scalability and elasticity to our infrastructure. Through the use of elastic load balancing, auto scaling groups, and RDS for relational databases, you'll be equipped with the services required to deploy scalable web applications on AWS. We'll also cover AWS Secrets Manager and KMS to cover the concepts of secrets management and the management of encryption keys.

This part contains the following chapters:

- *Chapter 5, Increasing Application Fault-Tolerance and Efficiency with Elastic Load Balancing*
- *Chapter 6, Increasing Application Performance Using AWS Auto Scaling*
- *Chapter 7, Scaling a Relational Database in the Cloud Using Amazon Relational Database Service (RDS)*
- *Chapter 8, Managing Secrets and Encryption Keys with AWS Secrets Manager and KMS*

5

Increasing Application Fault Tolerance and Efficiency with Elastic Load Balancing

In the previous chapter, we set up our first compute instances inside AWS using the **Elastic Compute Cloud (EC2)** service. As you have seen, these instances already expose a public IP address that we could use to serve our page. But what if we need more than one instance to handle the load? This is where **load balancing** – the distribution of traffic across a fleet of servers – comes into play.

In this chapter, we'll explore the different AWS offerings when it comes to load balancing, a collection of resources that are grouped under the term *Elastic Load Balancing*.

The topics covered in this chapter include the following:

- An introduction to elastic load balancing

- The different types of load balancers available on AWS

- Setting up an application load balancer

- Combining the network and application load balancers

- Examples of increasing security by serving HTTPS traffic

So, let's get started!

Technical requirements

To get the most out of this chapter, you should have a basic knowledge of the Amazon EC2 service.

You should have CloudFormation set up according to the instructions in *Chapter 1*.

The solution scripts for this chapter can be found at the following link:

`https://github.com/PacktPublishing/AWS-for-System-Administrators-Second-Edition`

The CiA video for this chapter can be found at `https://packt.link/3DfVe`

Understanding Elastic Load Balancing

The core job of any load balancer is to accept a connection from a user, for example, a web connection started by a browser, and distribute the traffic among a fleet of targets. This core idea can be summarized in the following figure, where users interact with a fleet of instances via an **Application Load Balancer (ALB)**.

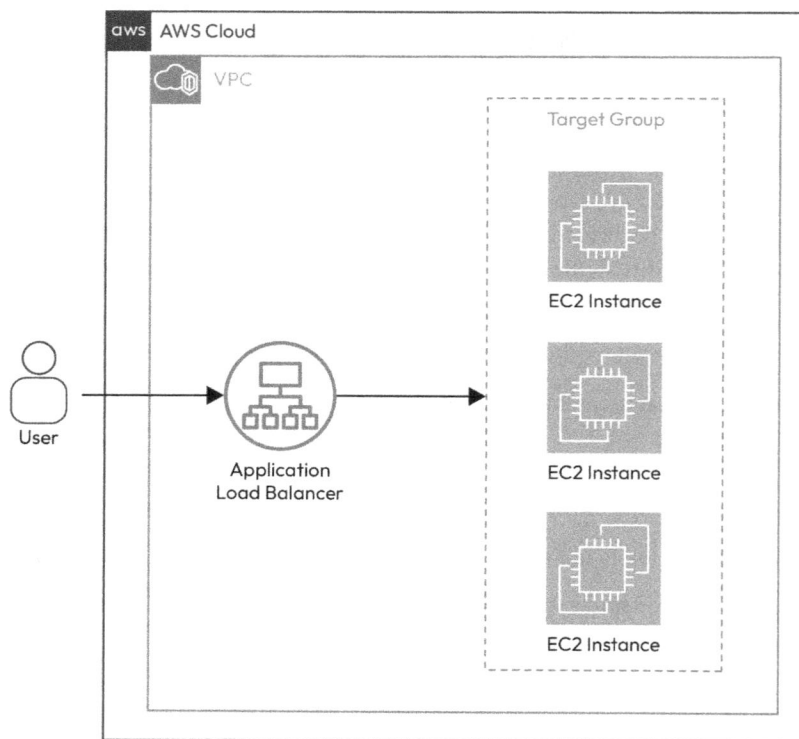

Figure 5.1 – Basic concept of a load balancer

Beyond this core functionality of distributing, or *balancing*, the traffic, load balancers can also be used for additional tasks such as terminating the TLS connection. We generally align load balancers with the layer in which they operate.

Before we get started, let's get a quick refresher on the **Open Systems Interconnection (OSI)** model for networked computer systems with the following figure.

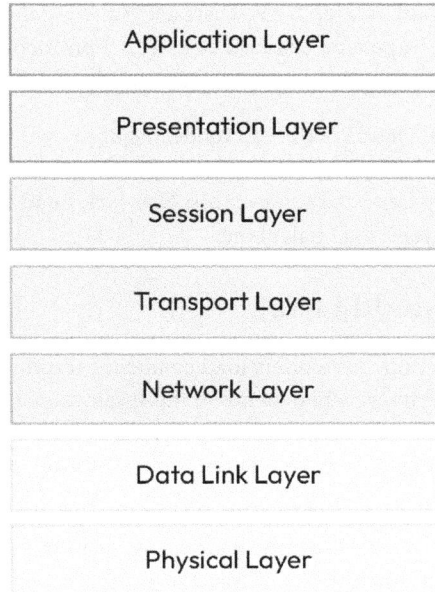

Application Layer

Presentation Layer

Session Layer

Transport Layer

Network Layer

Data Link Layer

Physical Layer

Figure 5.2 – The seven different layers of the OSI model

The OSI model defines seven different *layers* on which network protocols can operate. The details of these are as follows:

- **Physical layer**: Also known as **layer 1**, it handles the transmission of electric signals. This is the network card on your computer.

- **Data link layer**: Also called **layer 2**, it handles how the information from the upper layers is translated into data chunks to be put onto the physical wire.

- **Network layer**: Also known as **layer 3**, it can split the data received from the upper layers into *packets* and is also used to determine the best route to send a packet to. The most important protocol on this layer is the **Internet Protocol (IP)** protocol.

- **Transport layer**: Also called **layer 4**, it is responsible for turning the information passed from the upper layers into chunks called **segments**. On the receiving end of the connection, the transport layer is responsible for putting the segments back together and – if supported by the protocol – reassembling the packets in order. This is the layer of the **Transmission Control Protocol (TCP)** and the **User Datagram Protocol (UDP)**.

- **Session layer**: Also known as **layer 5**, it handles lasting connections between clients.

- **Presentation layer**: Also called **layer 6**, it takes the data from the upper layer and handles aspects such as a common understanding of things such as the encoding or compression of data.

- **Application layer**: Also known as **layer 7**, it is where applications define protocols to communicate with each other. The most important example of a layer 7 protocol is the **Hypertext Transfer Protocol** (**HTTP**), which web browsers use to communicate with a web server.

Load balancing happens on different layers of the OSI model. Typically, we'll do load balancing on either the application layer (layer 7) or the transport layer (layer 4). AWS offers us two different resources within the Elastic Load Balancing family to achieve this: **Network Load Balancers** (**NLBs**) for layer 4 load balancing and ALBs for layer 7 load balancing.

What load balancer should I use?

As mentioned in the previous section, AWS offers load balancing at different levels of the OSI stack. Which load-balancing technology to use will depend on the application architecture, and we can also chain load balancers acting on different levels depending on our needs. In this section, we'll quickly introduce the four different offerings that AWS – at the time of writing in July 2024 – has available.

The ALB acts as a layer 7 load balancer for HTTP and HTTPS traffic. Due to its understanding of the HTTP and HTTPS protocols, we can use information specific to this protocol to make our traffic distribution decisions. **Path-based routing** lets us make routing decisions based on the HTTP path. This means that, behind the same load balancer, we can send traffic that is requesting a path such as /home from the **Elastic Load Balancer** (**ELB**) to one set of instances while sending all traffic that is requesting a path such as /subscriptions to another set of instances. The set of instances that we are sending traffic to is also called a **target group**.

Besides routing requests based on the path, we can also use **host-based routing**, where the ALB will make traffic routing decisions based on the host header that is set in the request. So, requests for the host home.example.com can be routed to one target group while requests for subscriptions.example.com are routed to another target group.

Besides the routing, our ALB will also allow us to terminate TLS connections on it or return static responses.

When dealing with legacy applications within AWS, you might come across another type of layer 7 load balancer, called the **Classic Load Balancer** (**CLB**). CLBs, like ALBs, act on the application layer and support HTTP protocols. However, the CLB was the predecessor of the ALB and does not support things such as path-based or host-based routing. In general, you wouldn't use a CLB in any newly designed or deployed application.

The third option we have when it comes to load balancing is the NLB, which acts, as the name suggests, on the network layer (layer 4) of the OSI model. Due to its position on the OSI stack, it does not support load balancing based on layer 7 information such as the path. What it does support is a static IP address (per Availability Zone) and handling millions of requests per second. We can also set an

ALB as the target of an NLB. This pattern – which we'll look into later in this chapter, in the *Deploying an NLB in front of an ALB* section – allows us to get a static IP address for our application, which can be useful in enterprise environments that require the allow-listing of specific IP addresses in firewalls.

The fourth and final load balancer type that is available to you is the **Gateway Load Balancer (GWLB)**. This load balancer is used to deploy third-party security appliances (such as firewalls from vendors such as Fortinet or Check Point) into AWS. You'll usually not deploy a GWLB without this type of appliance as its target. The focus of the rest of the chapter will be on the ALB and NLB types.

Setting up our environment

Throughout this chapter, we'll use a lab setup to deploy instances that we can then target using our load balancers. The code for this is provided in the GitHub repository for this book, and in this section, we'll clone and set up the lab stack using Terraform. A version of this stack in AWS **Cloud Development Kit (CDK)** and CloudFormation is also available in the GitHub repository.

Follow these steps to set up your environment. You should have installed all the required tools as per the instructions in *Chapter 1*:

1. Clone the GitHub repository:

    ```
    git clone https://github.com/PacktPublishing/AWS-for-
    System-Administrators-Second-Edition && cd AWS-for-System-
    Administrators-Second-Edition/ch05/setup
    ```

2. Initialize the Terraform working directory:

    ```
    terraform init
    ```

3. Create the terraform plan for the resources. This command shows you which resources will be deployed by Terraform:

    ```
    terraform plan
    ```

4. Apply the plan to actually deploy the resources:

    ```
    terraform apply
    ```

What this Terraform code does is set up a VPC with public and private subnets in three Availability Zones in eu-central-1 (the Frankfurt Region). It also sets up instances that have an Apache web server running on them. We have covered all of these concepts in the previous chapters on cloud networking and the EC2 service. If you are curious, the GitHub repository contains a README with a more detailed outline of what the lab setup code does.

Now that we have our instances up and running, we can go ahead and create our first ALB.

> **Note**
>
> The infrastructure deployed in this section might incur costs when run. Due to this, be sure to decommission any infrastructure you deploy after you are done with your experimentation.
>
> For the parts set up by the lab, navigate to the same directory in which you cloned the lab infrastructure earlier in this section and run the following command to destroy the lab infrastructure that was set up for you: `terraform destroy`

Setting up the ALB

In this section, we are going to use Terraform and set up an ALB that can load-balance traffic to the instances we have created during the setup.

We'll modify the previously created `setup.tf` file in order to create our ALB. To do this, follow these steps:

1. Open up the `setup.tf` file in a code editor such as Visual Studio Code or Notepad++.

2. Navigate to the end of the file (*line 111*). You should see this comment:

   ```
   # start setting up your application load balancer here
   ```

3. The first resource we are going to create is the ALB itself. To do so, declare a resource of the `"aws_lb"` type. In this example, we'll call the resource `"main"`:

   ```
   resource "aws_lb" "main" {
   ```

4. Assign a name to the ALB. In this example, this is going to be `"main-alb"`:

   ```
   name                = "main-alb"
   ```

5. We want our ALB to be reachable from the internet and thus we'll define that it is not `internal` and that the ELB is of type `"application"`:

   ```
   internal            = false
   load_balancer_type  = "application"
   ```

6. Next, we assign the security group we had previously created. This security group allows for HTTP traffic to flow into this ALB:

   ```
   security_groups     = [aws_security_group.allow_http.id]
   ```

7. We then deploy the ALB into all of our public subnets:

   ```
   subnets             = aws_subnet.public[*].id
   ```

8. Finally, we give the ALB a name tag:

    ```
    tags = {
      Name = "Main ALB"
    }
    }
    ```

9. With the ALB created, we can go ahead and create a target group. The target group is where we'll later attach our instances and it is how we control to what instances a load balancer is routing traffic:

    ```
    resource "aws_lb_target_group" "main" {
    ```

10. We define the name and the port that this target group is listening on:

    ```
    name     = "main-tg"
    port     = 80
    ```

11. We will then define the protocol. Finally, we reference our VPC that this ALB is deployed into:

    ```
    protocol = "HTTP"
    vpc_id   = aws_vpc.main.id
    }
    ```

12. We now have a target group but we still need to tell the load balancer what to do with the traffic. This is done using listeners. Listeners define the action that should be taken by the ALB:

    ```
    resource "aws_lb_listener" "front_end" {
    ```

13. We reference our load balancer and define the protocol and port that this listener should act upon. You can attach multiple listeners to an ALB:

    ```
    load_balancer_arn = aws_lb.main.arn
    port              = "80"
    protocol          = "HTTP"
    ```

14. In this case, we'll use the default action – which matches all traffic – to forward to our previously created target group:

    ```
    default_action {
      type              = "forward"
      target_group_arn = aws_lb_target_group.main.arn
    }
    }
    ```

15. With the listener configured, the only thing missing is the association between the instances that our Terraform script has already predefined and the target group. We do this by attaching our instances to the previously created target group. We have a total of three instances deployed (one per Availability Zone) that we'll attach to our target group:

```
resource "aws_lb_target_group_attachment" "public" {
  count            = 3
```

16. We pass the ARN of the target group and use the index to assign all three of our instances in the public subnet:

```
target_group_arn = aws_lb_target_group.main.arn
target_id        = aws_instance.public[count.index].id
```

17. Finally, we define that our attachment is for port 80:

```
port             = 80
}
```

18. In order to be able to verify that our newly deployed ALB is working, we'll also add a Terraform output with the DNS name of our ALB:

```
output "alb_dns" {
    value = aws_lb.main.dns_name
}
```

19. You can now go ahead and create the ALB by running Terraform on the modified script:

```
terraform apply
```

In the command-line window, you'll see an output that contains the DNS name for our ALB. Copy this URL into a browser. Make sure to specify http as the protocol.

In your browser, you should be presented with the plain text Welcome from the instance!.

In this section, we have learned about the different types of load balancers available in AWS and seen how we can deploy an ALB. So far, our ALB is only able to handle unencrypted HTTP traffic. In the next section, we will see how we can add support for HTTPS to an ALB.

Handling HTTPS traffic with our ALB

When looking at the load balancer output from the previous section, there are two things you might notice:

- We have an AWS-provided hostname, ending in elb.amazonaws.com. While this might be fine for testing, we'll usually want to have this run behind our own domain.

- We currently use unencrypted HTTP traffic instead of encrypted HTTPS traffic.

In this section, we'll remediate both issues.

> **Note**
>
> In order for this section to work, you'll need a domain registered (ideally in **Route 53 (R53)**). Please follow the guides in the following documentation to either transfer a domain into your AWS account or buy a new domain.
>
> Here is the link to register a new domain: `https://docs.aws.amazon.com/Route53/latest/DeveloperGuide/domain-register.html`.

Before we can create an HTTPS listener in our load balancer, we'll need to do a few things:

- We need to associate a custom domain (`alb-test.<your_domain>`, in this example) with our previously deployed ALB. In order to do this, we'll need a DNS A record that *aliases* our custom domain name to our ALB.

- We need to request and verify an HTTPS certificate for our custom domain.

Let's begin the next step of this process.

Setting up a custom domain name for our ALB

We first need our custom domain. Assuming that you have either transferred a domain to your AWS account or you have bought a new domain within your AWS account, you can go ahead and set up a custom domain for your ALB:

1. Navigate to the R53 service in the AWS Management Console. R53 is the AWS DNS service that we'll use to create DNS records. In the left navigation menu, click on **Hosted zones**.

2. In the list, select the hosted zone of your domain (**squ4rks.link** in the following screenshot).

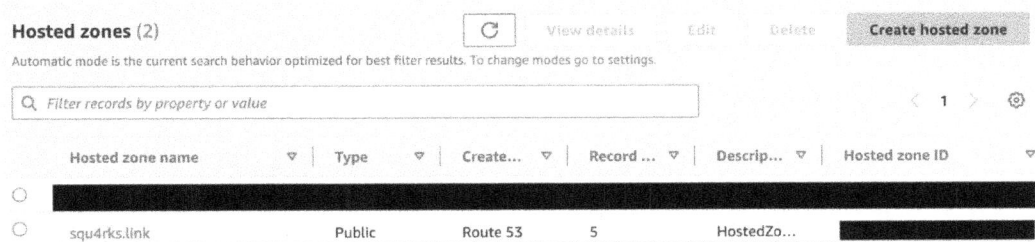

Hosted zones (2)							
Hosted zone name	Type	Create...	Record ...	Descrip...	Hosted zone ID		
squ4rks.link	Public	Route 53	5	HostedZo...			

Figure 5.3 – The list of available hosted zones

3. In the hosted zone, click the **Create record** button on the top right.

4. Fill in the information as shown in the following screenshot. This will create a DNS A record that aliases your chosen record name (aka *subdomain*) to your ELB:

Quick create record   Switch to wizard

▼ Record 1   Delete

Record name   Info   Record type   Info

| alb-test | .squ4rks.link | | A – Routes traffic to an IPv4 address and some AWS resources | ▼ |

Keep blank to create a record for the root domain.

🔘 Alias

Route traffic to   Info

| Alias to Application and Classic Load Balancer | ▼ |

| Europe (Frankfurt) | ▼ |

| 🔍 dualstack.main-alb-1636501428.eu-central-1.elb.amazonaws.com | ✕ |

Alias hosted zone ID: Z215JYRZR1TBD5

Routing policy   Info   Evaluate target health

| Simple routing | ▼ | 🔘 Yes

                                                                      [Add another record]

Figure 5.4 – Quick creation wizard for the A record connecting our subdomain with our ALB

With your domain configured, you should now be able to use your custom domain name to access the load balancer (via HTTP). In the next section, we'll create the certificate necessary to access the load balancer via HTTPS.

Requesting a new TLS certificate for our ALB

Now that we have mapped the domain name, we'll need to create a new HTTPS certificate. To do this, we'll use AWS Certificate Manager. This service allows us, as the name suggests, to create and manage certificates.

To create a new certificate for our newly created subdomain, follow these steps:

1. Navigate to the **AWS Certificate Manager** service in the AWS Management Console.

2. Click on the **Request** button.

3. When prompted for the certificate type you'd like to request, select **Request a public certificate**.

4. Fill in the information as shown in *Figure 5.5*.

    Under **Domain Names**, set the fully qualified domain name that you want to create a certificate for.

    In this example, this is **alb-test.squ4rks.link**. This should be the same subdomain you created in the previous section.

The **DNS validation - recommended** option means that your ownership of the domain will be verified by pushing some records into the DNS for your domain. If you have the domain in R53, this will be a one-click operation.

Under **Key algorithm**, select **RSA 2048**, which means that this certificate will be a 2,048-bit RSA key.

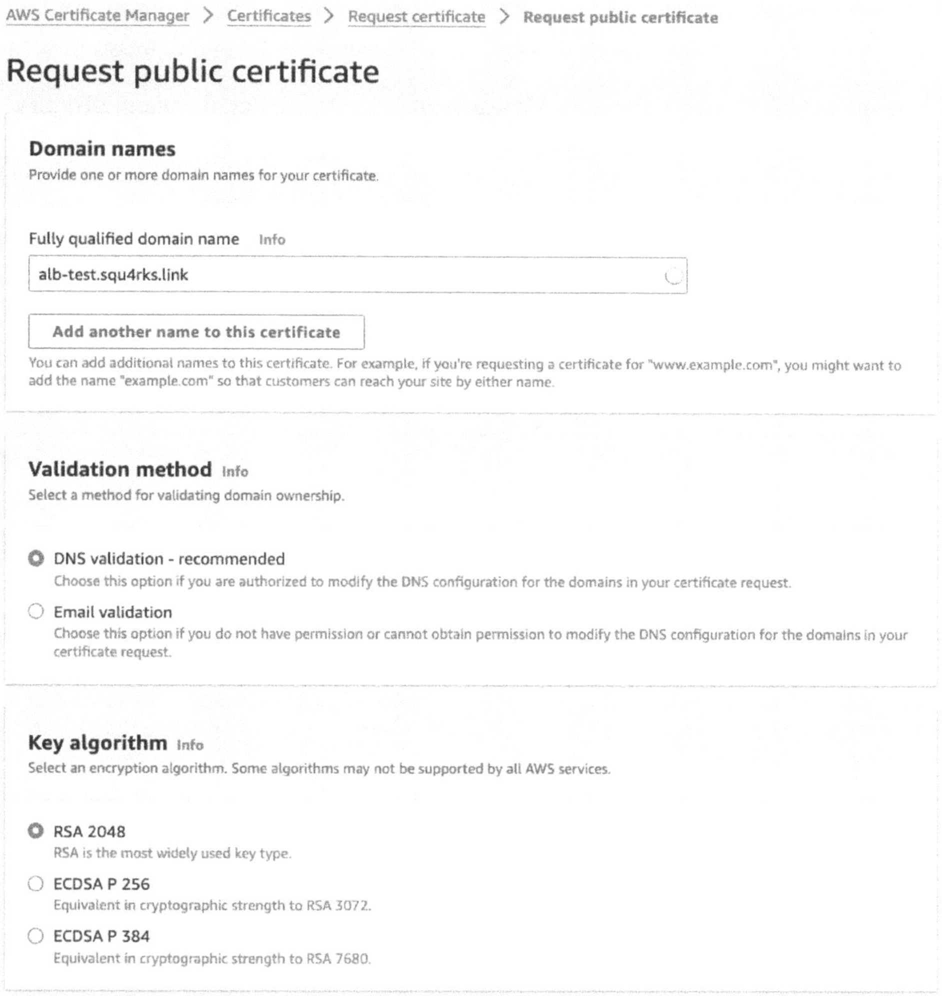

AWS Certificate Manager > Certificates > Request certificate > **Request public certificate**

Request public certificate

Domain names

Provide one or more domain names for your certificate.

Fully qualified domain name   Info

> alb-test.squ4rks.link

> **Add another name to this certificate**

You can add additional names to this certificate. For example, if you're requesting a certificate for "www.example.com", you might want to add the name "example.com" so that customers can reach your site by either name.

Validation method Info

Select a method for validating domain ownership.

● DNS validation - recommended

Choose this option if you are authorized to modify the DNS configuration for the domains in your certificate request.

○ Email validation

Choose this option if you do not have permission or cannot obtain permission to modify the DNS configuration for the domains in your certificate request.

Key algorithm Info

Select an encryption algorithm. Some algorithms may not be supported by all AWS services.

● RSA 2048

RSA is the most widely used key type.

○ ECDSA P 256

Equivalent in cryptographic strength to RSA 3072.

○ ECDSA P 384

Equivalent in cryptographic strength to RSA 7680.

Figure 5.5 – Information for the certificate request

5. Once you click **Create**, you'll be redirected to an overview page of your certificate request. Under the **Domains** section, click **Create records in Route 53** to create the required DNS records that prove your ownership of the domain.

Once you have created the DNS records, it can take a few minutes until the status of the certificate changes from **Pending validation** to **Issued**.

Once you have an issued certificate, we can get started with creating an HTTPS listener.

Adding an HTTPS listener

We can now add an HTTPS listener to our previously HTTP-only ALB. To do this, follow these steps:

1. Open up the EC2 service in the AWS Management Console and find the **main-alb** entry.

2. On the overview page, select **Add listener**.

3. For **Listener configuration**, select the values shown in the following screenshot:

Listener details: HTTPS:443

A listener checks for connection requests using the protocol and port that you configure. The default action and any additional rules that you create determine how the Application Load Balancer routes requests to its registered targets.

Listener configuration

The listener will be identified by the protocol and port.

Protocol
Used for connections from clients to the load balancer.

| HTTPS ▼ |

Port
The port on which the load balancer is listening for connections.

| 443 |

1-65535

Default actions   Info
The default action is used if no other rules apply. Choose the default action for traffic on this listener.

Authentication   Info
Authentication requires IPv4 connectivity to authentication endpoints. Learn more ⃗

☐ Use OpenID or Amazon Cognito
Include authentication using either OpenID Connect (OIDC) or Amazon Cognito.

Routing actions

| ● Forward to target groups | ○ Redirect to URL | ○ Return fixed response |

Forward to target group   Info
Choose a target group and specify routing weight or Create target group ⃗.

Target group			Weight	Percent
main-tg Target type: Instance, IPv4	HTTP ▼	C	1 ○ 0-999	100%

| Add target group |

You can add up to 4 more target groups.

Target group stickiness   Info
Enables the load balancer to bind a user's session to a specific target group. To use stickiness the client must support cookies. If you want to bind a user's session to a specific target, turn on the Target Group attribute Stickiness.

☐ Turn on target group stickiness

Figure 5.6 – Listener configuration for the HTTPS traffic

Let's learn about each of them in detail:

- **Protocol** is **HTTPS** since we want to serve HTTPS traffic.

- **Port** is **443**, the default port for HTTPS traffic.

- Under **Default actions**, we want to select **Forward to target groups** similar to how we did with the HTTP listener.

- For **Target group**, to forward traffic, we'll select **main-tg**, which was created by the Terraform script.

- For **Weight**, we keep a weight of **1**, which means that 100% of traffic is routed to this target group.

4. Next, we need to configure the security settings.

   For **Security policy**, we can use the recommended ELB security policy, which requires TLS version 1.2.

   For **Certificate source**, we select **From ACM** and then select the certificate we created in the previous step.

Secure listener settings Info

Security policy   Info
Your load balancer uses a Secure Socket Layer (SSL) negotiation configuration called a security policy to manage SSL connections with clients. Compare security policies [↗]

Security category	Policy name
All security policies ▼	ELBSecurityPolicy-TLS13-1-2-2021-06 (recommended) ▼

Default SSL/TLS server certificate
The certificate used if a client connects without SNI protocol, or if there are no matching certificates. You can source this certificate from AWS Certificate Manager (ACM), Amazon Identity and Access Management (IAM), or import a certificate. This certificate will automatically be added to your listener certificate list.

Certificate source

● From ACM	○ From IAM	○ Import certificate

Certificate (from ACM)
The selected certificate will be applied as the default SSL/TLS server certificate for this load balancer's secure listeners.

alb-test.squ4rks.link
bc2e3e96-4140-469c-8b25-036c... ▼   ⟳

Request new ACM certificate [↗]

Client certificate handling   Info
Client certificates are used to make authenticated requests to remote servers. Learn more [↗]

☐ Mutual authentication (mTLS)
  Mutual TLS (Transport Layer Security) authentication offers two-way peer authentication. It adds a layer of security over TLS and allows your services to verify the client that's making the connection.

Figure 5.7 – Secure listener settings for our HTTPS listener

We now have an HTTPS listener that listens on port 443. However, our ALB is currently configured (via security groups) to only allow traffic on port 80. In order to remediate this, we'll have to attach another security group that allows traffic to port 443. The Terraform script we ran at the beginning has already provisioned such a security group for us. To carry out the attaching process, follow these steps:

1. On the overview page of the load balancer, select the **Security** tab.

2. Under **Security groups**, select the edit button and then select the security group named **allow_https** in addition to the **allow_http** security group, as shown in the following screenshot:

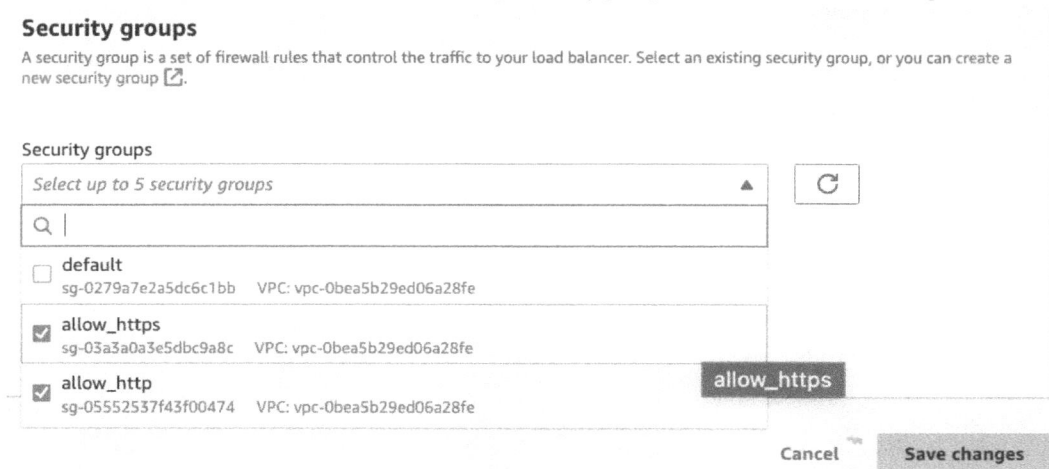

Security groups

A security group is a set of firewall rules that control the traffic to your load balancer. Select an existing security group, or you can create a new security group [⎘].

Security groups

| Select up to 5 security groups ▲ | ↻ |

🔍 |

☐ default
sg-0279a7e2a5dc6c1bb   VPC: vpc-0bea5b29ed06a28fe

☑ allow_https
sg-03a3a0a3e5dbc9a8c   VPC: vpc-0bea5b29ed06a28fe

☑ allow_http   allow_https
sg-05552537f43f00474   VPC: vpc-0bea5b29ed06a28fe

Cancel   **Save changes**

Figure 5.8 – Adding the allow_https security group to our ALB

With this done, we can now access the HTTPS version of our web page under our custom domain.

Deploying an NLB in front of an ALB

Sometimes, we'll need a static IP address for our application that serves as the entry point that can be allow-listed, for example, in a firewall.

The following figure shows the architecture diagram of an NLB in front of an ALB that then relays traffic to a target group of EC2 instances.

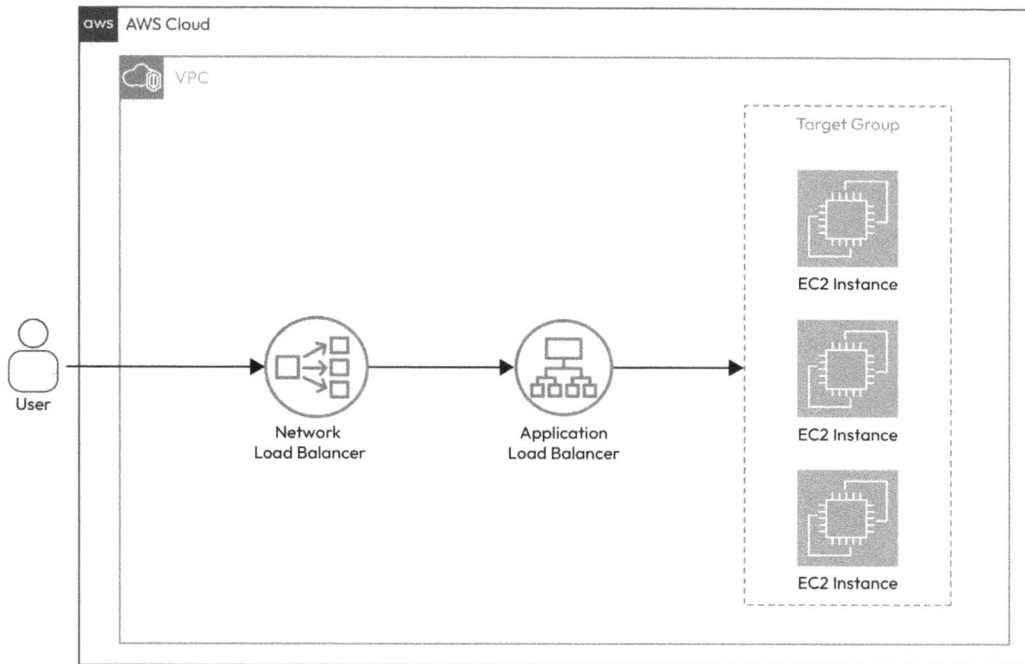

Figure 5.9 – Architecture diagram of an NLB deployed in front of an ALB

In this section, we'll deploy our NLB in the AWS Management Console since we have so far only deployed an ELB via Terraform. On the GitHub page, you can find versions of this deployment in Terraform, AWS CDK, and CloudFormation.

Follow these steps to create an NLB that will live in front of our ALB. We'll first create a target group that contains our ALB. Once we have the target group, we'll create an NLB that routes traffic to the previously created target group containing our ALB. Follow these steps:

1. Navigate to the EC2 service in the AWS Management Console and select **Load Balancers** in the left-hand navigation pane.

2. In the left-hand navigation, select **Target Groups** and click **Create target group**.

3. In the dialog, select the values shown here:

    -   **Choose a target type**: **Application Load Balancer**

    -   **Target group name**: Use any name you want to identify this target group

- **VPC**: Select the VPC that your ALB is located in

- **Port**: Select the port that your ALB is listening on

Basic configuration

Settings in this section can't be changed after the target group is created.

Choose a target type

○ Instances

- Supports load balancing to instances within a specific VPC.
- Facilitates the use of Amazon EC2 Auto Scaling [↗] to manage and scale your EC2 capacity.

○ IP addresses

- Supports load balancing to VPC and on-premises resources.
- Facilitates routing to multiple IP addresses and network interfaces on the same instance.
- Offers flexibility with microservice based architectures, simplifying inter-application communication.
- Supports IPv6 targets, enabling end-to-end IPv6 communication, and IPv4-to-IPv6 NAT.

○ Lambda function

- Facilitates routing to a single Lambda function.
- Accessible to Application Load Balancers only.

◉ Application Load Balancer

- Offers the flexibility for a Network Load Balancer to accept and route TCP requests within a specific VPC.
- Facilitates using static IP addresses and PrivateLink with an Application Load Balancer.

Target group name

```
alb-tg
```

A maximum of 32 alphanumeric characters including hyphens are allowed, but the name must not begin or end with a hyphen.

Protocol : Port

Choose a protocol for your target group that corresponds to the Load Balancer type that will route traffic to it. Some protocols now include anomaly detection for the targets and you can set mitigation options once your target group is created. This choice cannot be changed after creation

| TCP | ▼ | 80 | ⌄ |

1-65535

VPC

Select the VPC with the Application Load Balancer that you want to include in the target group.

```
main-vpc
vpc-0bea5b29ed06a28fe
IPv4 VPC CIDR: 10.0.0.0/16                                    ▼
```

Figure 5.10 – Configuration for the ALB target group

4. When asked to register an ALB, choose **Register now** and select our previously created ALB from the dropdown.

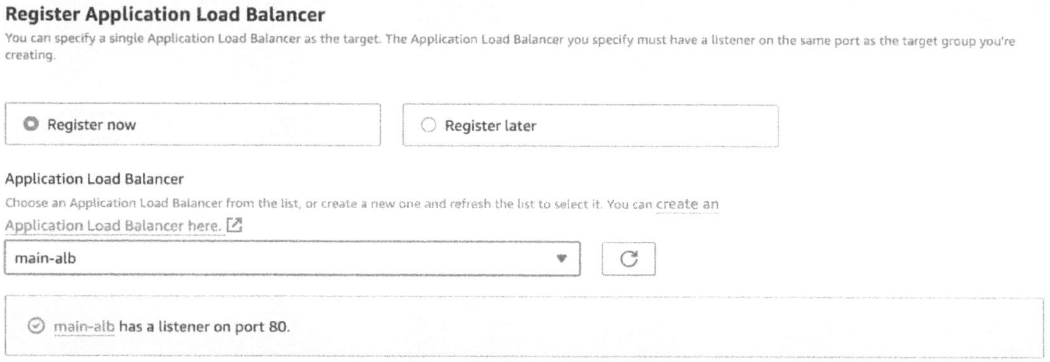

Register Application Load Balancer

You can specify a single Application Load Balancer as the target. The Application Load Balancer you specify must have a listener on the same port as the target group you're creating.

⦿ Register now	○ Register later

Application Load Balancer

Choose an Application Load Balancer from the list, or create a new one and refresh the list to select it. You can create an Application Load Balancer here. ☐

main-alb ▼	C

⊘ main-alb has a listener on port 80.

Figure 5.11 – Registration of the ALB for our target group

5. With the target group created, navigate back to the **Load Balancers** item in the left-hand navigation pane and, on the overview page, click the **Create Load Balancer** button.

6. Under **Load Balancer Type**, click the **Create** button under **Network Load Balancer**.

7. Give your load balancer a name and select **Internet-facing** for the scheme.

8. For the address type, you can leave it at **IPv4** but notice that the NLB also supports dual-stack (IPv6 + IPv4).

9. In the **Network mapping** section, select the VPC we have used throughout this chapter and deploy the NLB into all of the three Availability Zones.

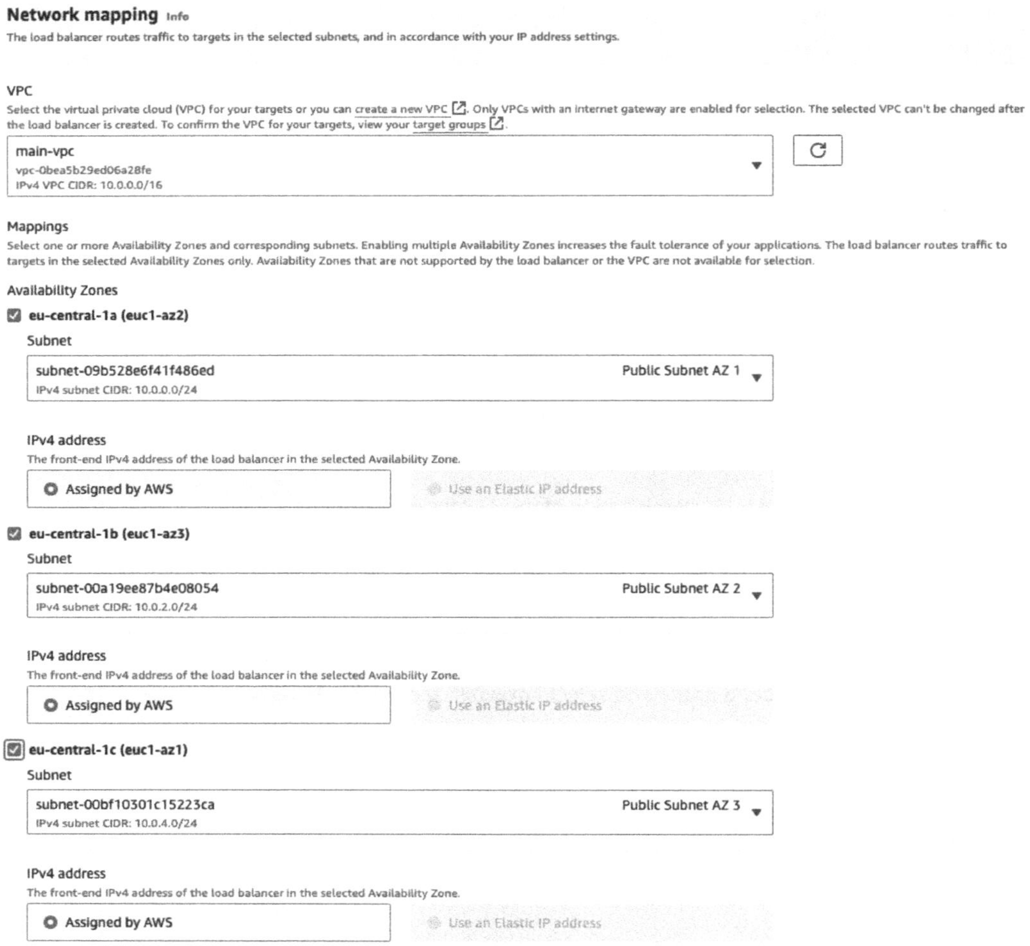

Network mapping Info

The load balancer routes traffic to targets in the selected subnets, and in accordance with your IP address settings.

VPC

Select the virtual private cloud (VPC) for your targets or you can create a new VPC 🗗. Only VPCs with an internet gateway are enabled for selection. The selected VPC can't be changed after the load balancer is created. To confirm the VPC for your targets, view your target groups 🗗.

```
main-vpc
vpc-0bea5b29ed06a28fe
IPv4 VPC CIDR: 10.0.0.0/16
```

Mappings

Select one or more Availability Zones and corresponding subnets. Enabling multiple Availability Zones increases the fault tolerance of your applications. The load balancer routes traffic to targets in the selected Availability Zones only. Availability Zones that are not supported by the load balancer or the VPC are not available for selection.

Availability Zones

☑ **eu-central-1a (euc1-az2)**

Subnet

```
subnet-09b528e6f41f486ed                    Public Subnet AZ 1
IPv4 subnet CIDR: 10.0.0.0/24
```

IPv4 address

The front-end IPv4 address of the load balancer in the selected Availability Zone.

⦿ Assigned by AWS   ⦿ Use an Elastic IP address

☑ **eu-central-1b (euc1-az3)**

Subnet

```
subnet-00a19ee87b4e08054                    Public Subnet AZ 2
IPv4 subnet CIDR: 10.0.2.0/24
```

IPv4 address

The front-end IPv4 address of the load balancer in the selected Availability Zone.

⦿ Assigned by AWS   ⦿ Use an Elastic IP address

☑ **eu-central-1c (euc1-az1)**

Subnet

```
subnet-00bf10301c15223ca                    Public Subnet AZ 3
IPv4 subnet CIDR: 10.0.4.0/24
```

IPv4 address

The front-end IPv4 address of the load balancer in the selected Availability Zone.

⦿ Assigned by AWS   ⦿ Use an Elastic IP address

Figure 5.12 – Exemplary network mapping

10. For the security groups, deselect the **Default** security group and add our **allow_http** security group to this listener.

11. Finally, for **Listeners and routing**, select **TCP** as the protocol and **80** as the port and forward all traffic to our previously created ALB target group.

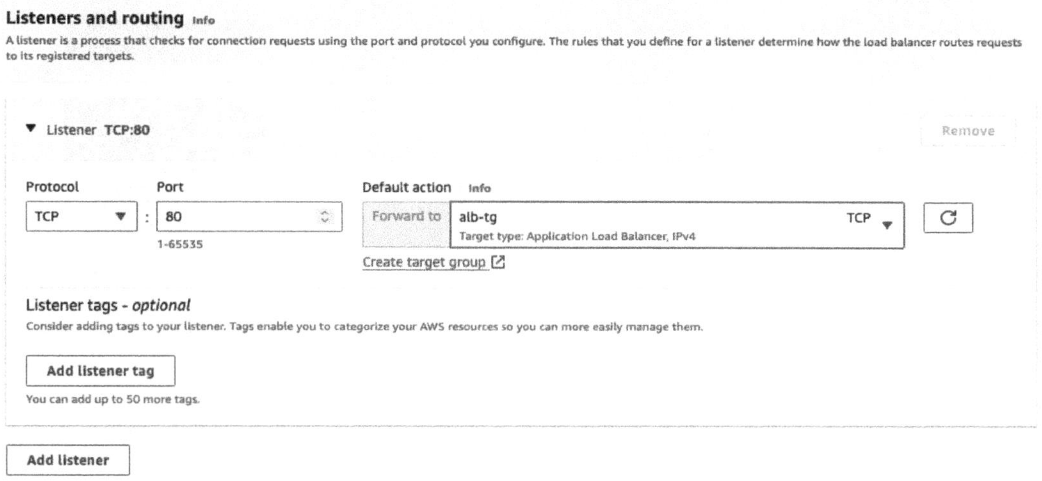

Listeners and routing Info

A listener is a process that checks for connection requests using the port and protocol you configure. The rules that you define for a listener determine how the load balancer routes requests to its registered targets.

Figure 5.13 – The listener config for our NLB

Once created, you'll have an NLB deployed that can be used to access the ALB. On the NLB page, there is a new DNS name that you can use to access your ALB. In this section, we have seen how we can add a custom domain and a TLS certificate to our load balancer. By doing so, we can now serve traffic both from a custom domain name and using TLS encryption.

Summary

In this chapter, we have covered how elastic load balancing can be used to distribute traffic among a group of instances. We explored the different types of load balancers available and discussed when to use which kind of load balancer. We then deployed ALBs and also an NLB before securing our traffic by implementing HTTPS.

With load balancers, we can get a public endpoint to which we can send our traffic. So far, we have had a set number of instances. We are missing one more piece to achieve scalable infrastructure – Auto Scaling groups. In the next chapter, we'll see how they can be used to automatically scale the compute instances behind our load balancer.

Get This Book's PDF Version and Exclusive Extras

Scan the QR code (or go to packtpub.com/unlock). Search for this book by name, confirm the edition, and then follow the steps on the page.

Note: Keep your invoice handly. Purchase made directly from packt don't require one.

Increasing Application Performance Using AWS Auto Scaling

In the previous chapters, we saw how the Amazon **Elastic Compute Cloud** (**EC2**) service can be used to dynamically spin up virtual machines in seconds. In *Chapter 5*, we also saw how **Elastic Load Balancing** (**ELB**) can be used to distribute traffic between a (possibly changing) number of instances. In this chapter, we'll add the final piece of the puzzle for scalable computing. One of the benefits of the cloud is the availability of on-demand capacity when we need it. However, it would be cumbersome for us as administrators and operators to manually check the load of our machines and add or remove compute capacity based on those manually checked load numbers. This is where auto-scaling comes into play.

AWS Auto Scaling will scale the number of instances based on demand. This means that if the load hits a critical point, new instances will be added, and once the load on our system goes down, instances will be terminated.

Besides making sure that the provided instances match our required capacity as closely as possible, Auto Scaling can also be used for fault tolerance. By connecting the scaling groups to health checks (for example, from our load balancer), we can make sure that unhealthy instances are terminated and replaced with new ones without any human interference.

In this chapter, we'll look into Auto Scaling and its different policies. We'll set up an Auto Scaling policy – first, in the console and then using Terraform.

The main topics covered in this chapter are as follows:

- Setting up auto scaling using the AWS console and Terraform
- Understanding the different auto scaling policies
- Scaling applications based on demand

Technical requirements

Before following this chapter, please create an AWS account for yourself. You can sign up at aws.amazon.com. A basic understanding of AWS – for example, what a service is – will be beneficial for following the chapter.

To get the most out of this chapter, an understanding of EC2 and load balancers in AWS is advisable.

All scripts from this section can be found at the following GitHub link:

`https://github.com/PacktPublishing/AWS-for-System-Administrators-Second-Edition`

The CiA video for this chapter can be found at `https://packt.link/tSPim`

You'll need a VPC and subnets to deploy your instances into. If you still have the subnets and VPCs created for the load balancers in the previous chapter, you can reuse these. Otherwise, deploy the Terraform script that you can find at the following GitHub link:

`https://github.com/PacktPublishing/AWS-for-System-Administrators-Second-Edition/blob/main/ch05/setup/setup.tf`

When should we use auto scaling?

Not all applications lend themselves to being scaled using auto scaling. Crucially, in order for auto scaling to work, we need our application to be *horizontally* scalable.

In general, there are two types of scaling when it comes to computing:

- **Vertical scaling**: This is the practice of adding more power to a single machine. This could be done by changing the instance type to a more powerful instance with more CPU and memory. This is sometimes also referred to as *scaling up*.
- **Horizontal scaling**: This is the practice of increasing the compute by adding additional instances. This is sometimes also referred to as *scaling out*.

The following figure shows the difference between scaling up and scaling out.

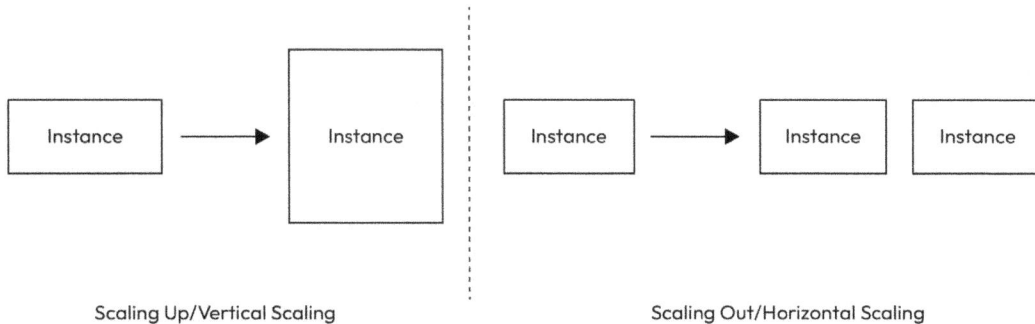

Figure 6.1 – Scaling up vs. scaling out

Whether or not we can use horizontal scaling (and thus auto scaling) for our application depends on the application architecture and on one crucial question: *Can a new request be handled by a new instance independently or are there any in-process dependencies?*

A classic example of applications that are difficult to scale horizontally are applications that require local disk I/O. Take the following simple architecture as an example:

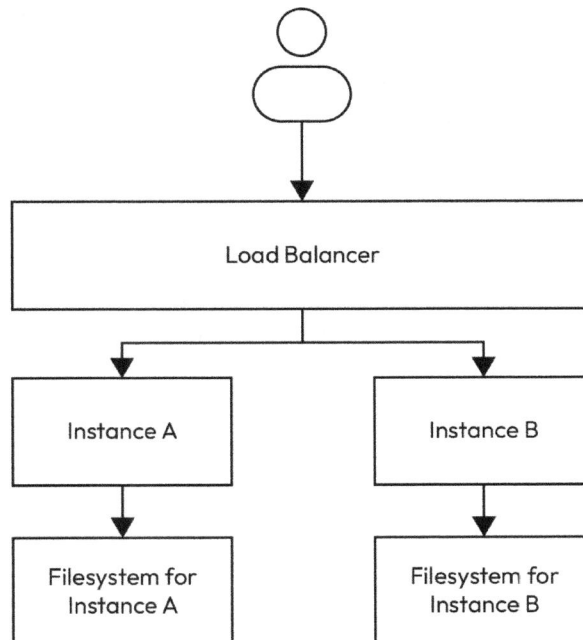

Figure 6.2 – Scenario for an application where horizontal scaling would be difficult

In this example, we have two instances, A and B, behind a load balancer. Each instance has an attached filesystem. Let's assume our application handles photo uploads and stores them on the local storage of the instance.

If the user now uploads a picture, the requests might randomly get routed to instance A where the picture gets stored on the local filesystem of instance A. Next, the user tries to retrieve the photo. This request is routed to instance B. This instance can't find the image and returns an error. The application won't be able to handle the request properly.

> **Note**
>
> The preceding example is even worse because it does not simply fulfill the request to retrieve a photo. It works only *sometimes*. Whenever a request to retrieve an image is sent to the instance that handled the upload, the request returns successfully. Next time, when the request is routed to the instance that didn't handle the upload, it will error out.
>
> This kind of behavior is known as intermittent failure or **bimodal behavior** and is one of the most undesirable states an application can be in because (from the point of the user) the application works *sometimes*.

For this simple example, there would be ways to fix this. One approach would be to introduce a shared filesystem that synchronizes the files between two or more instances. However, legacy applications, in particular, can struggle with this kind of scaling, and then scaling up or re-engineering the application to support horizontal scaling are the only options.

Assuming that our application can be scaled horizontally, we need to define a template of how our scaled instances should look – this is called a **launch template**.

Creating a launch template

When we previously created a virtual machine in AWS using EC2, there was a lot of information that we had to configure manually, such as the **Amazon Machine Image** (**AMI**), the instance type, and the amount of storage, to name a few. How do we do this in our **auto scaling group** (**ASG**)? We need a set of generalized information, such as a blueprint or template, that can be used to create new instances. This is what *launch templates* are for.

We'll first create a launch template in the AWS console and then via Terraform together with an ASG.

Creating a launch template in the AWS console

To create a launch template, follow these steps:

1. Navigate to the EC2 service in the AWS console and select **Instances | Launch Templates**.

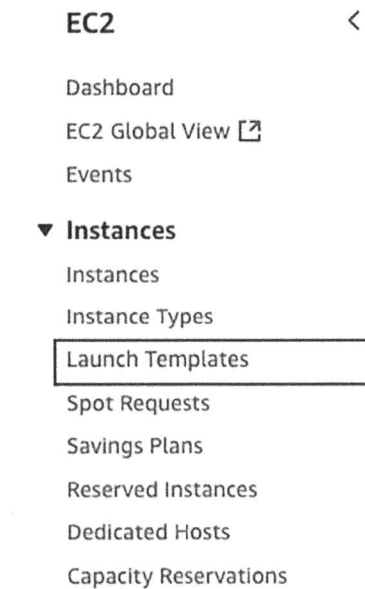

EC2   ＜

Dashboard
EC2 Global View [↗]
Events

▼ **Instances**

Instances
Instance Types
Launch Templates
Spot Requests
Savings Plans
Reserved Instances
Dedicated Hosts
Capacity Reservations

Figure 6.3 – The Launch Templates sub-menu

2. Click the **Create launch template** button.

3. In the next section, we'll fill out the details of our launch template. First, specify the following:

    -   **Launch template name**: This is the name of this launch template.

    -   **Template version description**: This is a description of this version of the launch template. Launch templates can have multiple versions that can be used independently from each other. This means that one ASG can use version 2 while another is already running version 3. Such a behavior is desirable when rolling out changes to a small subset of instances instead of all of them.

Create launch template

Creating a launch template allows you to create a saved instance configuration that can be reused, shared and launched at a later time. Templates can have multiple versions.

Launch template name and description

Launch template name - *required*

| MyTemplate |

Must be unique to this account. Max 128 chars. No spaces or special characters like '&', '*', '@'.

Template version description

| A prod webserver for MyApp |

Max 255 chars

Auto Scaling guidance   Info
Select this if you intend to use this template with EC2 Auto Scaling

☐ Provide guidance to help me set up a template that I can use with EC2 Auto Scaling

▶ Template tags

▶ Source template

Figure 6.4 – Launch template naming and description section

4. Specify the AMI this launch template should use. In this example, we'll be using the Amazon Linux AMI.

▼ **Application and OS Images (Amazon Machine Image)** Info

An AMI is a template that contains the software configuration (operating system, application server, and applications) required to launch your instance. Search or Browse for AMIs if you don't see what you are looking for below

| Q   Search our full catalog including 1000s of application and OS images |

Recents   **Quick Start**

Don't include in launch template	Amazon Linux	macOS	Ubuntu	Windows	Red Hat	SUSE Linux	Debian	Browse more AMIs
	aws	Mac	ubuntu®	Microsoft	Red Hat	SUSE	debian	Including AMIs from AWS, Marketplace and the Community

Amazon Machine Image (AMI)

Amazon Linux 2023 AMI	Free tier eligible
ami-00a929b66ed6e0de6 (64-bit (x86), uefi-preferred) / ami-05f417c208be02d4d (64-bit (Arm), uefi)	
Virtualization: hvm ENA enabled: true Root device type: ebs	

Description

Amazon Linux 2023 is a modern, general purpose Linux-based OS that comes with 5 years of long term support. It is optimized for AWS and designed to provide a secure, stable and high-performance execution environment to develop and run your cloud applications.

Amazon Linux 2023 AMI 2023.7.20250331.0 x86_64 HVM kernel-6.1

Architecture	Boot mode	AMI ID	Publish Date	Username ⓘ	
64-bit (x86) ▼	uefi-preferred	ami-00a929b66ed6e0de6	2025-03-29	ec2-user	Verified provider

Figure 6.5 – Dialog to select the desired AMI and CPU architecture

5. Next, we select the instance type that we want to use. In this example, we'll be using the free-tier eligible **t2.micro** instance.

Figure 6.6 – Dialog defining the EC2 instance type to be used in our launch template

6. Next, define which SSH keys should be used for the newly created instances.

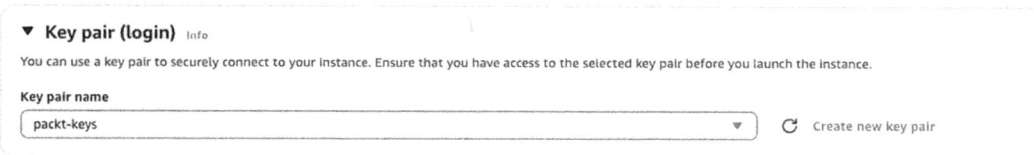

Figure 6.7 – Key pair used to log in to the instances created by this instance template

7. Finally, the **Network settings** options define the VPCs in which new instances will be added. Since we'll configure the AZs that instances should be placed into in the ASG, we'll need to leave the **Subnet** selection empty (remember that subnets are tied to AZs). For the security group, select the previously created **allow_http** group.

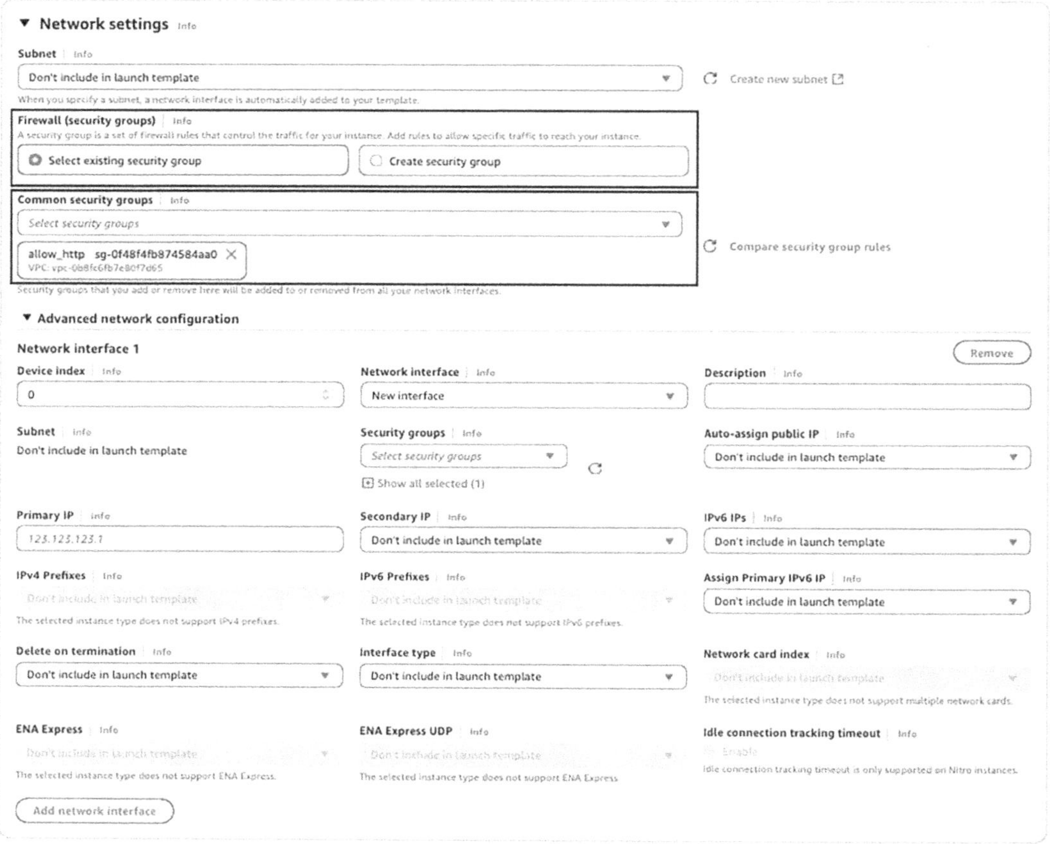

Figure 6.8 – Network settings in our launch template

8. For **Storage**, we'll leave it at the default 8-GiB gp3 EBS volumes.

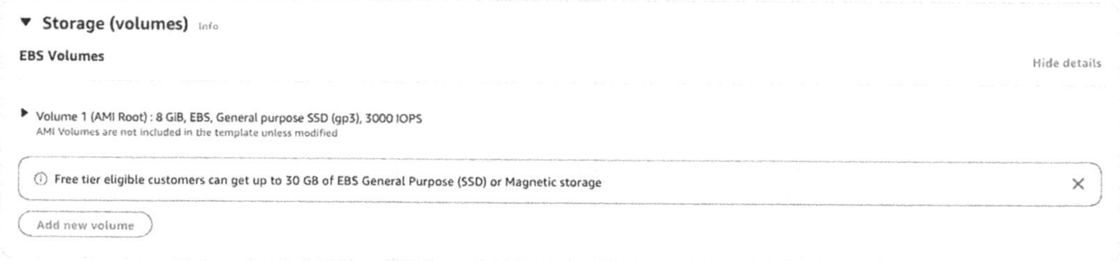

Figure 6.9 – Storage configuration for our launch template

9.   Finally, open up **Advanced settings** and scroll to the bottom. You should find a field called **User data**. Insert the following script in this field:

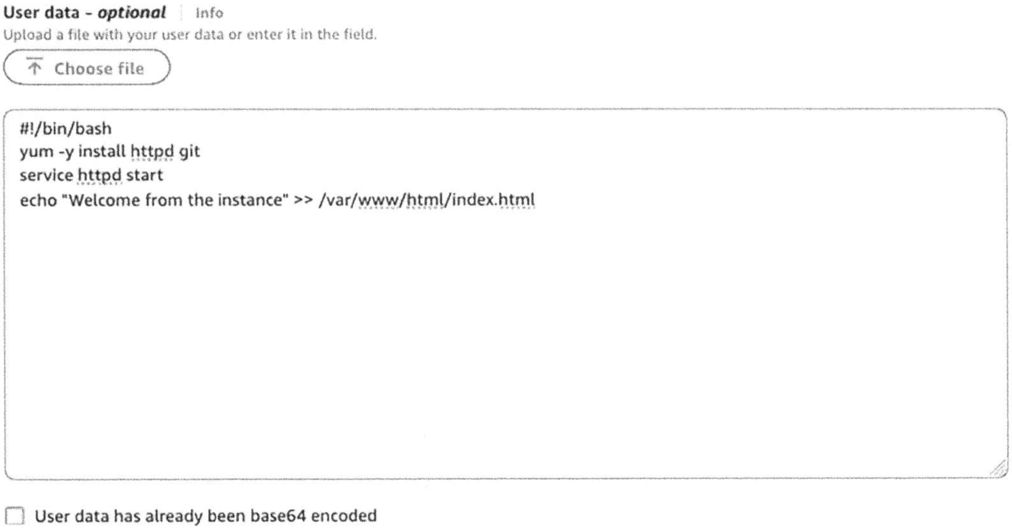

User data - *optional*   Info
Upload a file with your user data or enter it in the field.

(⤒ Choose file)

```
#!/bin/bash
yum -y install httpd git
service httpd start
echo "Welcome from the instance" >> /var/www/html/index.html
```

☐ User data has already been base64 encoded

Figure 6.10 – User data for our launch template

This is the user data for copying and pasting:

```
#!/bin/bash
yum -y install httpd git
service httpd start
echo "Welcome from the instance!" >> /var/www/html/index.html
```

Remember that the user data is a script that is being run upon instance creation. In this example, the script installs Apache 2 and Git, starts the Apache server, and then overwrites the default HTML with the message `Welcome from the instance!`.

With this, we now have a launch template that can be used with ASGs.

Creating an ASG in the AWS console

Now that we have our template, we can go ahead and create an ASG. In this chapter, we'll create an ASG in the AWS console before using Terraform to create both a launch template and an ASG.

Follow these steps to create a new ASG in the AWS console:

1. In the menu of the EC2 service, select **Auto Scaling Groups** under the **Auto Scaling** menu item.
2. Click the **Create Auto Scaling Group** button.
3. First, type a name for your ASG.

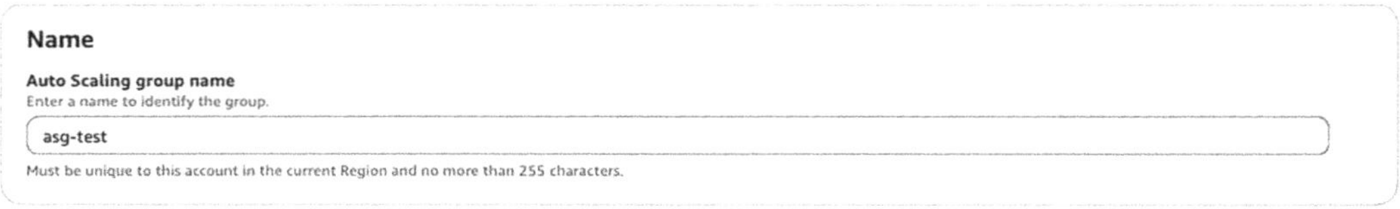

Name

Auto Scaling group name
Enter a name to identify the group.

```
asg-test
```

Must be unique to this account in the current Region and no more than 255 characters.

Figure 6.11 – Name dialog for the ASG

4. Next, select the previously created launch template. As you can see, you can change the version of the launch template here.

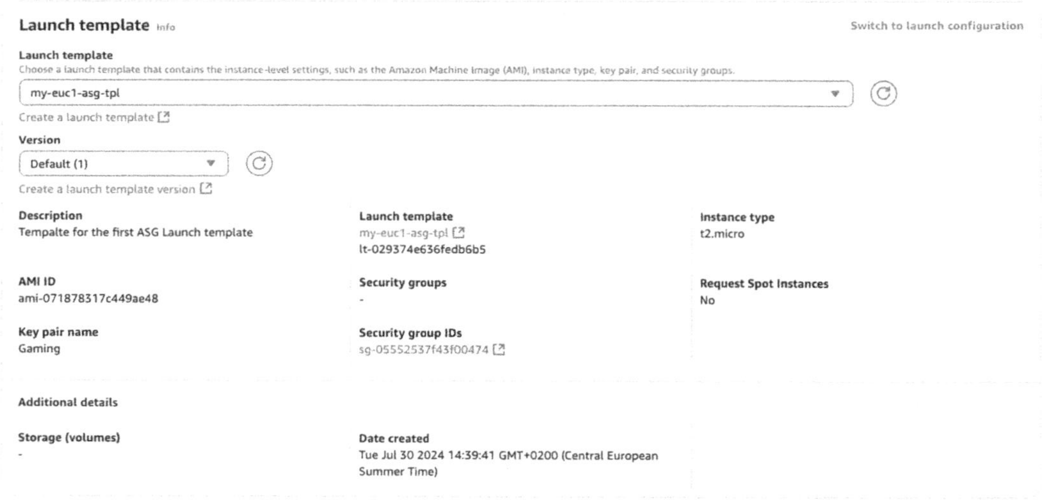

Launch template Info   Switch to launch configuration

Launch template
Choose a launch template that contains the instance-level settings, such as the Amazon Machine Image (AMI), instance type, key pair, and security groups.

```
my-euc1-asg-tpl
```

Create a launch template

Version

```
Default (1)
```

Create a launch template version

| **Description** | **Launch template** | **Instance type** |
| Templalte for the first ASG Launch template | my-euc1-asg-tpl <br> lt-029374e636fedb6b5 | t2.micro |

| **AMI ID** | **Security groups** | **Request Spot Instances** |
| ami-071878317c449ae48 | - | No |

| **Key pair name** | **Security group IDs** | |
| Gaming | sg-05552537f43f00474 | |

Additional details

| **Storage (volumes)** | **Date created** |
| - | Tue Jul 30 2024 14:39:41 GMT+0200 (Central European Summer Time) |

Figure 6.12 – Selected launch template repeating our selections from its creation

> **Note**
>
> You'll sometimes find the term *launch configuration*. **Launch configurations** are also templates to create instances used by ASGs. They are the predecessor of launch templates and are supported for backward compatibility, but accounts created after June 1, 2023, are not able to create new launch configurations.
>
> Any new application should use launch templates instead of launch configurations. As of October 1, 2024, accounts can't create new launch configurations.

5. Next, we can define the instance type and networking. Since our launch template already defines our desired instance type, we only need to define the networking selection. Recall that, in our launch template, we only defined a security group but no subnets since the subnets are dependent on the AZs.

6. In the **Network** section, select the `main-vpc` VPC that was either created in the previous chapter or by running the Terraform code in the *Technical requirements* section of this chapter. Select all three AZs and their corresponding subnets.

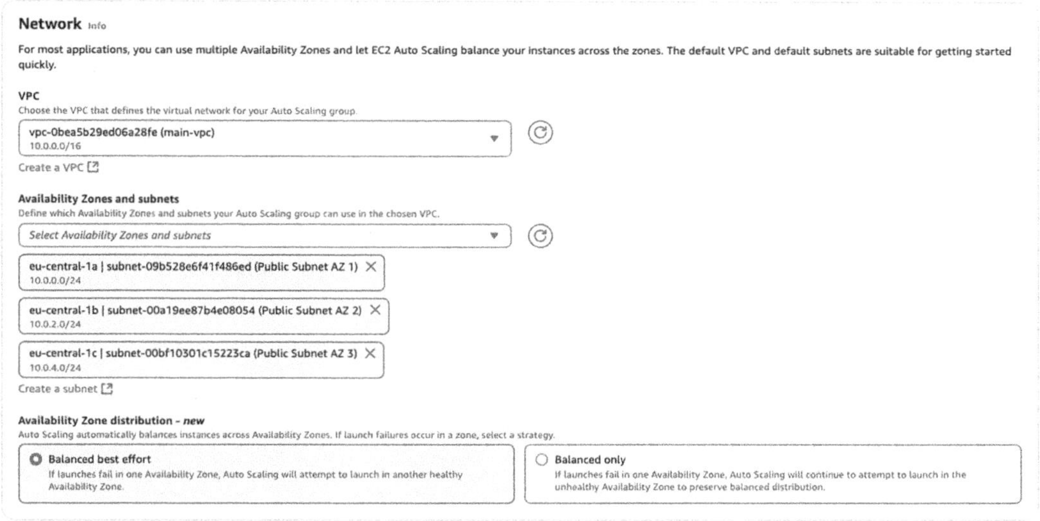

Figure 6.13 – Network selection of the VPC and subnets into which we want this ASG to deploy instances

7. Next, we can attach the ASG to our previously created load balancer. This will add the instances from the ASG to the target group of our load balancer. Any instances that are being scaled down (and thus terminated) are automatically removed from the target group, and any new instances added (by scaling up) are automatically added to the list of targets.

8. Select **Attach to an existing load balancer** and then select **Choose from your load balancer target groups**. In the dropdown, select the target group. If you are following the example, the name should be **main-tg**.

Integrate with other services - *optional* Info

Use a load balancer to distribute network traffic across multiple servers. Enable service-to-service communications with VPC Lattice. Shift resources away from impaired Availability Zones with zonal shift. You can also customize health check replacements and monitoring.

Load balancing Info

Use the options below to attach your Auto Scaling group to an existing load balancer, or to a new load balancer that you define.

○ No load balancer	● Attach to an existing load balancer	○ Attach to a new load balancer
Traffic to your Auto Scaling group will not be fronted by a load balancer.	Choose from your existing load balancers.	Quickly create a basic load balancer to attach to your Auto Scaling group.

Attach to an existing load balancer
Select the load balancers that you want to attach to your Auto Scaling group.

● Choose from your load balancer target groups	○ Choose from Classic Load Balancers
This option allows you to attach Application, Network, or Gateway Load Balancers.	

Existing load balancer target groups
Only instance target groups that belong to the same VPC as your Auto Scaling group are available for selection.

Select target groups ▼ ⟳

| main-tg | HTTP   ✕ |
| Application Load Balancer: main-alb |

Figure 6.14 – Selection of the load balancer we want our ASG to be part of in the target group

9. We'll ignore the **VPC Lattice integration options** and move straight to the **Health checks** section. (Amazon VPC Lattice is an application networking service that we won't be covering in this chapter.) In the **Health checks** section, put a checkmark next to the **Turn on Elastic Load Balancing health checks** option. This will enable unhealthy instances (determined based on the health checks from the load balancer) to be terminated and replaced.

Health checks
Health checks increase availability by replacing unhealthy instances. When you use multiple health checks, all are evaluated, and if at least one fails, instance replacement occurs.

EC2 health checks
ⓘ Always enabled

Additional health check types - *optional* Info

☑ Turn on Elastic Load Balancing health checks [Recommended]
Elastic Load Balancing monitors whether instances are available to handle requests. When it reports an unhealthy instance, EC2 Auto Scaling can replace it on its next periodic check.

| ⓘ EC2 Auto Scaling will start to detect and act on health checks performed by Elastic Load Balancing. To avoid unexpected terminations, first verify the settings of these health checks ✕ |
| in the Load Balancer console 🗗 |

☐ Turn on VPC Lattice health checks
VPC Lattice can monitor whether instances are available to handle requests. If it reports a target as failed a health check, EC2 Auto Scaling replaces it after its next periodic check.

☐ Turn on Amazon EBS health checks
EBS monitors whether an instance's root volume or attached volume stalls. When it reports an unhealthy volume, EC2 Auto Scaling can replace the instance on its next periodic health check.

Health check grace period Info
This time period delays the first health check until your instances finish initializing. It doesn't prevent an instance from terminating when placed into a non-running state.

[300 ⌄] seconds

Figure 6.15 – Health checks for ELB

10. Next, we can configure our desired minimum and maximum sizes, as well as our scaling policy.

11. Under **Group size**, define the desired capacity. This is the number of instances that our ASG should keep running under normal circumstances.

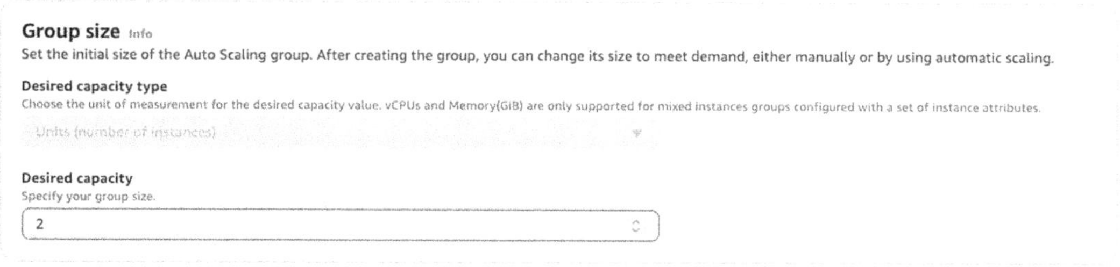

Group size Info
Set the initial size of the Auto Scaling group. After creating the group, you can change its size to meet demand, either manually or by using automatic scaling.

Desired capacity type
Choose the unit of measurement for the desired capacity value. vCPUs and Memory(GiB) are only supported for mixed instances groups configured with a set of instance attributes.

Units (number of instances)

Desired capacity
Specify your group size.

2

Figure 6.16 – Desired capacity

12. Then, we can define the scaling. The **Min desired capacity** field defines how many instances should be kept up and running at a minimum and **Max desired capacity** defines the maximum. By defining a maximum, we make sure that our application scaling doesn't get out of control, which could be too costly.

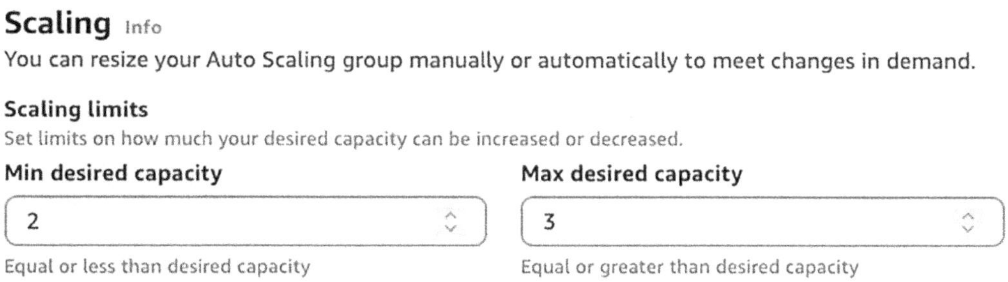

Scaling Info

You can resize your Auto Scaling group manually or automatically to meet changes in demand.

Scaling limits
Set limits on how much your desired capacity can be increased or decreased.

Min desired capacity

2

Equal or less than desired capacity

Max desired capacity

3

Equal or greater than desired capacity

Figure 6.17 – Scaling options for this ASG

13. Next, we need to define the dynamic scaling part. Select **Target tracking scaling policy**. Give the scaling policy a name and then, under **Metric type**, select **Average CPU utilization**. The metric type defines what machine metric should be used to trigger a scale in or scale out of this ASG. In this example, we are scaling in and out based on the CPU utilization. Our target is to have our instances run at 60%. If the instances exceed that threshold, new instances are added. If many instances go below that threshold, some of them are terminated to get the average utilization of all instances in the ASG back closer to 60%.

Automatic scaling - *optional*

Choose whether to use a target tracking policy   Info
You can set up other metric-based scaling policies and scheduled scaling after creating your Auto Scaling group.

○ No scaling policies	◉ Target tracking scaling policy
Your Auto Scaling group will remain at its initial size and will not dynamically resize to meet demand.	Choose a CloudWatch metric and target value and let the scaling policy adjust the desired capacity in proportion to the metric's value.

Scaling policy name

Target Tracking Policy

Metric type   Info
Monitored metric that determines if resource utilization is too low or high. If using EC2 metrics, consider enabling detailed monitoring for better scaling performance.

Average CPU utilization ▼

Target value

60

Instance warmup   Info

300   seconds

☐ Disable scale in to create only a scale-out policy

Figure 6.18 – Automatic scaling based on CPU utilization

14. Click **Next**. In the **Add notifications** dialog, also click **Next**. With notifications, we could send alerts every time a scaling event happens. This can be useful for monitoring and we'll revisit this when looking into monitoring later in the book.

Add notifications - *optional* Info

Send notifications to SNS topics whenever Amazon EC2 Auto Scaling launches or terminates the EC2 instances in your Auto Scaling group.

(Add notification)

Cancel   (Skip to review)   (Previous)   **Next**

Figure 6.19 – Add notifications dialog

15. Skip the addition of tags since we don't need to add additional meta information for this example. You can now review all the information put into the ASG before clicking **Create** to create the ASG.

With the ASG created, it will begin by starting instances that are then added to the target group of the load balancer. We can verify this by checking the target group in the AWS console.

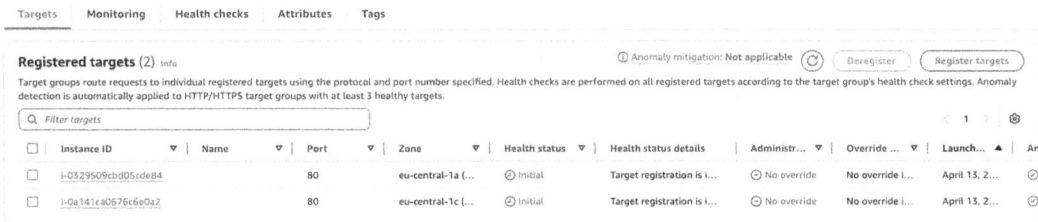

Figure 6.20 – Instances from the ASG have been added to the
registered targets of our Auto Load Balancer (ALB)

As you can see in the preceding screenshot, the three instances previously added are still part of the target (identified by their name) but there are two newly created instances. These are the instances coming from the ASG.

Exploring scaling policies

In the previous example, we set a dynamic scaling policy based on CPU utilization. Before moving on to creating the same with Terraform, let's briefly touch on the different policies available:

- **Dynamic scaling**: This tracks a metric such as the CPU utilization of your instances and, when a certain threshold is met, either scales the number of instances up or down. This is a *reactive* scaling policy because the load on the machines needs to increase in order for the scaling to trigger. For sharp increases in loads and with instances that take a long time to start (for example, due to a complicated setup process of your software), this type of scaling might not be able to adequately match the required capacity.

- **Predictive scaling**: This uses historical data to determine when to scale out (or scale down) your instances. As the name suggests, this is a *predictive* scaling policy that tries to anticipate the required number of instances based on historical data. You can use both predictive and dynamic scaling together. This means that the predictive scaling policy will try to anticipate the required load and make scaling decisions based on this prediction while the dynamic scaling policy will be able to react to real-time deviations from the forecasted load.

- **Scheduled actions**: These let you define a specific time frame, either once or as a repeating pattern, in which you want to adjust the number of instances. This can be useful for applications where the load is highly predictable. Take, for example, an HR system that gets very few visitors throughout the month except for payday, when all employees access the application to download their pay slips. This is an example of where you could use scheduled actions to accommodate the required load.

When talking about scaling, we have to also look into the metrics on which we can base our scaling decisions, as follows:

- **Average CPU utilization**: This is the average usage percentage of your CPU.

- **Network in/out**: This is the percentage of your network interface throughput that is being used. This can be used for network-intensive applications.

- **Application Load Balancer request count per target**: This tracks how many requests have been sent to each target. If the count exceeds the desired threshold, new instances are added. This can be a good metric when dealing with applications where the load is primarily determined by the number of requests handled by each instance.

Creating ASGs in Terraform

Now that we have seen how ASGs work, let's automate their creation using Terraform. The sample in this chapter is self-contained. This means that it will create a new VPC with subnets and an ALB. We'll very briefly cover the parts where the VPC and the ALB are created since these have been covered in the previous chapters.

You can find a finished version of this script on GitHub at this link: `https://github.com/ PacktPublishing/AWS-for-System-Administrators-Second-Edition/tree/ main/ch06`

To get started, follow these steps to create a new ASG using Terraform:

1. Create a new directory named `asg_sample` and navigate into it.

2. Inside the newly created directory, create a file called `install.sh` and open it in a code editor such as Visual Studio Code.

3. In `install.sh`, type the following code. This will be the user data that is passed to our instances:

    ```
    #!/bin/bash
    yum -y install httpd git
    service httpd start
    echo "Welcome from the instance!" >> /var/www/html/index.html
    ```

4. Now, in the same directory, create another file called `main.tf` and open it in a code editor such as Visual Studio Code.

5. In this Terraform file, we'll first define our VPC in the `eu-central-1` (Frankfurt) region and set up subnets in the three AZs, as well as internet gateways. Afterward, a security group that allows HTTP and SSH traffic is created, which will be used by our load balancer and our instances later on. Finally, a route table (and association) is created:

    ```
    provider "aws" {
      region = "eu-central-1"
    ```

```
}

# VPC
resource "aws_vpc" "asg" {
  cidr_block          = "10.0.0.0/16"
  enable_dns_hostnames = true
  enable_dns_support   = true

  tags = {
    Name = "asg-vpc"
  }
}

# Internet Gateway
resource "aws_internet_gateway" "asg" {
  vpc_id = aws_vpc.asg.id

  tags = {
    Name = "asg-igw"
  }
}

# Public Subnets
resource "aws_subnet" "public" {
  count               = 3
  vpc_id              = aws_vpc.asg.id
  cidr_block          = "10.0.${count.index}.0/24"
  availability_zone   = data.aws_availability_zones.
available.names[count.index]
  map_public_ip_on_launch = true

  tags = {
    Name = "asg-public-subnet-${count.index + 1}"
  }
}

# Route Table
resource "aws_route_table" "public" {
  vpc_id = aws_vpc.asg.id

  route {
    cidr_block = "0.0.0.0/0"
    gateway_id = aws_internet_gateway.asg.id
  }
```

```
      tags = {
        Name = "asg-public-rt"
      }
    }

    # Route Table Association
    resource "aws_route_table_association" "public" {
      count          = 3
      subnet_id      = aws_subnet.public[count.index].id
      route_table_id = aws_route_table.public.id
    }

    # Data source for AZs
    data "aws_availability_zones" "available" {
      state = "available"
    }

    # Security Group for EC2 instances
    resource "aws_security_group" "allow_http_ssh" {
      name        = "asg-allow-http-ssh"
      description = "Allow HTTP and SSH inbound traffic"
      vpc_id      = aws_vpc.asg.id

      ingress {
        description = "HTTP from anywhere"
        from_port   = 80
        to_port     = 80
        protocol    = "tcp"
        cidr_blocks = ["0.0.0.0/0"]
      }

      ingress {
        description = "SSH from anywhere"
        from_port   = 22
        to_port     = 22
        protocol    = "tcp"
        cidr_blocks = ["0.0.0.0/0"]
      }

      egress {
        from_port   = 0
        to_port     = 0
        protocol    = "-1"
        cidr_blocks = ["0.0.0.0/0"]
```

```
    }

    tags = {
      Name = "asg-allow-http-ssh"
    }
  }
```

6. With the boilerplate done, we can get started writing our launch template. We first define a data source that returns the latest Amazon Linux 2 AMI:

```
# Data source for latest Amazon Linux 2 AMI
data "aws_ami" "amazon_linux_2" {
  most_recent = true
  owners      = ["amazon"]

  filter {
    name   = "name"
    values = ["amzn2-ami-hvm-*-x86_64-gp2"]
  }
}
```

7. Next, we can define our launch template. Notice how we define the instance type, security groups for the networking interface, and user data in a similar way to how we did it previously in the AWS console:

```
# Launch Template
resource "aws_launch_template" "asg" {
  name_prefix   = "asg-template"
  image_id      = data.aws_ami.amazon_linux_2.id
  instance_type = "t2.micro"

  network_interfaces {
    associate_public_ip_address = true
    security_groups             = [aws_security_group.allow_
http_ssh.id]
  }

  user_data = base64encode(file("install.sh"))

  tag_specifications {
    resource_type = "instance"
    tags = {
      Name = "asg-instance"
    }
  }
}
```

8. With the launch template done, we can now define our ASG. We start by giving it a name and defining the VPC and subnets that this ASG should place instances into. We then also define our health check integration (using the health checks from our load balancer) as well as the target group. We'll create the load balancer and its corresponding target group later in the script:

```
# Auto Scaling Group
resource "aws_autoscaling_group" "asg" {
  name                = "asg-group"
  vpc_zone_identifier = aws_subnet.public[*].id
  target_group_arns   = [aws_lb_target_group.asg.arn]
  health_check_type   = "ELB"
```

9. Next, we define our desired capacity:

```
  min_size         = 2
  max_size         = 5
  desired_capacity = 2
```

10. Next, we define the launch template that we want to use by referencing the launch template created in the preceding script. We also add a name tag to the ASG:

```
  launch_template {
    id      = aws_launch_template.asg.id
    version = "$Latest"
  }

  tag {
    key                 = "Name"
    value               = "ASG-Instance"
    propagate_at_launch = true
  }
}
```

11. The only missing piece now is the scaling policy that tracks the average CPU utilization and scales to get the average back close to 60:

```
# Target Tracking Scaling Policy
resource "aws_autoscaling_policy" "target_tracking_policy" {
  name                   = "asg-target-tracking-policy"
  autoscaling_group_name = aws_autoscaling_group.asg.name
  policy_type            = "TargetTrackingScaling"

  target_tracking_configuration {
    predefined_metric_specification {
      predefined_metric_type = "ASGAverageCPUUtilization"
    }
```

```
      target_value = 60.0
    }
  }
}
```

12. With our ASG done, we need some more boilerplate code to create the ALB that will target the instances in our ASG:

```
# Application Load Balancer
resource "aws_lb" "asg" {
  name                = "asg-alb"
  internal            = false
  load_balancer_type  = "application"
  security_groups     = [aws_security_group.allow_http_ssh.id]
  subnets             = aws_subnet.public[*].id

  tags = {
    Name = "asg-alb"
  }
}

# ALB Listener
resource "aws_lb_listener" "asg" {
  load_balancer_arn = aws_lb.asg.arn
  port              = "80"
  protocol          = "HTTP"

  default_action {
    type            = "forward"
    target_group_arn = aws_lb_target_group.asg.arn
  }
}

# ALB Target Group
resource "aws_lb_target_group" "asg" {
  name     = "asg-tg"
  port     = 80
  protocol = "HTTP"
  vpc_id   = aws_vpc.asg.id

  health_check {
    path               = "/"
    healthy_threshold   = 2
    unhealthy_threshold = 10
  }
```

```
}
output "alb_dns" {
    value = aws_lb.asg.dns_name
}
```

This concludes our Terraform script to create a launch template and an ASG. We can now initiate our Terraform workspace by running the following command:

```
terraform init
```

Next, apply the changes to deploy our newly defined infrastructure:

```
terraform apply
```

Once the Terraform script has run through, you should see a new load balancer in the AWS console called `asg-alb`. You can use the DNS name that is outputted by the `apply` command to verify that everything is working.

You should see a web page saying **Welcome from the instance!**.

> **Note**
>
> Once you are done experimenting, don't forget to destroy/decommission all infrastructure you created by either deploying Terraform scripts or by using the AWS console.
>
> For the Terraform parts, run the following command:
>
> ```
> terraform destroy
> ```

Summary

In this chapter, we explored how ASGs can be used to dynamically scale our instances based on demand and how to increase fault tolerance in case one or more instances crash and become unhealthy. We now have all the compute needs to define a standard three-tier web application in AWS.

In the next chapter, we'll see how we can use Amazon **Relational Database Service** (RDS) – a managed database service – to add databases to our applications.

7

Scaling a Relational Database in the Cloud Using Amazon Relational Database Service (RDS)

In previous chapters, we covered EC2 and its adjacent services, such as ELBs for load balancing and ASGs for automatically scaling our compute infrastructure to meet our demands. If we think about a classic three-tier application with a frontend, backend, and database layer, we are missing one last component – the database layer.

This is where Amazon **Relational Database Service (RDS)** comes into play. RDS allows us to set up relational databases with a variety of engines in the cloud. If you come from a classical operations background, you might be wondering why we need this service. After all, we could just set up a database on an EC2 instance ourselves. This is true, and nothing is stopping you from doing so. However, if you have set up a production-grade database before, you will know that there are a bunch of tasks that need to be carried out, such as the following:

- Patching of the operating system of the instance running your database
- Patching and updating of the database engine
- Failover of your database in case an instance goes down
- Backup and recovery procedures

This list is not conclusive, and the idea of managed services in the cloud is that these different tasks can be delegated to a cloud provider (such as AWS).

In this chapter, we'll cover the following topics:

- An overview of Amazon RDS
- Setting up a PostgreSQL database in the AWS Management Console
- Automating the setup of an RDS database with Terraform

So, let's get started!

Technical requirements

To get the most out of this chapter, you should have a basic understanding of relational databases. You should be familiar with the term relational database. A basic knowledge of PostgreSQL, the relational database engine we'll be deploying, is beneficial.

To follow the **Infrastructure-as-Code (IaC)** portion of the chapter, basic familiarity with Terraform will be beneficial. If you haven't done so already, please follow the steps described in *Chapter 1* to set up a Terraform environment on your development machine.

The GitHub repository with the solution scripts for this chapter can be found at `https://github.com/PacktPublishing/AWS-for-System-Administrators-Second-Edition`.

The CiA video for this chapter can be found at `https://packt.link/tvWOw`

As with previous chapters, a CloudFormation and AWS CDK version of the Terraform script can be found in the GitHub repo linked previously.

What is Amazon RDS?

Amazon RDS, as a managed service for relational databases, automates administrative tasks such as the patching of the underlying operating system or the database software itself, which are handled by the service. In addition, RDS also offers automation for common tasks such as backing up and restoring your database. So, instead of having to write your own backup scripts that run periodically, you can use the technology offered by the AWS service.

When choosing a database, most organizations usually choose a database engine. These can be either commercial database engines such as Microsoft SQL Server or open source database engines such as MySQL. At the time of writing (August 2024), RDS supports the following database engines:

- Open source engines:

    - MySQL

    - MariaDB

    - PostgreSQL

- Commercial engines:

    - Oracle Enterprise Edition/Oracle Standard Edition

    - Microsoft SQL Server

    - IBM Db2

In addition to these, RDS also supports Aurora. Aurora is Amazon's own database engine that comes in two flavors. One is compatible with MySQL and the other is compatible with PostgreSQL.

Which database engine you choose will depend on the requirements of the software that you are building. Throughout this chapter, we'll be using PostgreSQL, but the workflow is similar for the other database engines.

So, let's create our first RDS database using the AWS Management Console.

Creating a PostgreSQL database in the AWS Management Console

In this section, we'll create – and then later delete – our first PostgreSQL database using the launch wizard in the AWS Management Console. In this walk-through, we'll create a simple multi-AZ deployment with a primary and a standby instance. This deployment means that we have our primary instance in one AZ and a secondary instance in another AZ that we can failover to if the instance in our primary AZ goes down.

Follow these steps to set up a PostgreSQL instance in RDS:

1. Navigate to the RDS service in the AWS Management Console by either searching for RDS or navigating to the following link: `https://eu-central-1.console.aws.amazon.com/rds/home?region=eu-central-1`.

2. On the overview page (see the following screenshot), you'll find an overview of databases you have previously created and also the orange **Create database** button that you need to click on to get to the wizard.

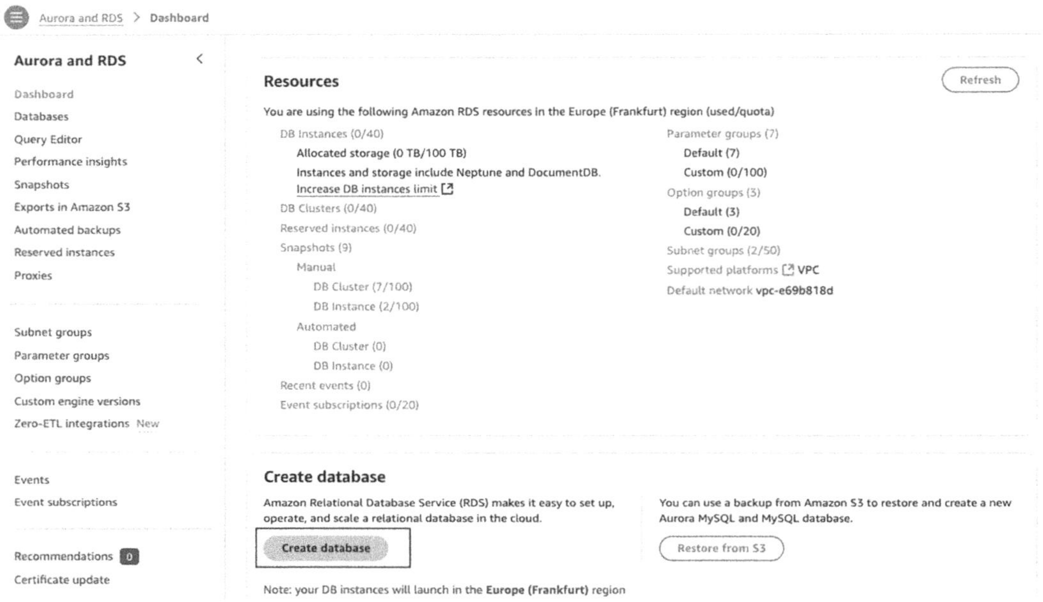

Figure 7.1 – Overview of database instances in RDS and the Create database button

3. We'll first need to choose a creation method. For this walk-through, we'll be using **Standard create**, which lets us freely configure our database.

Figure 7.2 – Our chosen creation method for this walk-through

4. Next, we need to select the database engine we want to use, as well as the version of that database engine. For this walk-through, select **PostgreSQL** as the engine and a version of your choice (for example, **PostgreSQL 16.3-R2**). As you can see by the length of the dropdown, RDS will support not only one but many different versions for each of the available engines.

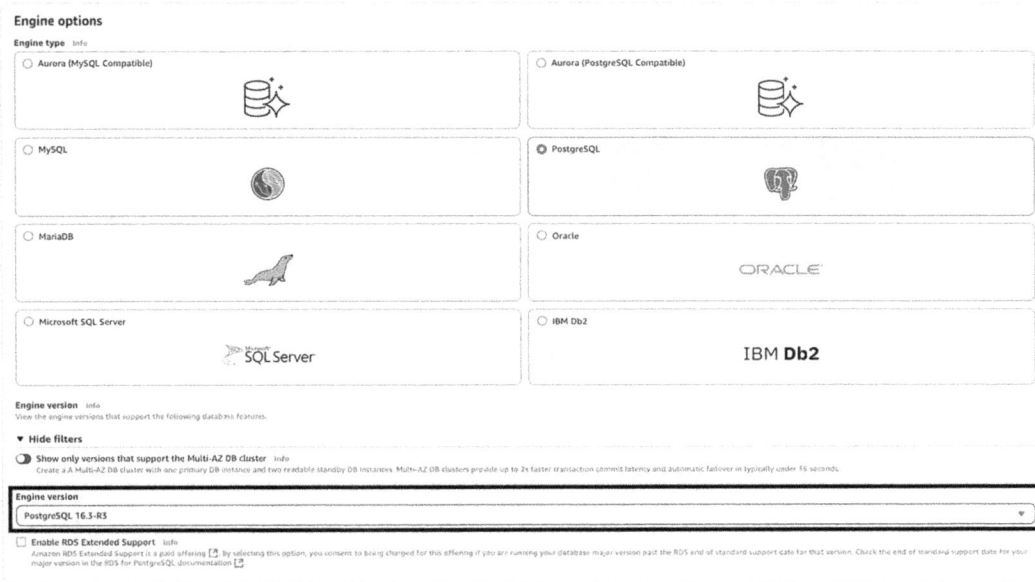

Figure 7.3 – Selection of the database engine and engine version

RDS offers a variety of best-practice templates. We can select which use case we are currently looking to implement. A production-grade database configuration will default to high-availability and performance options at the expense of higher costs. For this tutorial, we'll thus choose the **Dev/Test** option. This will keep the costs down while allowing us to configure features such as a multi-AZ deployment. These configurations are *not* available in the **Free tier** template.

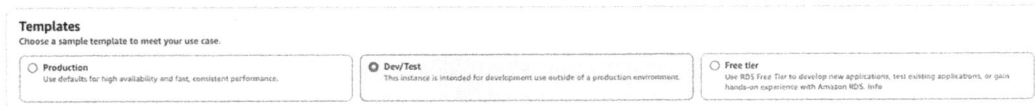

Figure 7.4 – Selection of the use case template

5. Next, we need to select an **Availability and durability** option. We'll select **Multi-AZ DB instance** here.

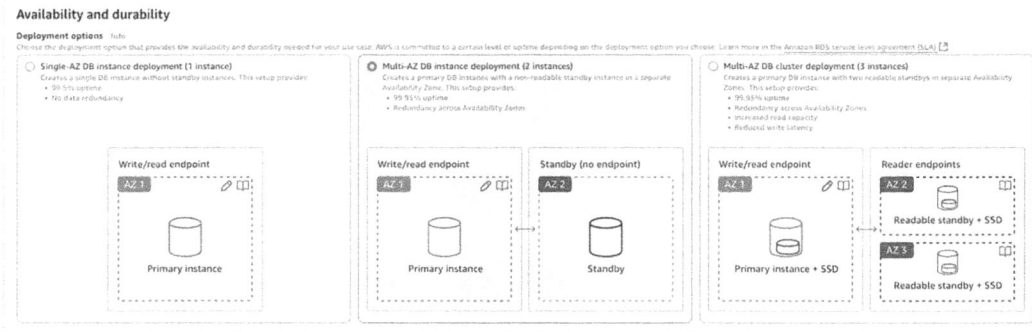

Figure 7.5 – Selecting our Availability and durability option

Before continuing, let's discuss the three options available to us for availability and durability:

- **Single DB instance**: This will deploy a single instance in one AZ. This is a great option for non-critical workloads where the business impact of the database being unreachable is low. This is commonly the case for development or testing environments that don't have any production workloads running on them.

- **Multi-AZ DB instance**: This will deploy a primary and secondary database spread across two different AZs. The data is automatically synchronized between these two instances. In a scenario where the primary instance goes down, this means that the secondary instance can take over and we thus minimize the downtime. This comes at a greater cost since we now have two instances instead of just one that we are paying for. We do not get any performance benefits since the secondary instance is a passive standby.

- **Multi-AZ DB Cluster**: These, similar to a multi-AZ DB instance, deploy instances across AZs and replicate the data to them. However, these secondary instances also become **read replicas**. This means that we have a primary endpoint that we can use to read and write while we have endpoints for the read replicas that we can only read from. This kind of setup is useful for use cases where we have read-heavy workloads (reporting and analytics workloads, for example) since we can take some of the read load off of the primary instance and shift it to the secondary instances. This performance and availability gain again come at a price since we are paying for multiple instances.

6. Next, we can configure the settings of our database, such as the name of our database (`my-first-database`, in this example) as well as the username and password.

    Under **Credentials management**, we'll choose **Self managed** for the creation of the password. We'll see how to integrate RDS with AWS Secrets Manager in *Chapter 8*.

You can then set a password for your database.

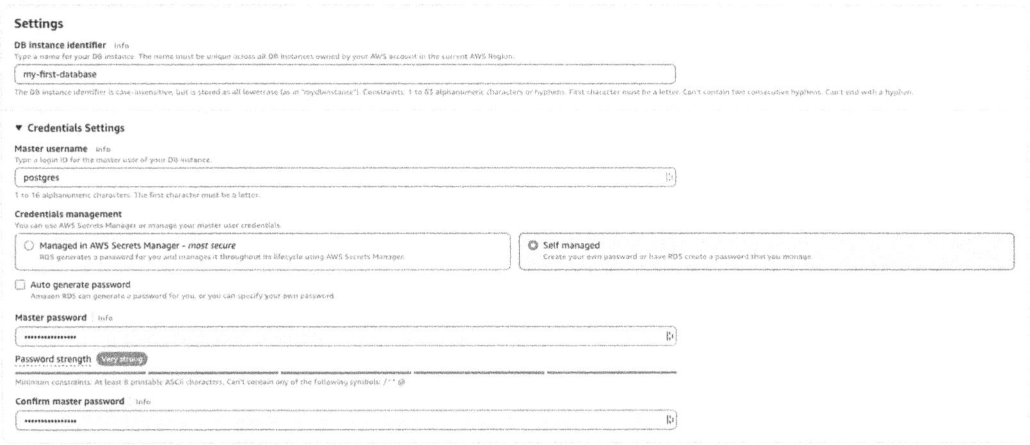

Figure 7.6 – Username and password settings for our database

7. With the username and password configuration done, we can move on to the instance configuration. Here, we select the type of instance we want RDS to use in the background. The more powerful our instance is, the more expensive our RDS deployment becomes. The type of instance depends on the performance requirements for your database.

For this example, we'll choose the **db.m6g.large** instance type.

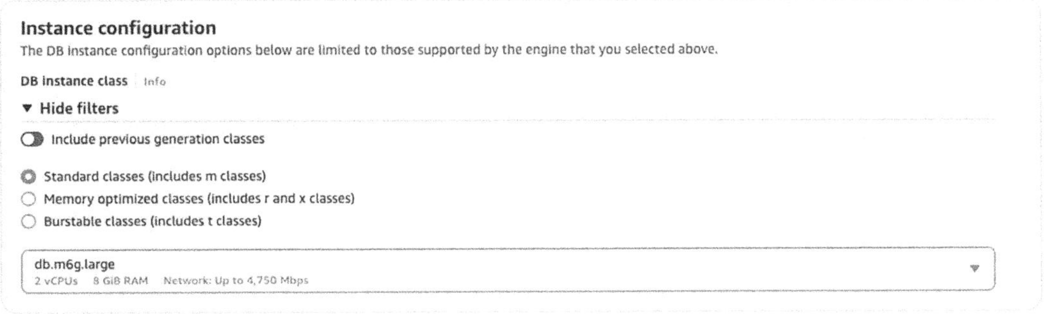

Figure 7.7 – The instance configuration for our RDS database

Notice the **g** in the instance name. This identifies instances that use the **Graviton** processor family from AWS. These ARM-based CPUs are generally more cost-efficient than using Intel or AMD-based CPUs. Since RDS is a managed service, it ensures that the database engine software runs smoothly on ARM-based systems, which is an easy way to save money.

8. With our compute selected, we can now select our preferred storage type and the size of our storage volume. In this example, we are going to select the **General Purpose SSD (gp3)** storage type and allocate the minimum required amount of storage of **20 GiB**.

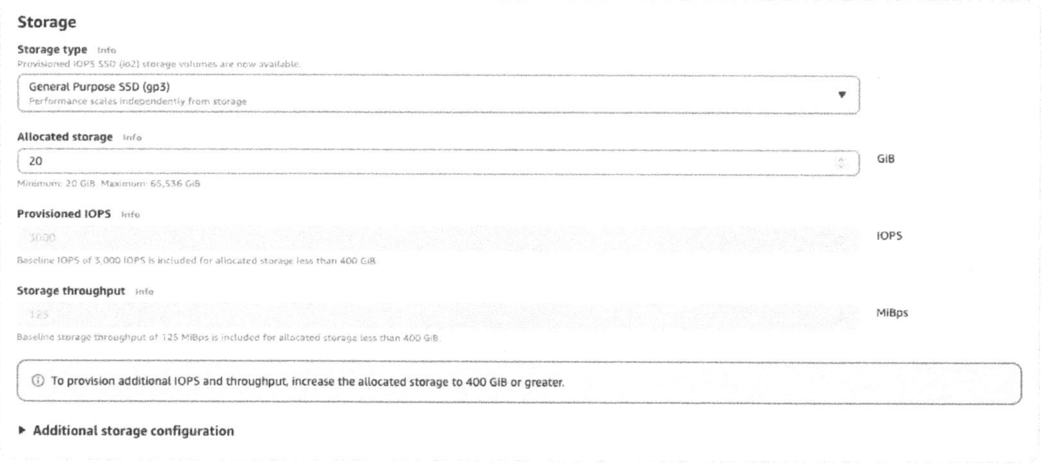

Figure 7.8 – Storage settings for our database instance

9. Next, we have the connectivity. RDS will deploy our instance into a VPC. The details of the configuration are as follows:

-   **Compute resource**: Select **Don't connect to an EC2 compute resource**.

-   **Network type**: Select **IPv4** since we don't need dual-stack (IPv6 and IPv4 connectivity) for this example.

-   **Virtual private cloud (VPC)**: Select a VPC that you want to deploy the database into. You can select **main-vpc** that was created in the previous chapters.

-   **DB subnet group**: Either select the subnet that you want this database to be deployed into or select **Create new DB Subnet Group**, which will set up a new subnet for you.

-   **Public access**: Select **No** here. This means that the database instances will be deployed into a private subnet that can't be reached from the public internet. This is generally the preferred way since you don't want public access to your database instance.

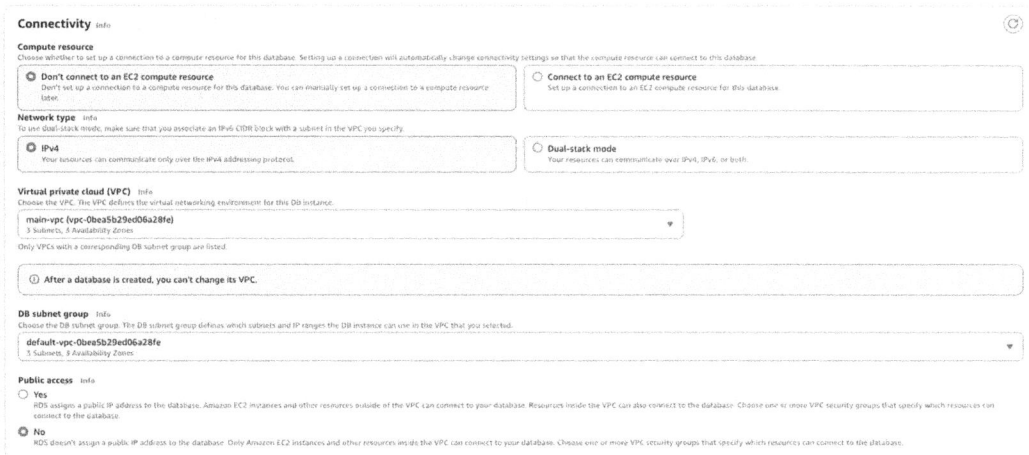

Figure 7.9 – Connectivity settings for our database instance

10. Within the VPC, we'll also need to create a security group that will be attached to our database instances. Select **Create new** to have the wizard create a new security group that, by default, allows for communication on the database port (5432 by default for Postgres).

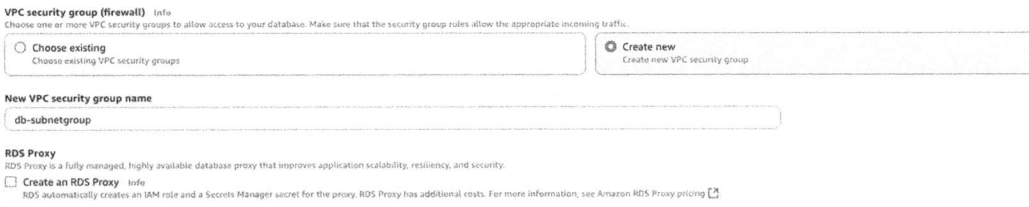

Figure 7.10 – Settings for our security group that will be attached to the database instances

11. For **Database authentication**, select **Password authentication**. We could also manage access to our database via IAM roles and permissions or using Kerberos. For this walk-through, we'll use **Password authentication** since this is still the most common way to authenticate with a database.

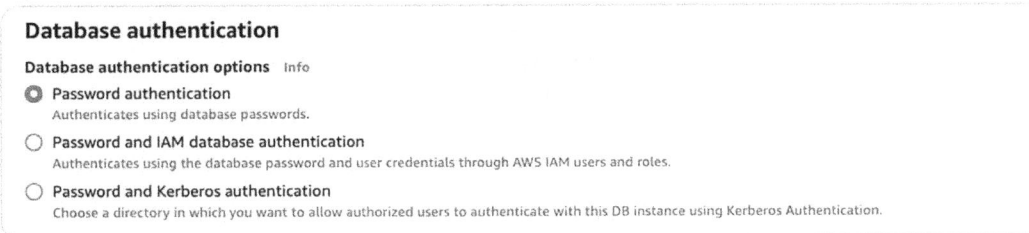

Figure 7.11 – Authentication settings for our database instance

12. For **Monitoring**, we can enable Performance Insights with the **7 days** retention period.

At the time of writing, these are part of the free tier. Performance Insights analyzes the performance metrics of your database and transforms them into an easy-to-understand load number that is presented in the AWS Management Console.

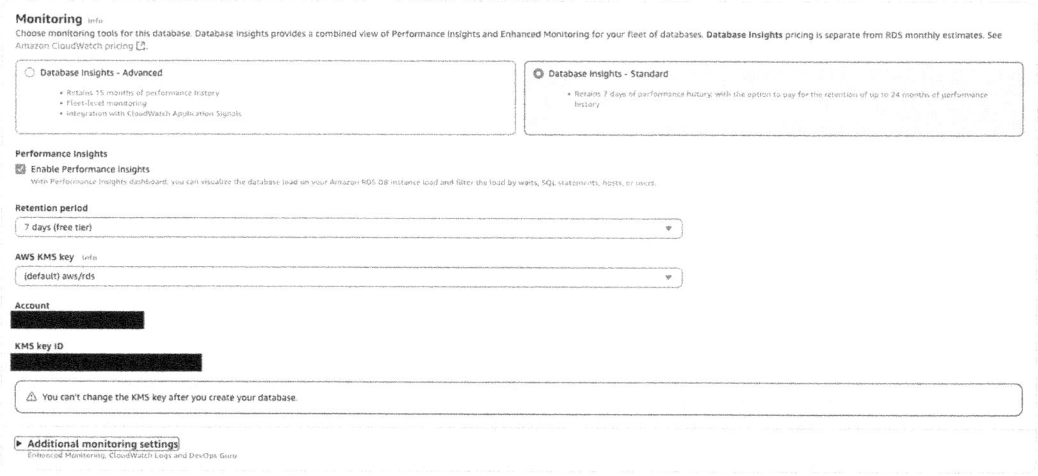

Figure 7.12 – Monitoring the settings for our RDS instance

13. Next, open up the **Additional configuration** tab. Most of the settings here are sensible defaults but we want to quickly walk through them to get an understanding of what RDS is doing in the background:

- **Initial database name** lets you specify a default database that RDS will create automatically.

- **DB parameter group** and **Option group** are the configuration and option parameters for our database engine.

- Under **Backup**, we can enable (or disable) automated backups and we can also define the time window during which we want the backup to take place, as well as the retention period for our backups.

- An optional setting (turned off in this example) is the replication to another Region. This means that our data gets replicated to another Region (say from **eu-central-1**, the Frankfurt Region, to **us-east-1**, the North Virgina Region). In the highly unlikely case of a full Region failure of the first region (**eu-central-1**, in this case), this would mean that we could restore our database from that backup.

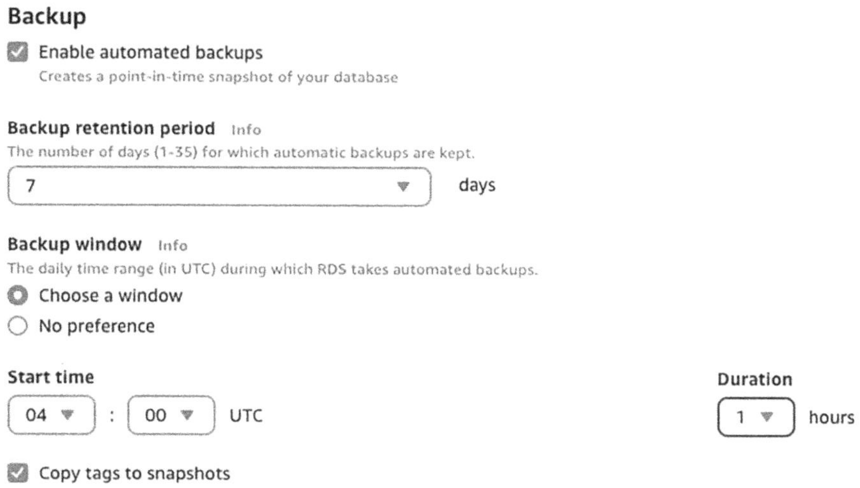

Backup

☑ **Enable automated backups**
Creates a point-in-time snapshot of your database

Backup retention period Info
The number of days (1-35) for which automatic backups are kept.

| 7 ▼ | days |

Backup window Info
The daily time range (in UTC) during which RDS takes automated backups.

◉ Choose a window
◯ No preference

Start time

| 04 ▼ | : | 00 ▼ | UTC

Duration

| 1 ▼ | hours

☑ Copy tags to snapshots

Figure 7.13 – Additional settings containing database options and backup

Also, under **Additional configuration**, we can find settings relating to encryption and maintenance.

We will talk more about encryption and AWS **Key Management Service** (**KMS**) in *Chapter 8*.

Under **Maintenance**, we can define that RDS is allowed to automatically apply minor version upgrades to our instance and we can – similar to the backup window – define a timeframe during which these updates are allowed to take place.

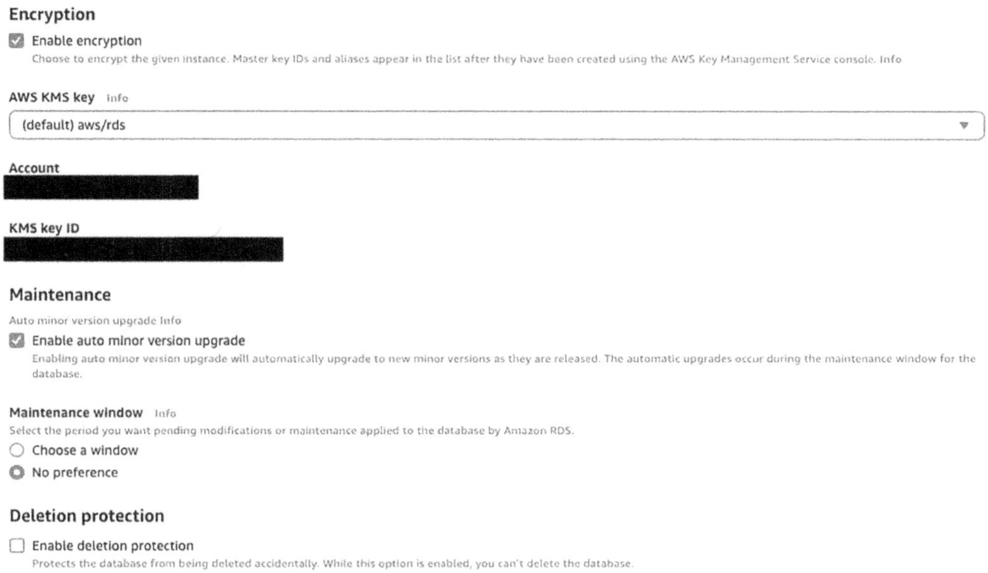

Encryption

☑ Enable encryption
Choose to encrypt the given instance. Master key IDs and aliases appear in the list after they have been created using the AWS Key Management Service console. Info

AWS KMS key Info

| (default) aws/rds | ▼ |

Account

KMS key ID

Maintenance

Auto minor version upgrade Info

☑ Enable auto minor version upgrade
Enabling auto minor version upgrade will automatically upgrade to new minor versions as they are released. The automatic upgrades occur during the maintenance window for the database.

Maintenance window Info
Select the period you want pending modifications or maintenance applied to the database by Amazon RDS.

◯ Choose a window
◉ No preference

Deletion protection

☐ Enable deletion protection
Protects the database from being deleted accidentally. While this option is enabled, you can't delete the database.

Figure 7.14 – Maintenance and encryption settings for our RDS instance

14. The last element in the wizard is an estimate of the monthly cost incurred by running this database. The cost is split across compute – the cost of running our database instances – and storage – the cost of our storage volumes. Depending on your previous selections, your numbers may differ here.

You can use this estimate to play around with the cost impact of, for example, adding more storage or selecting a different deployment type (**Multi-AZ Cluster** instead of **Multi-AZ instance**, for example).

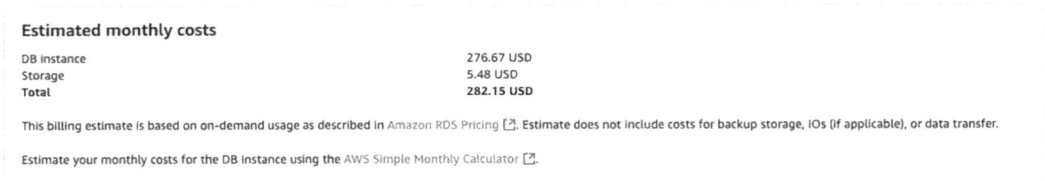

Estimated monthly costs

DB instance	276.67 USD
Storage	5.48 USD
Total	**282.15 USD**

This billing estimate is based on on-demand usage as described in Amazon RDS Pricing ☑. Estimate does not include costs for backup storage, IOs (if applicable), or data transfer.

Estimate your monthly costs for the DB instance using the AWS Simple Monthly Calculator ☑.

Figure 7.15 – Estimated monthly cost of our database configuration

15. With the configuration done, click on the **Create database** button

After a few minutes, you should see your newly created database on the overview page in RDS with an **Available** status.

Figure 7.16 – RDS overview page showing the newly created database

In this section, we have seen how to create a Postgres database in RDS and explored some of the features of RDS. Next, let's learn how to delete this database. Especially when exploring the functionality of RDS, it is important to not have unused database instances sitting in our account since, as you have seen in the previous estimate when creating the database, they incur a not insignificant cost. Thus, going through the list of databases from time to time and verifying whether they are still needed is also a good way to optimize costs as an organization.

Deleting a database in RDS

Since the database that we have just created is incurring some costs, we'll now go ahead and delete the database after taking a snapshot. A **snapshot** is a copy of our data at the time the snapshot was taken. We could use the snapshot to recreate the database if we needed to.

In order to delete the database after creating a snapshot, follow these steps:

1.   In the database overview, select your previously created database.

2.   Under **Actions** in the dropdown, select **Delete**.

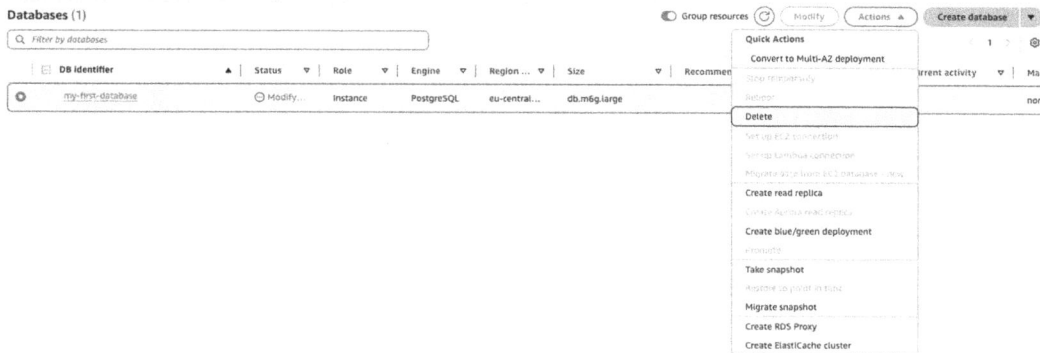

Figure 7.17 – Delete action for our newly created database

3.   You'll be presented with a popup that lets you select the option to create a final snapshot. The **Create final snapshot** checkbox should be selected by default. If it isn't, select it and provide a name for your final snapshot. You can also select the option to retain the automated backups for seven days after deletion. This will incur storage costs but would give you the option to restore your database to not only the final snapshot but also any point where a backup was taken.

     Once you have checked both boxes, type `delete me` into the text field at the bottom to confirm your intention to delete the database.

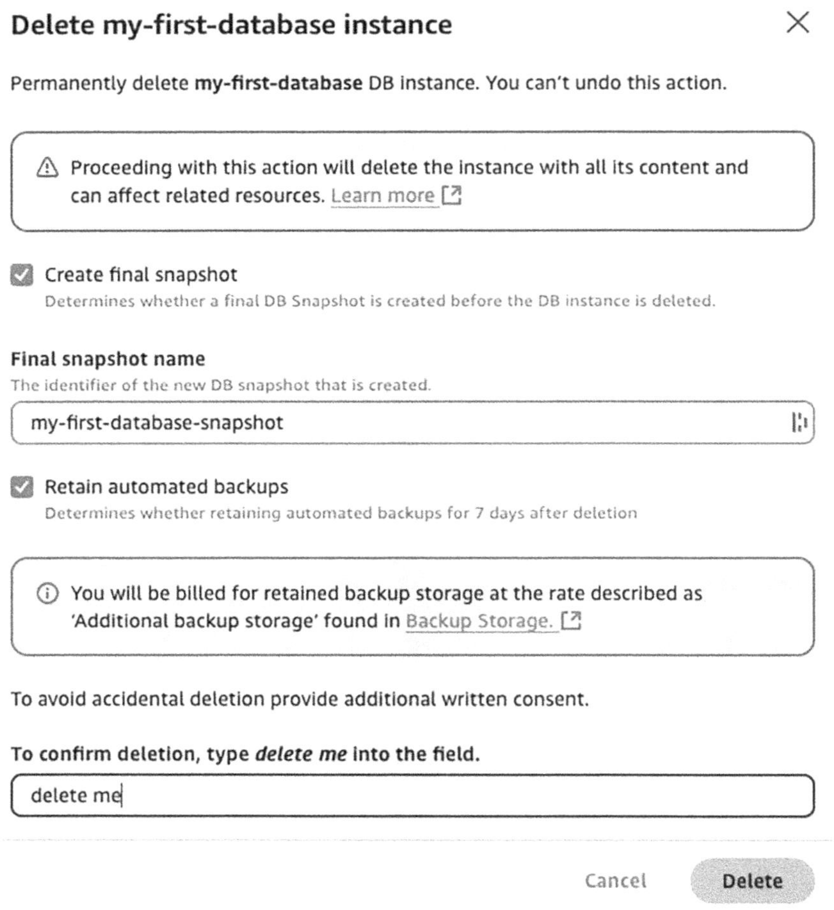

Figure 7.18 – Dialog to confirm the creation of a final snapshot of our
RDS database, as well as the retention of our backups

After you have confirmed the deletion, the database will become unreachable and will switch its state to **Deleting**.

While the database is deleting, you can navigate to **Snapshots** in the left-hand navigation menu. Here, you'll see a list of your snapshots and also the snapshot of the database that is being deleted.

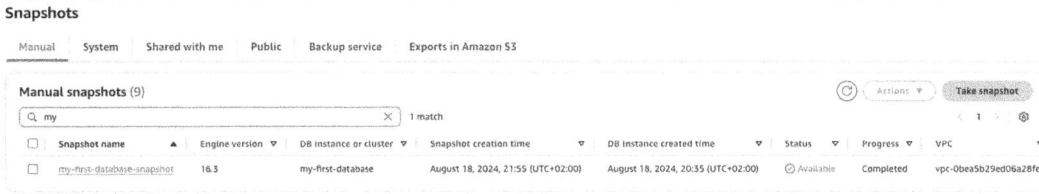

Snapshots

| Manual | System | Shared with me | Public | Backup service | Exports in Amazon S3 |

Manual snapshots (9)   Actions ▼   Take snapshot

Q my   ✕   1 match   ⟨ 1 ⟩ ⚙

| ☐ | Snapshot name ▲ | Engine version ▽ | DB instance or cluster ▽ | Snapshot creation time ▽ | DB instance created time ▽ | Status ▽ | Progress ▽ | VPC ▽ |
| ☐ | my-first-database-snapshot | 16.3 | my-first-database | August 18, 2024, 21:55 (UTC+02:00) | August 18, 2024, 20:35 (UTC+02:00) | ⊘ Available | Completed | vpc-0bea5b29ed06a28fe |

Figure 7.19 – Snapshots overview and the snapshot from our newly deleted database

Selecting a snapshot and choosing the **Restore Snapshot** action from the **Actions** dropdown would bring you to the creation wizard that we have just walked through. The only difference is that the instance wouldn't start with no data in it but rather with the data from the snapshot.

In this section, we have seen how we can delete a previously created database instance in the AWS Management Console. Before deleting, we also saw how we can leverage the **Snapshots** tool to make a backup of our data before deleting the database.

In the next section, we'll set up another RDS instance – but this time as a multi-AZ cluster with a read replica and using Terraform instead of the wizard in the AWS Management Console.

Deploying an RDS instance with Terraform

In this section, we'll create a Postgres instance in RDS using IaC in Terraform. The following walk-through contains some boilerplate code at the beginning to set up a new VPC and public and private subnets before setting up a new multi-AZ deployment with two read replicas.

Follow these steps to create an RDS instance for PostgreSQL in Terraform:

1. Create a file called `database.tf` and open it in a code editor such as Visual Studio Code or Notepad++.

2. We'll first need some boilerplate code to create a new VPC, as well as to create public and private subnets. For more details on the concepts in this code, please refer to the *Creating a VPC using the AWS Management Console* section of *Chapter 3*, where it was explained in detail:

```
provider "aws" {
  region = "eu-central-1"
}
data "aws_availability_zones" "available" {
  state = "available"
}
resource "aws_vpc" "main" {
```

```
  cidr_block              = "10.0.0.0/16"
  enable_dns_hostnames = true
  enable_dns_support      = true
}
resource "aws_internet_gateway" "main" {
  vpc_id = aws_vpc.main.id
}
resource "aws_subnet" "public" {
  count                   = 3
  vpc_id                  = aws_vpc.main.id
  cidr_block              = "10.0.${count.index}.0/24"
  availability_zone       = data.aws_availability_zones.
available.names[count.index]
  map_public_ip_on_launch = true
}
resource "aws_subnet" "private" {
  count             = 3
  vpc_id            = aws_vpc.main.id
  cidr_block        = "10.0.${count.index + 10}.0/24"
  availability_zone = data.aws_availability_zones.available.
names[count.index]
}
resource "aws_route_table" "public" {
  vpc_id = aws_vpc.main.id
  route {
    cidr_block = "0.0.0.0/0"
    gateway_id = aws_internet_gateway.main.id
  }
}
resource "aws_route_table_association" "public" {
  count          = 3
  subnet_id      = aws_subnet.public[count.index].id
  route_table_id = aws_route_table.public.id
}
```

3. With the boilerplate code done, we can next create a subnet group for our database instances to be placed into. We'll deploy our database instances into the previously created public subnets here:

```
resource "aws_db_subnet_group" "postgres_subnet_group" {
  name       = "postgres-subnet-group"
  subnet_ids = aws_subnet.private[*].id
}
```

4. Next, we define a security group in our previously created VPC and allow ingress traffic to port 5432 (the default port for Postgres):

```
resource "aws_security_group" "postgres" {
  name       = "postgres-sg"
  vpc_id     = aws_vpc.main.id
  ingress {
    from_port   = 5432
    to_port     = 5432
    protocol    = "tcp"
    cidr_blocks = [aws_vpc.main.cidr_block]
  }
  egress {
    from_port   = 0
    to_port     = 0
    protocol    = "-1"
    cidr_blocks = ["0.0.0.0/0"]
  }
}
```

5. Now we can create our primary database instance using the aws_db_instance resource. We first define information such as the name, the engine, and the engine version we want to use, as well as the instance type and storage configuration, similar to how we selected this in the wizard in the AWS Management Console:

```
resource "aws_db_instance" "postgres_primary" {
  identifier        = "postgres-primary"
  engine            = "postgres"
  engine_version    = "16.3"
  instance_class    = "db.m6g.large"
  allocated_storage = 20
  storage_type      = "gp3"
```

6. Next, we define our instance to be multi-AZ and configure a name for the database, a username, and a password:

```
  multi_az   = true
  db_name    = "mydb"
  username   = "postgres"
  password   = ""  # Insert your chosen password here
```

7. Then, we can associate this instance with the previously created database subnet group, as well as the security group we previously created:

```
  db_subnet_group_name = aws_db_subnet_group.postgres_subnet_
  group.name

  vpc_security_group_ids = [aws_security_group.postgres.id]
```

8. We can then define our backup and maintenance settings. Here, we instruct RDS to keep our backups for seven days and select a backup from 3 to 4 a.m. and a maintenance window on Mondays from 4 to 4.30 a.m:

```
backup_retention_period = 7
  backup_window          = "03:00-04:00"
  maintenance_window     = "mon:04:00-mon:04:30"
```

9. Since this is our primary database, we configure it to (upon deletion) take a final snapshot called `tf-final-snapshot`:

```
  skip_final_snapshot     = false
  final_snapshot_identifier = "tf-final-snapshot"
}
```

10. With our main instance done, we can configure our two read replicas (using the `count` parameter) and associate these to replicate the primary database. We define the same instance class and security group for our read replicas that we used for the primary instance.

    Since our read replicas only replicate the data from our primary, we skip the creation of a final snapshot on these instances:

```
resource "aws_db_instance" "postgres_replica" {
  count                   = 2
  identifier              = "postgres-replica-${count.index + 1}"
  instance_class          = "db.m6g.large"
  replicate_source_db     = aws_db_instance.postgres_primary.
identifier

  vpc_security_group_ids = [aws_security_group.postgres.id]
  backup_retention_period = 0
  skip_final_snapshot     = true
}
```

11. Finally, we define two outputs, one for the primary endpoint (for read/write operations) and one for the replica endpoints (for read-only operations):

```
output "primary_endpoint" {
  value = aws_db_instance.postgres_primary.endpoint
}
output "replica_endpoints" {
  value = aws_db_instance.postgres_replica[*].endpoint
}
```

12. To deploy the database, we need to first initiate Terraform:

```
terraform init
```

13. With Terraform ready, we can deploy the database by running the `apply` command. Note that this `apply` command could take several minutes to finish:

```
terraform apply
```

During the deployment, you can see the database being deployed in the AWS Management Console. Notice in the following screenshot how the two replicas are associated with our primary database instance.

Figure 7.20 – The RDS database overview page during the creation of
our mutli-AZ cluster with two read replicas from Terraform

Since the database will incur costs, it is recommended that you go ahead and delete the database using Terraform. This operation will also create a snapshot that you can verify in the **Snapshots** menu in the AWS Management Console:

```
terraform destroy
```

Summary

In this chapter, we have seen how Amazon RDS can be used to create managed relational databases. We created a PostgreSQL database – first in the console and then using Terraform.

In the next chapter, we'll learn about two services that have already been mentioned in this chapter: AWS KMS for the management of encryption keys and Secrets Manager to manage secrets. We'll also revisit RDS and configure it to use a customer-managed encryption key from KMS, as well as storing the database password in Secrets Manager.

Join the CloudPro Newsletter with 44000+ Subscribers

Want to know what's happening in cloud computing, DevOps, IT administration, networking, and more? Scan the QR code to subscribe to **CloudPro**, our weekly newsletter for 44,000+ tech professionals who want to stay informed and ahead of the curve.

https://packt.link/cloudpro

Managing Secrets and Encryption Keys with AWS Secrets Manager and KMS

In the previous chapters, we saw how to create scalable compute infrastructure using EC2 and managed databases with RDS. However, for an EC2 instance to be able to connect to a database, we'll usually need a username/password combination. This is also often the case when we want to connect to third-party services that are available via an API. In short, we need a way to create and retrieve these secrets without the need to manually add them to each of our systems.

Setting and retrieving a secret securely is already a very helpful feature, but what about password rotations? When dealing with credentials such as the connection details for a database instance, it is advisable to change or *rotate* these credentials on a regular basis. Let's say we want to rotate the password of all our database systems every seven days. This would mean that every seven days, we would have to remember to manually set a new password for each of our databases and then also remember to update all applications that need connectivity to that database system.

Handling these two topics, the storage and retrieval of secrets as well as the rotation of secrets, can be done using AWS Secrets Manager, which we are going to explore in this chapter.

The main topics covered in this chapter are as follows:

- Introduction to AWS Secrets Manager
- Creating a secret in Secrets Manager using both Terraform and the CDK
- Accessing a secret from an AWS Lambda function using Boto3
- Integrating Secrets Manager with Amazon RDS to automatically rotate passwords
- Introduction to AWS KMS
- Changing an existing S3 bucket to a customer-managed key

Technical requirements

Before moving further in this chapter, please create an AWS account for yourself. You can sign up at `aws.amazon.com`. A basic understanding of AWS, such as what a service is, will be beneficial.

A basic understanding of Python will help with the programming-based sections of this chapter.

A basic understanding of **infrastructure-as-code** (**IaC**) tools such as Terraform and CDK is beneficial.

All scripts from this section can be found at the following GitHub link:

`https://github.com/PacktPublishing/AWS-for-System-Administrators-Second-Edition`

The CiA video for this chapter can be found at `https://packt.link/9jEj3`

Storing secrets with AWS Secrets Manager

In this section, we'll look at AWS Secrets Manager and how we can use it to securely store our secrets in the AWS cloud. We'll see how we can programmatically create these secrets via IaC tools, and we'll also see, based on the example of Amazon RDS, how Secrets Manager integrates with other AWS services to store and rotate secrets.

With our secrets stored, we'll then see how to access these secrets using Boto3 and Python. So, let's get started!

What is AWS Secrets Manager?

When dealing with secrets, we need a centralized way of storing them. In AWS, this job is done by AWS Secrets Manager. Secrets are key/value pairs and the secret itself is represented as a JSON object. In theory, we can store any key-value pair we want in a Secrets Manager secret (if the value is JSON-serializable and does not contain an array – otherwise, you will get an error) but in practice, we usually just store credentials such as the username and password. Application configuration should reside in environment variables or tools such as AWS Systems Manager Parameter Store. We'll see an example of storing application configuration in Parameter Store in *Chapter 14*.

Secrets have two major sources:

- **Populated by a service**: This includes Amazon RDS or an Amazon Redshift data warehouse, among others

- **Provided by the user**: This is used when we want to store secrets such as API keys, OAuth tokens, or username/password combinations for systems that are either self-developed or are outside of AWS

Secrets also have a lifecycle, especially for passwords, as we want to rotate them regularly. Secrets Manager handles this for us and lets us define a rotation schedule as well as allow the manual rotation of a compromised secret.

With the basic ideas behind secrets and AWS Secrets Manager covered, let's go ahead and create a new secret using IaC in both the CDK and Terraform.

Creating secrets in the CDK

We can use IaC with the CDK to create a new secret. We'll then also use the CDK to write a Python-based Lambda function that retrieves the provided secret.

Note that you need a CDK setup as shown in *Chapter 1*. The solution script can be found in the GitHub repository.

To get started with the secret creation in CDK, follow these steps:

1. Using your command line, create a new directory called `secrets_sample` and change your working directory to the newly created directory using the `cd` command:

   ```
   mkdir secrets_sample
   cd secrets_sample
   ```

2. In the newly created directory, we need to create a CDK project. We'll be using Python as our programming language of choice here. To create a new project that uses Python, type the following command:

   ```
   cdk init app --language=python
   ```

3. The CDK automatically creates a new virtual environment for us that we need to activate:

   ```
   source .venv/bin/activate
   ```

4. Once the virtual environment is activated, we need to install all requirements for this CDK project. We can do this using `pip` and the `requirements.txt` file that the CDK created for us:

   ```
   python3 -m pip install -r requirements.txt
   ```

5. You should now have a directory structure like the following:

   ```
   ├── README.md
   ├── app.py
   ├── cdk.json
   ├── requirements-dev.txt
   ├── requirements.txt
   ├── secrets_sample
   │   ├── __init__.py
   ```

```
|    └── secrets_sample_stack.py
├── source.bat
└── tests
     ├── __init__.py
     └── unit
          ├── __init__.py
          └── test_secrets_sample_stack.py
```

6. With the setup done, we can start writing our CDK code. To do so, open the `secrets_sample/secrets_sample_stack.py` file with a text editor such as Visual Studio Code.

7. The CDK organizes its constructs by Python modules that correspond to AWS services. We'll need to import the module for Secrets Manager, which is called `aws_secretsmanager`. We'll import it as the shorthand, `sm`. In addition, we'll also import the built-in `json` module. Your `import` section should look like the following code snippet:

```python
import json
from aws_cdk import (
  Stack,
  aws_secretsmanager as sm,
)
from constructs import Construct
```

8. In the `SecretSampleStack` class and inside the constructor, we can now define our secret. We start by defining our generation configuration. `secret_string_template` is a JSON-formatted `dict` that contains all the additional properties we want to store inside of the secret, such as the username. These will be handled as plaintext and shown accordingly in the AWS console. It also contains, in the `generate_string_key` property, the key of the secret property. This property (the `Password` key, in our example) will be generated automatically:

```python
gen_config = {
          "secret_string_template": json.dumps({"Username":
"admin"}),
          "generate_string_key": "Password"
        }
```

9. Next, we can create our secret. In this example, we give the secret the CDK-internal `ExampleSecret` ID and pass the previously created `gen_config` as the `generate_secret_string` property:

```python
secret = sm.Secret(self, "ExampleSecret",
          generate_secret_string=gen_config
        )
```

Your entire class should look like this:

```
from aws_cdk import (
    Stack,
    aws_secretsmanager as sm,
)
import json
from constructs import Construct
class SecretsSampleStack(Stack):
    def __init__(self, scope: Construct, construct_id: str,
**kwargs) -> None:
        super().__init__(scope, construct_id, **kwargs)
        # The code that defines your stack goes here
        gen_config = {
            "secret_string_template": json.dumps({"Username":
"admin"}),
            "generate_string_key": "Password"
        }

        secret = sm.Secret(self, "ExampleSecret",
            generate_secret_string=gen_config
        )
```

10. Going back to the command line, we can now deploy this CDK stack. We first set the Region to which we want to deploy our CDK stack using the following export. In this example, the secret will be deployed into the eu-central-1 Region:

```
export AWS_DEFAULT_REGION=eu-central-1
```

11. If this is your first time using the CDK with this account and in this Region, you need to bootstrap the account. This will set up the resources that are required by the CDK to provision your infrastructure. This is only required once per account and Region. You can do so by running the following command:

```
cdk bootstrap
```

12. To deploy the stack, type the following deploy command:

```
cdk deploy
```

The output from the previous command should look similar to this:

```
SecretsSampleStack: deploying... [1/1]
SecretsSampleStack: creating CloudFormation changeset...
 ☑  SecretsSampleStack
 ✦  Deployment time: 11.79s
Stack ARN:
```

```
arn:aws:cloudformation:eu-central-1:<account_id>:stack/
SecretsSampleStack/12b866b0-6edc-11ef-acfc-0a0943c62f3b
✦  Total time: 28.17s
```

Once the CDK stack is deployed, we can see our newly created secret in the **Overview** tab in AWS Secrets Manager in the AWS console. The following screenshot shows the **Overview** tab of the secret page. It shows the secret, including our username as well as the password that was randomly generated.

| Overview | Rotation | Versions | Replication | Tags | | |

Secret value Info

Retrieve and view the secret value.

| Key/value | Plaintext |

Secret key	Secret value
Username	⧉ admin
Password	⧉ Yqrt":iRG1BvT]BE[Fo$`Hkruqm:H3.3

Figure 8.1 – The secret we created via the CDK

In this example, we have created a secret using the CDK. We also had the secret (in this case, the password) be auto-generated. But what about cases where we already have a password that we want to write into a secret? In the next section, we'll do that using Terraform.

Creating secrets in Terraform

When we look at configuring secrets from IaC, there is one issue that we need to solve. *How do we prevent the cleartext secrets from going into version control?* The whole purpose of Secrets Manager is to have a secure and access-restricted service where we can manage our secrets. Putting them into a source code repository with all the Terraform code would thus defeat the purpose. In the previous CDK example, you saw how a secret was generated. In this example, we'll use Terraform and environment variables to provision a secret such as a password that is not generated by Secrets Manager without it being written explicitly in the Terraform code.

To do this, follow these steps:

1. Create a new directory called `tf_secrets` and navigate into it using the `cd` command:

    ```
    mkdir tf_secrets
    cd tf_secrets
    ```

2. In it, create a file called `main.tf` and open it in a code editor such as Visual Studio Code.

3. Inside the file, we'll first define our provider and the desired Region (`eu-central-1`, in this example):

    ```
    provider "aws" {
      region = "eu-central-1"
    }
    ```

4. Next, we define a variable that will hold our secret value. Notice how we don't define a type or default value for it:

    ```
    variable "secret_value" {}
    ```

5. We can then create the secret itself using the `aws_secretsmanager_secret` resource. Here, we define the name and description of our secret:

    ```
    resource "aws_secretsmanager_secret" "tf_secret" {
      name        = "tf_secret"
      description = "Secret created from terraform"
    }
    ```

6. Secrets Manager versions its secrets. So, instead of putting the value of a secret inside the secret itself, in Terraform, we define `aws_secretmanager_secret_version`, which references our previously created secret resource and also passes the JSON we want to store inside of the secret. Here, we are passing a username and the password from the variable defined in the beginning:

    ```
    resource "aws_secretsmanager_secret_version" "tf_secret_version"
    {
      secret_id     = aws_secretsmanager_secret.tf_secret.id
      secret_string = jsonencode({
        Username = "admin"
        Password = var.secret_value
      })
    }
    ```

    With our Terraform code defined, we can now go ahead and deploy it. At this point, you might be wondering how we will pass the value into Terraform since, so far, `secret_value` is an empty variable. We can do this by defining an environment variable called `TF_VAR_secret_value` before running `terraform apply`. This works with any variable in Terraform. You just need to prefix the name of the variable in Terraform with `TF_VAR_` and use that as the name of the environment variable.

7. Next, run `terraform init` to set up your workspace and download the required providers:

    ```
    terraform init
    ```

8. Finally, we can run `terraform apply`. In the output shown in the following screenshot, notice how Terraform will mask the value of the secret by putting `(sensitive value)` instead of the actual string:

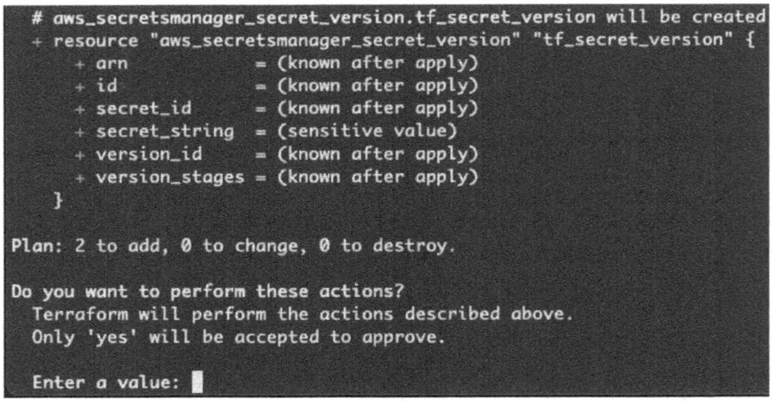

```
# aws_secretsmanager_secret_version.tf_secret_version will be created
+ resource "aws_secretsmanager_secret_version" "tf_secret_version" {
    + arn           = (known after apply)
    + id            = (known after apply)
    + secret_id     = (known after apply)
    + secret_string = (sensitive value)
    + version_id    = (known after apply)
    + version_stages = (known after apply)
  }

Plan: 2 to add, 0 to change, 0 to destroy.

Do you want to perform these actions?
  Terraform will perform the actions described above.
  Only 'yes' will be accepted to approve.

Enter a value:
```

Figure 8.2 – Terraform masking the secret value in its apply output

9. Once Terraform is done deploying the resources, we can see our new secret, similar to the following screenshot, in the AWS console.

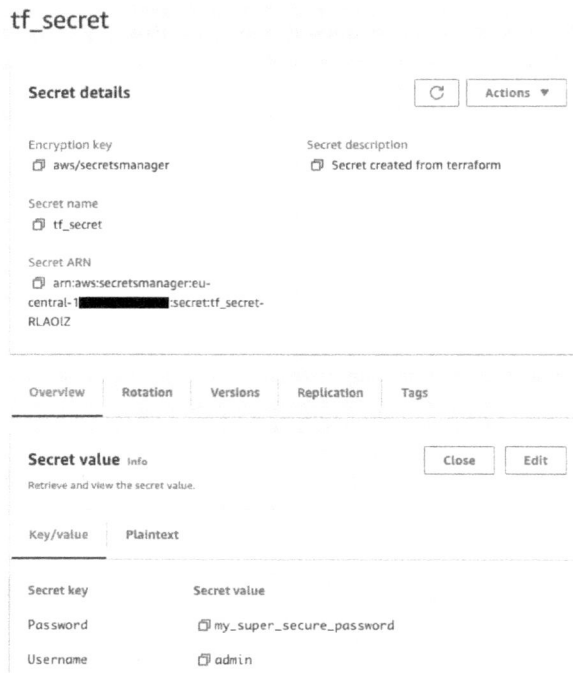

Figure 8.3 – The secret that was created using Terraform in the AWS console

Now that we have seen how we can use different IaC techniques to provision a secret, let's have a look at how we can retrieve such a secret.

Accessing secrets from an AWS Lambda function using Boto3

With our secrets programmatically created, we also need a way to programmatically retrieve them. In this section, we'll be retrieving secrets using the Boto3 SDK and Python. We'll be executing our Python code not on our machine but, rather, in an AWS Lambda function that we'll provision using the CDK.

To follow along in this section, please either download the solution from GitHub or follow the steps described in the previous section, *Creating secrets in the CDK*.

Before we get started with creating our Lambda function, let's do a quick summary of what Lambda is.

What is AWS Lambda?

AWS Lambda is a service that provides serverless compute and **function-as-a-service** (**FaaS**) functionality within AWS. When we think about compute infrastructure, an easy way to distinguish different types is by seeing how much of the underlying infrastructure you need to manage.

In the case of an EC2 instance, we are essentially managing the entire virtual machine. Containers go one level above that by abstracting the host operating system. Lambda and other FaaS services go one step above. In Lambda, we only have to manage the business logic we are writing. The service then takes care of hosting and scaling the underlying compute capacity for us.

> **Note**
>
> The underlying virtualization technology for Lambda is a virtualization technology called Firecracker. **Firecracker** is written in Rust and is open source. You can find the source code on GitHub at `https://github.com/firecracker-microvm/firecracker` and the documentation at `https://firecracker-microvm.github.io/`.

With Lambda, we can write functions in a variety of modern programming languages, such as Python, JavaScript, or Go, and run them on AWS.

Writing a Lambda function to read our previously created secret

To write the Lambda function, we'll need to go back into the CDK project we created for the previous section. To do so, open the folder in a code editor such as Visual Studio Code and then follow these steps:

1. Open up the `secrets_sample/secrets_sample_stack.py` file. At this point, the file should look like the following. Note the `Duration` and `lambda` imports that were added, as well as the addition of the `import os` statement:

    ```
    from aws_cdk import (
        Duration,
    ```

```
        Stack,
        aws_secretsmanager as sm,
        aws_lambda as lambda_
    )
    import json
    import os
    from constructs import Construct
    class SecretsSampleStack(Stack):
        def __init__(self, scope: Construct, construct_id: str,
    **kwargs) -> None:
            super().__init__(scope, construct_id, **kwargs)
            # The code that defines your stack goes here
            gen_config = {
                "secret_string_template": json.dumps({"Username":
    "admin"}),
                "generate_string_key": "Password"
            }

            secret = sm.Secret(self, "ExampleSecret",
                generate_secret_string=gen_config
            )
```

2. To better organize the code of our project, it is common to create a source code directory for the Lambda functions. Let's go ahead and create a new `src` folder and in it, another folder for our Lambda function called `get_secret_func`:

```
mkdir src
mkdir src/get_secret_func
```

3. Go back to the `secrets_sample_stack.py` file. In it, let's first write the code to define the location of our Lambda source code. We'll always make the paths relative to our `secrets_sample_stack.py` file. Inside the constructor of our `SecretSampleStack` class, right below the definition of our secret, add the following code, which retrieves the absolute path of the Python file. We can then use that absolute path to create a path that points toward our folder containing the source code for the Lambda function:

```
current_dir = os.path.dirname(os.path.abspath(__file__))
lambda_code_path = os.path.join(current_dir, "..", "src", "get_
secret_func")
```

4. Next, we can create a Lambda function using the `Function` construct. We first define the internal ID and set it to `RetrieveFunction`. Next, we pass a human-readable function with the name `GetSecretFunc` as the value of the `function_name` property. With the `code` property, we can define the path to the directory where our source code sits. The `handler` property defines the name of the handler. Here, `func.handler` means that the

entry point for our Lambda function will be a Python function called `handler` in a file called `func.py`. We then define a runtime for our code, in this case, Python version 3.11. We can also pass environment variables using the `environment` property. In this example, we are passing the **Amazon Resource Name (ARN)** of the previously created secret as an environment variable. Finally, we set the timeout of this function to `10` seconds:

```python
func = lambda_.Function(self, "RetrieveFunction",
        function_name="GetSecretFunc",
        code=lambda_.Code.from_asset(lambda_code_path),
        handler="func.handler",
        runtime=lambda_.Runtime.PYTHON_3_11,
        environment={
            "SECRET_ARN": secret.secret_arn
        },
        timeout=Duration.seconds(10)
    )
```

5. With the function defined, we could now go ahead and deploy the function. However, so far, the function doesn't have permission to access our secret.

6. The following is one of the big strengths of the CDK. For services where L2 constructs (such as `Function` or `Secret`) exist, least-privilege IAM permissions often come with them. Instead of writing an IAM policy that allows the Lambda execution role to retrieve our secret manually, we can use the `grant_read()` method of the `secret` object to generate this policy for us. Below the definition of our Lambda function, enter the following:

```python
secret.grant_read(func)
```

And that is it. Upon deployment of the stack, this will generate a new IAM policy that grants the Lambda function the right to have read-only access to our secret. Your final file should look like this:

```python
import os
import json
from aws_cdk import (
    Duration,
    Stack,
    # aws_sqs as sqs,
    aws_secretsmanager as sm,
    aws_lambda as lambda_,
)
from constructs import Construct
class SecretsSampleStack(Stack):
    def __init__(self, scope: Construct, construct_id: str,
**kwargs) -> None:
        super().__init__(scope, construct_id, **kwargs)
```

```
                   # The code that defines your stack goes here
              gen_config = {
                   "secret_string_template": json.dumps({"Username":
   "admin"}),
                   "generate_string_key": "Password"
              }
              secret = sm.Secret(self, "ExampleSecret",
                   generate_secret_string=gen_config
              )
              current_dir = os.path.dirname(os.path.abspath(__file__))
              lambda_code_path = os.path.join(current_dir, "..",
   "src", "get_secret_func")
              func = lambda_.Function(self, "RetrieveFunction",
                   function_name="GetSecretFunc",
                   code=lambda_.Code.from_asset(lambda_code_path),
                   handler="func.handler",
                   runtime=lambda_.Runtime.PYTHON_3_11,
                   environment={
                        "SECRET_ARN": secret.secret_arn
                   },
                   timeout=Duration.seconds(10)
              )
              secret.grant_read(func)
```

7. With the CDK code done, we can now write our Lambda function. Create a new file called func.py in the src/get_secret_func folder and open it in a text editor such as Visual Studio Code.

8. We'll first import a few functions, namely, the built-in os and json modules. The default runtime for Python in Lambda comes with boto3 pre-installed, so we don't have to install this package:

```
import os
import json
import boto3
```

9. Next, we use the os module to retrieve the environment variable we previously set in the CDK deployment and create a boto3 client for Secrets Manager. To do so, type the following:

```
SECRET_ARN = os.environ.get("SECRET_ARN")
sm_client = boto3.client("secretsmanager")
```

10. Next, we need to define the Python function that Lambda will call. As per the definition in our CDK code, this function needs to be called `handler`. It takes two arguments: `event` and a `context` dictionary.

11. Inside the function, we retrieve the secret value via the `GetSecretValue` API operation, read the contained JSON, and then return a string containing the password and the username from the secret. In a real-life application, you could use these credentials now to authenticate against another system such as a database:

```
resp = sm_client.get_secret_value(SecretId=SECRET_ARN)
secret_obj = json.loads(resp["SecretString"])
return "Read password: " + secret_obj["Password"] + " Read
username: " + secret_obj["Username"]
```

12. With the code of our Lambda function done, we can now deploy this stack. We first set the Region that this stack will be deployed into via the `AWS_DEFAULT_REGION` environment variable:

```
export AWS_DEFAULT_REGION=eu-central-1
```

13. If this is your first time using the CDK with this account and in this Region, you need to bootstrap it. This is only required once. You can do so by running the following command. Bootstrapping creates some resources, such as an S3 bucket to store your assets. You can find more information on bootstrapping in this documentation: `https://docs.aws.amazon.com/cdk/v2/guide/bootstrapping.html`.

Here's the command:

```
cdk bootstrap
```

14. Next, start the deployment by running the following command:

```
cdk deploy
```

When the CDK detects that it is creating new IAM permissions (as is the case in this example, where we are granting our Lambda function access to our secret), the CDK shows a summary table of all the changes that are proposed and asks us to confirm these.

The following screenshot shows the proposed changes. As you can see in the first row, we grant the principal of the execution role of our Lambda function the `DescribeSecret` and `GetSecretValue` API actions on the resource of our example secret:

	Resource	Effect	Action	Principal	Condition
+	${ExampleSecret}	Allow	secretsmanager:DescribeSecret secretsmanager:GetSecretValue	AWS:${RetrieveFunction/ServiceRole}	
+	${RetrieveFunction/ServiceRole.Arn}	Allow	sts:AssumeRole	Service:lambda.amazonaws.com	

IAM Policy Changes

	Resource	Managed Policy ARN
+	${RetrieveFunction/ServiceRole}	arn:${AWS::Partition}:iam::aws:policy/service-role/AWSLambdaBasicExecutionRole

(NOTE: There may be security-related changes not in this list. See https://github.com/aws/aws-cdk/issues/1299)

Do you wish to deploy these changes (y/n)?

Figure 8.4 – Output from the CDK when applying a change that involves the creation of an IAM policy

Once the CDK stack is deployed, the terminal will show a result similar to this:

```
SecretsSampleStack: deploying... [1/1]
SecretsSampleStack: creating CloudFormation changeset...
✓    SecretsSampleStack
✦  Deployment time: 22.35s
Stack ARN:
arn:aws:cloudformation:eu-central-1:317322385701:stack/
SecretsSampleStack/12b866b0-6edc-11ef-acfc-0a0943c62f3b
✦  Total time: 36.49s
```

15. With our function deployed, we can test it by running the Lambda function from the command line. Note that this will execute the function in the AWS cloud and not on our local machine. We use the `invoke` command in the AWS CLI. As arguments, we need to pass the function name (`GetSecretFunc`) and a file (`out.txt`, in this example) to which the output of the function will be written:

```
aws lambda invoke --function-name GetSecretFunc out.txt
```

16. When running this command, you'll get a result like the following. A status code of 200 means that the function executed successfully, and you should see a new file called out.txt:

```
{
    "StatusCode": 200,
    "ExecutedVersion": "$LATEST"
}
```

17. We can have a look at the output from the function by using the cat command:

```
cat out.txt
```

18. The output then looks similar to the following. Notice how this is the same secret value that we previously saw in the AWS console:

```
"Read password: Yqrt\":iRG1BvT]BE[Fo$`Hkruqm:H3.3 Read username:
admin"
```

In this section, you have seen how to programmatically access a secret in a Lambda function and use the Boto3 SDK for Python. Of course, this doesn't only work for secrets we have previously created but also for secrets that were created by another service such as RDS. In the next section, you'll see how we can integrate RDS to add the credentials for a database into Secrets Manager.

Integrating Amazon RDS with AWS Secrets Manager to rotate database credentials

We have seen how we can programmatically create and retrieve a secret. But what about the usage of Secrets Manager together with other services such as RDS? Since the use case of storing and rotating the username and password of a database system is so common, there is an integration between Amazon RDS (which we introduced in the previous chapter) and Secrets Manager. In this section, we are going to create an RDS cluster and delegate the creation and rotation of the secret to Secrets Manager.

To create a new RDS cluster with credentials managed by Secrets Manager, follow these steps:

1. In the AWS console, navigate to the RDS service page.

2. Click on the **Create database** button.

3. Since the focus of this section is the integration of RDS with Secrets Manager, in the database creation method, select **Easy create**, as shown in the following screenshot. If you want a more detailed explanation of the different options available in RDS, have a look at *Chapter 7*, where we created a database cluster using the **Standard create** mode.

RDS > Create database

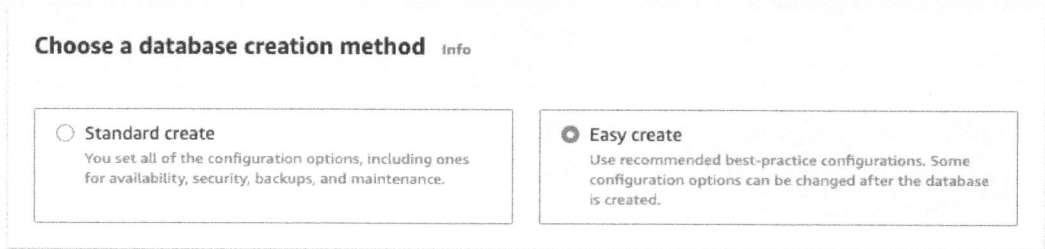

Create database

Choose a database creation method Info

○ **Standard create**
You set all of the configuration options, including ones for availability, security, backups, and maintenance.

◉ **Easy create**
Use recommended best-practice configurations. Some configuration options can be changed after the database is created.

Figure 8.5 – Selecting Easy create for our simple RDS cluster

4. For engine options, select **Aurora (PostgreSQL Compatible)**, as shown in the following screenshot:

Configuration

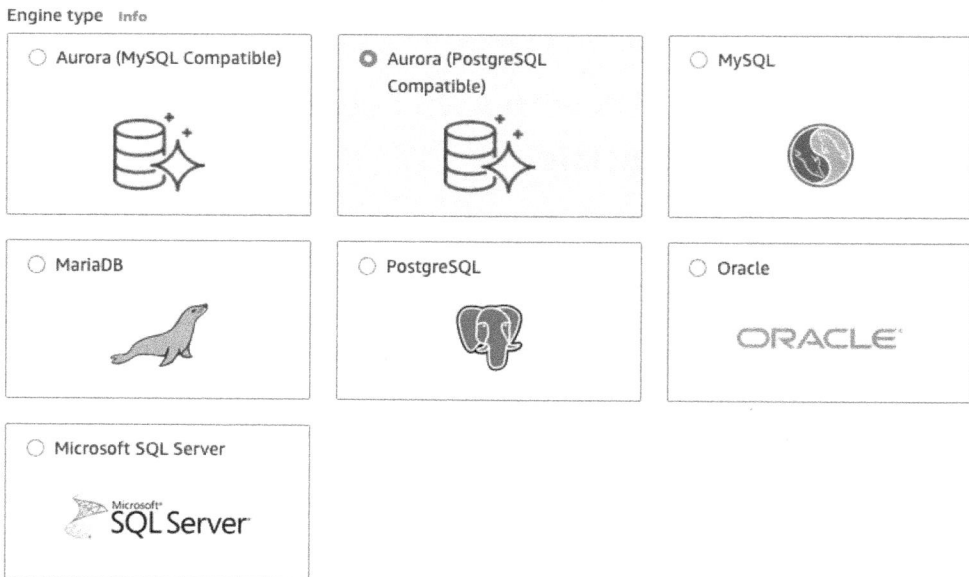

Engine type Info

○ Aurora (MySQL Compatible)

◉ Aurora (PostgreSQL Compatible)

○ MySQL

○ MariaDB

○ PostgreSQL

○ Oracle

ORACLE

○ Microsoft SQL Server

Microsoft
SQL Server

Figure 8.6 – Selecting our database engine

5. Under **Templates**, select **Dev/Test**, as shown in the following screenshot. Since this cluster is just for testing the integration, we can use an economical development and testing configuration for the compute instances behind our database cluster.

DB instance size

○ Production	◉ Dev/Test
db.r6g.2xlarge	db.t4g.large
8 vCPUs	2 vCPUs
64 GiB RAM	8 GiB RAM
1.253 USD/hour	0.170 USD/hour

Figure 8.7 – Using a development template for the compute instances of this database cluster

Next, we can define the name of our database cluster and also the configuration for our secrets. The following screenshot shows the configuration needed to let Secrets Manager handle our password generation and lifecycle:

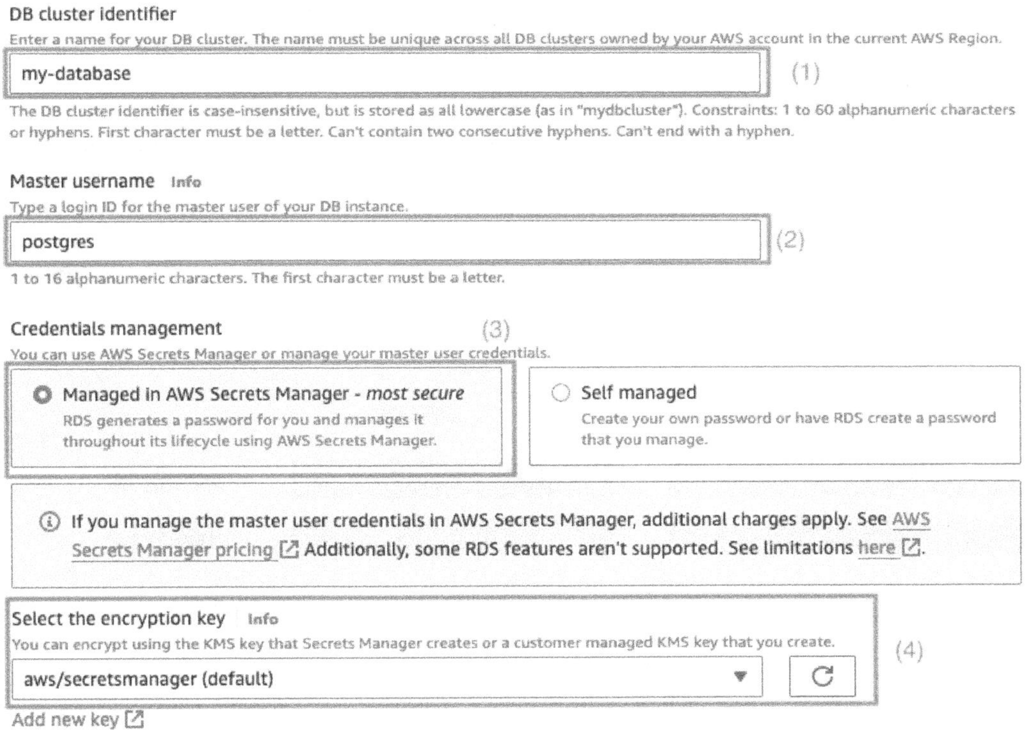

DB cluster identifier

Enter a name for your DB cluster. The name must be unique across all DB clusters owned by your AWS account in the current AWS Region.

> my-database   (1)

The DB cluster identifier is case-insensitive, but is stored as all lowercase (as in "mydbcluster"). Constraints: 1 to 60 alphanumeric characters or hyphens. First character must be a letter. Can't contain two consecutive hyphens. Can't end with a hyphen.

Master username   Info

Type a login ID for the master user of your DB instance.

> postgres   (2)

1 to 16 alphanumeric characters. The first character must be a letter.

Credentials management   (3)

You can use AWS Secrets Manager or manage your master user credentials.

◉ **Managed in AWS Secrets Manager** - *most secure*	○ Self managed
RDS generates a password for you and manages it throughout its lifecycle using AWS Secrets Manager.	Create your own password or have RDS create a password that you manage.

ⓘ If you manage the master user credentials in AWS Secrets Manager, additional charges apply. See AWS Secrets Manager pricing ☑ Additionally, some RDS features aren't supported. See limitations here ☑.

Select the encryption key   Info

You can encrypt using the KMS key that Secrets Manager creates or a customer managed KMS key that you create.   (4)

> aws/secretsmanager (default)   ▼   ↻

Add new key ☑

Figure 8.8 – The secrets configuration for our database

Here are some things to note in the preceding figure:

- Under **DB cluster identifier** (number **1** in the figure), we define the name/identifier for the cluster.

- Under **Master username** (number **2** in the figure), we define the username used to authenticate with this cluster. The username will be included as part of the secret that is stored in Secrets Manager.

- Under **Credentials management** (number **3** in the figure), select **Managed in AWS Secrets Manager** to instruct RDS to use Secrets Manager for the generation, storage, and rotation of these secrets.

- Under **Select the encryption key** (number **4** in the figure), select **aws/secretsmanager (default)** to use the AWS-managed key. We'll learn more about KMS-managed encryption keys later on in this chapter.

6. Next, click the **Create database** button at the bottom of the page.

7. Navigate to Secrets Manager in the AWS console.

8. In the overview, you should see the newly created secret. The ARN of your database should be included in the description of the secret. The following screenshot shows an example of the overview:

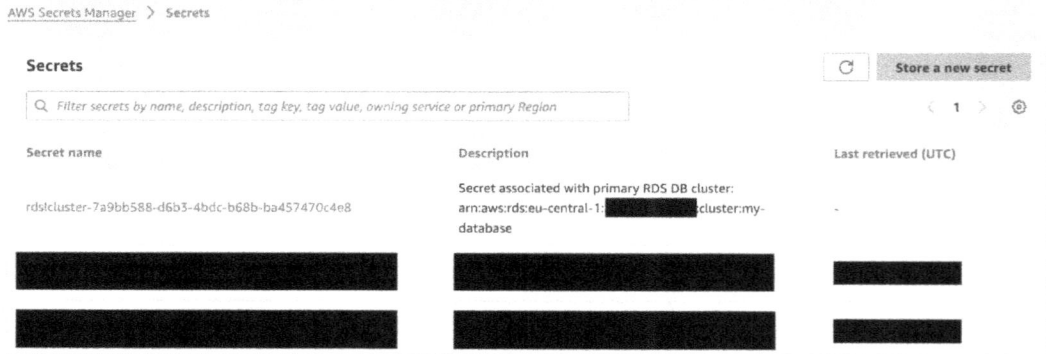

Figure 8.9 – List of available secrets, including the secret created by RDS

9. By clicking on the secret name, you'll get a detailed overview of the secret. Click the **Retrieve secret value** button, as highlighted in the following screenshot, to reveal the secret that was set:

Figure 8.10 – Using the Retrieve secret value button to unveil the
username and password stored in this secret

10. The overview now shows the key-value pairs associated with this secret. This password could be retrieved programmatically, as shown in the example using Boto3 and Lambda in the *Writing a Lambda function to read our previously created secret* section. You can see, in the following screenshot, how the secret contains the username we set in the RDS configuration dialog as well as an auto-generated password string:

Overview	Rotation	Versions	Replication	Tags

Secret value Info   Close   Edit
Retrieve and view the secret value.

Key/value	Plaintext

Secret key	Secret value
username	postgres
password	+-2bpp9jkWNg#fCCn]U*I+G)QZ2x

Figure 8.11 – The unveiled username and password

11. By clicking on the **Rotation** tab, we see the default rotation settings. In the following screenshot, you can see that rotation is enabled and that the password will be rotated every 7 days. If we know that a password was compromised, we can also use the **Rotate secret immediately** button to trigger an immediate rotation of our secret.

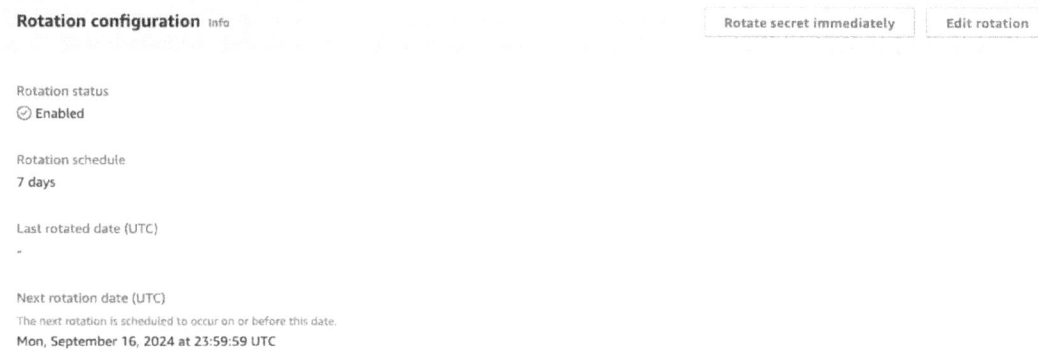

Rotation configuration Info   Rotate secret immediately   Edit rotation

Rotation status
⊘ Enabled

Rotation schedule
7 days

Last rotated date (UTC)
-

Next rotation date (UTC)
The next rotation is scheduled to occur on or before this date.
Mon, September 16, 2024 at 23:59:59 UTC

Figure 8.12 – The rotation configuration, indicating our rotation schedule and rotation status

So far in this chapter, we have seen how to create secrets using IaC, how to retrieve them programmatically in Python, and finally, how to integrate RDS with Secrets Manager for automated secrets management and rotation.

> **Note**
>
> In the previous section, we saw how to create a secret in the CDK. When dealing with secrets that were created using the AWS console or by a service such as RDS, the following snippet shows how you could import a secret via its ARN. You could then use the same `grant_read()` function to allow a Lambda function (or any other role in the CDK) to read the secret:
>
> ```
> secret_arn = "<insert_arn_of_secret_here>"
> secret = Secret.fromSecretCompleteArn(self, "ImportedSecret",
> secret_arn)
> ```

Next, we'll have a closer look at another AWS service, called **AWS Key Management Service** (**KMS**), which is used for managing our encryption keys in AWS.

Handling encryption keys with AWS KMS

Data encryption is a central aspect of the cloud and, in AWS, encryption is mainly done via KMS. We have previously seen KMS as an option. For example, in the previous section, when selecting the encryption key for our secrets, we saw the option to define a different KMS key. In this section, we'll get a brief overview of KMS before using it to configure a different encryption key for an S3 bucket to show how KMS is integrated into a variety of services.

> **Note**
>
> This section assumes that you have a basic understanding of public/private key cryptography. If that is not the case, you can acquaint yourself with the concept by visiting `https://docs.aws.amazon.com/crypto/latest/userguide/cryptography-concepts.html`.

What is KMS?

When we talk about encryption, we usually talk about the storage and usage of encryption keys. Before talking about how we can create and use keys, let's briefly discuss storage. KMS stores its encryption keys in **hardware security modules** (**HSMs**) in a way that they can't be accessed externally. The HSMs are validated under the United States **National Institute of Standards and Technology** (**NIST**) **Federal Information Processing Standards** (**FIPS**) 140-2 Cryptographic Module Validation Program. With FIPS 140-2, NIST has a standard for the requirements of cryptographic modules.

> **Note**
>
> The details of how KMS handles keys as well as the cryptographic concepts underneath it could fill an entire book. If you want to learn more, AWS has published a summary paper that can be found at `https://docs.aws.amazon.com/kms/latest/cryptographic-details/intro.html`.

In KMS, we generally differentiate between two different types of keys: AWS-managed keys and **customer-managed keys (CMKs)**. As the name suggests, AWS-managed keys are managed by the service. We saw such a key in the previous section when we selected the `aws/secretsmanager` key for encrypting our database secrets.

Services such as Amazon S3 use AWS-managed keys by default but we can configure them to use CMKs.

KMS keys are regional by default. This means that, by default, a key only exists in the Region it was created in. If that Region were to go down, all access to data that was encrypted using that key would be inaccessible for the duration that the Region is unreachable. We can work around this by creating a multi-Region key. We will see how to do this in *Chapter 11*.

Changing an S3 bucket to use a CMK

So, let's see CMKs in action. In this section, we'll create a CMK and then use it to encrypt objects in a bucket. Before we do this, let's first create a bucket with default encryption (meaning server-side encryption using AWS-managed keys) and upload a file to it:

1. In the command line, use the following command to create a new bucket:

   ```
   aws s3 mb s3://<your_bucket_name>
   ```

2. We can check the current encryption of our bucket by running the following command:

   ```
   aws s3api get-bucket-encryption --bucket <your_bucket_name>
   ```

3. The output will look like the following:

   ```
   {
       "ServerSideEncryptionConfiguration": {
           "Rules": [
               {
                   "ApplyServerSideEncryptionByDefault": {
                       "SSEAlgorithm": "AES256"
                   },
                   "BucketKeyEnabled": false
               }
           ]
       }
   }
   ```

   Notice the `SSEAlgorithm` property defining the encryption to be `AES256`, which is the value for AWS-managed encryption (also known as SSE-S3).

4. Let's create a text file, add some placeholder text to it, and then upload it to our previously created S3 bucket:

```
touch test.txt
echo "test1233445" >> test.txt
aws s3 cp test.txt s3://<your_bucket_name>/
```

5. Now that we have a bucket that is currently using the AWS-managed key, let's go to KMS and create our own CMK. To do so, open the AWS console and search for KMS or follow this link: https://eu-central-1.console.aws.amazon.com/kms/home?region=eu-central-1#/kms/home.

6. On the KMS overview page, click the **Create a key** button to create a new key.

7. In the wizard, select **Symmetric** for **Key type** and **Encrypt and decrypt** for **Key usage**, as shown in the following screenshot:

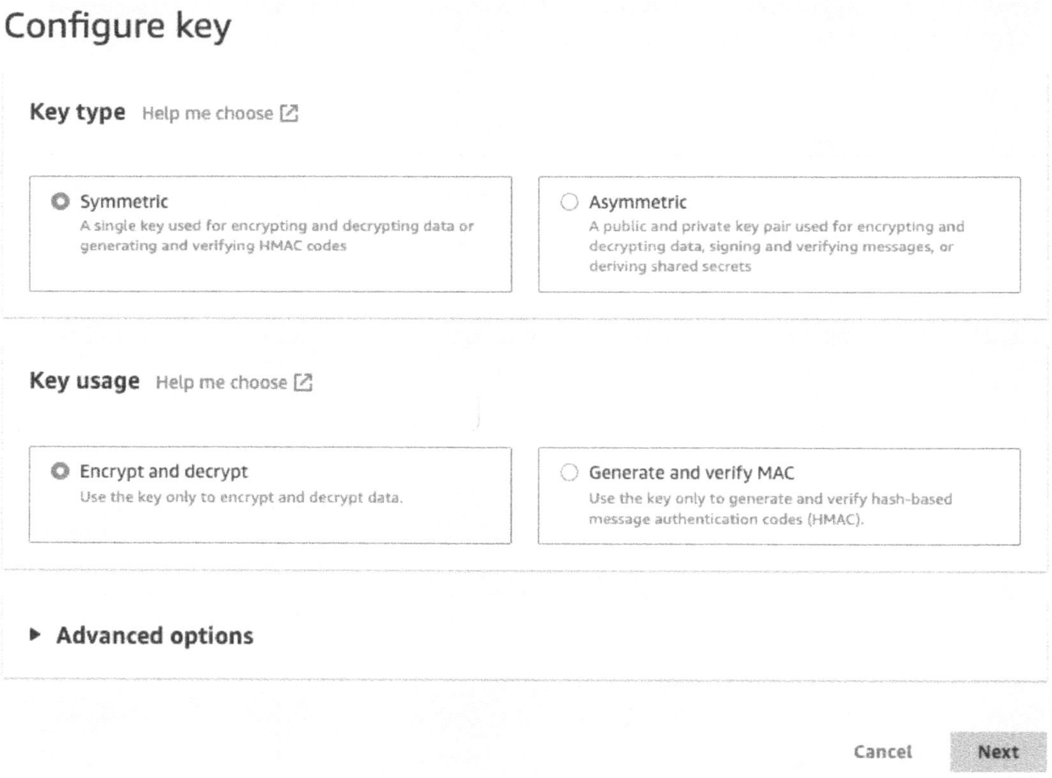

Configure key

Key type Help me choose ☒

⦿ Symmetric
A single key used for encrypting and decrypting data or generating and verifying HMAC codes

◯ Asymmetric
A public and private key pair used for encrypting and decrypting data, signing and verifying messages, or deriving shared secrets

Key usage Help me choose ☒

⦿ Encrypt and decrypt
Use the key only to encrypt and decrypt data.

◯ Generate and verify MAC
Use the key only to generate and verify hash-based message authentication codes (HMAC).

▶ **Advanced options**

Cancel   Next

Figure 8.13 – The key configuration for our new KMS key

8.   Next, define a name (or alias) for this key:

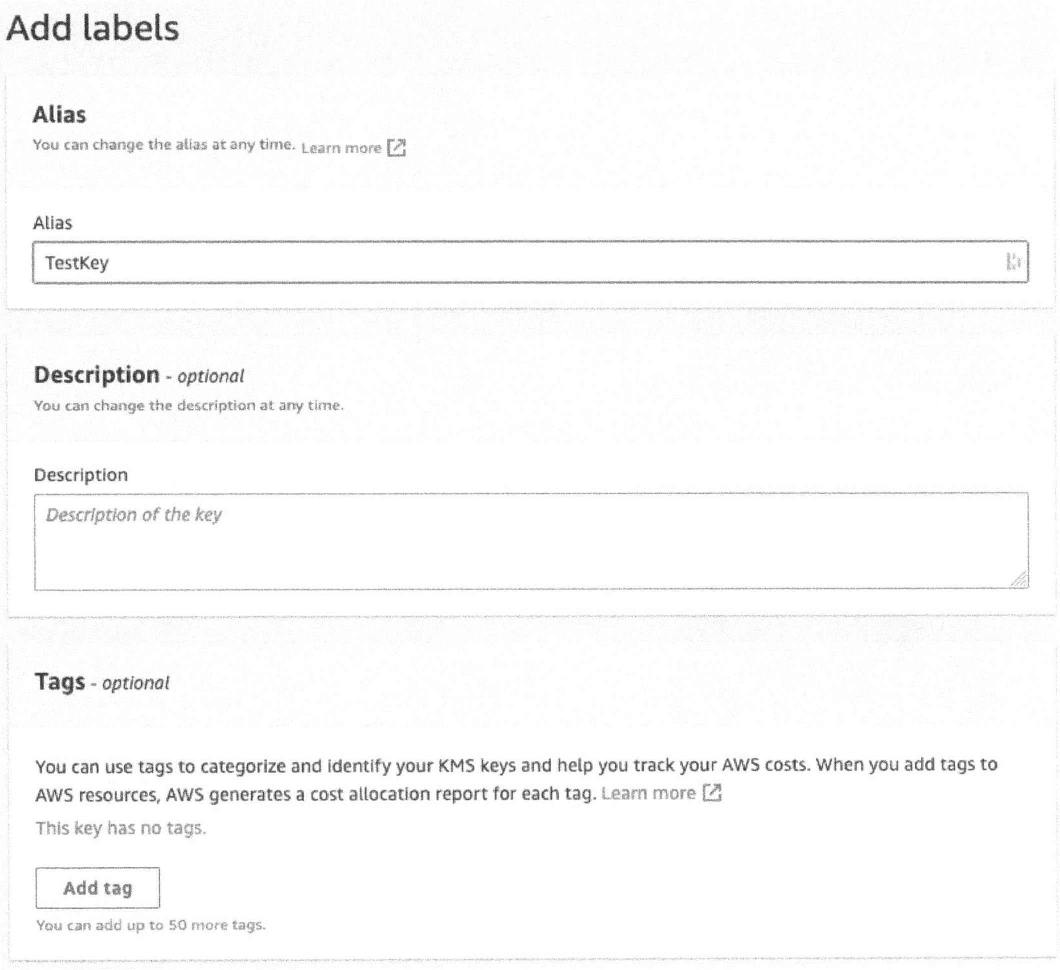

Add labels

Alias
You can change the alias at any time. Learn more [↗]

Alias

| TestKey |

Description - *optional*
You can change the description at any time.

Description

| Description of the key |

Tags - *optional*

You can use tags to categorize and identify your KMS keys and help you track your AWS costs. When you add tags to AWS resources, AWS generates a cost allocation report for each tag. Learn more [↗]

This key has no tags.

| Add tag |

You can add up to 50 more tags.

Figure 8.14 – Defining the alias of our key

9.   On the next two pages, you define the admin users that have the right to manage (including deleting) your key. Note that KMS keys are not directly deleted. When a `delete` operation on a KMS key is issued, it is deactivated but kept for a time threshold. This is to prevent accidental deletion of keys. In the dialog, select the users that you want to have admin rights to your key. Choose the IAM user that you are using:

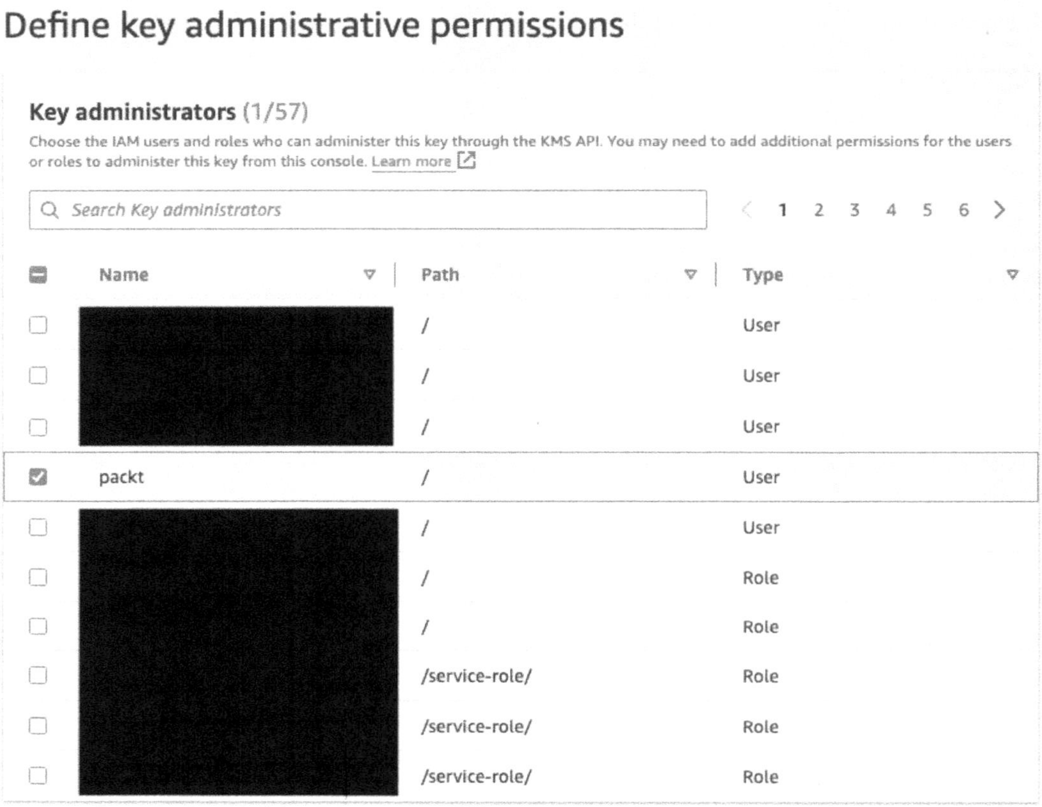

Define key administrative permissions

Key administrators (1/57)

Choose the IAM users and roles who can administer this key through the KMS API. You may need to add additional permissions for the users or roles to administer this key from this console. Learn more [↗]

	Name ▽	Path ▽	Type ▽
☐		/	User
☐		/	User
☐		/	User
☑	packt	/	User
☐		/	User
☐		/	Role
☐		/	Role
☐		/service-role/	Role
☐		/service-role/	Role
☐		/service-role/	Role

Figure 8.15 – Definition of the key administrator

10. Click **Create Key** to create the new KMS key.

11. Now, we can navigate to S3 and change our bucket. Search for S3 in the AWS console.

12. In the list that appears in the AWS console, find your previously created bucket and click on its name.

13. Navigate to the **Properties** tab and find the **Default encryption** panel, as shown in the following screenshot. In this panel, you can see that the bucket currently uses SSE-S3 (so AWS-managed keys) for encryption. Click the **Edit** button to change the default encryption.

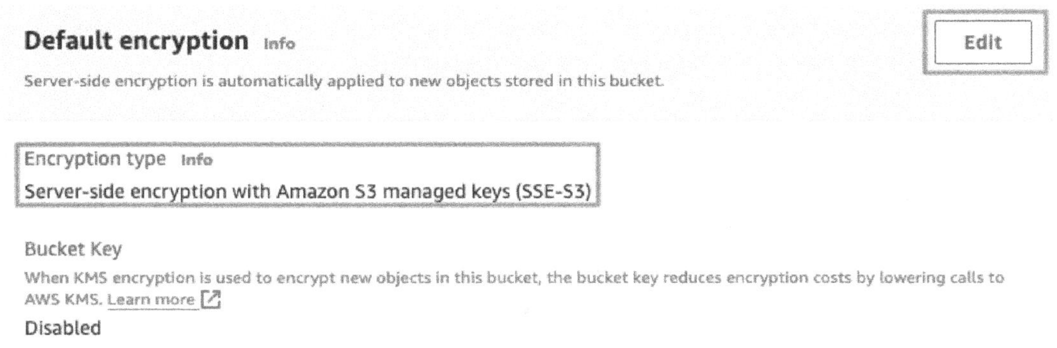

Default encryption Info

Edit

Server-side encryption is automatically applied to new objects stored in this bucket.

Encryption type Info

Server-side encryption with Amazon S3 managed keys (SSE-S3)

Bucket Key

When KMS encryption is used to encrypt new objects in this bucket, the bucket key reduces encryption costs by lowering calls to AWS KMS. Learn more [↗]

Disabled

Figure 8.16 – Default encryption for our bucket

14. In the dialog, select **Server-side encryption with AWS Key Management Service keys (SSE-KMS)**. Next, select **Choose from your AWS KMS keys** and, in the dropdown, select the previously created key. Also, select **Enable** for the **Bucket Key** field. These selections are shown in the following screenshot:

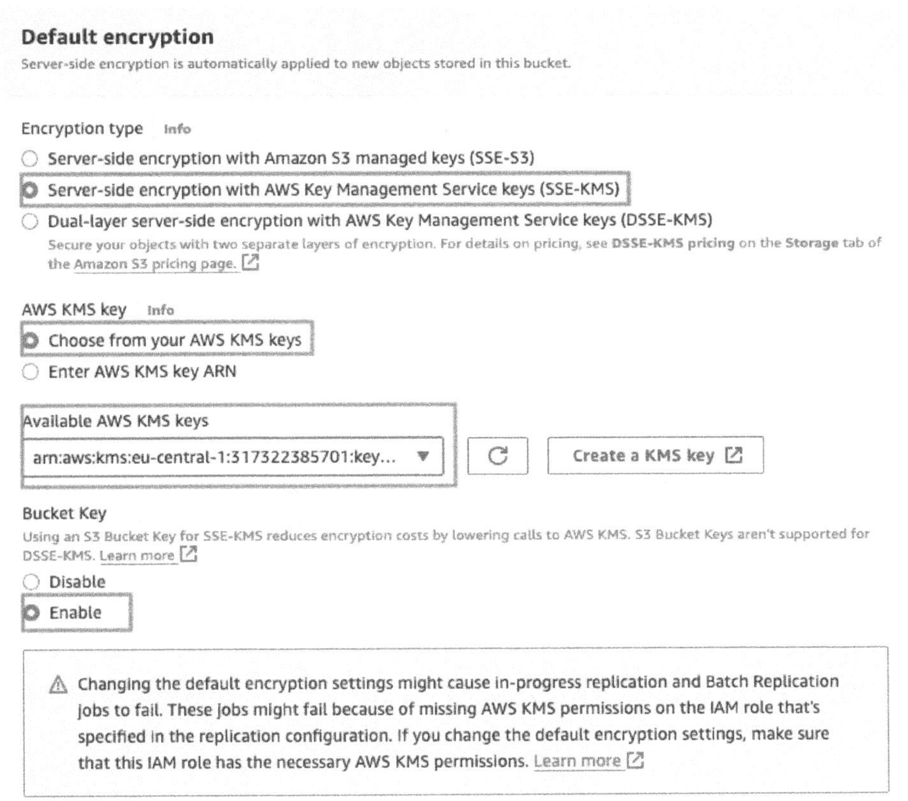

Default encryption

Server-side encryption is automatically applied to new objects stored in this bucket.

Encryption type   Info

○ Server-side encryption with Amazon S3 managed keys (SSE-S3)

◉ Server-side encryption with AWS Key Management Service keys (SSE-KMS)

○ Dual-layer server-side encryption with AWS Key Management Service keys (DSSE-KMS)
　Secure your objects with two separate layers of encryption. For details on pricing, see **DSSE-KMS pricing** on the **Storage** tab of the Amazon S3 pricing page. [↗]

AWS KMS key   Info

◉ Choose from your AWS KMS keys

○ Enter AWS KMS key ARN

Available AWS KMS keys

arn:aws:kms:eu-central-1:317322385701:key... ▼   ↻   Create a KMS key [↗]

Bucket Key

Using an S3 Bucket Key for SSE-KMS reduces encryption costs by lowering calls to AWS KMS. S3 Bucket Keys aren't supported for DSSE-KMS. Learn more [↗]

○ Disable

◉ Enable

⚠ Changing the default encryption settings might cause in-progress replication and Batch Replication jobs to fail. These jobs might fail because of missing AWS KMS permissions on the IAM role that's specified in the replication configuration. If you change the default encryption settings, make sure that this IAM role has the necessary AWS KMS permissions. Learn more [↗]

Figure 8.17 – Selections for changing the bucket encryption settings

15. With the changes done, we can rerun our encryption command to see that the encryption was changed on our bucket. To do so, run the following command:

```
aws s3api get-bucket-encryption --bucket <your_bucket_name>
```

16. The output should look similar to this:

```
{
    "ServerSideEncryptionConfiguration": {
        "Rules": [
            {
                "ApplyServerSideEncryptionByDefault": {
                    "SSEAlgorithm": "aws:kms",
                    "KMSMasterKeyID": "arn:aws:kms:eu-central-
1:<account_id>:key/8e7266f2-<redacted>"
                },
                "BucketKeyEnabled": true
            }
        ]
    }
}
```

All new objects will now be encrypted using our new CMK. But what about the one previously updated? We can simply copy all objects from our bucket back into the same bucket. This will trigger re-encryption with the new key. This can be particularly useful when we want to retire an old CMK:

```
aws s3 cp s3://<bucket_name> s3://<bucket_name> --recursive
```

With that, we have successfully changed our bucket to use a CMK from KMS and seen how KMS provides encryption keys to services across AWS.

Summary

In this chapter, we have explored two services: AWS Secrets Manager and KMS. AWS Secrets Manager lets you manage your secrets, such as database credentials. We have seen how to programmatically create secrets with different IaC tools (such as the CDK or Terraform), how Secrets Manager is integrated into services such as RDS, and how we can retrieve secrets in a Lambda function.

Then, we saw how KMS is used to manage encryption keys in AWS, how we can create our own encryption keys, and finally, how we can configure S3 to use such a CMK.

In the next chapter, we'll have a deeper look at monitoring our AWS services using CloudWatch and SNS.

Get This Book's PDF Version and Exclusive Extras

UNLOCK NOW

Scan the QR code (or go to `packtpub.com/unlock`). Search for this book by name, confirm the edition, and then follow the steps on the page.

Note: Keep your invoice handly. Purchase made directly from packt don't require one.

Part 4: Monitoring, Metrics, and the Backup Layer

The fourth part discusses how we can implement observability, metrics, alerting, and centralized logging through the use of CloudWatch and SNS. Equipped with the right tools to observe our infrastructure, we'll then see how we can efficiently implement backup plans for our infrastructure, what disaster recovery options are available to us, and how we can test the resilience of our deployed infrastructure through chaos engineering.

This part contains the following chapters:

- *Chapter 9, Centralized Logging and Monitoring with Amazon CloudWatch*

- *Chapter 10, Centralizing Cloud Backup Solutions*

- *Chapter 11, Disaster Recovery Options with AWS*

- *Chapter 12, Testing the Resilience of Your Infrastructure and Architecture with AWS Fault Injection Service*

Centralized Logging and Monitoring with Amazon CloudWatch

So far, we have seen how we can use AWS to build the infrastructure required for deploying modern applications. But what about monitoring our application and infrastructure once it is deployed? With the often distributed nature of applications on AWS, this can become a challenge.

In this chapter, we'll look into AWS CloudWatch, a logging and metrics service provided by AWS that can serve as the centralized dashboard for all our infrastructure and application metrics.

CloudWatch has two key types of operational data that can be ingested and viewed: logs and metrics. **Logs** are all the textual outputs (such as debug messages or error messages) that your application and infrastructure produce while **metrics** are performance numbers, such as the CPU utilization or the number of requests per second being handled by your application. These metrics can serve a variety of purposes from automated scaling of your infrastructure to alerting you of unusual activities such as a spike in CPU utilization, which could indicate issues with your application or infrastructure.

In the book we have so far seen how we can use AWS to build the infrastructure required for deploying modern applications. But what about monitoring our application and infrastructure once it is deployed? Especially due to the often distributed nature of applications on AWS this can become a challenge.

In this chapter, we'll have a look at both the metrics and log side of CloudWatch.

The topics covered in this chapter are:

- An introduction to CloudWatch monitoring
- Why do we need log management
- Instrumenting an EC2 instance to ingest custom metrics and send custom logs
- An introduction to **Simple Notification Service (SNS)**
- Automated notifications to email and Slack

Technical requirements

Before following this section, please create an AWS account for yourself. You can sign-up at `https://aws.amazon.com`. A basic understanding of AWS (for example, knowing what a service is) will be beneficial.

A basic understanding of Python will help with the programming-based sections of this chapter.

This chapter also assumes that you have a running EC2 instance that can be accessed via SSH. You can refer to the instructions in *Chapter 4* if you need a step-by-step guide on setting up a new instance.

All scripts from this section can be found at the following GitHub link: `https://github.com/PacktPublishing/AWS-for-System-Administrators-Second-Edition`

The CiA video for this chapter can be found at `https://packt.link/KmPdt`

An introduction to CloudWatch for metrics

CloudWatch is well integrated with most AWS services such that they publish performance metrics into CloudWatch. In order to keep things organized, metrics are published under service-specific namespaces. A namespace (for example, `AWS/EC2`) contains all the metrics related to the EC2 service. Typically, the metrics can be further subdivided into groups. For example, in EC2, we usually want to look at all metrics that are related to an instance (`Per-instance` metrics) or all metrics related to an Auto Scaling group (`Per-Auto Scaling group` metrics).

> **Note**
>
> You can find a list of all the possible metrics at the following URL: `https://docs.aws.amazon.com/AmazonCloudWatch/latest/monitoring/aws-services-cloudwatch-metrics.html`.

The types of metrics that are available will depend on the service. For each instance, EC2 publishes host-level metrics such as the following:

- CPU utilization
- Network packets/data in and out
- Disk read/write
- Status checks

The following figure shows the CloudWatch metrics graph for the CPU utilization of an EC2 instance.

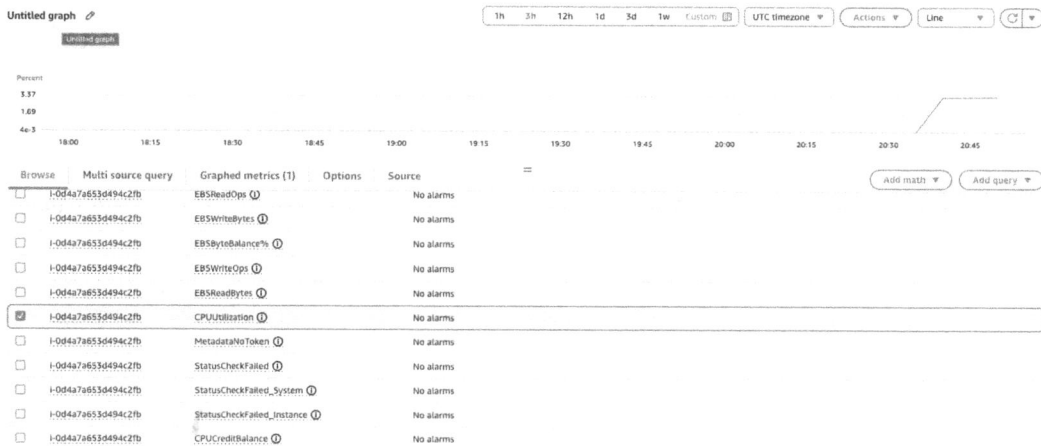

Figure 9.1 – Graphical overview of the CPU utilization of our EC2 instance over 3 hours

A metric that is curiously absent from the preceding list is the memory usage of our EC2 instance. To understand why, we have to recall that EC2 instances are virtual machines that emulate physical hardware such as the CPU, disk, and RAM via a hypervisor. While metrics such as CPU utilization can be determined on the hypervisor – and thus the EC2 service can publish them into CloudWatch for us – this is not possible for RAM. Memory allocation is handled by the guest operating system (for example, Ubuntu or Windows Server running on our EC2 instance) and it can't be inferred on a hypervisor level.

What we need, therefore, is an agent that runs on our instance itself and lets us publish these custom metrics to CloudWatch.

Before setting up our instance for custom metrics, let's first explore another important CloudWatch feature, the logs.

Why do we need log management?

When troubleshooting software system issues, logs are usually the first place we investigate. Both applications and the underlying infrastructure generate log messages, and we typically distinguish between two types:

- **Application logs**: Messages produced by applications running on our servers (for example, a web server like Apache2).

- **System logs**: Messages generated by the server's operating system (for example, a Linux distribution).

Application logs don't necessarily report only errors. For instance, Apache2 also produces access logs that record every web request processed by the server.

Logs are usually either written to STDOUT or to a log file. A basic approach to troubleshooting during an outage is to log into the system, for example, a server, where these log files reside and analyze them using command-line tools like `cat`, `grep`, or `sed` to look for patterns.

This approach, however, has a few downsides:

- In large-scale deployments, where we might have hundreds or thousands of servers, logging into each server individually to analyze logs is not feasible.

- The server that stores our logs could be unreachable, meaning we can no longer access the files.

One of the most important challenges comes with the distributed nature of many modern software systems. In a scenario such as a microservices architecture, the entire software system is made up of multiple subsystems that interact with each other to provide services to users.

The following figure shows a simplified version of a microservices architecture for a social networking application:

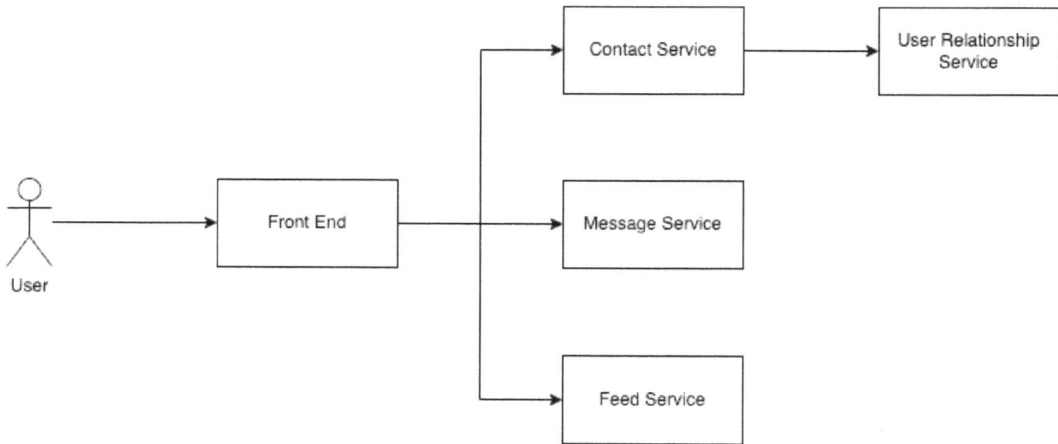

Figure 9.2 – A simple component overview for a social network application

In this architecture, each box represents a service. A user accesses the functionality provided by the software, for example, the ability to send a message to another user, through the front end. The front end then communicates with backend services that provide the actual functionality. Each rectangle represents its own software system running on its own infrastructure.

Imagine a user approaches you with a problem regarding sending a message. To troubleshoot it, you would have to log into each of the services, find the relevant logs, and use that information to solve the issue.

> **Additional Information**
>
> The issue of logging within a distributed system is one of the most cited examples of a cross-cutting concern. Such concerns occur when functionality, like tracing a user's request through a system, cannot be addressed by looking into a single component but rather cuts across multiple components.

This is where centralized log management becomes crucial. By storing logs in a central place, we get a single pane of glass to index, search, and analyze our logs.

Until now, we have discussed centralized logging in the abstract. Let's now get more specific with AWS.

In AWS, we have an additional category of logs, logs from managed services. In *Chapter 7*, we saw how to set up a database instance using RDS. But where can we see the logs created by that RDS instance? In AWS, managed services, such as RDS or Lambda, usually push their logs into CloudWatch Logs.

An introduction to CloudWatch for logs

Logs in CloudWatch are organized into **log groups**. Each log group has a name that identifies it. Since log groups are regional resources, the name must be unique within the same region.

This means two different log groups in the `eu-central-1` region cannot both be called `AppLogs`, although you could have a group named `AppLogs` in `eu-central-1` and another in `us-east-1`.

Log group names can be between 1 and 512 characters long. While there is no enforced naming convention, AWS typically follows a path-based pattern:

- Log groups created by RDS start with the prefix `aws/rds/`.
- Logs for Lambda functions are found under `aws/lambda/`.

As a result, when defining names for your log groups, you cannot start them with the prefix `aws/`.

In theory, logs can be stored forever, however, logs typically tend to become less relevant as they become older. To accommodate this, CloudWatch lets you configure a retention period for the logs within your log group. This ranges, at the time of writing, from 1 day to 10 years, or you can choose to never expire your logs.

Since every log has a timestamp, CloudWatch will retain your logs up to their retention period and then delete them. Retention periods can be changed after the creation of a log group and can be used to optimize costs. In CloudWatch Logs, at the time of writing, you pay for every gigabyte of logs stored, so having CloudWatch automatically delete old and unneeded logs will save you money.

One final concept when discussing log groups is the storage class. Similar to how Amazon S3 offers different storage classes when creating a bucket, CloudWatch lets you choose between, at the time of writing in May 2025, two different log classes, Standard and Infrequent Access.

- Standard is the default class that provides all the features of CloudWatch Logs, like ingestion, querying, and exporting logs to S3.

- Infrequent Access lets you store and query your logs but does not support some advanced features, such as natural language-based queries.

The benefit of using Infrequent Access is the lower price. For example, at the time of writing, the price per GB of stored logs for the Standard tier in the `eu-central-1` (Frankfurt) region is $0.63 per GB, while the Infrequent Access tier costs only $0.315 per GB.

This makes the Infrequent Access tier ideal for any log groups where you do not require the more advanced features. However, especially when considering long-term storage of logs, for example, for compliance audits, it can be cheaper to export them to S3, a feature only available with the Standard storage class.

> **Note**
> At the time of writing, it is not possible to change the log class of a log group after its creation.

- For an up-to-date comparison table of which CloudWatch features are supported by which storage class, you can follow this link: `https://docs.aws.amazon.com/AmazonCloudWatch/latest/logs/CloudWatch_Logs_Log_Classes.html#Log_Class_Features`.

- And for a pricing comparison, you can check the official pricing table here: `https://aws.amazon.com/cloudwatch/pricing/`

- With the theory of log groups covered, let's go ahead and create one.

Creating a log group in CloudWatch

In this section, we will create a new log group in CloudWatch. Later on in the chapter, we will use the CloudWatch agent to send our logs to the newly created log group.

For creating the log group, follow these steps:

1. Navigate to the CloudWatch console by either searching for `CloudWatch` in the AWS Console or by using this link: `https://console.aws.amazon.com/cloudwatch`.

2. In the left-hand menu, select **Log groups** under **Logs**.

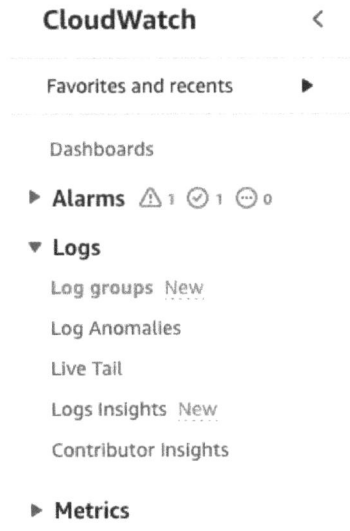

Figure 9.3 – Log groups in the menu

3. On the overview page, you will see a list of all your existing log groups. By default, you can have up to 1 million log groups. At the top right, click the **Create log group** button.

Figure 9.4 – Button to create a new log group in the log group overview page

1. In the **Create log group** wizard, we need to set a name, retention period, and log class for our new log group.

   • For the **Log group name**, we will use /ServerLogs.

   • Retention is set to **1 week (7 days)**, so logs older than one week will be deleted.

   • **Log class** is set to **Standard**.

- The **KMS key ARN** is left empty. We could provide the ARN of a KMS key here to specify a customer-managed key that will be used for encrypting the log files.

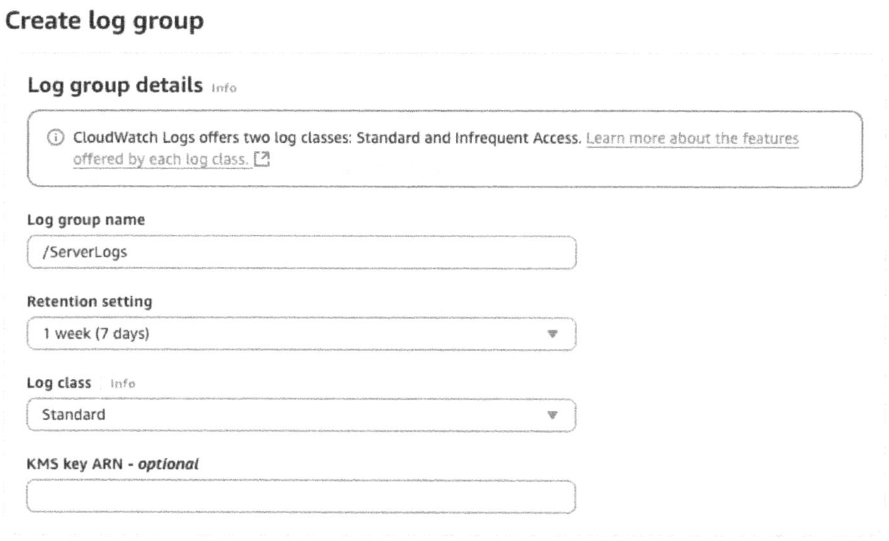

Create log group

Log group details Info

ⓘ CloudWatch Logs offers two log classes: Standard and Infrequent Access. Learn more about the features offered by each log class. ↗

Log group name

/ServerLogs

Retention setting

1 week (7 days)   ▼

Log class   Info

Standard   ▼

KMS key ARN - *optional*

Figure 9.5 – Filled out form to create a new log group

2. Click the **Create** button at the bottom right to create your new log group.

3. In the search bar, type the name of your newly created log group. In this example, the name was /ServerLogs. You should find the new log group.

Figure 9.6 – Searching for the new log group

4. By clicking on the name of the log group, you will be taken to the overview page shown in the following screenshot:

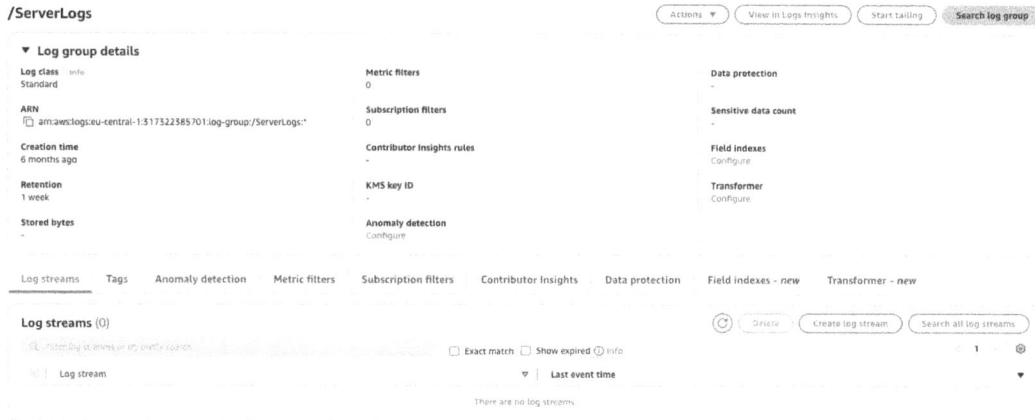

/ServerLogs

▼ Log group details

Log class info	Metric filters	Data protection
Standard	0	-
ARN	**Subscription filters**	**Sensitive data count**
arn:aws:logs:eu-central-1:517322585701:log-group:/ServerLogs:*	0	-
Creation time	**Contributor Insights rules**	**Field indexes**
6 months ago	-	Configure
Retention	**KMS key ID**	**Transformer**
1 week	-	Configure
Stored bytes	**Anomaly detection**	
-	Configure	

Log streams Tags Anomaly detection Metric filters Subscription filters Contributor Insights Data protection Field indexes – *new* Transformer – *new*

Log streams (0)

| Log stream | Last event time |

There are no log streams.

Figure 9.7 – Overview page of the new log group

In the overview of your new log group, you can find basic information such as the log class, retention period, and the amount of bytes currently stored within the log group.

At the bottom of the log group, you will find the list of log streams. Each log group is made up of log streams. A log stream bundles all log events from one source, for example, an EC2 instance or a Lambda function.

Additional Information

You may wonder why the log group of a single Lambda function has multiple log streams attached to it. This is because each version of the Lambda function gets its own log stream.

Every time you change the source code of your Lambda function, it will create a new version that gets its own new log stream in the log group of the Lambda function.

With our new log group created, we now need a source of logs to send to the group.

We have previously discussed the value of having all logs from our application, the underlying system logs, and the logs from all AWS services like RDS that make up our application, in one place. To get the logs from an EC2 instance, we will next use and configure the CloudWatch agent to stream the logs to CloudWatch.

Monitoring custom metrics and sending log files using CloudWatch Agent

The agent we need to install in our operating system is called the **CloudWatch agent**. It is available for a variety of modern operating systems, from most Linux distributions such as Ubuntu and Red Hat Enterprise Linux to macOS X and Windows. You can find a list of all operating systems that are supported in the table at this URL, along with the links to download the CloudWatch agent for each one: https://docs.aws.amazon.com/AmazonCloudWatch/latest/monitoring/download-cloudwatch-agent-commandline.html.

In this chapter, we'll see the steps needed to install the CloudWatch agent on our instance.

> **Note**
>
> To follow the steps described in this section, you will need a running EC2 instance that you can connect to.
>
> You can follow the steps in *Chapter 4* to set up such an EC2 instance. Note that the following instructions assume that you are using Amazon Linux 2 as your operating system. Other Linux distributions (such as Ubuntu) might have a different default username.

To get started, follow these steps:

1. Log in to your EC2 instance by running the following command in your terminal. You'll need to fill in the details such as the path to your key file or the IP of your instance:

    ```
    ssh -i <path_to_key_file> ec2-user@<server public ip>
    ```

2. Download the installer for the CloudWatch agent. The URL depends on the operating system you are using and the Region in which your instance is running. You can find the list of download links in the URL shared in the preceding paragraphs. AWS offers two different download links: a general one and a Region-specific one. Using the Region-specific link will potentially speed up the download since the file will be retrieved from the same Region. Remember to replace the red Region placeholders with the AWS Region you are running your instance in, for example, eu-central-1.

    In this example, we'll be using the general download link for Amazon Linux 2023 and Amazon Linux 2:

    ```
    wget https://amazoncloudwatch-agent.s3.amazonaws.com/amazon_
    linux/amd64/latest/amazon-cloudwatch-agent.rpm
    ```

3. After the download is finished, we can start the installation of the package by using the following command:

```
sudo rpm -ivh amazon-cloudwatch-agent.rpm
```

4. The output of this command should look similar to the following:

```
Verifying...
############################### [100%]
Preparing...
############################### [100%]
create group cwagent, result: 0
create user cwagent, result: 0
Updating / installing...
   1:amazon-cloudwatch-agent-1.300044.
############################### [100%]
```

With the CloudWatch agent installed, we are almost ready to configure it to collect metrics. However, we haven't given our instance the correct permissions yet to transmit metrics. We will do this by creating an IAM role that has the correct permissions attached. This role will then be attached to our instance.

To do this, follow these steps:

1. Navigate to IAM by either searching for it in the AWS console or by using the following link: https://us-east-1.console.aws.amazon.com/iam/home#/home. In the navigation bar on the left, click **Roles** and then **Create role**.

2. For **Trusted entity type** (as shown in the following figure), select **AWS service**.

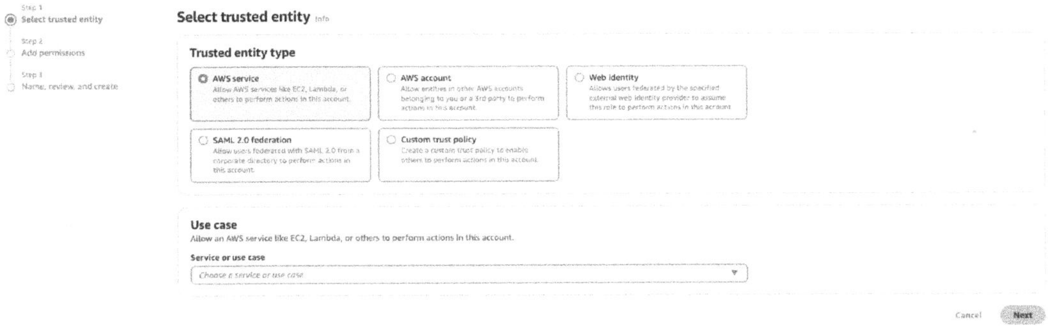

Figure 9.8 - Setting the trusted entity type for our new role

3.   Under **Use case**, in the dropdown, select **EC2** and then select the radio button next to **EC2**, as shown in the following screenshot. We do this since this role will be attached to an EC2 instance.

Use case
Allow an AWS service like EC2, Lambda, or others to perform actions in this account.

Service or use case

> EC2   ▼

Choose a use case for the specified service.
Use case
◉ EC2
   Allows EC2 instances to call AWS services on your behalf.
○ EC2 Role for AWS Systems Manager
   Allows EC2 instances to call AWS services like CloudWatch and Systems Manager on your behalf.
○ EC2 Spot Fleet Role
   Allows EC2 Spot Fleet to request and terminate Spot Instances on your behalf.
○ EC2 - Spot Fleet Auto Scaling
   Allows Auto Scaling to access and update EC2 spot fleets on your behalf.
○ EC2 - Spot Fleet Tagging
   Allows EC2 to launch spot instances and attach tags to the launched instances on your behalf.
○ EC2 - Spot Instances
   Allows EC2 Spot Instances to launch and manage spot instances on your behalf.
○ EC2 - Spot Fleet
   Allows EC2 Spot Fleet to launch and manage spot fleet instances on your behalf.
○ EC2 - Scheduled Instances
   Allows EC2 Scheduled Instances to manage instances on your behalf.

Figure 9.9 - Selection of our use case for this newly created role.

4.   Click **Next**.

5.   Under **Permissions policies**, search for CloudWatchAgentServer. You should find an AWS-managed policy with the name **CloudWatchAgentServerPolicy**. Click the checkmark next to the name, as shown in the following figure:

Add permissions Info

Permissions policies (1/1064) Info
Choose one or more policies to attach to your new role.

	Q CloudWatchAgent	✕	Filter by Type All types ▼	2 matches	‹ 1 › ⚙
☐	Policy name ☑	▲	Type	▽	Description
☐	⊞ CloudWatchAgentAdminPolicy		AWS managed		Full permissions required to use Amaz...
☑	⊞ CloudWatchAgentServerPolicy		AWS managed		Permissions required to use AmazonCl...

▶ Set permissions boundary - *optional*

                                                        Cancel   Previous   **Next**

Figure 9.10 - Selection of our permissions policy

6.   Click **Next**.

7.   Under **Role details**, you need to give your new role a name, such as Ec2InstancePolicy, as shown in the following screenshot:

Role details

Role name
Enter a meaningful name to identify this role.

Ec2InstancePolicy

Maximum 64 characters. Use alphanumeric and '+=,.@-_' characters.

Description
Add a short explanation for this role.

Allows EC2 instances to call AWS services on your behalf.

Maximum 1000 characters. Use letters (A-Z and a-z), numbers (0-9), tabs, new lines, or any of the following characters: _+=,.@-/\[]{}!e$%^*().;'"

Figure 9.11 - Naming of our new role

8. Below the name and description of our new role, you'll find the trust policy. Recall that this policy tells AWS who – or in this case, what service – can assume this role. Your trust policy should look similar to the following, which instructs IAM to allow the `ec2.amazonaws.com` service principal (which is the service principal behind the EC2 service) to call the `sts:AssumeRole` action, and thus allows it to assume this newly created role:

```
{
    "Version": "2012-10-17",
    "Statement": [
        {
            "Effect": "Allow",
            "Action": [
                "sts:AssumeRole"
            ],
            "Principal": {
                "Service": [
                    "ec2.amazonaws.com"
                ]
            }
        }
    ]
}
```

9. The next part contains the overview of permissions. In our case, as shown in the next screenshot, this only contains the AWS-managed permission called **CloudWatchAgentServerPolicy**.

Step 2: Add permissions   (Edit)

Permissions policy summary

Policy name 🗗	▲	Type	▽	Attached as	▽
CloudWatchAgentServerPolicy		AWS managed		Permissions policy	

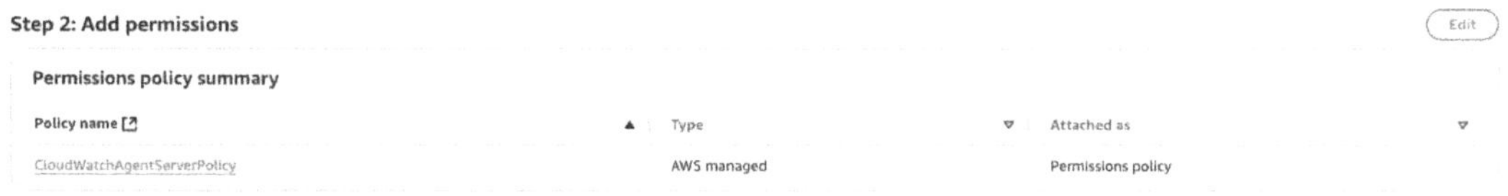

Figure 9.12 - Overview of the permissions policies attached to our role.

10. Click **Create role** at the bottom of the page.

11. With the new role created, we can attach it to our instance. To do so, go back to the details page of your EC2 instance. Here, click **Actions** and then select **Security** and **Modify IAM role**, as shown in the following screenshot:

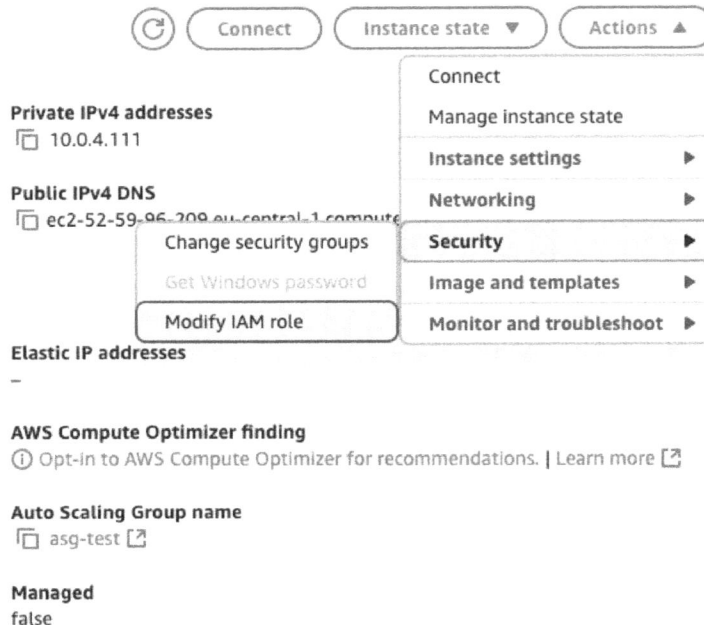

Figure 9.13 - Steps needed to attach an IAM role to this instance.

12. In the following dropdown, select the previously created role, then click **Update IAM role**, as shown in the following screenshot:

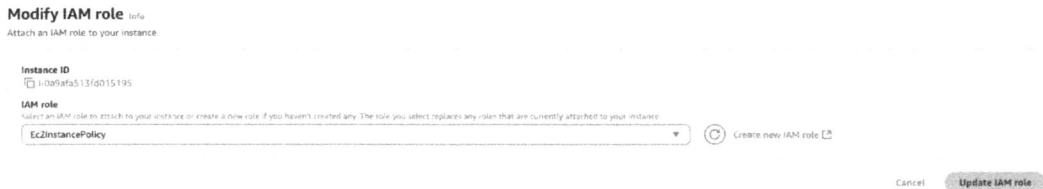

Figure 9.14 - Selection of our previously created IAM role

We now have attached a role with the necessary permissions on to our EC2 instance. Next, we can configure the CloudWatch agent to start pushing metrics and logs from our instance.

This is handled by a configuration file on the instance. AWS offers a configuration wizard that we can run to generate the configuration for our instance. Log back on to the EC2 instance to which you have previously attached the role and then follow these steps:

1. Run the following command to start the Amazon CloudWatch agent configuration wizard:

```
sudo /opt/aws/amazon-cloudwatch-agent/bin/amazon-cloudwatch-
agent-config-wizard
```

2. In the dialog, we are first asked where the agent is being run. In this case, our OS is Linux, so choice 1:

```
On which OS are you planning to use the agent?
1. linux
2. windows
3. darwin
default choice: [1]:
1
```

3. Since this instance is running in EC2, for the selection of where the instances run, we'll select option 1, which is EC2:

```
Are you using EC2 or On-Premises hosts?
1. EC2
2. On-Premises
default choice: [1]:
1
```

4. We'll then choose the default options for the following selections, so running the agent as the cwagent user, enable StatsD daemon, and have it listen on port 8125 with a collection interval of 10s (option 1) and an aggregation interval of 60s (option 4):

```
Do you want to turn on StatsD daemon?
1. yes
2. no
default choice: [1]:
1
Which port do you want StatsD daemon to listen to?
default choice: [8125]
8125
What is the collect interval for StatsD daemon?
1. 10s
2. 30s
3. 60s
default choice: [1]:
1
What is the aggregation interval for metrics collected by StatsD
daemon?
1. Do not aggregate
2. 10s
```

```
3. 30s
4. 60s
default choice: [4]:
4
```

5. Next, we'll prevent the collection of metrics from **CollectD**. CollectD is an agent that can collect application metrics but it needs to be installed in order for it to work. Since we are focused on the instance metrics from CloudWatch agents, we'll not use this feature here:

```
Do you want to monitor metrics from CollectD? WARNING: CollectD
must be installed or the Agent will fail to start
1. yes
2. no
default choice: [1]:
2
```

6. We'll then enable host-level metrics, monitor CPU metrics per core, add EC2 dimensions such as ImageId or InstanceId to the metrics where this information is available, and aggregate metrics based on InstanceId:

```
Do you want to monitor any host metrics? e.g. CPU, memory, etc.
1. yes
2. no
default choice: [1]:
1
Do you want to monitor cpu metrics per core?
1. yes
2. no
default choice: [1]:
1
Do you want to add ec2 dimensions (ImageId, InstanceId,
InstanceType, AutoScalingGroupName) into all of your metrics if
the info is available?
1. yes
2. no
default choice: [1]:
1
Do you want to aggregate ec2 dimensions (InstanceId)?
1. yes
2. no
default choice: [1]:
1
```

7. With the agent, we can increase the resolution of our metrics to a sub-minute interval. This can be useful when dealing with systems that have very spiky load patterns. In this case, the default 60s interval might not be sufficient to quickly catch a load increase. For this example, we'll keep the default value of a 60-second interval:

```
Would you like to collect your metrics at high resolution
(sub-minute resolution)? This enables sub-minute resolution for
all metrics, but you can customize for specific metrics in the
output json file.
1. 1s
2. 10s
3. 30s
4. 60s
default choice: [4]:
4
```

8. For the default metrics configuration, we'll select Advanced (Option 3). This will generate our configuration file in JSON format. The configuration shows the metrics we are now collecting. Take a look at the highlighted part in the following example, which highlights the memory metrics we are publishing as mem_used_percent. Notice how each measurement has its own interval. So, you could also gather the memory usage every 10 seconds while gathering disk metrics only every 120 seconds. In the following page, the output of other dimensions (such as disk I/O or CPU) is left out for brevity.

```
Which default metrics config do you want?
1. Basic
2. Standard
3. Advanced
4. None
default choice: [1]:
3
```

9. The agent part shows the configurations we have selected for our agent. In this case, the 60 second metrics collection interval, as well as the user that the agent should run as (cwagent in this case).

Current config as follows:

```
{
    "agent": {
        "metrics_collection_interval": 60,
        "run_as_user": "cwagent"
    },
```

10. We then find the `metrics` block. This defines all the metrics that we have configured before. The aggregated dimensions will later, in the CloudWatch interface, allow us to aggregate the values by them. For example, we can aggregate the memory usage for all of the instances.

```
"metrics": {
    "aggregation_dimensions": [
        [
            "InstanceId"
        ]
    ],
    "append_dimensions": {
        "AutoScalingGroupName":
"${aws:AutoScalingGroupName}",
        "ImageId": "${aws:ImageId}",
        "InstanceId": "${aws:InstanceId}",
        "InstanceType": "${aws:InstanceType}"
    },
```

11. The next block defines the metrics we have collected. As previously mentioned, we have abbreviated some metrics for brevity. As you can see, each metric, mem in this case, has a list of measurements. These measurements are what is actually measured. In this example, for the memory metric, we are measuring the percentage of memory used. You can also see that each metric has its own collection interval. This means that we could collect the mem_used_percent at a 5-second interval while collecting the `tcp_wait_time` (part of the `netstat` metric shown next) measurement at a 60-second interval. This gives us more flexibility when dealing with metrics that can change rapidly (like network load or memory usage) and metrics that usually only change gradually (like disk usage on a system whose primary purpose is not storage).

```
"metrics_collected": {
    // Abbreviated for brevity
    "mem": {
        "measurement": [
            "mem_used_percent"
        ],
        "metrics_collection_interval": 60
    },
    "netstat": {
        "measurement": [
```

```
                    "tcp_established",
                    "tcp_time_wait"
                ],
                "metrics_collection_interval": 60
            },
            // Left out for brevity
        }
    }
}
```

12. Select that you are satisfied with the preceding configuration (Option 1)

```
Are you satisfied with the above config? Note: it can be
manually customized after the wizard completes to add additional
items.
1. yes
2. no
default choice: [1]:
1
```

13. When asked about the existing CloudWatch agent configuration, select the no option since we are setting up the CloudWatch agent for the first time:

```
Do you have any existing CloudWatch Log Agent (http://docs.aws.
amazon.com/AmazonCloudWatch/latest/logs/AgentReference.html)
configuration file to import for migration?
1. yes
2. no
default choice: [2]:
2
```

14. With the metrics done, we can now configure our agent to send log files. Select option 1.

```
Do you want to monitor any log files?
1. yes
2. no
default choice: [1]:
1
```

15. Next, we define the path to the log files. Before we define it, let's take a quick excursion into how we can specify the path to our log files.

CloudWatch agent supports wildcards, so we can use `/var/messages/*.log` to indicate all files ending in `.log` in the directory `/var/messages`. In addition, it also supports `**` or a **super asterisk**. This can be used to match all files in a directory tree. A directory tree is all the files in a directory, as well as all subdirectories. Take a directory structure like the following one as an example. If we point the CloudWatch agent to collect all logs in `/var/logs/*.log`, it will only collect the `app.log` file. If we instead use the super asterisk and instruct the agent to collect all logs in `/var/logs/**.log`, it will go through all subdirectories, such as `httpd` in this example, and also find the `access.log` file that is under the `httpd/` directory.

```
var/
├─ logs/
│   ├─ app.log
│   ├─ httpd/
│   │   ├─ access.log
```

16. For our path, we define `/var/logs/**.log`.

```
Log file path:
/var/logs/**.log
```

17. Next, we need to define our log group name. In our example, this will be the log group we previously created, which is `/ServerLogs`.

```
Log group name:
default choice: [messages]
/ServerLogs
```

18. For the log group class, we define the same class we used when creating the log group, so STANDARD (choice 1).

```
Log group class:
1. STANDARD
2. INFREQUENT_ACCESS
default choice: [1]:
1
```

19. Next, we need to define the name of our log stream. As previously mentioned, the log stream should group logs that come from the same source, so we will usually define a name that uniquely identifies this EC2 instance.

To do this, we have a few variables available to us:

- `{instance_id}` is the ID of our instance
- `{hostname}` retrieves the hostname from EC2 metadata
- `{local_hostname}` uses the locally configured network hostname
- `{ip_address}` is the IP address of our instance

For our example, we'll use the default instance id.

```
Log stream name:
default choice: [{instance_id}]
```

20. Next, we can configure our log group retention and set it to the same value we used when setting up the log group (7 days, or choice 5).

```
Log Group Retention in days
1. -1
2. 1
3. 3
4. 5
5. 7
// Other options left out for brevity
default choice: [1]:
5
```

21. We then decline to specify any other log files to monitor by selecting choice 2, no.

```
Do you want to specify any additional log files to monitor?
1. yes
2. no
default choice: [1]:
2
```

22. We are then asked to configure X-Ray traces. X-Ray is beyond the scope of this book, so we select option 2, no, as our choice.

```
Do you want the CloudWatch agent to also retrieve X-ray traces?
1. yes
2. no
default choice: [1]:
2
```

23. The configuration wizard will now repeat the entire configuration file (which we have omitted here for brevity) and ask you to store this file in Parameter Store. This can be useful when sharing a configuration between a group of instances. For now, select no (Option 2). The program then exits and a configuration file is created:

```
Please check the above content of the config.
The config file is also located at /opt/aws/amazon-cloudwatch-
agent/bin/config.json.
Edit it manually if needed.
Do you want to store the config in the SSM parameter store?
1. yes
2. no
```

```
default choice: [1]:
2
Program exits now.
```

24. To validate that everything worked, we can use the CloudWatch agent control to fetch the configuration. This verifies the configuration and creates a symlink for the CloudWatch agent service:

```
sudo /opt/aws/amazon-cloudwatch-agent/bin/amazon-cloudwatch-
agent-ctl -a fetch-config -m ec2 -c file:/opt/aws/amazon-
cloudwatch-agent/bin/config.json -s
```

25. The output should look similar to the following. You should see a message indicating that the schema of our configuration file is valid and then that the validation has succeeded. The bold text in the following code snippet highlights the parts to pay attention to in the output.

```
****** processing amazon-cloudwatch-agent ******
// Omitted for brevity
Successfully fetched the config and saved in /opt/aws/amazon-
cloudwatch-agent/etc/amazon-cloudwatch-agent.d/file_config.json.
tmp
Start configuration validation...
2024/09/22 19:54:59 Reading json config file path: /opt/aws/
amazon-cloudwatch-agent/etc/amazon-cloudwatch-agent.d/file_
config.json.tmp ...
2024/09/22 19:54:59 I! Valid Json input schema.
// Output ommited for brevity
2024/09/22 19:54:59 Configuration validation first phase
succeeded
I! Detecting run_as_user...
// Ommited for brevity
Configuration validation second phase succeeded
Configuration validation succeeded
amazon-cloudwatch-agent has already been stopped
Created symlink /etc/systemd/system/multi-user.target.wants/
amazon-cloudwatch-agent.service → /etc/systemd/system/amazon-
cloudwatch-agent.service.
```

26. Restart the CloudWatch agent to load the new configuration by using the following command. This command has no output.

```
sudo systemctl restart amazon-cloudwatch-agent.service
```

27. You can verify that everything worked and that the agent was reloaded successfully by running the following command. The output should show **Active: active (running)**.

```
sudo systemctl status amazon-cloudwatch-agent.service
```

With the agent configured to send all of our logs to CloudWatch, you can navigate back to the log group in the instance and watch the logs from your server flow in.

Additional Information

In the previous configuration, as well as in the menu of the CloudWatch section in the AWS Console, we have seen the mention of X-Ray. X-Ray is an AWS service that allows for the tracing of requests in a microservices architecture. When dealing with an architecture like the one shown at the beginning of the chapter in *Figure 10.1*, it can be hard to correlate the logs of a user request across all systems. X-Ray, and other distributed tracing tools, solve this by attaching a unique identifier to a request. This unique ID is usually called a **trace ID**. As the request is forwarded from one service, for example, from the front-end service to the Message Service and back, that unique identifier is preserved and can be added to any logs. This way, if a user provides the trace ID, we can quickly search for all logs related to that trace across all our systems.

---

28. To verify that the CloudWatch agent is running successfully, run the following command:

```
sudo systemctl amazon-cloudwatch-agent.service
```

The output should look similar to the following:

```
• amazon-cloudwatch-agent.service - Amazon CloudWatch Agent
     Loaded: loaded (/etc/systemd/system/amazon-cloudwatch-
agent.service; enabl>
     Active: active (running) since Sun 2024-09-22 19:55:00 UTC;
1min 50s ago
   Main PID: 5097 (amazon-cloudwat)
      Tasks: 6 (limit: 1112)
     Memory: 23.6M
        CPU: 393ms
     CGroup: /system.slice/amazon-cloudwatch-agent.service
             └─5097 /opt/aws/amazon-cloudwatch-agent/bin/amazon-
cloudwatch-agen>

// Omitted for brevity
```

We can now verify that everything worked by navigating back to our CloudWatch **Metrics** overview. In the following figure, you can see a new custom namespace called **CWAgent**, which contains all the metrics we have defined in our configuration:

Figure 9.15 - Overview of our newly available custom metrics namespace

We can now also go to the logs part of the console and verify that our log group exists and after some time (it can take a few minutes for logs to show up) you should see some logs here.

With our custom metrics now available we'll next look into notifications and alarming. To do so we'll first introduce another service, **Simple Notification Service** (**SNS**).

Introduction to SNS

SNS is a service that lets you send notifications via email, text message, or webhook, based on events or via an API call. In SNS, you have three main components:

- **Topic**: A topic is used to separate messages. You could, for example, have an SNS topic for infrastructure alerts.

- **Publisher**: A publisher sends a message to a topic. Many AWS services can act as publishers for SNS topics out of the box or you can use Lambda functions to send messages.

- **Consumer**: A consumer receives all messages that are published to a topic. Consumers can be humans who are notified via email or text message, as well as automations that are invoked via a webhook or by invoking a Lambda function.

Let's start by creating a new topic that will be used to notify us of change events. To do so, follow these steps:

1. Go to the SNS service in the AWS console by searching for it or by using the following link: `https://eu-central-1.console.aws.amazon.com/sns/v3/home?region=eu-central-1#/homepage`.

2. In the left navigation bar, select **Topics** and then click **Create topics**.

3. We first need to select the type of SNS topic we want to create. At the time of writing, there are two different types of topics: **FIFO (first-in, first-out)** and **Standard**. Select **Standard** and

give the topic a name (`InfrastructureEvents`, in this example) and an optional display name, as shown in the following screenshot:

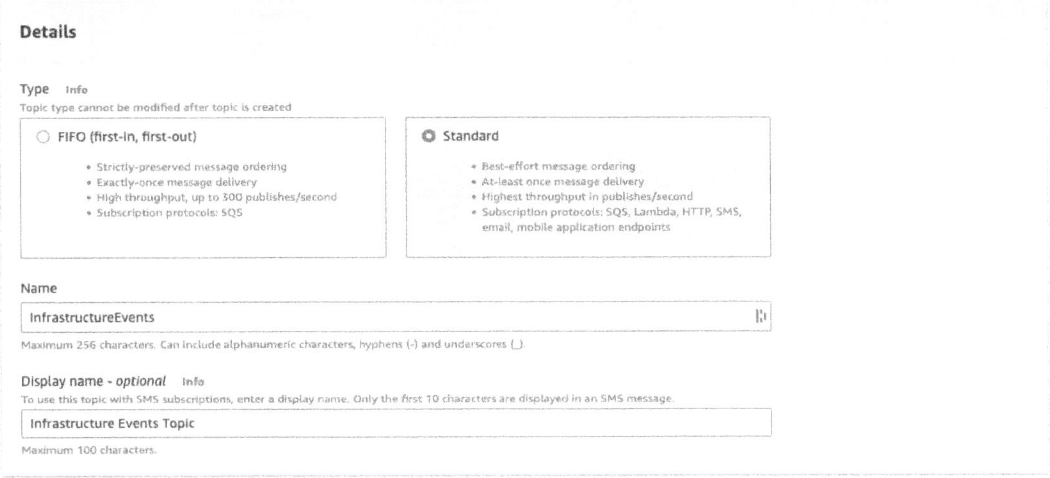

Details

Type   Info
Topic type cannot be modified after topic is created

○ FIFO (first-in, first-out)
- Strictly-preserved message ordering
- Exactly-once message delivery
- High throughput, up to 300 publishes/second
- Subscription protocols: SQS

◉ Standard
- Best-effort message ordering
- At-least once message delivery
- Highest throughput in publishes/second
- Subscription protocols: SQS, Lambda, HTTP, SMS, email, mobile application endpoints

Name

`InfrastructureEvents`

Maximum 256 characters. Can include alphanumeric characters, hyphens (-) and underscores (_).

Display name - *optional*   Info
To use this topic with SMS subscriptions, enter a display name. Only the first 10 characters are displayed in an SMS message.

`Infrastructure Events Topic`

Maximum 100 characters.

Figure 9.16 – Information needed to create a new SNS topic

> **Note**
>
> FIFO topics preserve the ordering of messages and ensure that a message will be delivered only once. This type of topic can be useful for use cases where the ordering and exactly-once delivery of a message plays an important role. Think, for example, about a banking application that handles withdrawal requests from an ATM. We'd all prefer the request to be handled in order so that we can use money that has been deposited shortly before and also that withdrawals happen only exactly once.
>
> The downside of FIFO topics is their reduced throughput. Standard topics in us-east-1 can support up to 30,000 messages per second while FIFO topics can only handle 3,000 messages per second. You can learn more about these limitations (and also see the numbers for your preferred Region) here: `https://docs.aws.amazon.com/general/latest/gr/sns.html`.
>
> In addition, at the time of writing in September 2024, FIFO topics only support **Simple Queue Service (SQS)** as the target for sending notifications.

4. Once we have the topic created, we can create a new subscription. This is how we associate a new consumer with our topic.

   To do so, on the overview page of your topic, select the **Create subscription** button.

5. When creating a subscription, we'll need to select a protocol. In this case, we want email notifications, and we'll thus select **Email** for **Protocol**. For **Endpoint**, enter a valid email address of yours. Be aware that you'll have to confirm the subscription. See the following screenshot for an example configuration:

Create subscription

Details

Topic ARN

Q arn:aws:sns:eu-central-1: ▇▇▇▇▇ :InfrastructureEvents   ✕

Protocol
The type of endpoint to subscribe

Email   ▼

Endpoint
An email address that can receive notifications from Amazon SNS.

▇▇▇▇▇ @ ▇▇▇▇   ⌸

ⓘ After your subscription is created, you must confirm it. Info

Figure 9.17 – Configuration for our new subscription

6. Click the **Create subscription** button at the bottom of the page. You'll need to check your emails for one that contains a confirmation link to open.

With the topic created and our email subscription activated, let's create an alert that gets triggered from our metrics and sends us an email.

Creating a CloudWatch metric alert that pushes a notification to SNS

In this section, we'll now set up a CloudWatch alarm that monitors a metric and then pushes a notification into SNS. To do this, follow these steps:

1. Navigate to the CloudWatch service by either searching for CloudWatch in the AWS console and then selecting **All Alarms** in the left navigation or going to the following link: `https://eu-central-1.console.aws.amazon.com/cloudwatch/home?region=eu-central-1#alarmsV2`.

2. This page lists all the alarms you have enabled. To create a new alarm, click the **Create alarm** button on the right.

3. In the following agent, you'll have to first select a metric. Click the **Select metric** button and then choose the **CWAgent** namespace. You'll then see all the aggregations we have configured in the CloudWatch agent. Select **InstanceId**, as shown in the following screenshot:

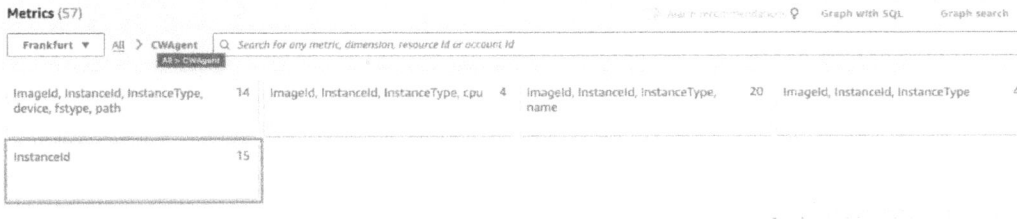

Figure 9.18 – Selecting the aggregation under which our metric will be selected

4. In the next table, you can find all available metrics for this instance. Find and select the **mem_used_percent** metric.

Figure 9.19 – Selection of the metric used for this alarm

5. Next, we configure the condition. Under **Metric**, you can select the statistical function (in this example, **Average**) you want applied to the metric. There are other functions, such as **p90** available. You can also configure the period over which the function will be applied. With the configuration shown in the following screenshot, the average will be taken over a 5-minute window:

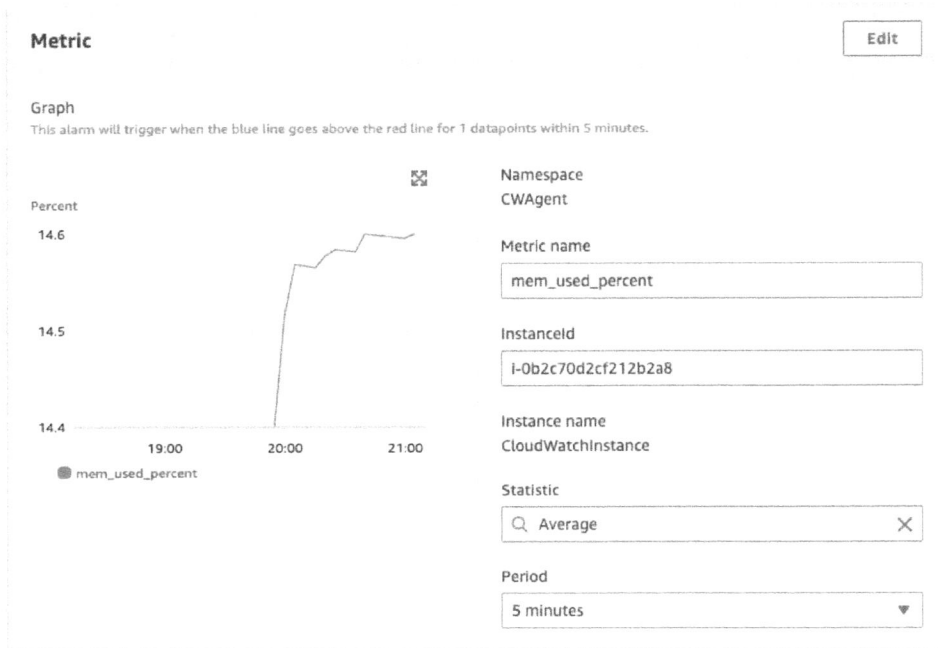

Figure 9.20 – Configuration for the metric in our alert

6. Next, we can define the condition that needs to be met for our alert to trigger. Here, we define a **Static** threshold type. This allows us to configure a simple threshold number. We then define that this alert should trigger when our value is greater than our threshold value of 14. Note that this threshold is set deliberately low so that we can immediately see the alarm being triggered. Under **Additional configuration**, we can set the number of datapoints that need to be in breach in order for the alert to be triggered. In this example, we will keep this at **1 out of 1**:

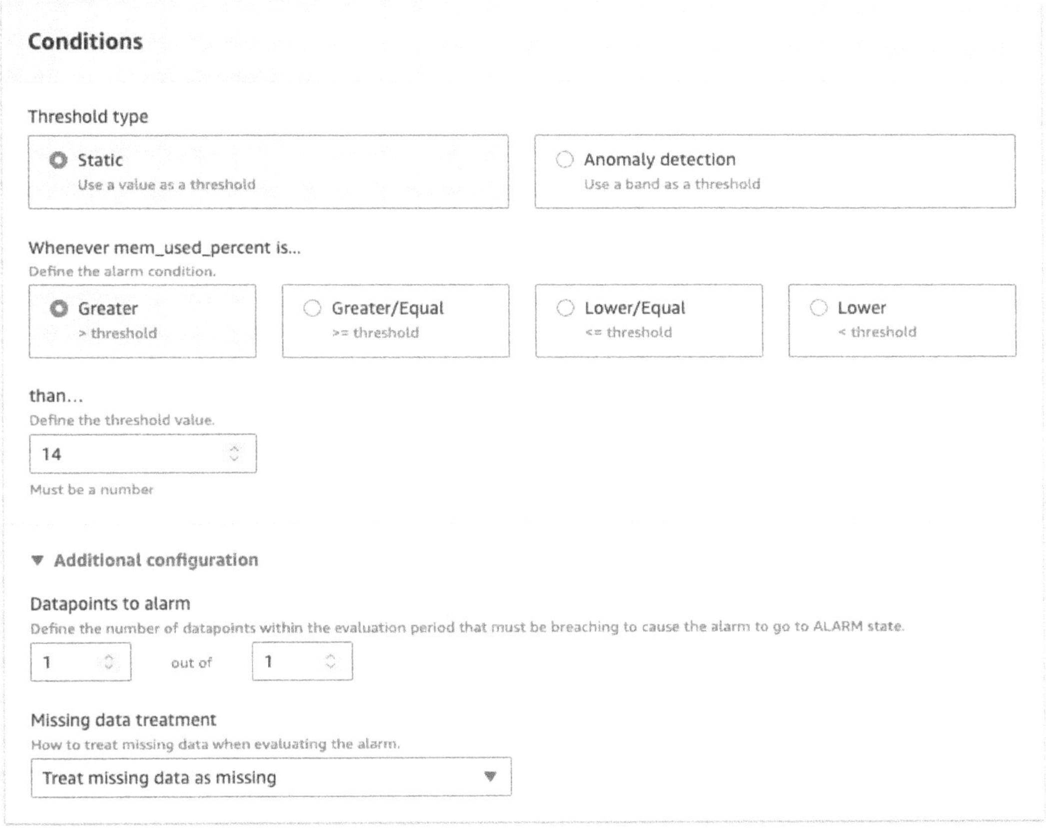

Figure 9.21 – Conditions for our threshold

7. Next, we define where our data is sent. We select to trigger the notification when the status changes to **In alarm** (so when the metric is outside of the threshold) and we then select our previously created SNS topic.

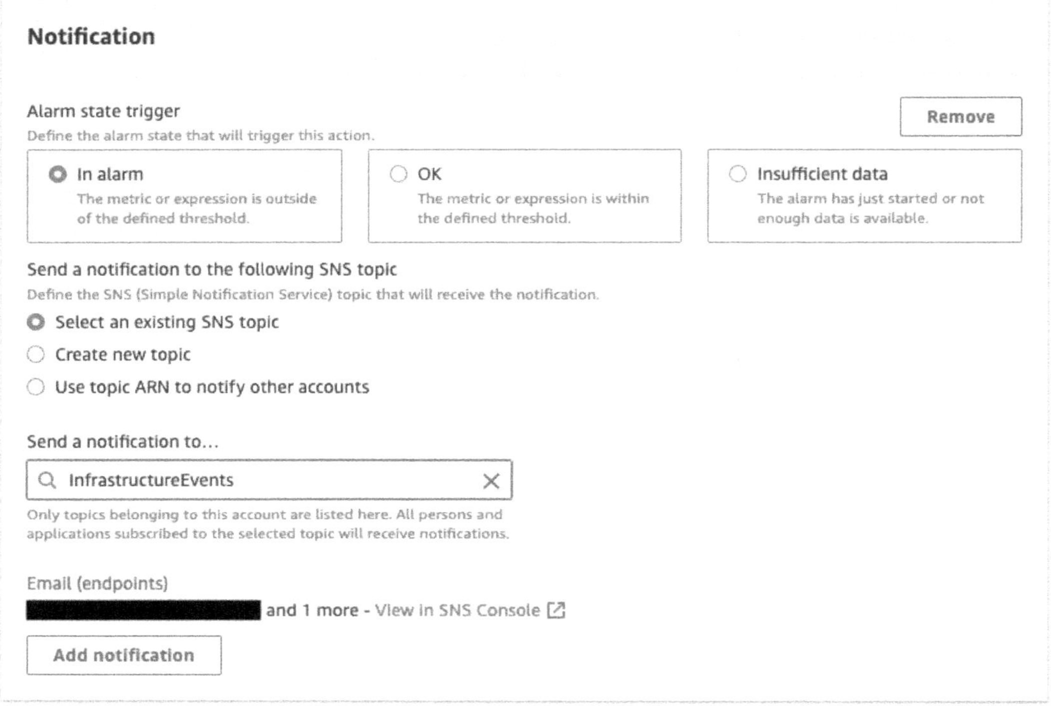

Notification

Alarm state trigger
Define the alarm state that will trigger this action.   Remove

○ **In alarm**   ○ OK   ○ Insufficient data
The metric or expression is outside   The metric or expression is within   The alarm has just started or not
of the defined threshold.   the defined threshold.   enough data is available.

Send a notification to the following SNS topic
Define the SNS (Simple Notification Service) topic that will receive the notification.
○ Select an existing SNS topic
○ Create new topic
○ Use topic ARN to notify other accounts

Send a notification to...

🔍 InfrastructureEvents   ✕

Only topics belonging to this account are listed here. All persons and
applications subscribed to the selected topic will receive notifications.

Email (endpoints)
███████████████ and 1 more - View in SNS Console ↗

Add notification

Figure 9.22 – Settings for our notifications to SNS

8. Click **Next** and define a name for your alert, for example, `MemUsageAlert`. Then, click **Create alert**

Once your alarm has been triggered, you'll receive an email containing the details of your alert.

With email alerts, we can already have the alert sent to a common mailing list that everyone on the DevOps team is a part of. However, we can also go a step further. Most companies these days use some sort of collaboration/chat platform. Wouldn't it be better to have all of our alerts sent to this common platform?

Sending SNS notifications to Slack

Email is supported as a native consumer for SNS notifications. Common enterprise communications platforms such as Slack or Microsoft Teams are not supported. So, in this example, we'll work around this limitation by using a Lambda function.

> **Note**
> In this example, we're only forwarding messages via our Lambda function. In *Chapter 10*, we'll see how to take automated action upon receiving a notification.

To do this, we'll first have to create a Slack app. In order to follow this section, you'll need a Slack account and workspace. A free workspace/account is sufficient.

In Slack, we'll use a concept called **webhooks**. A webhook is a space-specific URL to which we can send a JSON payload. This payload contains the message we want to send.

Follow these steps to set up a webhook for Slack:

1. Navigate to `https://api.slack.com/apps/new` and select **From scratch** when asked what type of app you want to create.

2. In the next dialog, give your app a name and select the workspace to which the messages should be sent.

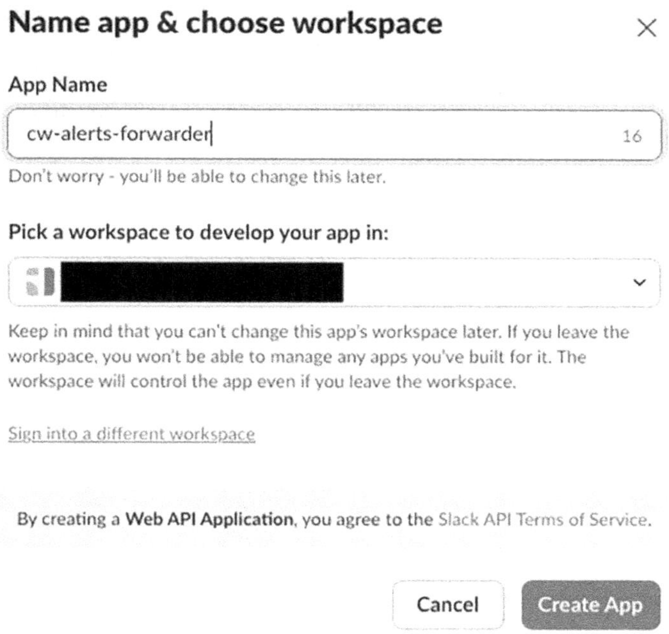

Figure 9.23 – Naming our app

3. On the overview page of your new application, select **Incoming Webhooks** and, at the top right, toggle the button next to **Activate Webhook** to *on*. At the bottom of the page, you'll then find an **Add New Webhook to Workspace** button. Click this button.

4. You'll then be asked to select the channel to which the message will be posted. Select the channel from the dropdown menu and click **Allow**.

5. With this done, you can now see the webhook URL. Copy this URL as we'll need it in our Lambda function.

Next, we will write a small Lambda function that takes an SNS notification and forwards it to Slack.

Writing a forwarding Lambda function

With our webhook set up and ready, we can now write the Lambda function that will be invoked by SNS, which then pushes our notifications to Slack.

Follow these steps to write the Lambda function:

1. Navigate to the Lambda console by either searching for the Lambda service in the AWS console or by going to the following URL: `https://eu-central-1.console.aws.amazon.com/lambda/home?region=eu-central-1#/functions`.

2. Click on **Create function** at the top right and select **Author from scratch**. For **Basic information**, give your function a name (for example, `SlackForwarder`) and select the latest Python version (at the time of writing, this is Python 3.12) as the runtime. For **Architecture**, select **arm64** to use the cost-efficient graviton CPUs for our runtime. Then, click **Create function**.

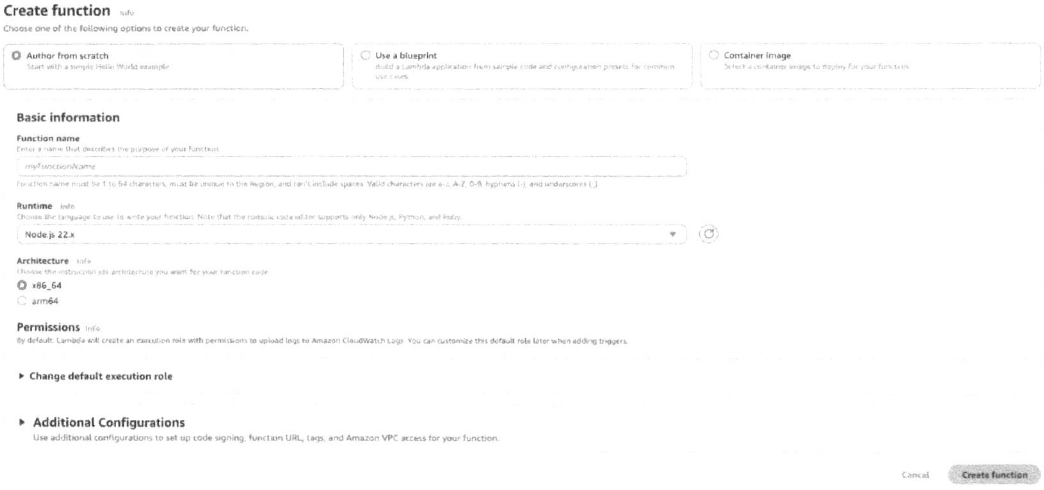

Figure 9.24 – Basic configuration of our Lambda function

3. Next, we need to write the code for our Lambda function. AWS provides example Lambda functions for many different chat applications at the following URL: `https://repost.aws/knowledge-center/sns-lambda-webhooks-chime-slack-teams`.

We'll be using the code provided for the Slack integration under **Example Python code snippet for Slack** and modify it. The sample snippet hard-codes the webhook URL and channel name. In our version, these will be read from the environment variables.

4. Open the code source by selecting the **Code** tab in the Lambda console and then type the following code. All modifications are marked in bold. We import the `os` package to get access to environment variables and then pull the `SLACK_WEBHOOK` and `SLACK_CHANNEL` environment variables. Before the definition of the handler, we then check that neither of these two variables is `None`, which indicates that they have not been set properly:

```python
import urllib3
import json
import os
http = urllib3.PoolManager()
SLACK_HOOK = os.environ.get("SLACK_WEBHOOK", None)
SLACK_CHANNEL = os.environ.get("SLACK_CHANNEL", None)
if not SLACK_HOOK or not SLACK_CHANNEL:
    raise Exception("Missing Slack hook or slack channel")
def lambda_handler(event, context):
    url = SLACK_HOOK
    msg = {
        "channel": SLACK_CHANNEL,
        "username": "WEBHOOK_USERNAME",
        "text": event["Records"][0]["Sns"]["Message"],
        "icon_emoji": "",
    }
    encoded_msg = json.dumps(msg).encode("utf-8")
    resp = http.request("POST", url, body=encoded_msg)
    print(
        {
            "message": event["Records"][0]["Sns"]["Message"],
            "status_code": resp.status,
            "response": resp.data,
        }
    )
```

5. The following screenshot shows the source code in the editor and also highlights the **Deploy** button that needs to be pressed to publish a new version of the Lambda function:

Figure 9.25 – Source code and the Deploy button for publishing a new version

6. We now need to set our environment variables. Click the **Configuration** tab and then select **Environment variables** in the left navigation, as shown in the following screenshot:

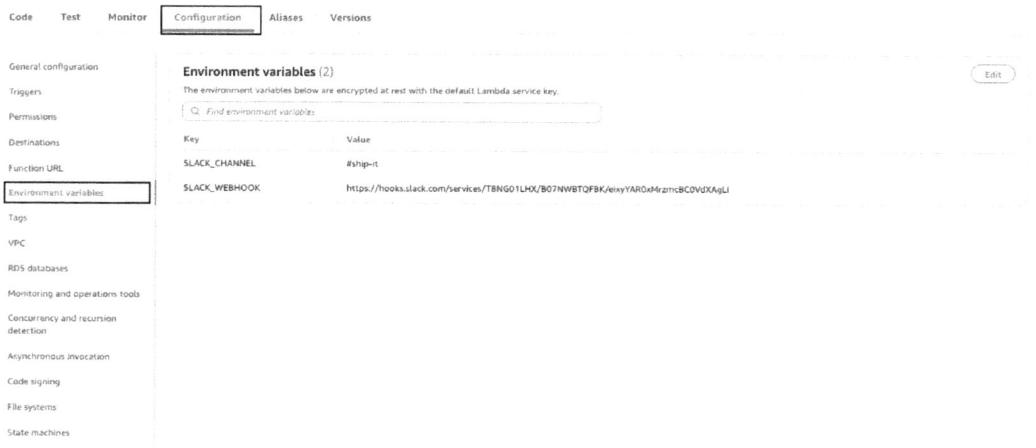

Figure 9.26 – Setting environment variables for our Lambda function

7. Click **Edit** and then **Add environment variable** to set the two environment variables with the channel name and webhook URL you previously got from Slack.

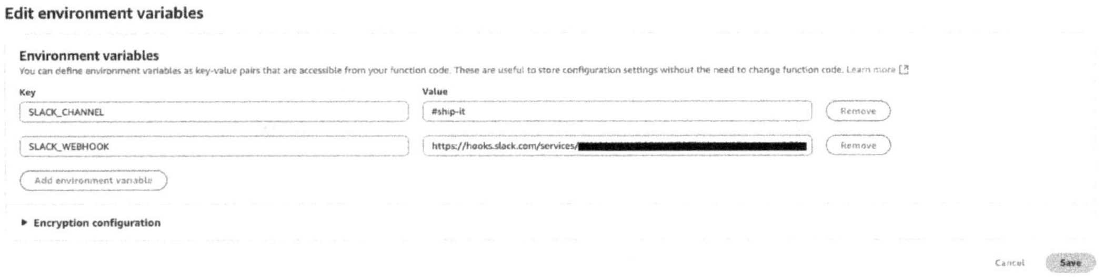

Edit environment variables

Environment variables
You can define environment variables as key-value pairs that are accessible from your function code. These are useful to store configuration settings without the need to change function code. Learn more

Key	Value	
SLACK_CHANNEL	#ship-it	Remove
SLACK_WEBHOOK	https://hooks.slack.com/services/	Remove

Add environment variable

▶ **Encryption configuration**

Cancel   Save

Figure 9.27 – Setting the values of our environment variables

8. Finally, we need to trigger the Lambda function from our SNS topic. Click the **Add trigger** button, as shown in the following screenshot:

SlackForwarder

Throttle   Copy ARN   Actions ▼

▼ Function overview   Info

Export to Infrastructure Composer   Download ▼

Diagram   Template

SlackForwarder

Layers   (0)

Description
-

Last modified
7 months ago

Function ARN
📋 arn:aws:lambda:eu-central-1: function:SlackForwarder

+ Add trigger

+ Add destination

Function URL   Info
-

Figure 9.28 – The button to add a new trigger such as an SNS topic

9. In the dropdown, search for and select **SNS** as the trigger source and then select the SNS topic we previously created.

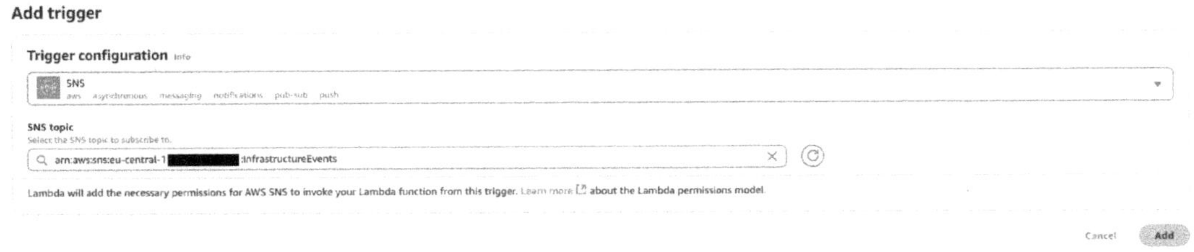

Add trigger

Trigger configuration   Info

SNS
arn   asynchronous   messaging   notifications   pub-sub   push   ▼

SNS topic
Select the SNS topic to subscribe to.

🔍 arn:aws:sns:eu-central-1:   :InfrastructureEvents   ✕   ⟳

Lambda will add the necessary permissions for AWS SNS to invoke your Lambda function from this trigger. Learn more about the Lambda permissions model.

Cancel   Add

Figure 9.29 – SNS topic configuration as our trigger source

With this, we'll now receive notifications on Slack and via email whenever our alert is triggered.

Summary

Monitoring is a critical part of operating any type of infrastructure. With the dynamic nature of AWS, we can use CloudWatch to proactively monitor and be alerted when our infrastructure metrics cross a certain threshold. We got a quick overview of the important terminology and components of CloudWatch for logging, such as log groups, log classes, retention periods, and log streams.

We then covered, based on the example of EC2, how CloudWatch can be used out of the box to monitor metrics exposed by AWS services. Afterwards, we set up the CloudWatch agent to get more detailed metrics from our application, as well as how we can stream the log files from our instance to AWS.

After a short introduction to SNS, we then configured our first topic that was notified when our infrastructure triggered a custom alert. We then saw how we could use a Lambda function to forward infrastructure alerts to Slack.

In the next chapter, we will cover another important aspect of operating in the cloud: the techniques and services needed to build a centralized backup for our cloud-deployed solutions.

10

Centralizing Cloud Backup Solutions

The importance of backups is well understood in the modern IT world. Whenever our IT system is dealing with data, we must ask the question: *What happens if we lose this data?* Depending on the answer, we'll choose to create a backup from our data source that enables us to restore the data. *When* and *what* to back up is a discussion that is mainly decided by the business requirements of the application you are operating. But the *how* is often a critical task when setting up the infrastructure for a new or existing application.

This chapter will explore a few ways that backups can be implemented within the context of AWS. We'll first discuss why we are backing up data, before going deeper into **AWS Backup**, a backup service provided by AWS. In AWS Backup, we'll use Terraform to automate the creation of a backup policy and see how we can use tags to automatically add EBS volumes to the previously created backup policy.

We'll then see how we can set up life cycle policies to store old files – such as old backups – in a cheaper storage tier of S3 called Glacier. Finally, we are going to explore the concept of bunker accounts, which can be useful to safeguard your backups.

In this chapter, we're going to cover the following main topics:

- Introduction to the backup offerings in AWS – in particular, AWS Backup
- Automating the creation of backup plans and policies
- Exploring bunker accounts for safeguarding our backups

So, let's get started!

Technical requirements

Before following this chapter's tutorials, please create an AWS account for yourself. You can sign up at `https://aws.amazon.com`. A basic understanding of AWS – for example, what a service is – will be beneficial.

You'll need a working installation and a basic understanding of Terraform when running through the code samples.

All scripts from this chapter can be found in this book's GitHub repository:

`https://github.com/PacktPublishing/AWS-for-System-Administrators-Second-Edition`

The CiA video for this chapter can be found at `https://packt.link/AkfsG`

Backups in AWS

When dealing with solutions in AWS, we quite often have multiple services involved. With the topic of backups, this can lead to some difficulty. While in the old data center world we might just take periodic snapshot data of all our servers and call it a day, in AWS, our data is often spread across multiple services.

Some data might be stored in a relational database in RDS, some on EBS volumes attached to a subset of our servers, some other data stored in a NoSQL database such as DynamoDB, and some data – such as image uploads – on an S3 bucket.

This spread of data can lead to complex backup solutions since each of these services provides its own way of backing up data.

In EBS, we can create periodic snapshots of our volumes. S3 lets us replicate entire buckets or enable versioning to allow us to jump back to a previous version of a file. RDS also lets us take snapshots that can then be stored on S3.

Creating backups with AWS Backup

With the variety of backup methods available in the different services, it makes sense for there to be a centralized service we can use to configure our backups. In AWS, this service is AWS Backup. With this service, we can create and manage central backup plans that allow us to take backups at varying times and across multiple types of resources from S3 buckets to EBS volumes.

Before jumping in and creating our first backup, let's first review some key concepts within AWS Backup:

- **Vault**: Every backup is stored in a vault. This vault is a container in which all our backups are stored. You can think of a vault like a safebox into which our belongings are deposited for safekeeping.

- **Backup plan**: This contains the schedule on which the backups are created, the target vault to store the backups in, as well as the collection of resources that should be included.

- **Resource**: This is an AWS resource, such as an EBS volume or an S3 bucket, that should be included in a backup job. Resources can be included in a backup plan by using resource selections. A resource selection defines a condition – for example, a resource with a certain tag attached to it. If a resource matches this condition, it will be automatically included in the backup plan.

- **Backup job**: An asynchronous job that performs the actual backup operation.

A note on storage

AWS Backup uses incremental backups. This means that only for the first run on a resource will a full copy be performed. Afterward, only the incremental changes to the resource are stored. This allows us to make frequent backups while keeping the cost of storage low.

AWS Backup – at the time of writing in May 2025 – supports Amazon S3, Amazon EBS, Amazon EFS, Amazon RDS, Amazon DynamoDB, and many more services and their resources for backup. To get a complete list of services and resources that are supported, you can use the following link: `https://docs.aws.amazon.com/aws-backup/latest/devguide/whatisbackup.html#supported-resources`.

Automating the creation of backups with Terraform and tags

We have seen the core components of the AWS Backup service. But how can we automate the creation of backups? In this section, we are going to first use Terraform to create a new backup vault and backup plan. The backup plan will contain two backup rules that create a daily and a weekly backup – each of them with different retention periods. Together with tags, we can thus automate the creation of backups for our resources.

As a test, we'll then use Terraform to create a new EBS volume with the corresponding tags to test our backup policy.

To create a new backup vault and policy in Terraform, follow these steps:

1. Create a new directory called `backup_plans` and navigate into it using the following commands:

    ```
    mkdir backup_plans
    cd backup_plans
    ```

2. In the new directory, create a new file called `main.tf` and open it with a text editor such as Notepad++ or Visual Studio Code.

3. In the file, we are going to first define the provider block that tells Terraform what Region to use. In this example, we are going to create the provider to use the `eu-central-1` (Frankfurt) Region. Remember which Region you selected here when later checking for the backup vault and plans in the console:

    ```
    provider "aws" {
      region = "eu-central-1"
    }
    ```

4. Next, we can create a new backup vault. We are going to give it the name `tf-backup-vault`:

    ```
    resource "aws_backup_vault" "backup_vault" {
      name = "tf-backup-vault"
    }
    ```

5. With the vault in place, we can start with the creation of our backup plan. We'll start by giving it a name – `prod-ebs-backups`, in this case. Ideally, your names should be chosen such that they explain what this backup plan (or any other resource for that matter) does:

    ```
    resource "aws_backup_plan" "prod_ebs_backups" {
      name = "prod-ebs-backups"
    ```

6. Next, we define our rule. A rule is composed of a name, for example, `daily_ebs_backup_rule`. We also need to define a target vault – identified by the vault's name and a schedule. Schedules in AWS Backups are written using the syntax for cron jobs. In this example, we are going to create a backup at 3 a.m. UTC every day. The corresponding cron syntax is `cron(0 3 ? * * *)`. Since the size of these backups can accumulate, we also define a life cycle policy that will delete our daily backups after seven days:

    ```
    rule {
        rule_name         = "daily_ebs_backup_rule"
        target_vault_name = aws_backup_vault.backup_vault.name
        schedule          = "cron(0 3 ? * * *)"
        lifecycle {
          delete_after = 7
        }
      }
    ```

7. We'll do a similar rule for our weekly EBS backups. Notice how the life cycle has changed to delete these backups after 30 days instead of 7. Also, the cron expression for the schedule has changed:

```
rule {
    rule_name          = "weekly_ebs_backup_rule"
    target_vault_name = aws_backup_vault.backup_vault.name
    schedule           = "cron(0 3 ? * 1 *)"
    lifecycle {
      delete_after = 30
    }
}
```

8. With our rules created and our backup plan complete, we need to allow the AWS Backup service to access resources in our account. To do this, we first need to create a new role that allows the `backup.amazonaws.com` service principal to assume our newly created role:

```
resource "aws_iam_role" "backup_role" {
  name = "aws-backup-service-role"
  assume_role_policy = jsonencode({
    Version = "2012-10-17"
    Statement = [
      {
        Action = "sts:AssumeRole"
        Effect = "Allow"
        Principal = {
          Service = "backup.amazonaws.com"
        }
      }
    ]
  })
}
```

9. So far, AWS Backup can access (or assume) this role – but the role itself does not have any rights to do anything, such as accessing our EBS volumes to create the backups. To allow this, we need to attach an IAM policy to the role. In this example, we are going to rely on the AWS-managed policy called `AWSBackupServiceRolePolicyForBackup`. To do this in Terraform, we are using an IAM role policy attachment resource that references the ARN of the AWS-managed policy and our previously created role name:

```
resource "aws_iam_role_policy_attachment" "backup_policy" {
  policy_arn = "arn:aws:iam::aws:policy/service-role/
AWSBackupServiceRolePolicyForBackup"
  role       = aws_iam_role.backup_role.name
}
```

Additional information

If you want to have a look at what kind of access this managed policy has, you can find the JSON policy document at the following link: `https://docs.aws.amazon.com/aws-managed-policy/latest/reference/AWSBackupServiceRolePolicyForBackup.html`.

---

10. With our backup plan configured, we can now create the new vault and backup policy. To do this, we first need to initialize the Terraform working directory using the `init` command. Your output should look like the following:

```
terraform init
Initializing the backend...
Initializing provider plugins...
- Reusing previous version of hashicorp/aws from the dependency
lock file
- Using previously-installed hashicorp/aws v5.73.0
Terraform has been successfully initialized!
```

11. Next, apply the changes using `terraform apply`. Terraform will show you the resources it plans to create. You should recognize some, such as the backup vault or the IAM role:

```
terraform apply
Terraform used the selected providers to generate the following
execution plan.
Resource actions are indicated with the following symbols:
  + create
Terraform will perform the following actions:
  # aws_backup_plan.prod_ebs_backups will be created
  + resource "aws_backup_plan" "prod_ebs_backups" {
      + arn      = (known after apply)
      + id       = (known after apply)
      + name     = "prod-ebs-backups"
      + tags_all = (known after apply)
      + version  = (known after apply)
      + rule {
# rest omitted for brevity
Plan: 3 to add, 0 to change, 0 to destroy.
Do you want to perform these actions?
  Terraform will perform the actions described above.
  Only 'yes' will be accepted to approve.
  Enter a value: yes
aws_backup_vault.backup_vault: Creating...
# Omitted for brevity
Apply complete! Resources: 3 added, 0 changed, 0 destroyed.
```

After Terraform has been applied, we can navigate to our AWS Management Console and search for the AWS Backup service. Under **Backup plans**, we'll now find the newly created **prod-ebs-backups** plan.

The following screenshot shows the details view of this backup plan, including its two associated backup rules.

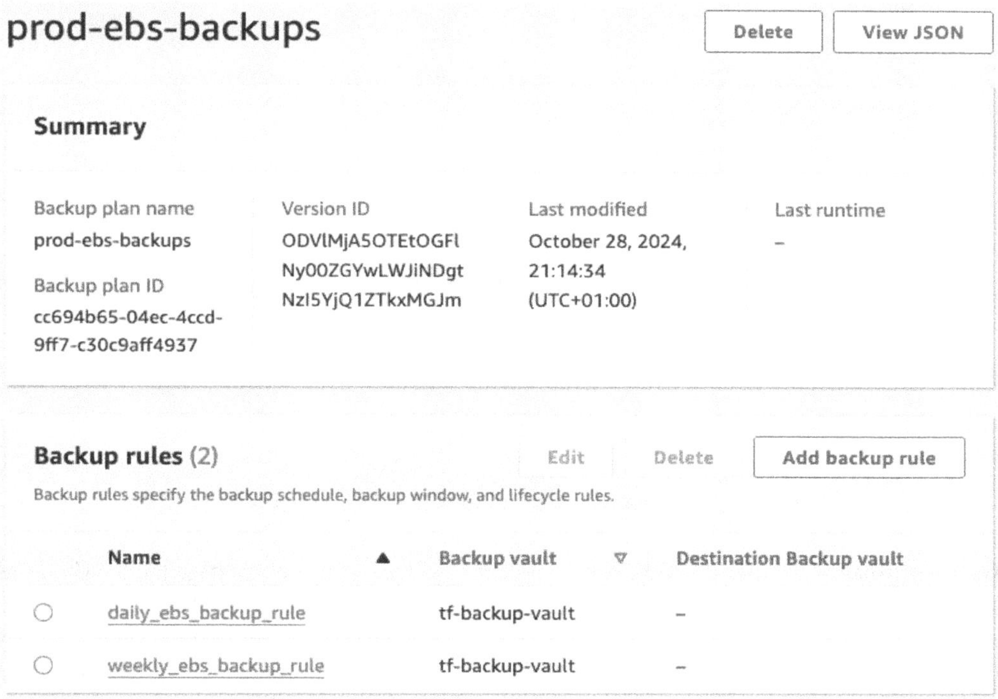

prod-ebs-backups

| Delete | View JSON |

Summary

Backup plan name	Version ID	Last modified	Last runtime
prod-ebs-backups	ODVlMjA5OTEtOGFl Ny00ZGYwLWJiNDgt NzI5YjQ1ZTkxMGJm	October 28, 2024, 21:14:34 (UTC+01:00)	–
Backup plan ID cc694b65-04ec-4ccd-9ff7-c30c9aff4937			

Backup rules (2)

| Edit | Delete | Add backup rule |

Backup rules specify the backup schedule, backup window, and lifecycle rules.

Name ▲	Backup vault ▽	Destination Backup vault
○ daily_ebs_backup_rule	tf-backup-vault	–
○ weekly_ebs_backup_rule	tf-backup-vault	–

Figure 10.1 – Details view of the backup plan

We can also click on one of the backup rules and see the details for the rule itself. The following screenshot shows the details of the weekly EBS backup rule we created using Terraform.

You can see the result of the schedule cron expression within the **Frequency** column, as well as the result of our life cycle configuration under **Total retention period**.

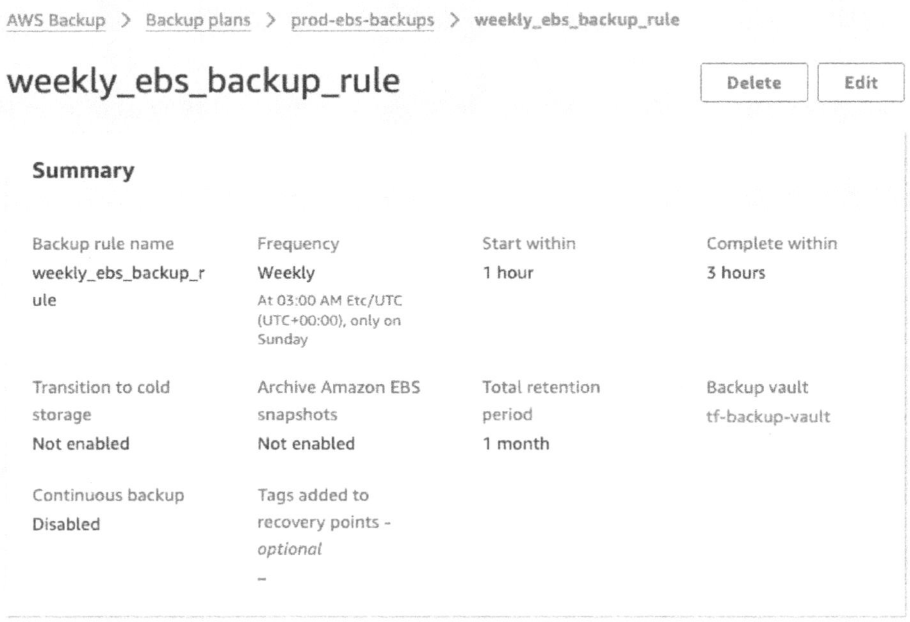

AWS Backup > Backup plans > prod-ebs-backups > weekly_ebs_backup_rule

weekly_ebs_backup_rule   Delete   Edit

Summary

Backup rule name	Frequency	Start within	Complete within
weekly_ebs_backup_r ule	Weekly At 03:00 AM Etc/UTC (UTC+00:00), only on Sunday	1 hour	3 hours

Transition to cold storage	Archive Amazon EBS snapshots	Total retention period	Backup vault
Not enabled	Not enabled	1 month	tf-backup-vault

Continuous backup	Tags added to recovery points - *optional*		
Disabled	–		

Figure 10.2 – Details view of our weekly EBS backup rule

The **Start within** and **Complete within** times you can also see on the details page tell us when the backup will be started and completed. Just because we define it to run at 3 a.m. UTC time, does not mean that it will start at exactly that moment. Rather, there is a one-hour time window (from 3 a.m. to 4 a.m.) in which the backup will start and a three-hour time window in which the backup completes.

> **Additional information**
>
> Backup jobs can fail – for example, due to the underlying volume being removed. You can find an example of how to set up a notification (using SNS) using the following link: `https://repost.aws/knowledge-center/backup-eventbridge-notifications`.

We have now successfully created a new backup vault, as well as weekly and daily rules to run our backup. But what about resources to back up? This is where the `aws_backup_selection` resource in Terraform comes into play, which we'll now use to automatically back up all EBS volumes with a specific tag.

Follow these steps to create a new AWS backup selection and an exemplary EBS volume:

1. Open up the previously created `main.tf` file. We'll add a few more resources to the end of it.

2. Start by defining the `aws_backup_selection` resource. We are going to give it a name (`ebs-backup-selection`, in this example), the ID of the backup plan we want this selection to be associated with, and the IAM role ARN we want this selection to use. Notice that this IAM role will need access to the resources that you want to back up. We have granted this by associating the `AWSBackupServiceRolePolicyForBackup` managed policy with our role. This policy contains (among others) access rights to create and copy snapshots of our EBS volumes. If you write your own role policy, make sure to include the required access rights:

    ```
    resource "aws_backup_selection" "ebs_backup_selection" {
      name         = "ebs-backup-selection"
      iam_role_arn = aws_iam_role.backup_role.arn
      plan_id      = aws_backup_plan.prod_ebs_backups.id
    ```

3. So far, we haven't automated the selection. This can be done using a `selection_tag` block. In this block, we define the type, `STRINGEQUALS`, to check that the key and value exactly match our defined values, and then the name of the key and the value of the tag that our resource needs in order to be associated with this selection. In this example, we are going to use a key named `ProdBackup` and a value of `true`:

    ```
      selection_tag {
        type  = "STRINGEQUALS"
        key   = "ProdBackup"
        value = "true"
      }
    }
    ```

4. To now test this setup, we'll also create a new EBS volume. The volume will have a total storage volume of 50 GB, be encrypted, and be of type `gp3`. Remember to adjust the name of the **Availability Zone (AZ)** you are creating this resource in in case you have chosen a different Region, such as `us-east-1`:

    ```
    resource "aws_ebs_volume" "example_volume" {
      availability_zone = "eu-central-1a"
      size              = 50  # Size in GiB
      type              = "gp3"  # General Purpose SSD
      encrypted         = true
    ```

5. So far, this EBS volume is not tagged and thus not properly associated with our backup plan. To do so, we need to add a tag with the `ProdBackup` key and a value of `true` to our resource. In this example, we are also adding a `Name` tag with the value `example-volume`. This name is not relevant to the backup selection process:

```
tags = {
  Name     = "example-volume"
  ProdBackup = "true"
}
}
```

6. With our selection created and our example EBS volume created in Terraform, we now need to apply these changes to our infrastructure. In order to do so, we need to run the `apply` command again:

`terraform apply`

After the successful application of our new version of the Terraform code, we can navigate back to our backup plan in the AWS Management Console. Under **Resource assignments**, we can find the newly created **ebs-backup-selection**. The following screenshot shows the resource assignment in the backup plan overview.

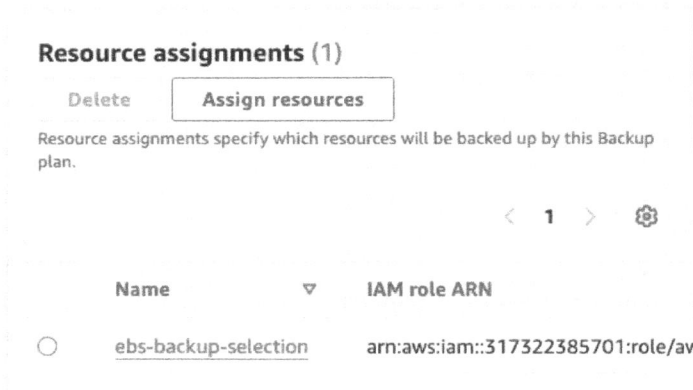

Resource assignments (1)

| Delete | Assign resources |

Resource assignments specify which resources will be backed up by this Backup plan.

‹ **1** › ⚙

	Name	▽	IAM role ARN
○	ebs-backup-selection		arn:aws:iam::317322385701:role/aw

Figure 10.3 – Resource selection in the AWS Management Console

With this, we have now automated the creation, modification, and deletion of our backup vault and policy using Terraform. By using the backup selection feature and tags, we can now automate the creation of backups.

S3 life cycle policies to transition data into S3 Glacier

A common trade-off when dealing with backups is the cost of storage. In theory, we would like to keep our backups forever; however, this would lead to an ever-increasing amount of data that we need to pay for. The reality is also that backups usually lose their value after some time. It is more common to access and restore a backup that was created seven days ago than it is to access a backup that was created seven years ago.

Especially in a disaster recovery case, we usually realize that there is an issue with our system and that the data needs to be restored in a shorter timeframe. Still, there are sometimes requirements – such as compliance rules – that require us to keep data or a backup of data for long periods of time.

One way to optimize storage costs is by using a purpose-built storage service such as Amazon S3. Instead of keeping a file on an EBS volume that is constantly backed up, we can keep the same file in S3.

S3 offers different storage classes. In this chapter, we'll briefly introduce four of them before showing you how to create a life cycle policy that rotates unaccessed items from one storage tier to another.

S3 storage classes

Storage classes in S3 define the price as well as performance metrics and resiliency of the data stored in it. By using the most suitable storage class for your requirements, you can lower the cost of your S3 storage.

A list of all storage classes, as well as a performance chart, is available at this link: `https://aws.amazon.com/s3/storage-classes/`. We will introduce the S3 Standard, S3 Standard-IA, S3 One Zone-IA, and S3 Glacier Instant Retrieval storage classes.

> **Additional information**
>
> If you are interested in the inner workings of S3, you can find a blog post called *Building and operating a pretty big storage system called S3* (Andy Warfield, 2023, *All Things Distributed* blog, `https://www.allthingsdistributed.com/2023/07/building-and-operating-a-pretty-big-storage-system.html`). If you are interested in the design principles of distributed systems, this is a fascinating read.

The first storage class is **S3 Standard**. This is the default storage class and is great for frequently accessed data that has a requirement for low latency and high throughput. When creating a new bucket without specifying a different storage class, this is the class that the bucket will have. With S3 Standard, a file is replicated across at least three AZs within a Region. This means that even if two AZs in a Region are lost, you'd still have access to your file.

For files that are less frequently accessed, we have **S3 Standard Infrequent Access** (or **S3 Standard-IA**). This storage class is cheaper than S3 Standard and is well suited for files – such as backups – that are not accessed frequently but where we need instant access just in case. With S3 Standard-IA, you pay a retrieval fee.

But what if our data is not *that* important? Think, for example, about temporary logs and things that, if lost, could be recreated. For this case, we can use **S3 One Zone Instant-Access**. Contrary to S3 Standard and Standard-IA, the data in this storage tier is only stored in one AZ within the Region. This means that data is still fast to retrieve but only stored in one AZ and thus lacks the durability of S3 Standard and S3 Standard-IA.

Finally, we have the storage classes for archival – the **Glacier** family. These storage classes are designed for the archival of data that is rarely accessed. A typical example of where this storage class could be used is the long-term storage of documents – such as invoices – that need to be stored for multiple years but are only accessed in the case of an audit:

- **Amazon S3 Glacier Instant Retrieval** offers low storage prices and – for a fee – the ability to instantly retrieve these files from the deep archive if needed.

- **Amazon S3 Glacier Flexible Retrieval** allows you to retrieve data within minutes to a few hours or do asynchronous bulk data retrieval. This storage class has a lower storage cost than the Glacier Instant Retrieval class but you will have to wait for your files upon retrieval.

- **Amazon S3 Glacier Deep Archive** is the lowest-cost storage tier. It is usually used for multi-year storage of data. Retrieval of data in this class can take up to 12 hours.

As you can tell, there are a lot of options available when selecting a storage tier. One pattern we can observe is that files that are accessed less frequently are usually better suited with a storage tier that offers cheaper storage prices at the cost of longer retrieval times or a fee for instant retrieval.

This means that we need to look at each object in our S3 bucket and – based on metadata such as the last time it was accessed – transition it to a different storage tier. This is something we *could* implement via Boto3; however, with this being a very common use case, AWS has implemented a solution called **S3 life cycle policies** to make this easier.

Life cycle policies define time intervals in which an object has not been accessed. For example, we can say that if an object hasn't been accessed for 30 days, it should be transitioned into a different storage tier. We are now going to configure such a life cycle policy in the AWS Management Console:

1. Open up the AWS Management Console and navigate to the S3 service.

2. In the overview, on the top right, click on **Create bucket** to open up the dialog to create a new bucket. Define a name (remember that the name of an S3 bucket must be unique) and leave all the default settings on before clicking **Create bucket** at the bottom of the page.

3. Use the search bar – as shown in the following screenshot – to find your bucket and click on the name to get to the details page of the previously created bucket.

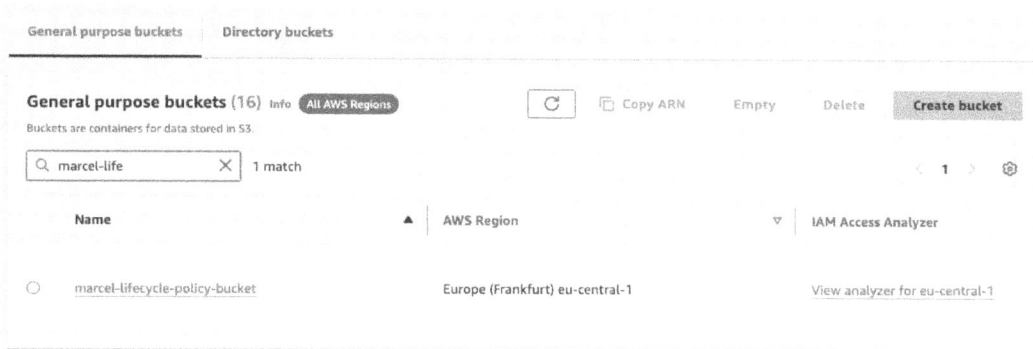

Figure 10.4 – Search field to find our newly created bucket

4. On the details page, navigate to the section on life cycle rule configuration.

5. Under **Lifecycle rule configuration**, define a name for your life cycle rule. In this example, the name we have used is `test-lifecycle`.

    You'll also need to select to which objects you want this life cycle rule to apply. You could limit the scope of the rule to only apply to objects with a specific prefix or to only objects that have a certain tag. In this example, we are going to apply the life cycle rule to all objects in this bucket, so select **Apply to all objects in the bucket** and acknowledge this in the "warning box," which you can also see in the following screenshot:

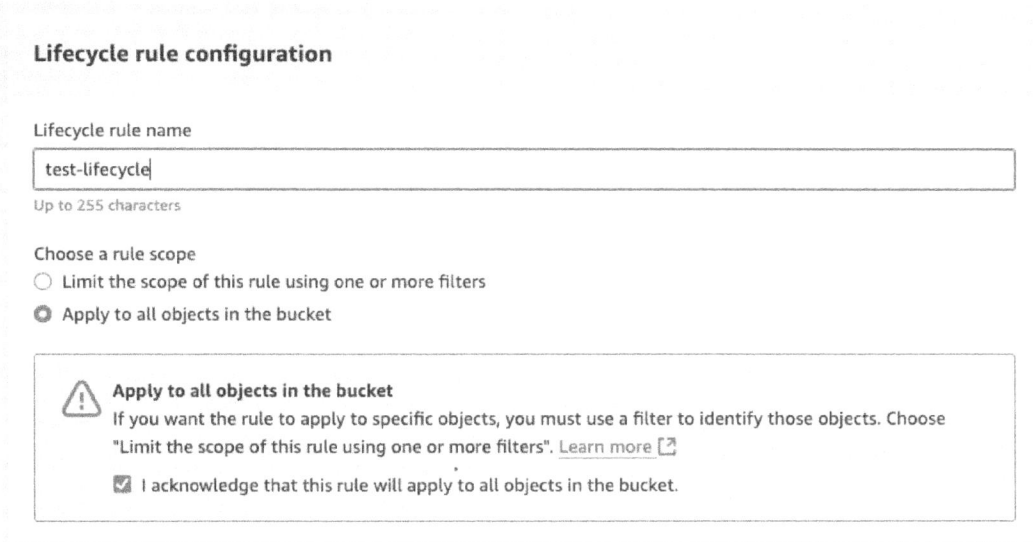

Figure 10.5 – Name and role scope configuration for our new life cycle rule

6. Next, we need to define the actions we want to take as shown in the following screenshot:

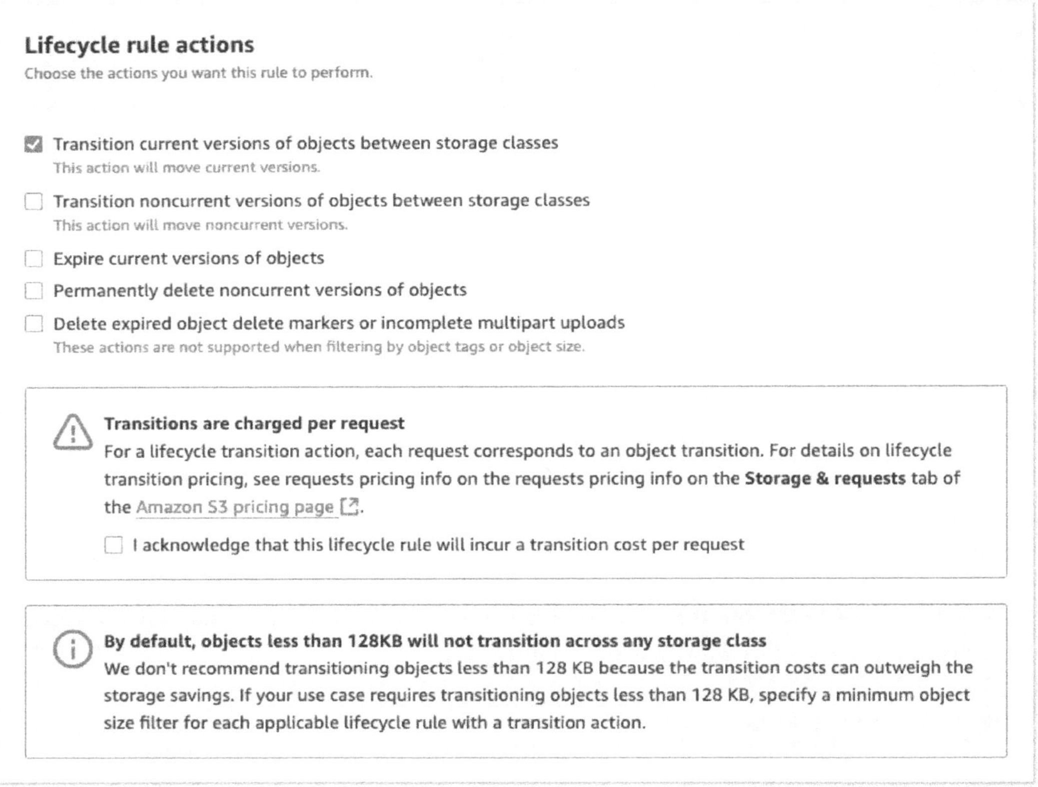

Lifecycle rule actions
Choose the actions you want this rule to perform.

☑ Transition current versions of objects between storage classes
   This action will move current versions.

☐ Transition noncurrent versions of objects between storage classes
   This action will move noncurrent versions.

☐ Expire current versions of objects

☐ Permanently delete noncurrent versions of objects

☐ Delete expired object delete markers or incomplete multipart uploads
   These actions are not supported when filtering by object tags or object size.

⚠ **Transitions are charged per request**
For a lifecycle transition action, each request corresponds to an object transition. For details on lifecycle transition pricing, see requests pricing info on the requests pricing info on the **Storage & requests** tab of the Amazon S3 pricing page [↗].

   ☐ I acknowledge that this lifecycle rule will incur a transition cost per request

ⓘ **By default, objects less than 128KB will not transition across any storage class**
We don't recommend transitioning objects less than 128 KB because the transition costs can outweigh the storage savings. If your use case requires transitioning objects less than 128 KB, specify a minimum object size filter for each applicable lifecycle rule with a transition action.

Figure 10.6 – Available life cycle rule actions

AWS allows us to take a variety of actions on our objects. Let's look at each of them:

- **Transition current versions of objects between storage classes**: Lets us change the storage class of the current version of an object based on the duration it was in a storage tier

- **Transition noncurrent versions of objects between storage classes**: Lets us change the storage class of old versions of a file based on the duration it was stored in a storage tier

- **Expire current versions of objects**: Lets us delete the current version of an object

- **Permanently delete noncurrent versions of objects**: Lets us delete old versions of an object

- **Delete expired object delete markers or incomplete multipart uploads**: Lets us permanently delete objects that were previously marked as expired

For our example, select **Transition current versions of objects between storage classes** and acknowledge the fact that we want to do this in the yellow box.

> **Additional information**
>
> In the previous explanation, the concept of *current* and *noncurrent* versions of an object, as well as delete markers, came up. S3 supports versioning of its files. So, when we upload a file with an existing name – for example, a new version of a picture – the old version will not be overwritten but rather become a noncurrent version of the file.
>
> Similarly, when deleting an object when versioning is enabled, the object is not actually deleted. Instead, a *delete marker* is put as the current version of the object but previous versions are still available and a delete can thus be undone.
>
> Versioned objects are a great way to protect our data from accidental deletion; however, we still need to pay for the storage of all noncurrent versions. It can thus be advisable to either transfer them to a low-cost storage tier or expire them completely.

7. Next, we define the transition of our current object versions. We'll keep the object in the **Standard-IA** tier for 30 days after its creation. Then, we'll transition it into the **Glacier Instant Retrieval** tier after 90 days and, finally, after half a year, the file will be transitioned into **Glacier Deep Archive**.

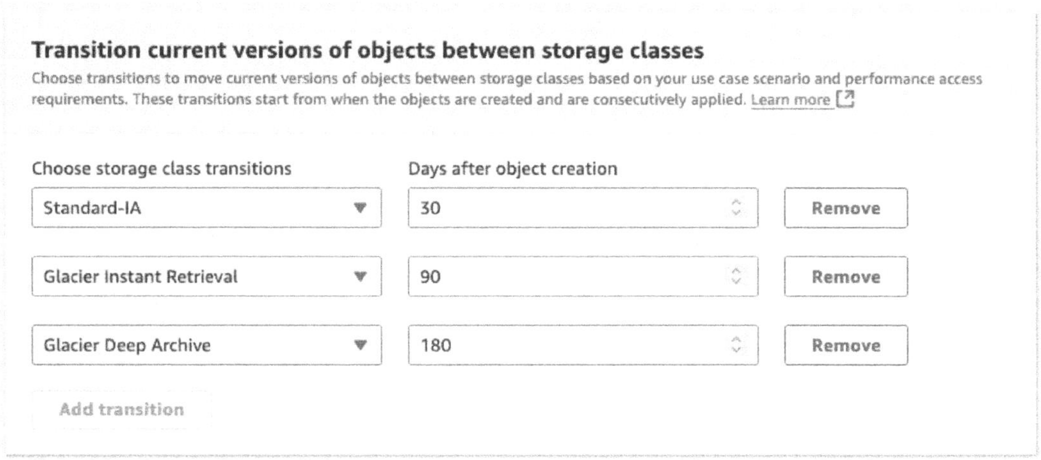

Figure 10.7 – Transition configuration for our life cycle policy

Finally, we can review our transition and expiration policy at the bottom of the page before clicking the **Create lifecycle rule button** to create our policy.

The following screenshot shows the previously defined transition configuration.

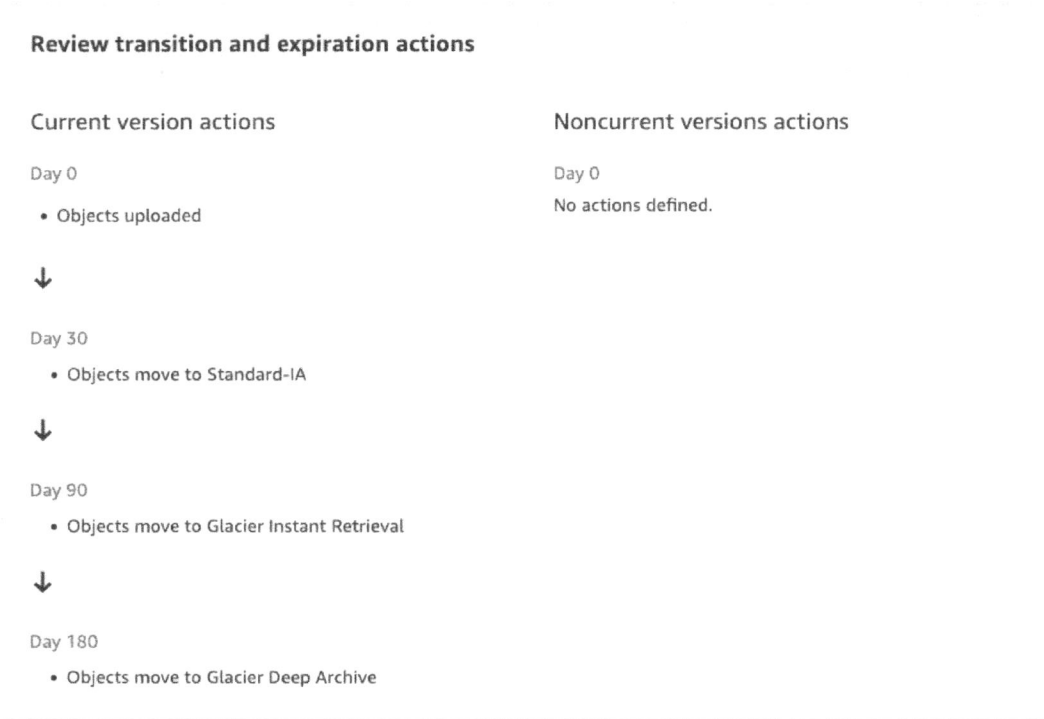

Review transition and expiration actions

Current version actions	Noncurrent versions actions
Day 0	Day 0
• Objects uploaded	No actions defined.
↓	
Day 30	
• Objects move to Standard-IA	
↓	
Day 90	
• Objects move to Glacier Instant Retrieval	
↓	
Day 180	
• Objects move to Glacier Deep Archive	

Figure 10.8 – Review of our life cycle policy

With this, we have now defined a life cycle policy that will automatically transition our objects from one tier to another based on the time since the object was created. To test this, you can upload a file – it needs to be at least 128 KB in size – to the folder and wait for the transition to happen after 30 days.

The reason for the file size of at least 128 KB is that AWS will – per our configuration and the default – only transition files that are at least that size. The reasoning behind this is that the cost of transitioning the files for smaller sizes is higher than the storage cost of such small files.

We have now seen how we can use S3 and the different storage classes to optimize our storage costs. Next, we will look into the concept of bunker accounts before concluding this chapter.

Exploring bunker accounts for backups

We have so far looked at AWS Backup and how we can use it to create backups that are stored in the same account as the resource. This type of setup is ideal for quick restoral of the data. The problem with this approach is, however, that an attacker – if they can compromise the account – could also just delete the backup. This doesn't necessarily need to be an attacker either. Another systems engineer or a careless developer writing an automation script that deletes the wrong resources could easily trigger the deletion of a backup.

One concept to guard against this is that of the **bunker account**. A bunker account is a separate AWS account that our backups are copied into. The following screenshot shows the basic architecture of a bunker account.

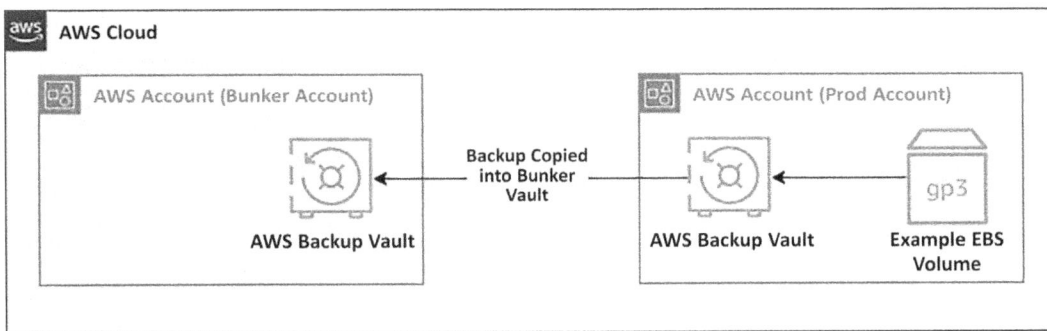

Figure 10.9 – Bunker and prod accounts in an architecture

Here, the backup of our resource, for example, an **EBS volume**, is first stored in the **AWS Backup vault** within the production account. The backup is then copied across into another AWS account – the **bunker account** – for additional storage. Even if an attacker or unattentive employee were to wipe both the EBS volume and the vault in the production account, we could still restore the data from the bunker account.

In this setup, the IAM policies that govern the cross-account access of the production account into the bunker account only allow the creation of backups but not their deletion. So, even with administrative rights in the **prod account**, an attacker couldn't delete the backups kept in the bunker account.

Since this pattern requires cross-account access, we'll revisit it in *Chapter 16* on operating in a multi-account environment.

Summary

In this chapter, you have seen how to use AWS Backup as a centralized solution for your cloud backups. We automated the creation and configuration of backup vaults, plans, and rules with Terraform and tags before exploring the different storage tiers in S3 and how a life cycle policy can be used to transition objects between the tiers.

Finally, we saw the concept of bunker accounts and how they can introduce another layer of security for our backups against negligence or bad actors.

In the next chapter, we'll cover the topic of disaster recovery (where taking backups plays an integral role).

Get This Book's PDF Version and Exclusive Extras

UNLOCK NOW

Scan the QR code (or go to `packtpub.com/unlock`). Search for this book by name, confirm the edition, and then follow the steps on the page.

Note: Keep your invoice handly. Purchase made directly from packt don't require one.

11

Disaster Recovery Options with AWS

In our path in the cloud so far, we have only dealt with the *happy path*. Everything we have set up so far always just worked. But what if it did not? What if we roll out a configuration change that prevents traffic from reaching our database? What if a disgruntled employee tries to harm our company by deleting all of our production instances?

You might argue that we can put controls into place and that no bug can get past rigorous testing. Even if that is the case, what about natural disasters? What about an earthquake hitting the location of our data center or the fiber cables of an **internet service provider** (**ISP**) going down?

Dr. Werner Vogels, chief technology officer at Amazon, famously quipped "*Everything fails all the time*." The meaning behind this goes beyond the simple words. What Vogels is acknowledging here is that any distributed system (or any system, for that matter) might eventually fail due to something going wrong. We have to accept this fact and design our systems in such a way that they can either proactively detect and mitigate a failure, be resilient against those we can anticipate, and recover from the disasters that occur.

This chapter is about the strategies and architectures we can employ to build a workload that can recover from a disaster. As with everything in IT, there is no *free lunch* so we'll also discuss the cost and complexity implications associated with the architectural choices we make. This chapter serves as the theoretical background to the more practical resilience and chaos engineering part, which we'll cover and see in action in *Chapter 12, Testing the Resilience of Your Infrastructure and Architecture with AWS Fault Injection Service*.

In this chapter, we're going to cover the following main topics:

- An introduction to **recovery time objective** (RTO) and **recovery point objective** (RPO) as the business metrics that define disaster recovery strategies
- An introduction to disaster recovery strategies
- The architecture of backup and restore
- The architecture of pilot light
- The architecture of warm standby
- The architecture of multi-site active/active

So, let's get started!

Technical requirements

Since we'll be dealing with architecture only in this chapter, there are no technical requirements. It is beneficial if you are aware of the idea of disaster recovery in the general sense of the term but we'll introduce it briefly in the first section.

For this chapter, there is no Code in Action (CiA) video available.

Defining our disaster recovery strategy

AWS defines disaster recovery as follows:

"Disaster recovery is the process by which an organization anticipates and addresses technology-related disasters. The process of preparing for and recovering from any event that prevents a workload or system [from fulfilling its business objectives in its primary deployed location], such as power outages, natural events, or security issues."

> **Note**
> The preceding quote is taken from `https://aws.amazon.com/what-is/disaster-recovery/`. The text in square brackets was added by the author and is not in the original quote.

We can summarize this description as the process an organization puts into place to prevent and react to technology-related disasters. But who decides what the correct process is? And how do we measure it?

RPO and RTO – the key metrics for DR

Most modern IT systems serve some sort of direct or indirect business purpose – either your company provides a software solution to your customers (say, in the form of a webshop) or you run applications that are critical to your company's function, such as a machine control system in an automotive parts company in the cloud.

At the other end of the spectrum, you might also run applications that are not very important. For example, let's say the online lunch plan of your company cafeteria is unavailable. It would certainly be an inconvenience but everyone could still just go to the cafeteria, see what is offered, and proceed with their lunch.

As we can see from these examples, different applications require different types of disaster recovery strategies. Based on the level of importance, the applications need to be guarded against different disaster events. It's much more likely that a single server crashes than it is that an entire region in AWS becomes unreachable but, depending on the criticality of our workload, we might need to guard against the failure of an entire region, however unlikely it is.

As you can see, our discussion on disaster recovery is very vague so far. If you go to the product owner or business counterpart and ask them how long their application can be down, the most likely answer is going to be "never." So, how can we quantify the requirements for disaster recovery? We generally use RPO and RTO. The following figure shows the relation between RPO, RTO, and the time of our disaster.

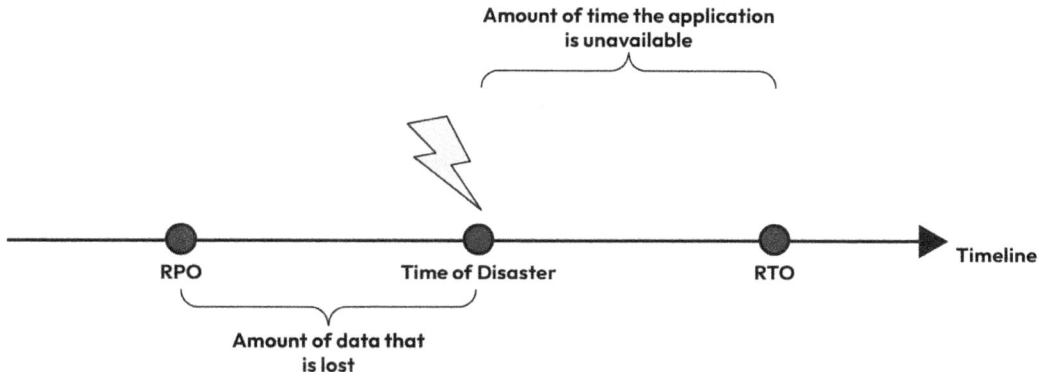

Figure 11.1 – The relationship between RTO/RPO and the time of disaster

RPO

RPO describes the amount of data that is acceptable to be lost in the case of a disaster. Let's assume our software saves all of its data in one place – a database server. If we only do a daily backup/snapshot of the data at 2 AM, our RPO will be one day. In the worst-case scenario, our database server dies at 1:59 AM right before the start of the next backup. In that case, we would lose all the data that has been written to the database server since the previous snapshot was taken.

With our application now impaired due to the unavailability of our database server, the second metric comes into play – RTO.

RTO

RTO describes the time it takes after a disaster has occurred until your application is fully functional and fully available again. This can also be described as your downtime.

Let's stay with the previously described example of the web application with a database server that goes down. After the server is down, we need to do the following:

1. Detect that our application is impaired.

2. Detect that the unreachable database server is at fault for our application not being available.

3. Start a new database server.

4. Restore our data from the backup to the new database server.

5. Change our application to use the new database server.

All of these steps take time and will factor into our RTO.

There are architectural patterns (which we will see later in this chapter) that can be implemented to have RTO and RPO values of nearly zero. However, this comes at a cost. The rule of thumb is that the lower the RTO and RPO, the higher the cost and complexity of our infrastructure and application architecture.

What RTO and RPO to choose is ultimately up to your business requirements. As mentioned in the introduction, a business-critical application without which all of your manufacturing robots can't function might warrant a much lower RTO and RPO than the lunch menu.

When arguing with your business counterparts about the cost associated with one or the other architecture in terms of DR, you can reframe the conversation into the question, *How much would x hours of downtime cost us?* This, combined with the likelihood of a disaster event occurring, will inform the architectural pattern to select. To stay with our previous example, the answer to that question for our manufacturing robots' control software could be in the millions while the answer for the lunch plan would probably be close to zero.

We are now going to do a quick overview of four architectural patterns you'll often encounter when dealing with disaster recovery:

*   Backup and restore

*   Pilot light

*   Warm standby

*   Multi-region active/active

After the overview, we'll then discuss each of the architectures in more detail and talk about cost and complexity implications when choosing that pattern. In *Chapter 13*, you'll see an application evolving from a *backup and restore* configuration to a *multi-region active/active* deployment and see how to test its resilience against failures using chaos experiments.

An introduction to disaster recovery strategies

As pointed out in the AWS definition of disaster recovery we saw at the beginning of the chapter, DR is triggered in the case that an application isn't functional from *its primary deployed location* anymore. This means that most DR strategies will involve one or more secondary locations from which the application could either be restored or to which traffic could be redirected.

We can thus generally differentiate between *active* and *passive* locations. An active location (for example, a Region in AWS) is actively used to serve traffic while a passive location isn't used to serve any production traffic. Our DR strategies can then be divided into active/passive and active/active setups.

A common depiction of the different disaster recovery strategies is to align them along a spectrum, as shown in the next figure:

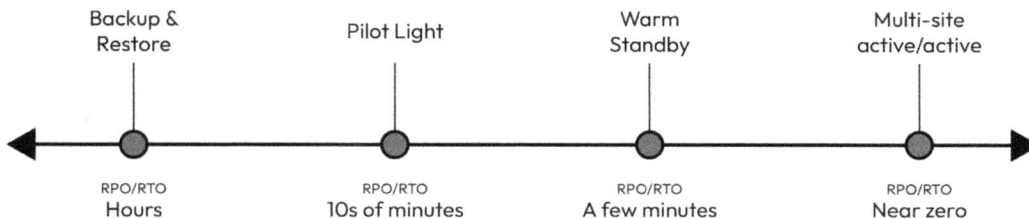

Figure 11.2 – The spectrum of disaster recovery patterns

The main disaster recovery strategies include:

- **Backup and restore** means that we keep a backup of our data and restore the service in the case of a disaster.

- In **pilot light,** we have a secondary deployment of our entire application (for example, in another AWS Region) but keep the infrastructure (for example, EC2 instances) stopped. In the case of a disaster, we only need to start the previously turned-off instances.

- **Warm standby** is similar to pilot light with the only difference being that the infrastructure in our passive site is only partially turned off.

- In **multi-site active/active,** we have two (or more) fully active sites that could take over the traffic from the other site at any moment without any interruptions.

To reiterate the previous distinction between active/passive and active/active patterns, backup and restore, pilot light, and warm standby are active/passive patterns since the DR site is inactive for production traffic. Multi-site active/active is, as the name suggests, an active/active pattern since both sites are active and available for traffic.

As we move from left to right with the strategies, we can see how the estimated RTO/RPO goes from hours to near zero.

To get a better understanding of these architectures, let's see the architecture diagram for each of them and discuss the cost and complexity implications when it comes to an exemplary web application.

The application we are going to use as an example is a standard API application. A load balancer distributes traffic to a fleet of instances. In the background, there is a database server from which data is pulled. The following figure shows the basic application architecture as we would see it in AWS:

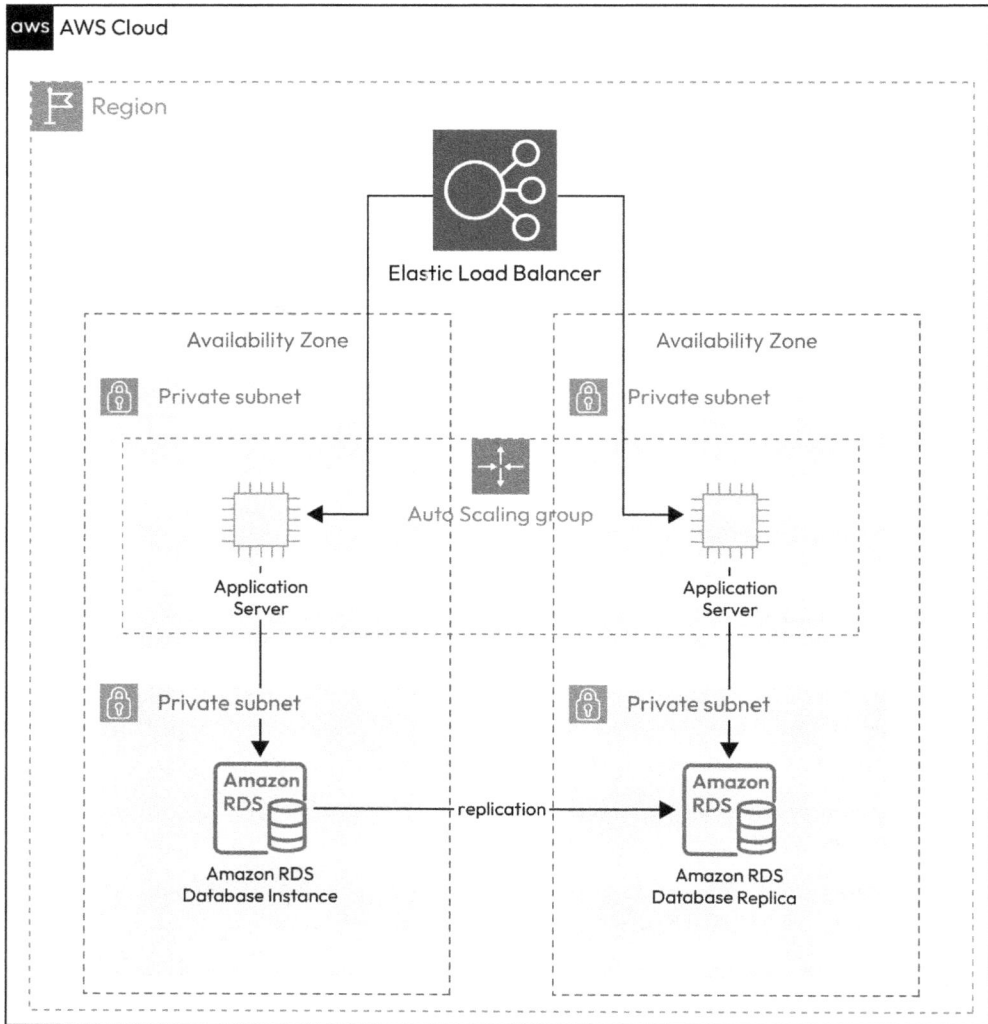

Figure 11.3 – Basic architecture of our application

As you can see in the architecture sketch, we have already taken some resiliency-related precautions by using concepts you have seen previously in the book. The application has instances deployed in

Auto Scaling groups across two **Availability Zones** (**AZs**) within the same Region. The auto scaling groups allow the system to respond to a surge in traffic while also being able to detect unhealthy instances, terminate them, and spin up a new instance for our application server. We use an elastic load balancer together with health checks to distribute traffic between the instances in the two AZs.

For the database, we have opted for a database in Amazon **Relational Database Service** (**RDS**), which supports cross-zone replicas (for example, Aurora Postgres allows this). That means that the data is synchronized between the two AZs.

This architecture should already be resilient against the failure of a single AZ. If the left AZ in our architecture goes down, the right AZ would still have all the data and resources to serve the traffic.

Backup and restore DR strategy

With backup and restore, the strategy is to take regular backups and restore our application from these backups in the case of a disaster. The following figure shows the architecture diagram for a backup and restore solution. We discussed the concept of a bunker account in the previous chapter on backups.

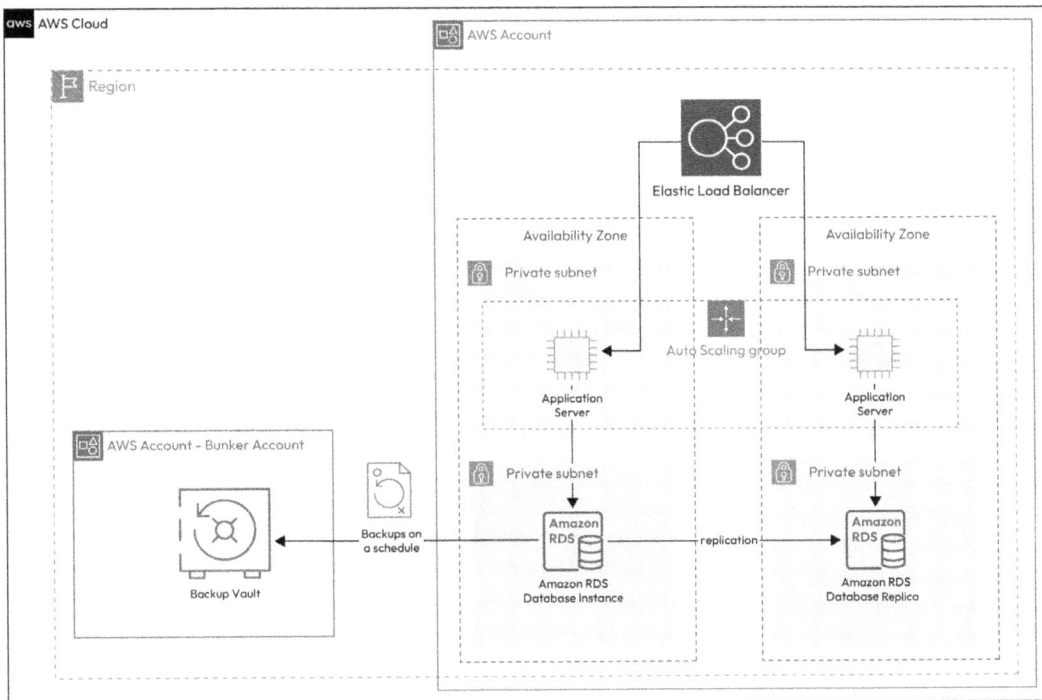

Figure 11.4 – Backup and restore setup with a bunker account to store the backups in

In the case of a disaster, we'd spin up a new deployment of our infrastructure and restore the state of the database from the backup vault.

The big benefit of the backup and restore strategy is its relative ease of implementation and the low cost. We only pay for the storage of our backups, and we have no infrastructure that sits idle waiting for a disaster to happen.

The downside is the time it takes to restore our application upon a disaster. There is another devil in the details here. With a backup and restore strategy, it can be very easy to rely on the backup but never test it. The AWS Well-Architected Framework explicitly calls out the need to test the restoration of your backups regularly to be sure that you are truly backing up all the data that you need for a full restore. In order to facilitate this, it is generally advisable to automate the process of restoring a backup so that you can test restores regularly.

Looking at the diagram, there is another disaster case that is not handled with this architecture. With the current proposal, we'd store our backups in the same region as the original application. If the entire region goes down, we might not have access to our data and thus it might be possible that we can't restore from our backup. We could mitigate this by replicating our backup not only cross-account (from our workload account to our backup bunker account) but also cross-region.

Additional information

AWS keeps a public record of **Post-Event Summaries (PESs)** for each issue that had a significant impact on customers. *A significant impact on customers* does not mean that it was a regional failure.

For example, the PES on a service event in the Sydney region on the 4th of June, 2016 explains the impact a service event had on the EC2 instances and EBS volumes in one of the AZs of the Sydney region.

You can find all PESs at this link: `https://aws.amazon.com/premiumsupport/technology/pes/`.

While backup and restore offers a cost-efficient solution for applications that can handle downtime of hours (or even days), there might be cases where we need to be able to restore faster at a slightly higher cost. Let's next look at the idea behind the pilot light strategy. Before doing this, we'll need to modify our application architecture a bit. Going forward, we'll deal with architectures where there are two load balancers, and thus two different entry points, to our software. We'll thus add a **Domain Name System (DNS)** service to our architecture. In this example, we'll add the AWS DNS service, called Amazon Route 53, to the architecture. The following figure shows the adapted basic architecture with Route 53 added:

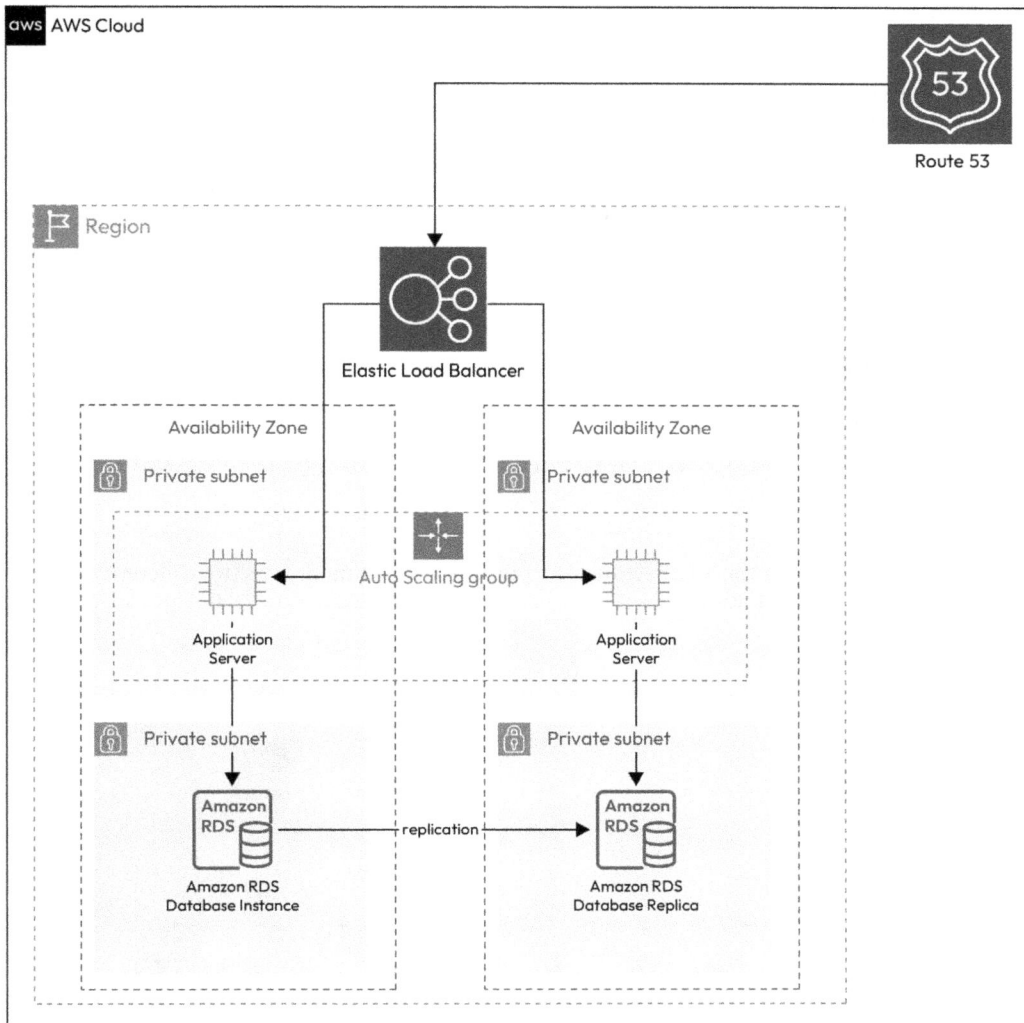

Figure 11.5 – Architecture of our application including Route 53 for DNS

Here, Route 53 just routes all traffic to our one elastic load balancer in our single region.

Pilot Light

In a pilot light strategy, we generally have a secondary passive site. In the case of AWS, this passive site is usually a secondary region. In that passive site, we have our infrastructure (for example, the EC2 instances used to serve our application) provisioned but turned off. The only running infrastructure in our secondary region is those components that hold any data, such as the database servers. Due to the latency between regions being too high to facilitate cross-region synchronous replication, the replication of our data will happen asynchronously. RDS and storage services such as S3 offer asynchronous cross-region replication.

Additional information

For a list of all database engines that support cross-region replication in RDS, you can follow this link: `https://docs.aws.amazon.com/AmazonRDS/latest/UserGuide/Concepts.RDS_Fea_Regions_DB-eng.Feature.CrossRegionReadReplicas.html`.

The following diagram shows the architecture for a pilot light deployment with two different regions:

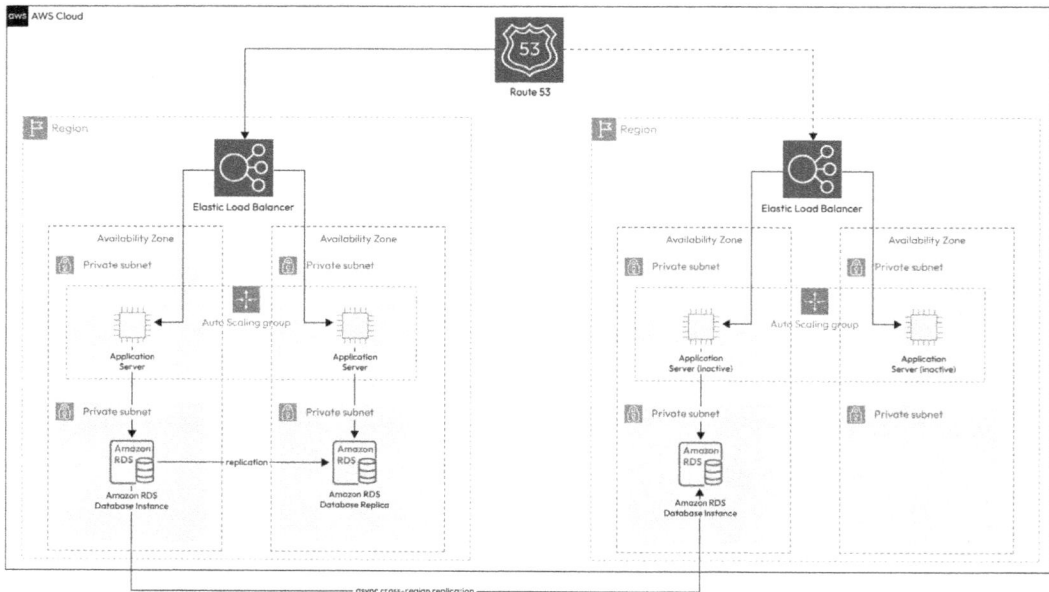

Figure 11.6 – Pilot light deployment across two regions

As you can see in the diagram, the path to the secondary region from Route 53 is dotted to indicate its inactive status. The application servers in the auto scaling group are inactive and the only active components in the secondary region are the load balancer and the database.

We also use asynchronous cross-region replication to replicate our data from the primary to the secondary region.

The benefit of this deployment is its relatively low RTO while being cost-efficient since only the minimal required infrastructure (the database and load balancer) is running.

The downside of pilot light, besides the increase in cost, is the added operational and architectural complexity. When selecting a database service, for example, we now need to make sure we use an engine that supports the required cross-region replication. Whenever we update our application in the primary region, we need to make sure that we also update the turned-off instances in our secondary region.

In the case of a disaster that requires us to switch over to our pilot light region, there is another problem. While the data is replicated and available in our new region, the infrastructure to serve that data still needs to be started up. This means that our customers will still encounter some unavailability from our API. When dealing with complex applications, spinning up all the instances could require significant time.

This is where our next strategy, warm standby, comes into play.

Warm standby

Warm standby looks very similar to pilot light. We also have a secondary region to which our infrastructure is deployed and our data is replicated. No production traffic is served from our secondary site. The following figure shows the architecture diagram for a warm standby.

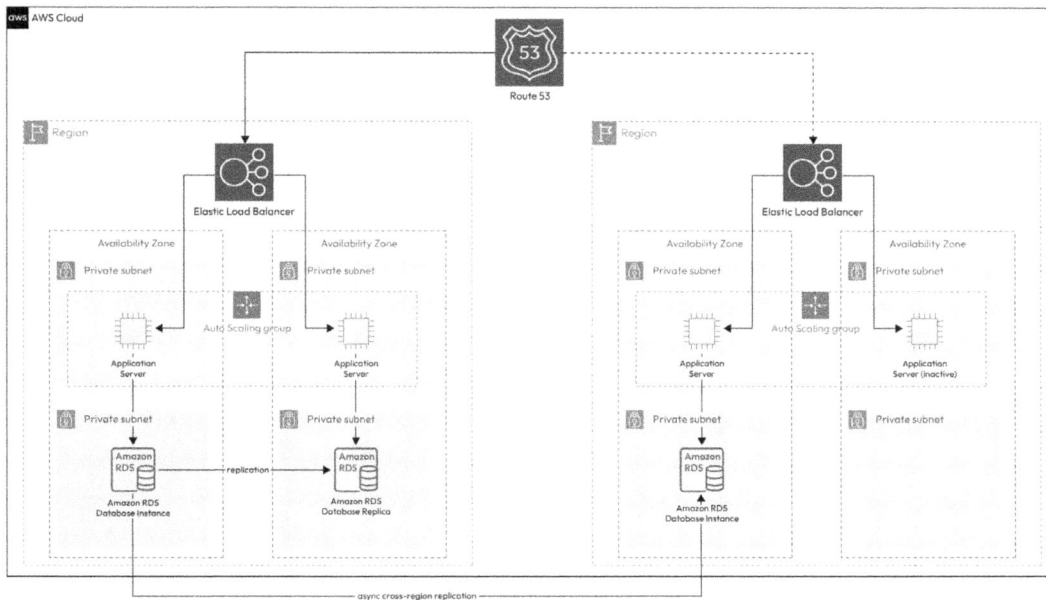

Figure 11.7 – Warm standby architecture

The difference between pilot light and warm standby lies in the fact that we have active instances in our secondary site. In the case of a disaster, this means that we can switch over our traffic to the secondary site and, instead of waiting for the instances to boot, we can already use our existing provisioned application server infrastructure to serve requests while the auto-scaling group takes care of scaling out our infrastructure to be able to handle the entire load.

Besides the implication that we need data storage services that allow cross-regional replication, the warm standby approach has obvious cost implications. We'll have resources that idle the entire time – until a disaster happens.

Pilot light and warm standby are, due to their relatively low-cost overhead, very efficient solutions for applications that require fast recovery times and low data loss. When opting for such an approach, we do need to take architectural considerations into account, mainly in the fact that all our data-storing components (such as databases or object storage such as S3) need to support cross-region replication. We also have implications for our operations since we now need to make sure that the deployments in our two regions are in sync.

But what if we can tolerate near-zero downtime? This is where multi-site active/active comes in.

Multi-site active/active

As the name suggests, multi-site active-active is the only architectural pattern on the list that is an active/active instead of an active/passive pattern.

In an active/active deployment, both sites accept production requests, and both serve them. If one of the regions is impaired, traffic is simply shifted over to the other active region. The following figure shows an example of such an architecture.

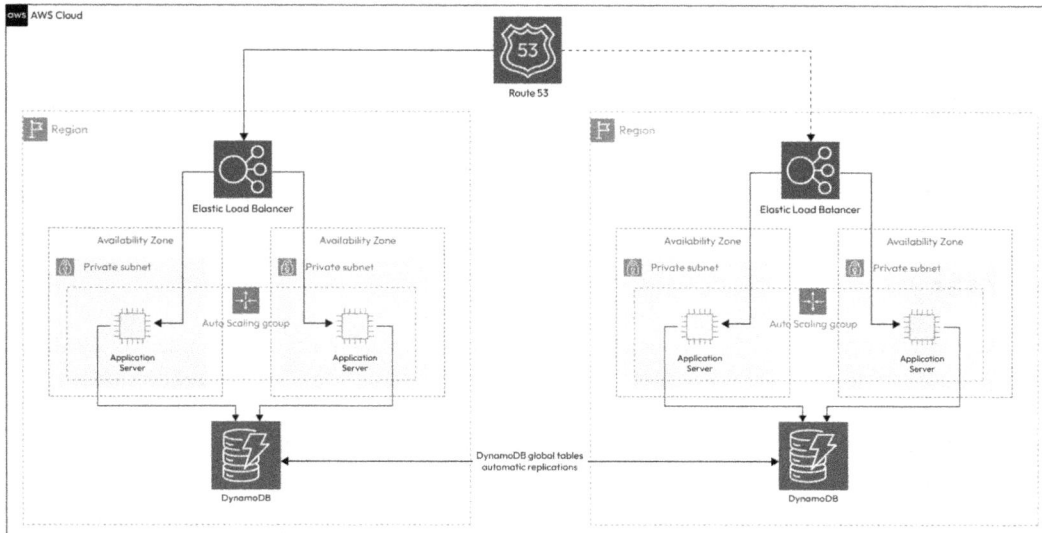

Figure 11.8 – Multi-site active/active architecture

What might look like a small change when drawn up on a whiteboard has significant implications for our application architecture. Compared to active/passive deployments where the data only needed to be copied from the active to the passive region, in an active/active setup, we also have write requests in our secondary region. We can solve this issue either by redirecting all write requests to one region or by using a database engine such as Amazon DynamoDB, which has features for eventual consistency that allow us to write in one region and have that change propagate to all other regions where the table is used.

As you can see, operating in such an environment has significant implications not only for our infrastructure setup but also for our software architecture. In addition, we have cost implications since we now have two active regions instead of only one.

The benefits of this approach are the near-zero RTO and RPO. Ideally, users don't even realize when the failover to another region/site happens.

> **Additional information**
>
> Netflix is famous for implementing a multi-region active/active setup. If you want to read about the challenges and the solutions to those challenges that the engineering team there encountered when setting this up, you can check out the following post on the Netflix engineering blog: https://netflixtechblog.com/active-active-for-multi-regional-resiliency-c47719f6685b.

Summary

In this chapter, we have covered the theoretical background and the different building blocks of disaster recovery. We introduced the two key metrics, RPO and RTO, to define what DR requirements we had. We then looked into four different architectural patterns: backup and restore, pilot light, warm standby, and multi-site active/active. We discussed the pros and cons of each of these solutions when it comes to engineering overhead and spending on infrastructure.

With this background covered, in the next chapter, we'll evolve an actual application from a backup and restore deployment to a multi-site active/active deployment and see how we can use chaos engineering and chaos experiments to test that features such as database failovers *actually* work as we intend them to.

Get This Book's PDF Version and Exclusive Extras

UNLOCK NOW

Scan the QR code (or go to packtpub.com/unlock). Search for this book by name, confirm the edition, and then follow the steps on the page.

Note: Keep your invoice handly. Purchase made directly from packt don't require one.

Join the CloudPro Newsletter with 44000+ Subscribers

Want to know what's happening in cloud computing, DevOps, IT administration, networking, and more? Scan the QR code to subscribe to **CloudPro**, our weekly newsletter for 44,000+ tech professionals who want to stay informed and ahead of the curve.

https://packt.link/cloudpro

12

Testing the Resilience of Your Infrastructure and Architecture with AWS Fault Injection Service

In the previous chapter, we introduced four different architectural patterns or strategies that can be used to deploy resilient applications in the cloud. However, it is hard to judge the resiliency of an application just from its architecture. Much depends on how the architecture is implemented. In this chapter, we'll introduce a method to test whether the disaster recovery configurations we have implemented would work in the case of a failure.

For this, we'll introduce AWS **Fault Injection Service** (**FIS**). AWS FIS is a tool for running chaos engineering experiments against your infrastructure deployed on AWS.

In this chapter, we'll cover the following:

- Introduction to chaos engineering and chaos experiments
- Introduction to AWS FIS
- Building a chaos experiment in AWS FIS

Technical requirements

A basic understanding of RDS, as given in the previous chapter, is beneficial since we'll be triggering a database failover of RDS.

A basic understanding of Terraform, which we'll use to provision the underlying infrastructure for our chaos experiment, is required.

All scripts from this section can be found at the following GitHub link: `https://github.com/PacktPublishing/AWS-for-System-Administrators-Second-Edition`.

For this chapter, there is no Code in Action (CiA) video available.

Introduction to chaos engineering and chaos experiments

How do we test the resiliency of our application and verify that mechanisms such as database failovers work? One way we could do this is by building a long checklist of best practices and checking our workload – maybe programmatically – against this. On such a checklist, you might find a line that says *Check that RDS is deployed in multiple AZs*. We'd then go into our AWS console and verify that RDS is indeed deployed in a high-availability mode into multiple AZs. But is our software also properly configured to use this multi-AZ deployment? And how long will it take for our application to recover after a failure? Will it recover at all?

To answer these questions, we'll need to try it out. This is where chaos engineering and chaos experiments come into play.

The idea of **chaos engineering** is to purposely inject faults and failures into a system to test its resiliency and ability to withstand and recover from them. In other words, we purposely inject chaos into our application infrastructure. The goal of chaos engineering, however, is not to just destroy all our infrastructure. Instead, we run experiments that simulate a behavior that we might encounter in the real world and that our architecture is built against.

Let's look at a more concrete example. The following figure shows the architecture of a basic two-tier web application with a web server and a database server, which we have already seen in the previous chapter:

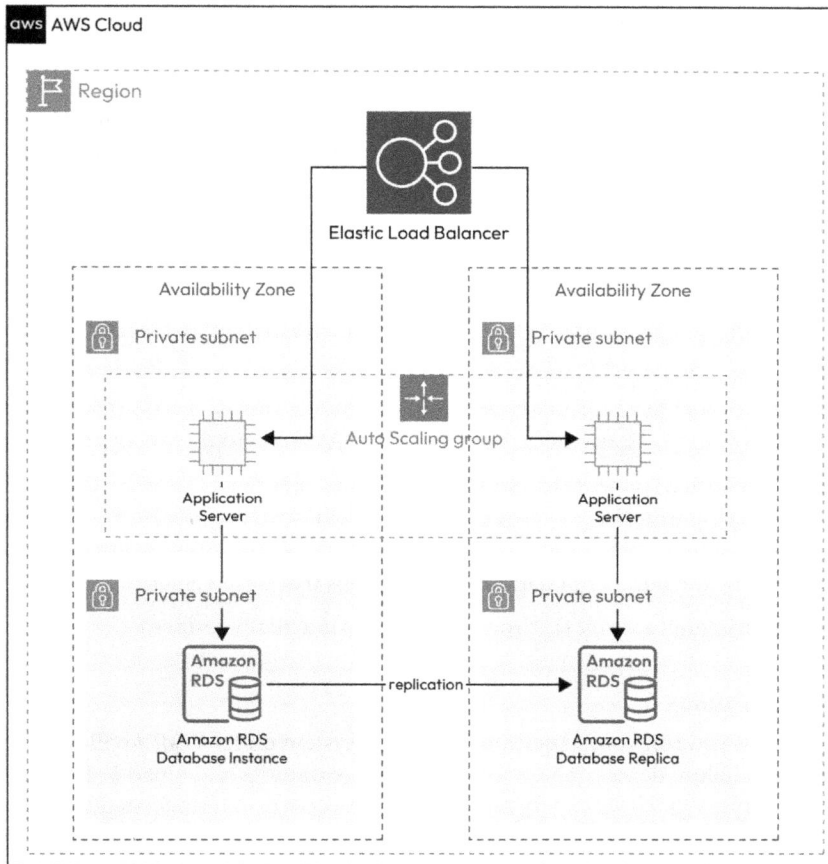

Figure 12.1 – Basic architecture of a web application on AWS

This architecture uses a multi-AZ deployment of its database using Amazon RDS and is deployed into a single Region.

What kind of failures would we expect this application to be able to withstand? From the architecture, we'd expect the application to be able to handle the failure of an entire AZ without a long degradation of services. If the AZ with the primary database server goes down, we'd expect RDS to handle the failover to the secondary database server. The load balancer should direct incoming traffic to the remaining health instances.

However, we do not expect this architecture to withstand an entire Region failure, for example. With the entire application being deployed only into a single Region, this is not a failure scenario that we have architected for.

A good chaos experiment could be to check whether our application can gracefully handle a database failover. Here, we would hypothesize that we expect the application to continue performing due to the automated failover of our database server. A bad chaos experiment would be the aforementioned Region failure. The only thing we would prove with that is that an architecture that isn't designed to withstand Region failure and is deployed into a single Region can't withstand a Region failure.

So how do we design these chaos experiments?

1. We start with a hypothesis. This hypothesis is usually an assumption about what your architecture should be able to withstand. For example, a hypothesis could be *My application will continue to function if 20% of my instances have a failure and terminate*. Architecturally, you might have mitigated this scenario via an Auto Scaling group.

2. Design an experiment that tests this hypothesis. This means you will need a service to randomly terminate 20% of the EC2 instances. We'll introduce AWS FIS to do exactly this next.

3. Define the metrics that you want to monitor during your experiment to assess the health of your application. Staying with the previous example, a useful metric could be the number of 5XX errors returned to users by your web server. In a scenario where we are failing over a database, a metric could be the number of database connections that were denied.

4. Run your experiment to verify that your architecture is actually resilient.

> **Additional information**
>
> It is important that you run your experiment against a system under load. Applications react very differently to failure depending on whether they are under a lot of load or just idling. If you don't want to run your chaos experiments in production (which is understandable), a great place to run them is during your scenario or load tests where the application is experiencing simulated but real requests.

AWS FIS for chaos experiments

In theory, we could run these chaos experiments in AWS by just using API scripts. Many actions, such as the failover of a database cluster, can be triggered via the API. However, what if we want to run these experiments over and over again, ideally with centralized logging and a visualization? This is where AWS FIS comes in. AWS FIS is a service for resiliency testing and building chaos engineering experiments. It comes with predefined sets of actions, such as the failover of an RDS database cluster or the random termination of EC2 instances. We can then orchestrate these actions into a sequence of actions that simulate a real failure.

A word of caution here. FIS used to be called Fault Injection *Simulator*. This might be a bit misleading as the service does not simulate the termination of EC2 instances or the failover of a database cluster and the simulation of the results. It actually triggers a shutdown or failover on your real and running infrastructure. While you can run this in your production, as Netflix famously does for their chaos engineering work, it is generally advisable to begin by running these in your testing or integration environment. A great time in your deployment cycle to run these experiments might be during scenario or load tests when there is simulated traffic on the system under test.

Building a chaos experiment with AWS FIS

In this section, we'll be building an actual chaos experiment with AWS FIS. This experiment will trigger a failover in our database cluster to simulate a partial database failure. To do so, we'll create an experiment template that contains the failover action we want to trigger. From this template, we'll then launch a new experiment and see the chaos in action.

Before we begin with this section, we'll need some infrastructure to run our experiment against. You can find the Terraform code to set up the testing infrastructure in the source code repository under `ch12/main.tf`. This script does the following:

- Creates a new VPC and private subnets in the `eu-central-1` (Frankfurt) Region in AWS

- Creates a multi-AZ deployed RDS cluster with Aurora PostgreSQL as the database engine

- Creates a new CloudWatch Logs group that we'll use to write the logs from our chaos experiment into

To create the sample infrastructure, follow these steps:

1. In your terminal, navigate to the `ch12` folder from the GitHub repository.

2. In the folder, run the following command to initiate your Terraform directory:

   ```
   terraform init
   ```

3. Run the `terraform apply` command to create your new infrastructure:

   ```
   terraform apply
   ```

It can take a couple of minutes for the RDS cluster and its accompanying instances to be created and Terraform to finish.

Caution

Due to the nature of multi-AZ deployments, the preceding deployed sample infrastructure can be costly. To minimize the cost impact, after running your chaos experiment, remember to delete the VPC, RDS cluster, RDS instances, and CloudWatch Logs group by using the `terraform destroy` command.

With the infrastructure that we want to run our experiment against deployed, let's get started with creating our chaos experiment. To do so, follow these steps:

1. Open the AWS console and search for FIS. Alternatively, you can use this link to open up the console page: https://eu-central-1.console.aws.amazon.com/fis/home?region=eu-central-1#Home.

2. On the console, select the **Experiment templates** menu entry in the left-hand menu, as shown in the following figure:

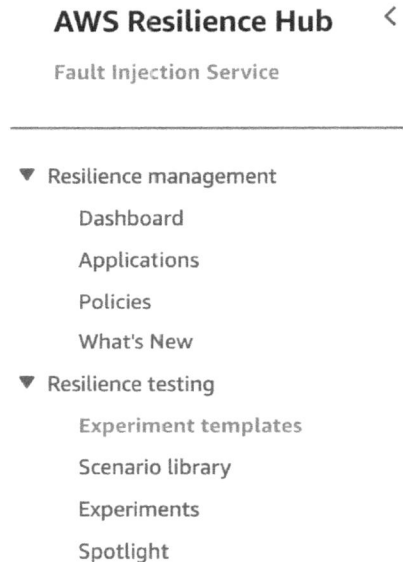

AWS Resilience Hub   <

Fault Injection Service

▼ Resilience management

Dashboard

Applications

Policies

What's New

▼ Resilience testing

Experiment templates

Scenario library

Experiments

Spotlight

Figure 12.2 – Experiment templates under Fault Injection Service in the Resilience testing section

3. You'll be presented with a (most likely empty) list of existing experiment templates. Click the orange **Create experiment template** button to open the wizard to create a new experiment template.

4. You'll first be asked to provide a name and description of your experiment. In this example, we will use RDS Failover Test for the description and RDS Failover as the name. The content of your name and description should be descriptive so that other DevOps engineers can understand what this experiment does.

    You'll also be asked what account the target workload is under. Since it is not uncommon for workloads on AWS to be spread across multiple AWS accounts, we could select targets for our actions from our current as well as multiple other accounts. Since our current target resources – namely, our previously created RDS cluster – run in the same account that we run our experiment, we'll select the **This AWS account…** option, as shown in the following figure:

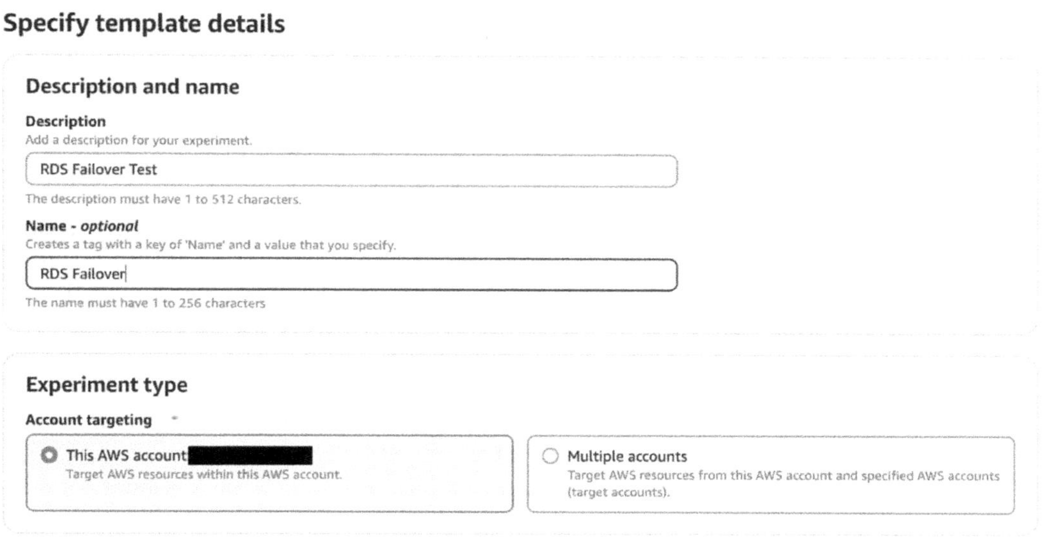

Specify template details

Description and name

Description
Add a description for your experiment.

> RDS Failover Test

The description must have 1 to 512 characters.

Name - *optional*
Creates a tag with a key of 'Name' and a value that you specify.

> RDS Failover|

The name must have 1 to 256 characters

Experiment type

Account targeting

- ◉ **This AWS account**▓▓▓▓▓▓▓
  Target AWS resources within this AWS account.

- ○ **Multiple accounts**
  Target AWS resources from this AWS account and specified AWS accounts (target accounts).

Figure 12.3 – The template details such as the description, name, and account target

5. In the next step, we need to define our actions and targets. This is the heart of the chaos experiment:

    - **Targets** are the groups of resources (for example, EC2 instances, RDS clusters, or Auto Scaling groups) that we will run our experiment against

    - **Actions** are the actions, such as terminating an instance, triggering an RDS failover, or injecting an insufficient instance capacity error into an Auto Scaling group when it tries to scale out

    The following screenshot shows the interface before we start creating targets and actions:

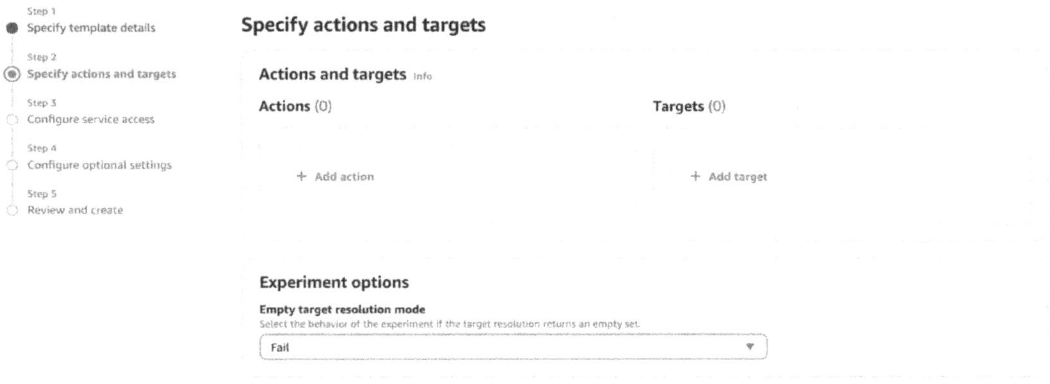

Step 1
● Specify template details

Step 2
◉ Specify actions and targets

Step 3
○ Configure service access

Step 4
○ Configure optional settings

Step 5
○ Review and create

Specify actions and targets

Actions and targets Info

Actions (0)   **Targets** (0)

\+ Add action   \+ Add target

Experiment options

Empty target resolution mode
Select the behavior of the experiment if the target resolution returns an empty set.

> Fail   ▼

Figure 12.4 – Chaos experiment template wizard showing the targets and actions (currently empty)

6. We'll first create a new target for our experiment, so select the + **Add target** button to open up the target creation wizard.

7. In the target creation wizard, define the following properties for our target:

    *   **Name** is the name of our target. Use something descriptive, such as RDS-Cluster.

    *   **Resource type** defines the type of resource we are targeting, such as an RDS cluster or EC2 instance. Select **aws:rds:cluster** here.

8. We then need to define how to select our targets under **Target method**. We can either directly provide the resource IDs (i.e., the ARNs of the cluster we want to target) or select them via a tag. For this example, we'll use the explicit naming of each resource using the resource IDs.

    Under **Resource IDs**, select the previously created RDS cluster. It should start with the prefix aurora-cluster-demo.

    Under **Selection mode**, choose **All**. The selection mode lets us define how the resources that are targeted are selected. With the **All** option, the defined action (for example, the database failover) will run against every database cluster in this target group. With the **Count** option, you can randomly select up to a certain number of resources that are part of this target, and with the **Percentage** option, you can have AWS FIS choose a percentage of resources as the target. The count and percentage method are useful if you want to simulate something such as 60% of your instances terminating.

    You can view the selected options in the following screenshot:

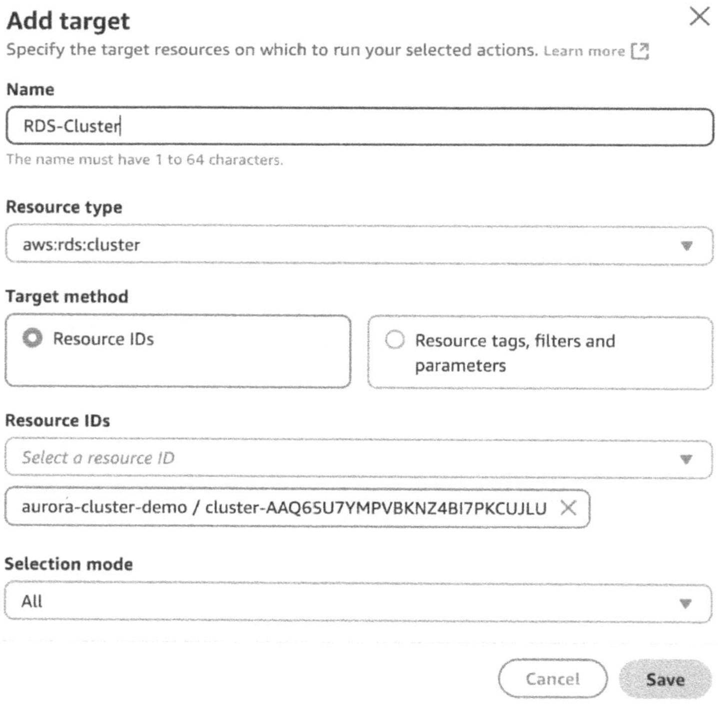

Figure 12.5 – Target selection wizard for our chaos experiment template

9. With our targets defined, we can go ahead and create the actions that we want to run against these targets:

- **Name** defines the name of our action. Use something descriptive, such as `Failover-RDS`, in this example.

- **Action type** defines the kind of action we want to carry out. Actions are grouped by their target service. In the first dropdown, select **RDS** since we want to trigger a database failover. In the second dropdown, select **aws:rds:failover-db-cluster** as the action.

- With **Start after**, you can define an action that needs to be finished before this action can run. This can be useful when building scenarios where failures build upon each other. We'll leave this empty since this is our only action in this experiment.

- For **Target**, select our previously created target, called **RDS-Cluster**.

You can see the entire filled-out wizard in the following screenshot:

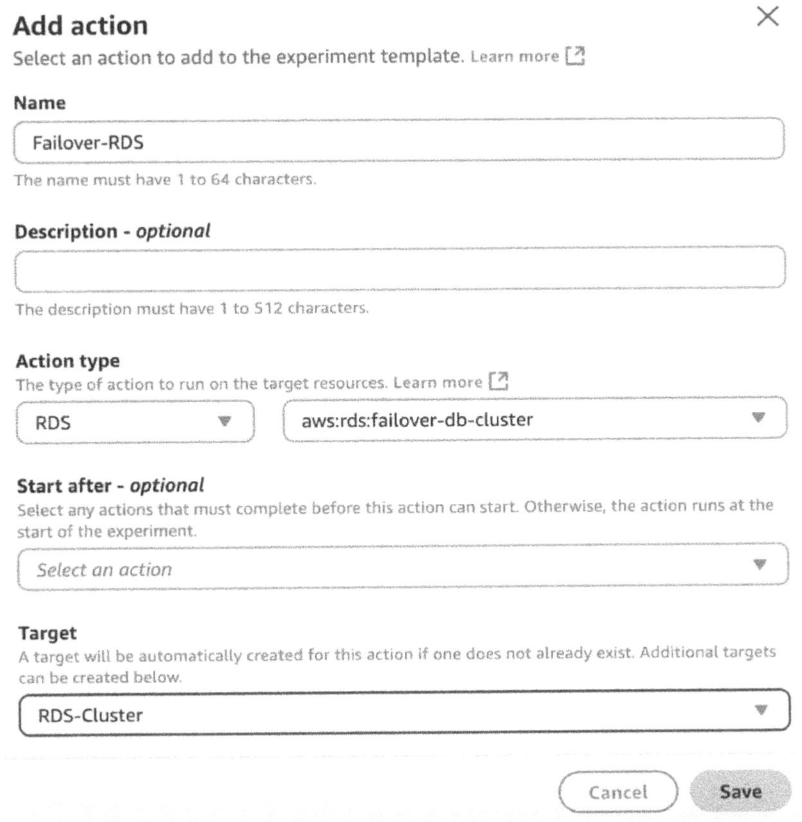

Add action ✕

Select an action to add to the experiment template. Learn more [↗]

Name

> Failover-RDS

The name must have 1 to 64 characters.

Description - *optional*

The description must have 1 to 512 characters.

Action type

The type of action to run on the target resources. Learn more [↗]

| RDS ▼ | aws:rds:failover-db-cluster ▼ |

Start after - *optional*

Select any actions that must complete before this action can start. Otherwise, the action runs at the start of the experiment.

> *Select an action* ▼

Target

A target will be automatically created for this action if one does not already exist. Additional targets can be created below.

> RDS-Cluster ▼

Cancel   Save

Figure 12.6 – Wizard for creating our action

10. With this, we now have the structure of our chaos experiment defined. Your **Actions and targets** pane should look like the following screenshot:

Specify actions and targets

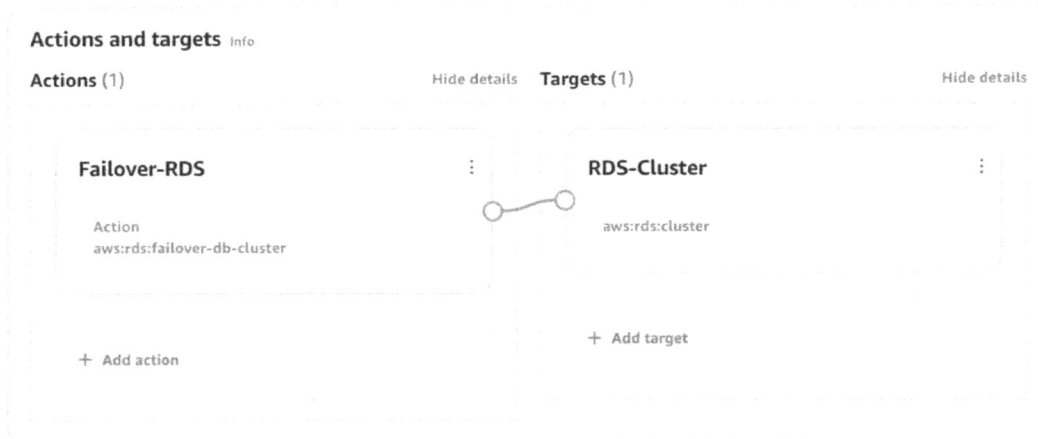

Figure 12.7 – Actions and targets after we have created our RDS failover scenario

11. We'll also need to select what should happen to this experiment if the target is empty. In this example, we'll fail the experiment, so let's select **Fail** in the dropdown under **Empty target resolution mode** and click **Next**.

12. Next, we need to configure the service access. In order for AWS FIS to be able to carry out the required actions against our resource, we need to create an IAM role that has the required permissions. We can either let AWS FIS create a new role with the correct set of permissions for us or specify a role if we already created one. Note that you generally don't want to run AWS FIS experiments with more permissions than required, so refrain from using your administrator role or similar here.

For this example, we'll select **Create new role for the experiment template** to have AWS FIS create a new role for us. AWS FIS will automatically generate a random role name with the prefix `AWSFISIAMRole-`, as shown in the following screenshot. Click **Next**.

Service access

FIS requires permission to conduct experiments on your behalf

⦿ Create a new role for the experiment template

◉ Use an existing IAM role

Service role name

AWSFISIAMRole-1733773237943

(View details)

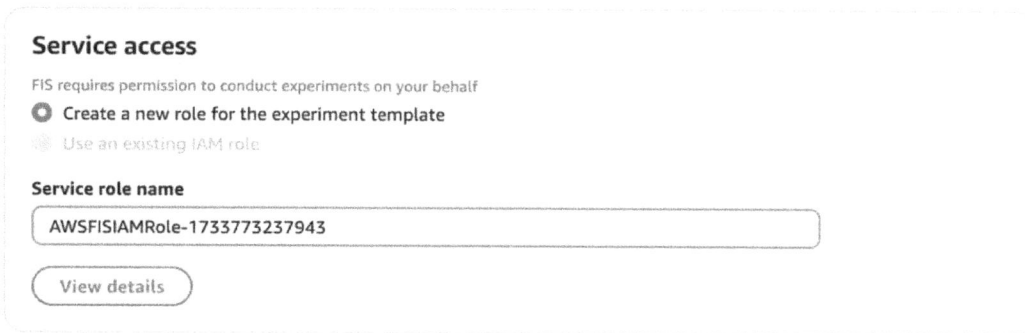

Figure 12.8 – Creation of the role that will be used to give AWS FIS the required IAM permissions

13. Next, we can configure optional settings.

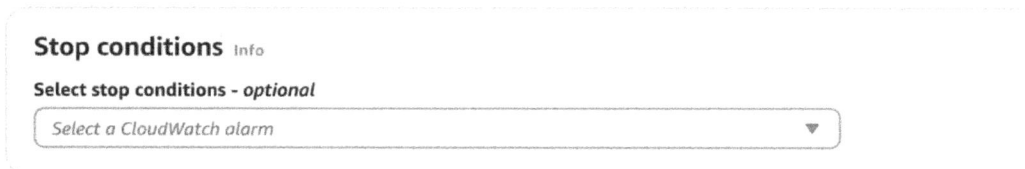

    The first optional setting we have is **Stop conditions**. We can use CloudWatch alarms to automatically stop a chaos experiment if a certain threshold is used. For example, if you have a metric that tracks the number of 5XX error codes returned to users, you could use this metric to automatically turn off the experiment if a certain threshold is reached. This can be very useful if you decide to run chaos experiments in production to avoid completely taking down the application.

    Since we don't have this kind of metric in our scenario, we'll leave it empty, as shown in the following screenshot:

Configure optional settings

Stop conditions Info

Select stop conditions - *optional*

Select a CloudWatch alarm ▾

Figure 12.9 – The optional Stop conditions configuration

14. AWS FIS can also generate a report of the chaos experiment in PDF format, which can be used as evidence that resiliency testing was carried out. The PDF will be uploaded to an S3 bucket of your choice. For this example, we'll also leave this optional feature off, as shown in the following screenshot:

Report configuration - *new, optional* Info

AWS FIS generates experiment reports as evidence of resilience testing. Configure report settings so that a FIS experiment report is delivered to an S3 bucket. You can download the PDF once the experiment is completed. FIS generates reports with an associated cost. See Amazon FIS pricing ↗

Report destination

Choose an S3 destination for the report. Ingestion and storage charges apply. See Amazon S3 pricing ↗

| Q bucket-name/prefix/ | View ↗ | Browse S3 |

Format: <bucket>/<optional-prefix-with-path>/

> ⓘ **Permissions required for FIS reporting**
> To generate and store reports, ensure your FIS experiment IAM role has CloudWatch and S3 permissions. Learn more ↗   (View permission details)   ✕

Embed CloudWatch metric snapshot graphs

You have the option to include snapshot graphs of Amazon CloudWatch metrics in the report by selecting a CloudWatch dashboard. The snapshot graphs will reflect the experiment impact on your key metrics over a time period that you specify. CloudWatch request charges apply.

☐ Include CloudWatch metrics in this report

Figure 12.10 – Optional AWS FIS reporting feature turned off

15. Finally, AWS FIS allows us to specify an S3 bucket or CloudWatch Logs group to send the logs from our chaos experiment. Here, we are going to check the checkbox next to **Send to CloudWatch Logs** to send them to CloudWatch, and under **Log group ARN**, use the **Browse** button to select the log group that was previously created by the Terraform script. It should be called `/chaos-experiments`. Your wizard should then look like the following:

▼ Logs

Destination - *optional*

The destination that receives the experiment log data. Amazon FIS doesn't charge for sending the logs. However, ingestion and storage charges apply based on the destination.

☐ Send to an Amazon S3 bucket

☑ Send to CloudWatch Logs

Log group ARN

| Q ▮▮▮▮▮▮:log-group:/chaos-experiments:* ✕ | View ↗ | Browse |

Log version

| Version 2   ▼ |

Figure 12.11 – Log delivery settings for our chaos experiment

16. With the logs configured, click the **Next** button to get to a final summary page. At the bottom of the summary, click **Create experiment template** to create our new experiment template. During this, you'll be prompted to confirm that you want to create an experiment without a stop condition, as shown in the following screenshot:

Create experiment template   ✕

> ⚠ You have not specified a stop condition for your experiment template. A stop condition can help to prevent your experiment from going out of bounds by stopping it automatically. Learn more [↗]

To confirm that you want to create an experiment template without a stop condition, enter *create* **in the field:**

    create

                                  Cancel   Create experiment template

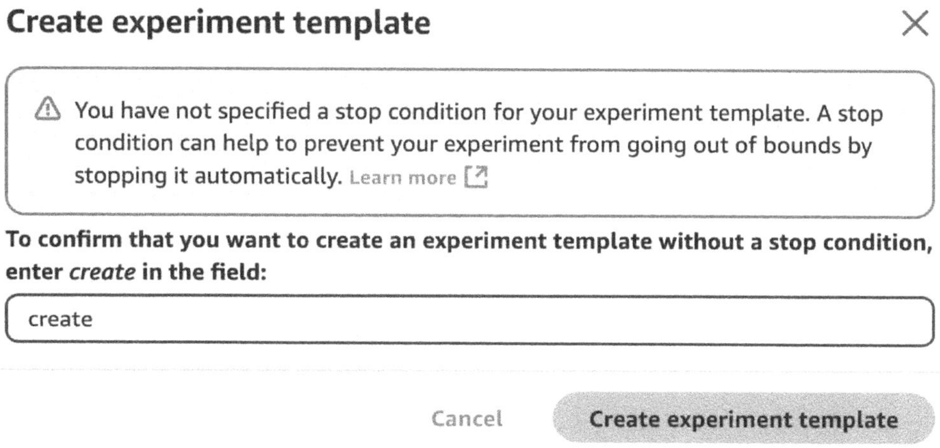

Figure 12.12 – Warning indicating that we are creating an experiment template without a stop condition

With our experiment template created, we are ready to run the experiment. To do this, follow these steps:

1. Open up the RDS console in a new tab by searching for it in the search bar or opening it up using this link: `https://eu-central-1.console.aws.amazon.com/rds/home?region=eu-central-1#databases`. We'll use this new tab to see the actual failover happen.

2. In the AWS FIS console, navigate to the **Experiment templates** entry in the left-hand menu, where you should see your previously created experiment template. Select it, as shown in the following screenshot, and click the **Start experiment** button:

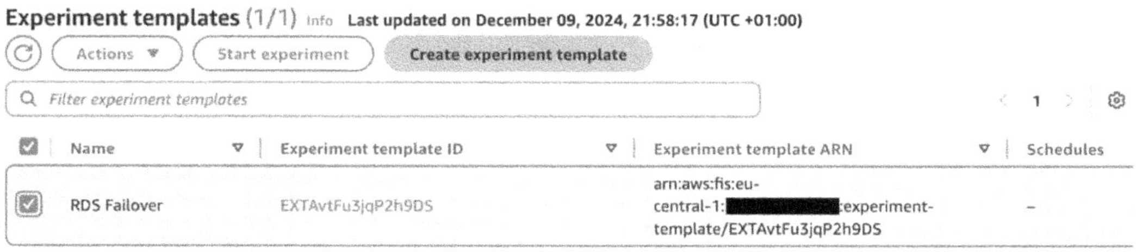

Experiment templates (1/1) Info Last updated on December 09, 2024, 21:58:17 (UTC +01:00)

☑	Name	▽	Experiment template ID	▽	Experiment template ARN	▽	Schedules
☑	RDS Failover		EXTAvtFu3jqP2h9DS		arn:aws:fis:eu-central-1:█████████:experiment-template/EXTAvtFu3jqP2h9DS		–

Actions ▾   Start experiment   Create experiment template

Figure 12.13 – Selection of our experiment template to create a new experiment from

3. In the next dialog, click the **Start experiment** button. You'll have to once again confirm that you want to start the experiment without a stop condition, as shown in the following screenshot:

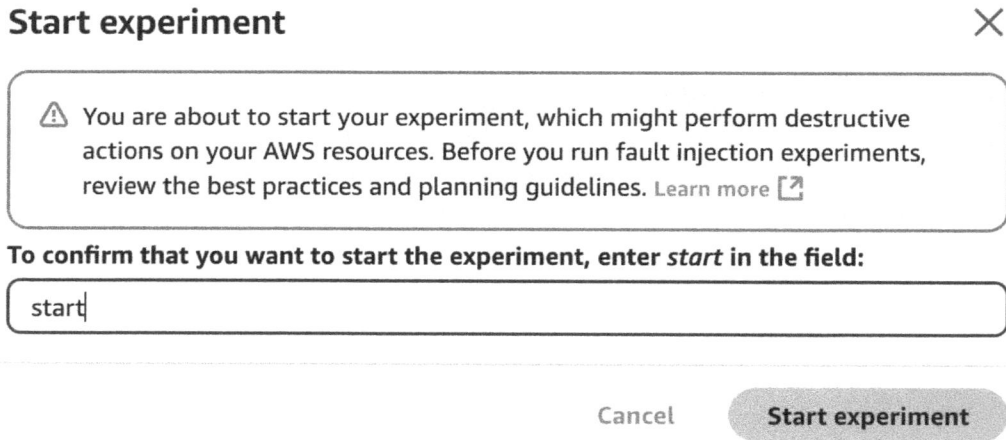

Start experiment   ✕

> ⚠ You are about to start your experiment, which might perform destructive actions on your AWS resources. Before you run fault injection experiments, review the best practices and planning guidelines. Learn more [↗]

To confirm that you want to start the experiment, enter *start* in the field:

start|

Cancel   **Start experiment**

Figure 12.14 – Confirmation that you want to run the experiment without a stop condition

4. While the experiment is now running, you can navigate over to RDS. Here, under your database clusters, you'll see the database failover happening, as shown in the following screenshot:

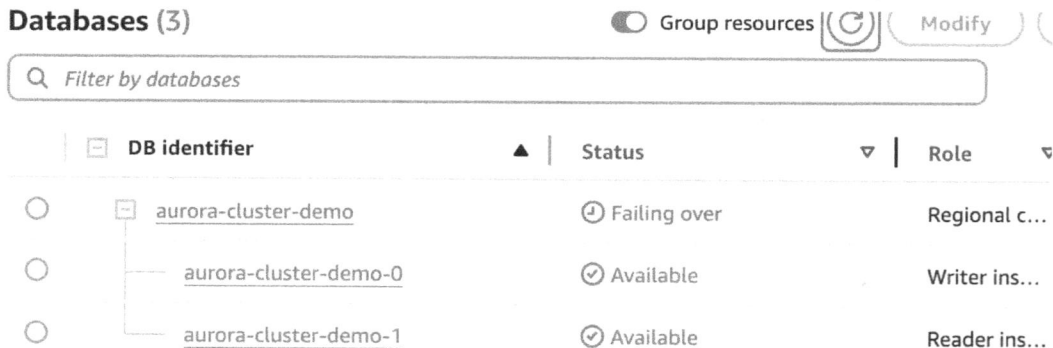

Databases (3)   ◯ Group resources |(C)| (Modify) (

Q *Filter by databases*

DB identifier ▲	Status ▽	Role ▽
☐ aurora-cluster-demo	⏱ Failing over	Regional c...
├── aurora-cluster-demo-0	⊘ Available	Writer ins...
└── aurora-cluster-demo-1	⊘ Available	Reader ins...

Figure 12.15 – RDS console showing the cluster failover triggered by our chaos experiment

5. Once the experiment is finished, the AWS FIS console will show you a summary of actions (under **Actions summary**), how long they took to carry out, and what resources were affected (under **Resources**), as shown in the following screenshot:

Actions summary (1)

Action name ▽	Status ▽	Action ID ▽	Start time ▽	End time ▽
RDS-Failover	⊘ Comp leted	aws:rds:failover-db-cluster	December 09, 2024, 22:06:41 (UTC +01:00)	December 09, 2024, 22:06:41 (UTC +01:00)

Resource overview

Resources targeted	Region	Resource types
1	eu-central-1	1

Resources (1)   ⟳ (Download)

🔍 *Filter resolved targets*   ‹ 1 › ⚙

Target information ▽	Resource type ▽	Target name ▽	Account ID
arn:aws:rds:eu-central-1:▮▮▮▮:cluster:aurora-cluster-demo ⎘	aws:rds:cluster	RDS-Cluster	▮▮▮▮

Figure 12.16 – Summary of the actions and affected resources

6. If you navigate to CloudWatch Logs and find the previously created log group (called /chaos-experiments), you'll find a new log stream under it that contains the logs from the chaos experiment run. It includes logs from all the stages, such as target resolution, actions starting, and the experiment ending. You can see an example of the log file in the following screenshot:

/chaos-experiments › /aws/fis/EXPR7ERnU9wJwJm4p2

Log events   ⟳ (Actions ▼) (Start tailing) Create metric filter

You can use the filter bar below to search for and match terms, phrases, or values in your log events. Learn more about filter patterns ⎘

🔍 *Filter events - press enter to search*   (1m 1h 📅) (UTC timezone ▼) (Display ▼)   ⚙

▶	Timestamp	Message
		No older events at this moment. *Retry*
▼	2024-12-09T21:06:29.486Z	{"id":"EXPR7ERnU9wJwJm4p2","log_type":"experiment-start","event_timestamp":"2024-12-09T21:06:29.486Z","versio...

```
{
    "id": "EXPR7ERnU9wJwJm4p2",
    "log_type": "experiment-start",
    "event_timestamp": "2024-12-09T21:06:29.486Z",
    "version": "2",
    "details": {
        "experiment_template_id": "EXTZMYX0hPUMwiln",
        "experiment_start_time": "2024-12-09T21:06:13.640Z"
    }
}
```

Figure 12.17 – CloudWatch Logs group with the detailed log messages from our experiment run

> **Additional information**
>
> Under **Experiments**, you'll find a button called **Stop all experiments**. This is a safety lever that you can pull. It will terminate all running experiments and will prevent any new experiments from being run (either started manually or automatically on a schedule) until you click the **Disengage safety lever** button. This can be useful when experiments are running that are threatening your production workload.

With this, we have successfully created our first chaos experiment. You can have a look at this documentation page to get an overview of all the actions that are available to you: `https://docs.aws.amazon.com/fis/latest/userguide/fis-actions-reference.html`.

When designing experiments, remember to make them realistic and adhere to a real-world scenario that your architecture should be resilient to.

Summary

In this chapter, we learned how to implement chaos engineering experiments using AWS FIS. We had a quick introduction to chaos engineering and chaos experiments before showcasing such a simple yet powerful experiment with a database failover.

In the next chapters, we'll cover how we can manage more complex multi-account setups. We'll start by introducing continuous deployment and continuous integration into our toolset.

Get This Book's PDF Version and Exclusive Extras

UNLOCK NOW

Scan the QR code (or go to `packtpub.com/unlock`). Search for this book by name, confirm the edition, and then follow the steps on the page.

Note: Keep your invoice handly. Purchase made directly from packt don't require one.

Part 5:
Deployments at Scale

In the fifth part of the book, we discuss common patterns when dealing with deploying infrastructure on AWS at scale. The part discusses patterns to design reusable Infrastructure-as-Code components and continuously deploy your infrastructure using CI/CD tools.

Finally, we combine all the learnings of the book to see how the end-to-end deployment of an application is handled.

This part contains the following chapters:

- *Chapter 13, Deploying Infrastructure Using CI/CD Pipelines*
- *Chapter 14, Building Reusable Infrastructure-as-Code Components*
- *Chapter 15, Ensuring Compliance Using AWS Config and SCPs*
- *Chapter 16, Operating in a Multi-Account Environment*
- *Chapter 17, End-to-End Deployment of an Application*

13

Deploying Infrastructure Using CI/CD Pipelines

A common theme throughout this book has been the usage of **infrastructure as code** (**IaC**). We have opted to describe and then automate the deployment of our infrastructure using tools such as Terraform and CloudFormation.

But one treatment that is usually applied to modern applications – the concept of continuously building and releasing the software – hasn't been applied to our infrastructure so far.

This chapter starts with a short introduction to CI/CD followed by a practical guide to deploying the Terraform scripts saved in a Git repository – hosted on GitHub – to our AWS environment.

In this chapter, we're going to cover the following main topics:

- Introduction to CI/CD
- Connecting AWS and GitHub
- Creating a pipeline to automatically run Terraform deployments

So, let's get started!

Technical requirements

Before following this section, please create an AWS account for yourself. You can sign up at aws. amazon.com. A basic understanding of AWS – for example, knowing what a service is – will be beneficial.

A basic understanding of IaC tools such as Terraform is beneficial. An understanding of version control with Git is required. You'll need to have Git set up on your local machine.

To follow the practical parts, a GitHub account is required.

All scripts from this section can be found at the following GitHub link:

`https://github.com/PacktPublishing/AWS-for-System-Administrators-Second-Edition.`

The CiA video for this chapter can be found at `https://packt.link/dpzgo`

A short introduction to CI/CD

Continuous integration/continuous delivery (CI/CD) is a practice in software engineering. The idea is that, instead of building (or integrating) our software project once every few months when releasing a new version, we continuously build our software as new changes are added to the repository. CD then takes these continually integrated changes and automatically prepares them for deployment and can also automatically deploy a new version.

This practice of continuously updating software instead of only doing one big change every few months helps with making our releases smaller and more manageable with a faster development cycle.

With IaC, we already treat our infrastructure the same way we would treat a software project. So, we can also apply the same practice of CI/CD to our infrastructure code.

In this chapter, we'll cover an AWS service, AWS CodeBuild, to do the job of running a set of commands on the new version of the code upon a change to the code in our version control system.

Automated deployment with Terraform and AWS CodeBuild

Before we can get started with setting up our deployment infrastructure, we need to perform two preliminary steps. First, we need to connect our GitHub account to our AWS account, and then we'll need to set up a backend to save our Terraform state.

Connecting your GitHub account

In this walkthrough, we'll store our code in a Git repository on GitHub and create a connection between our AWS account and our GitHub account.

> **Note**
>
> If you have previously used AWS, you might be familiar with its CodeCommit service for creating Git repositories. In this book, we are using GitHub to host our Git repositories instead of CodeCommit. This is because, in the summer of 2024, AWS announced that CodeCommit would no longer be usable to new customers. You can see the announcement at the beginning of the blog post here: `https://aws.amazon.com/blogs/devops/how-to-migrate-your-aws-codecommit-repository-to-another-git-provider/`.

Creating a new repository for our code

We'll first need a new repository to hold our Terraform code in. To create a new repository, follow these steps:

1. Navigate to `github.com` and log in to your account

2. On your dashboard, click the green **New** button to get to the dialog for creating a new repository:

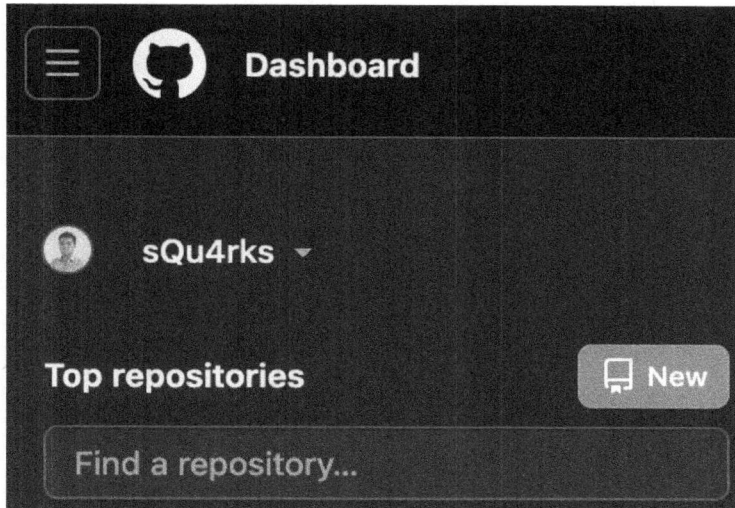

Figure 13.1 – Interface to create a new repository in GitHub

3. In the repository creation dialog (see the following figure), you'll need to provide a name and repository type. For this example, the name is `infra-demo` and the repository type is **Private**. Leave the **Add a README file** box unchecked since we won't need a README file for this demo application. Under **Add .gitignore**, in the dropdown, search for and select **Terraform**. This will make GitHub include a `.gitignore` file that already ignores the typical Terraform-specific files.

With the settings done to your liking, click the green **Create repository** button in the lower-right corner.

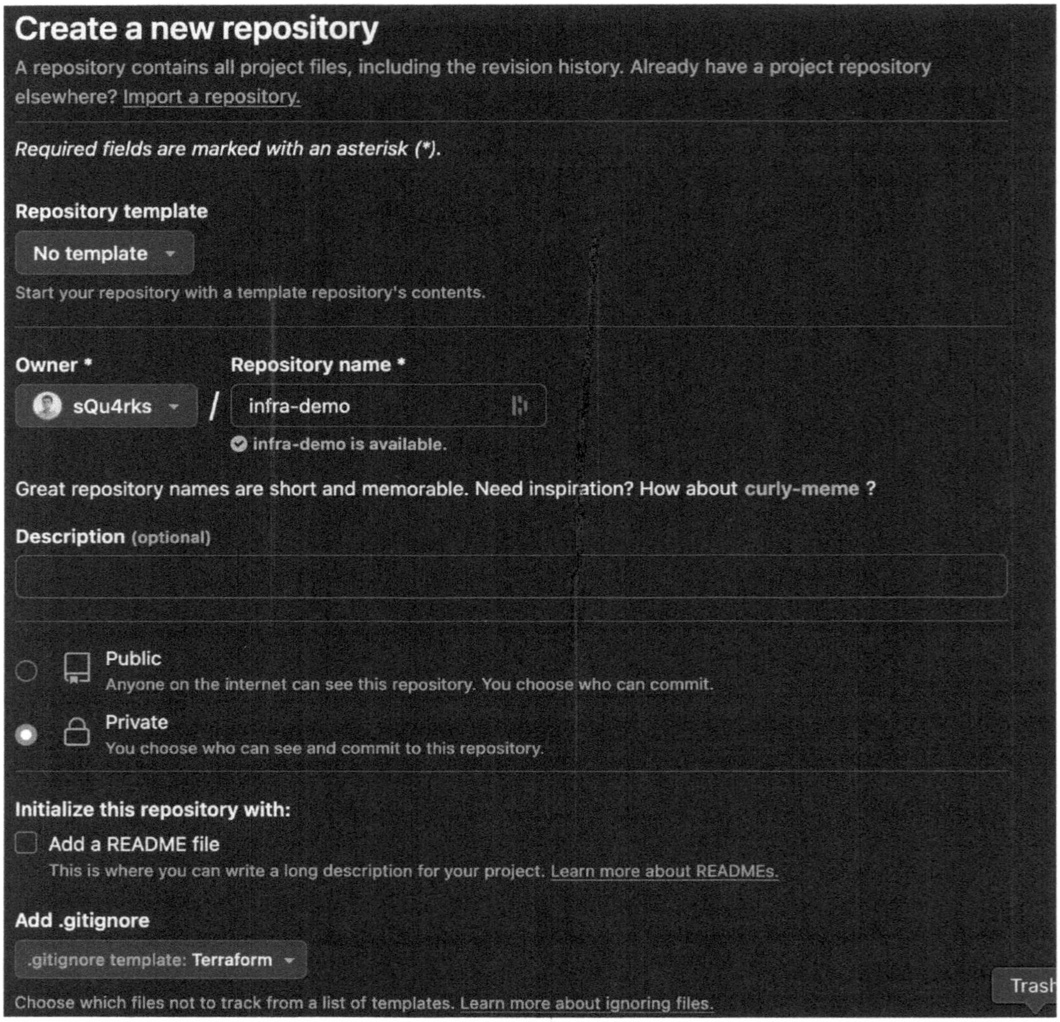

Create a new repository

A repository contains all project files, including the revision history. Already have a project repository elsewhere? Import a repository.

Required fields are marked with an asterisk (*).

Repository template

No template ▾

Start your repository with a template repository's contents.

Owner *   **Repository name ***

🙂 sQu4rks ▾   /   infra-demo   ⬚

⊘ infra-demo is available.

Great repository names are short and memorable. Need inspiration? How about **curly-meme** ?

Description (optional)

○ 🖳 **Public**
   Anyone on the internet can see this repository. You choose who can commit.

◉ 🔒 **Private**
   You choose who can see and commit to this repository.

Initialize this repository with:

Add a README file
   This is where you can write a long description for your project. Learn more about READMEs.

Add .gitignore

.gitignore template: **Terraform** ▾

Choose which files not to track from a list of templates. Learn more about ignoring files.

Trash

Figure 13.2 – The dialog to create the new GitHub repository

4.   With the repo configured, go ahead and clone it to your local machine. To do so, run the following command in your console. Don't forget to replace the placeholders with your GitHub username and repository name:

```
git clone https://github.com/<your-git-user>/<your-git-repo-
name>
```

5.   You should see a new folder with the same name as your repository.

With the repository that will hold our project created successfully, we can next create the connection that will allow the Code* services to pull from this repository.

Creating the connection between GitHub and AWS

We are now going to create a connection between AWS and our GitHub account. To do this, follow these steps:

1.   Before you begin, make sure that you are logged in to your GitHub account.

2.   To create the connection, open the AWS console in your web browser and search for CodeBuild. You'll be redirected to the **Developer Tools** service. In the left-hand navigation bar, select **Connections** under **Settings**, as shown in the following screenshot:

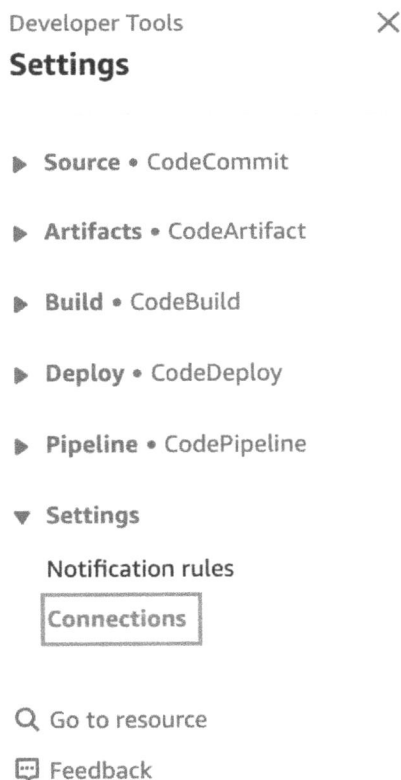

Developer Tools   ✕

Settings

▶ **Source** • CodeCommit

▶ **Artifacts** • CodeArtifact

▶ **Build** • CodeBuild

▶ **Deploy** • CodeDeploy

▶ **Pipeline** • CodePipeline

▼ **Settings**

Notification rules

Connections

Q Go to resource

▢ Feedback

Figure 13.3 – The Connections settings item in the Developer Tools service

3. In the menu, select **Create connection** at the top right to get to the dialog to create a new connection.

4. In the first field, we need to select the repository hosting provider we want to connect to. Aside from GitHub (and GitHub Enterprise), we could also connect to GitLab (both the SaaS service and a self-hosted instance) and Bitbucket. For our demo, we'll use GitHub, so select **GitHub** (not **GitHub Enterprise Server**) as the provider.

5. Type a name for your connection. In this example, we'll use `GitHubTest`. Both the provider choice and name are shown in the following screenshot:

Create a connection info

Select a provider

Bitbucket	○ GitHub	GitHub Enterprise Server
GitLab	GitLab self-managed	

Create GitHub App connection Info

Connection name

GitHubTest

▶ **Tags** - *optional*

Connect to GitHub

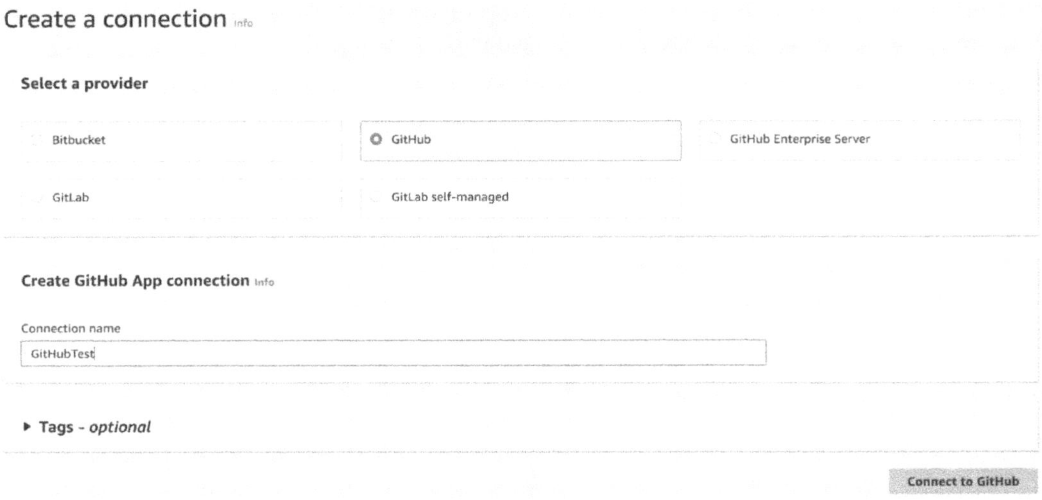

Figure 13.4 – Choice of provider and connection name

6. Click **Connect to GitHub** and you'll be redirected to GitHub, where you'll need to grant the AWS Connector for GitHub access to your GitHub account, as shown in the following screenshot. To do the authorization, click **Authorize AWS Connector for GitHub**. This will grant the integration from AWS the ability to see your repositories.

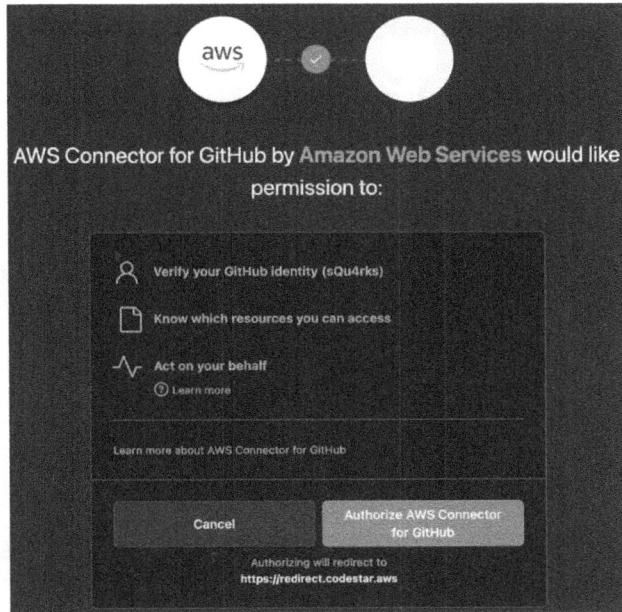

Figure 13.5 – Authorization of the AWS Connector for GitHub

7. You'll be redirected back to AWS where we can now install an app. This app will use your established connection between AWS and GitHub to create a new connection to a specific set of repositories using a bot integration. On the interface (shown in the following screenshot), click the **Install a new app** button:

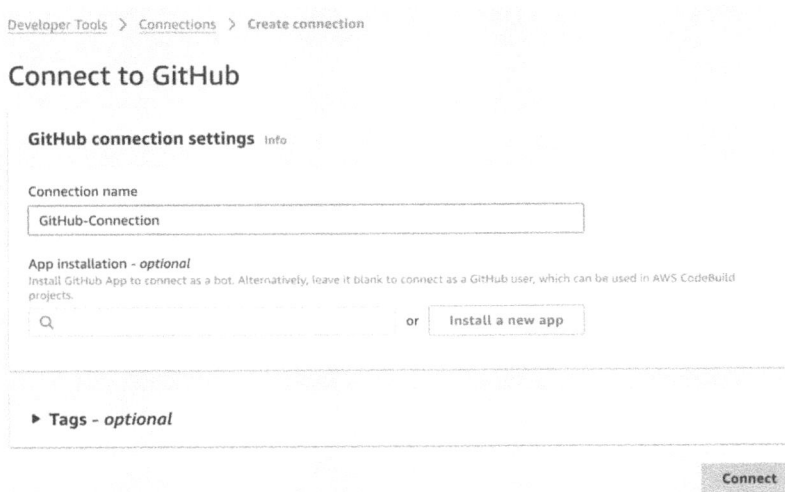

Figure 13.6 – Dialog to install the GitHub app

8. You'll again be redirected to GitHub. On GitHub, you'll be prompted to select where you want to install the app. The choice here is your personal account or any GitHub organization that you are a part of (**PacktPublishing**, in my example). Select your personal username (**sQu4rks**, in my case), as shown in the following screenshot:

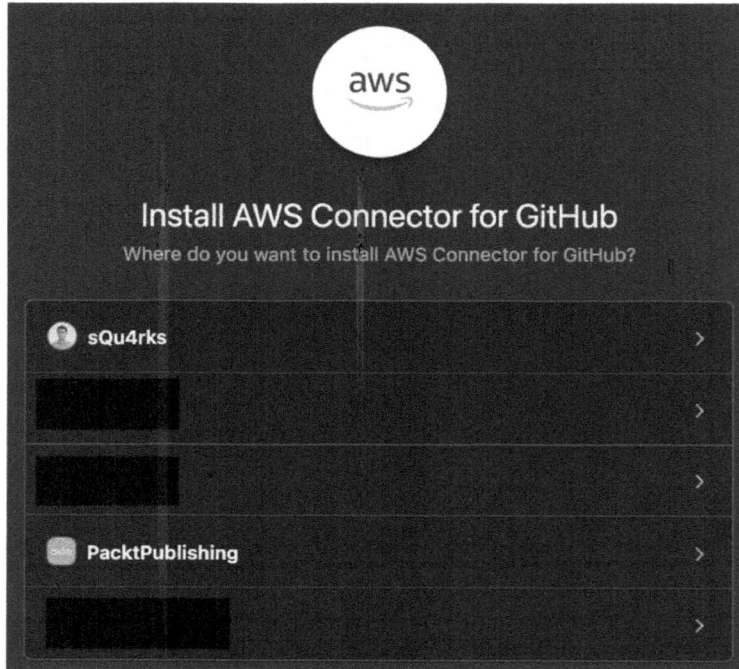

Figure 13.7 – GitHub location selector for the app

9. Next, we need to install and authorize the AWS connector. This is where we'll select which repositories the integration should have access to. We'll grant the integration access only to the previously created repo. To do this, select **Only select repositories** and, in the dropdown below, select your previously created repository – **sQu4rks/infra-demo**, in my example – as shown in the following screenshot. Then, click the **Install & Authorize** button, which will redirect you back to AWS.

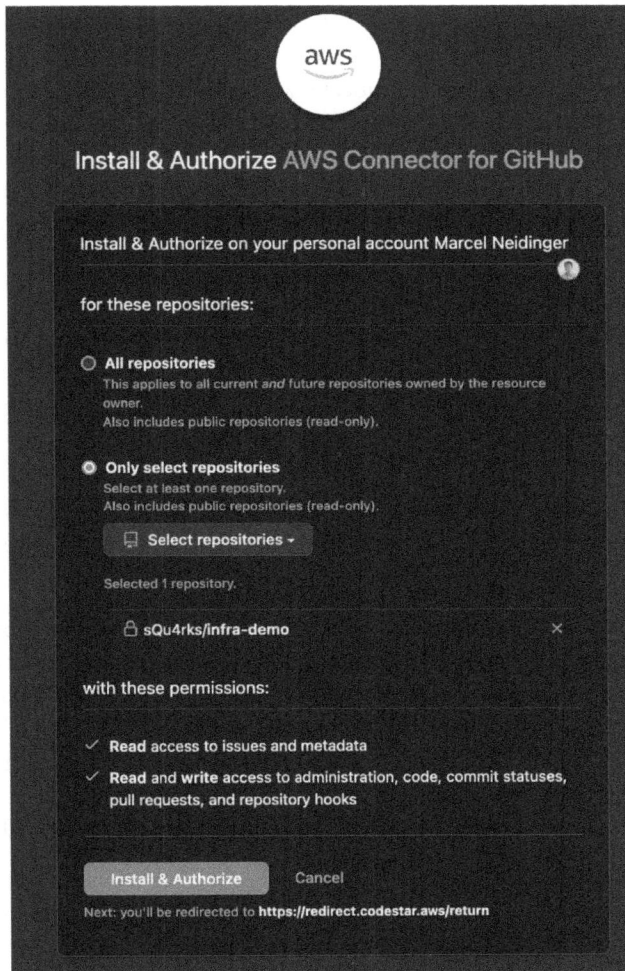

Figure 13.8 – Repository selection for our connection to GitHub

10. Back in the AWS console, we can now use our newly created app. The **App Installation** option should already be filled out with a number so you can click **Connect** to finish the process.

With the connection between GitHub and AWS established, we can now create the necessary infrastructure for Terraform.

Setting up a Terraform backend

So far, we have always run Terraform from our local machine as this made one thing very easy: *state management*. The Terraform state is a list of the state of your resources. This means that the state keeps track of which resources have been created as part of the Terraform project and how they are configured. When changing an attribute in Terraform or adding a new resource, the `plan` command will determine how the state – and thus the AWS infrastructure – needs to be altered.

> **Additional information**
>
> This state isn't something magical. Have a look at any of the previous examples where we used Terraform to create resources. You'll find a file called `terraform.tfstate` in the directory. This file is in JSON format and contains the list of resources that are deployed and managed by Terraform for that project.

But how do we keep this state file in sync if we have multiple people working on the same infrastructure? And how do we make sure that the CI/CD workers deploying our infrastructure have the correct version of the state file to use?

This is where remote backends in Terraform come into play. The backend is a Terraform construct that is used to define where the state file should be retrieved from and saved. If we do not define a backend, Terraform will use the default backend, which is local. The local backend stores all information in a local file. There is a variety of backends available. You can have a look at all the options here: `https://developer.hashicorp.com/terraform/language/backend`. In this example, we'll be using the S3 backend. With this backend, the state file will be stored on and retrieved from S3. In addition, we are going to use the NoSQL serverless DynamoDB for locking the state file.

Locking in this context means that only one deployment (be it from a human or an automated CI/CD pipeline) can access and modify the state file at the same time. This is useful for consistency so that we don't get two parallel updates messing up the state.

> **Additional information**
>
> This book has also introduced CloudFormation and the CDK, which generates CloudFormation in the background, as IaC tools. In CloudFormation, state management is handled by the tool itself, and we don't need to configure a remote backend. This is why we cover Terraform in this chapter.

To be able to use the S3 backend in our projects, we'll need two resources: an S3 bucket and a DynamoDB table for storing our locks. We'll now use Terraform to create these resources. Notice that you only need to do this once for an account and that you can then use the same bucket and DynamoDB table for multiple projects.

To set up the required infrastructure, follow these steps:

1.   Open a code editor such as Visual Studio Code and create a new file called `setup_tf.tf`.

2. In the newly created file, we'll first set up the Terraform provider. These concepts were covered in more depth in *Chapter 1, Setting Up the AWS Environment*:

```
terraform {
  required_providers {
    aws = {
      source  = "hashicorp/aws"
      version = "~> 5.0"
    }
  }
}
provider "aws" {
  region = "eu-central-1"
}
```

3. Next, we create the bucket that will hold our state file:

```
resource "aws_s3_bucket" "terraform_state_bucket" {
  bucket = "mn-tf-state-bucket"
}
```

4. Next, we'll enable bucket versioning. This tells S3 to version any file in this bucket. If someone accidentally deletes the state file from S3, this means that the file can be recovered. We'll do this using the aws_s3_bucket_versioning resource type:

```
resource "aws_s3_bucket_versioning" "terraform_state" {
  bucket = aws_s3_bucket.terraform_state_bucket.id
  versioning_configuration {
    status = "Enabled"
  }
}
```

5. And finally, we can create the DynamoDB table that will hold our lock. We'll use the serverless variant of DynamoDB (via the PAY_PER_REQUEST option) and define a table schema with a single attribute. This attribute needs to be called LockID and be of the S type (for *string*):

```
resource "aws_dynamodb_table" "terraform_state_lock_table" {
  name         = "mn-tf-state-table"
  billing_mode = "PAY_PER_REQUEST"
  hash_key     = "LockID"
  attribute {
    name = "LockID"
    type = "S"
  }
}
```

6. With our script done, we can start deploying the infrastructure. To do this, open up your console and first initialize the Terraform project. This will download the required AWS Terraform provider for you:

    ```
    terraform init
    ```

7. Once the initialization is done, you can create the infrastructure using the following command:

    ```
    terraform apply
    ```

With our DynamoDB table and S3 bucket set up to store our state, we can finally deploy our code.

Deploying your code

With the connection and state management handled, we can get started with creating our CodeBuild project to deploy our infrastructure upon changes in our source repository.

To do this, follow these steps:

1. Open up the AWS console and search for CodeBuild. In the left navigation, navigate to **Build projects**. Here, you'll find a list of all your build projects. In the top-right corner, click the **Create project** button to create a new project, as shown in the following screenshot:

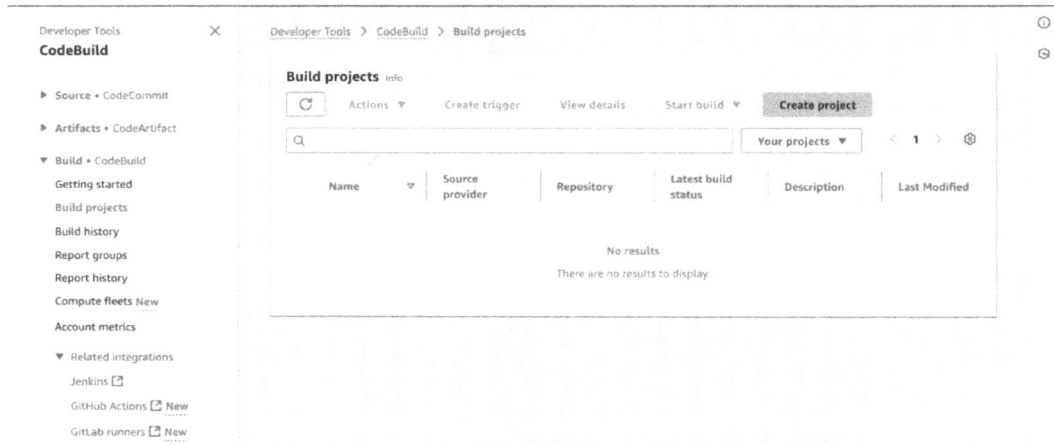

Figure 13.9 – Overview of our current build projects

2. We first need to define a name for our build project. In this example, we'll be using `TerraformDeploy`, as shown in the following screenshot:

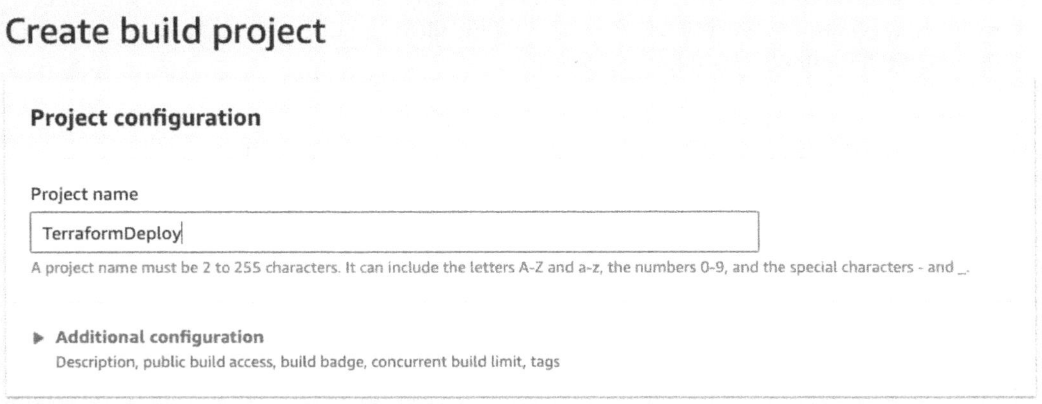

Create build project

Project configuration

Project name

TerraformDeploy|

A project name must be 2 to 255 characters. It can include the letters A-Z and a-z, the numbers 0-9, and the special characters - and _.

▶ **Additional configuration**
Description, public build access, build badge, concurrent build limit, tags

Figure 13.10 – The name of our build project

3. Next, we need to configure our source code provider. Select **GitHub** as the source provider. Then, select **Custom source credential** and **GitHub App** as the credential type. This will allow us to use the GitHub app integration we previously configured. Under **Connection**, select the previously created GitHub connection.

4. We can then select the repository to pull from. Since we want a repository in our account as opposed to one for a public GitHub repo, we'll select **Repository in my GitHub account**.

5.   In the search menu, type the first few characters of your previously created GitHub repo (infra-demo, in our example) and select it. Leave **Source version** empty. This optional field would allow you to scope the project to certain branches or tags, but we want our project to run on any commit to any branch. You can find the filled-out information for this section of the project definition in the following screenshot:

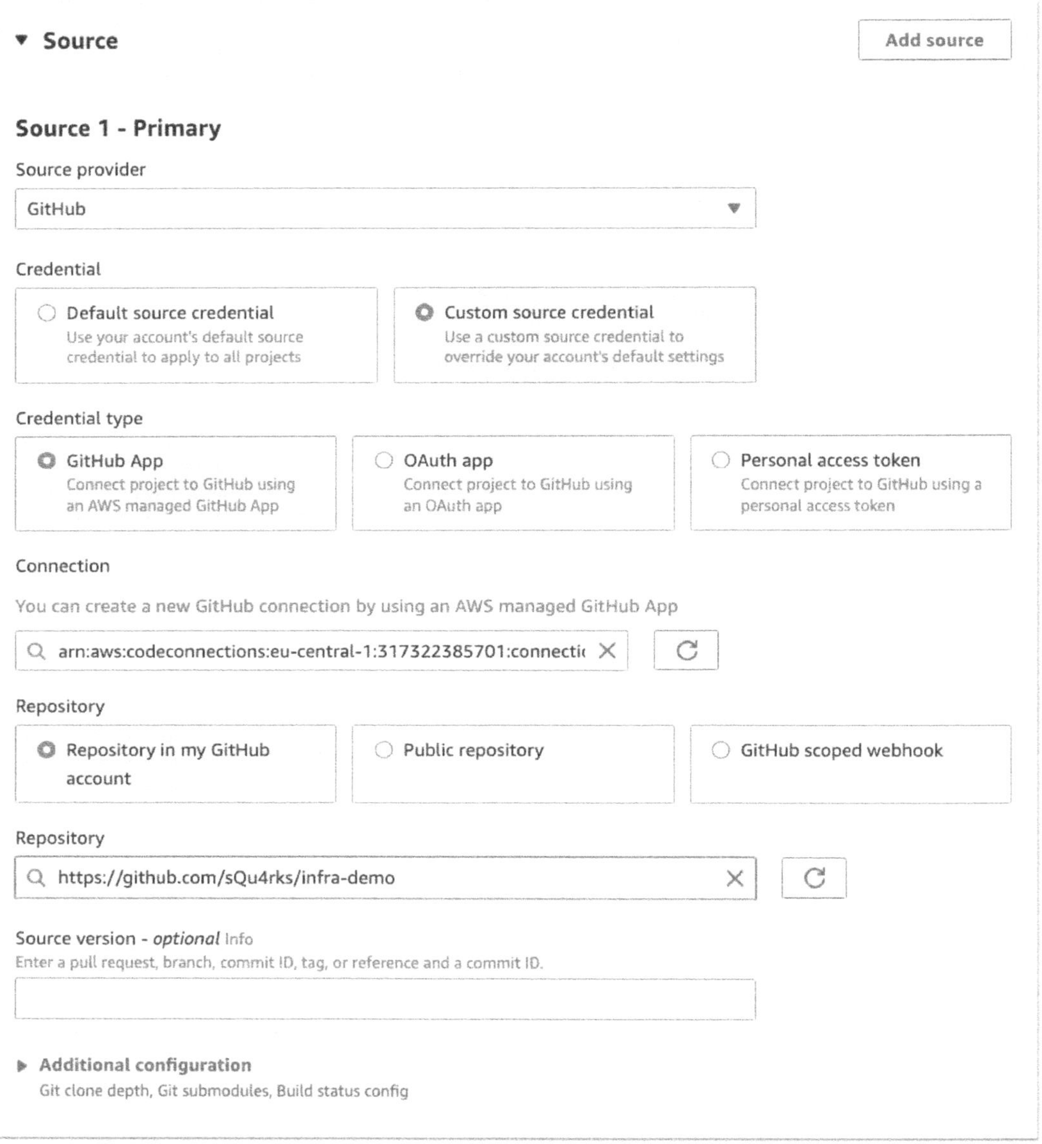

Figure 13.11 – Source configuration

6. For the primary source webhook, we'll select it to rebuild on every code change and to trigger a single build, as shown in the following screenshot:

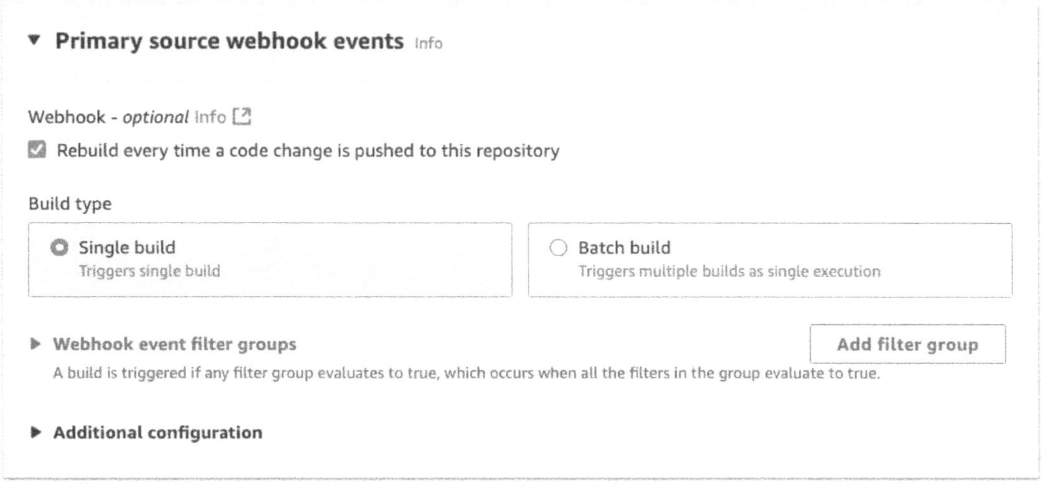

Figure 13.12 – Webhook event configuration for our CodeBuild project

7. Next up is the environment. This configures the compute that will be used to run the command we specify in our CodeBuild project.

   We'll choose **On-demand** as the provisioning model. This will let AWS automatically start and stop instances that will run our commands using the on-demand pricing model, where we pay for the time used.

8. **Environment image** defines the Docker image that will be used to run our commands. We'll leave this as **Managed image**. A custom image could be used if you have very specific build dependencies (such as internal libraries) that can't be easily installed using an install script.

9. For **Compute**, select **EC2** to tell CodeBuild to run our code on an EC2 instance instead of Lambda. Depending on the size of your build project, you could also use Lambda to provide the required compute capacity. We'll also leave the **Use GPU-enhanced compute** checkbox unchecked since we don't need a (more expensive) GPU-based instance to run our Terraform commands.

10. We'll leave the operating system as **Amazon Linux**, the runtime as **Standard**, and use the default image version for this demo. If you have specific build dependencies or setup scripts that are written for a different Linux distribution (such as Ubuntu), you can also select this here, but usually, you won't need to change these settings. The full configuration can be seen in the following screenshot:

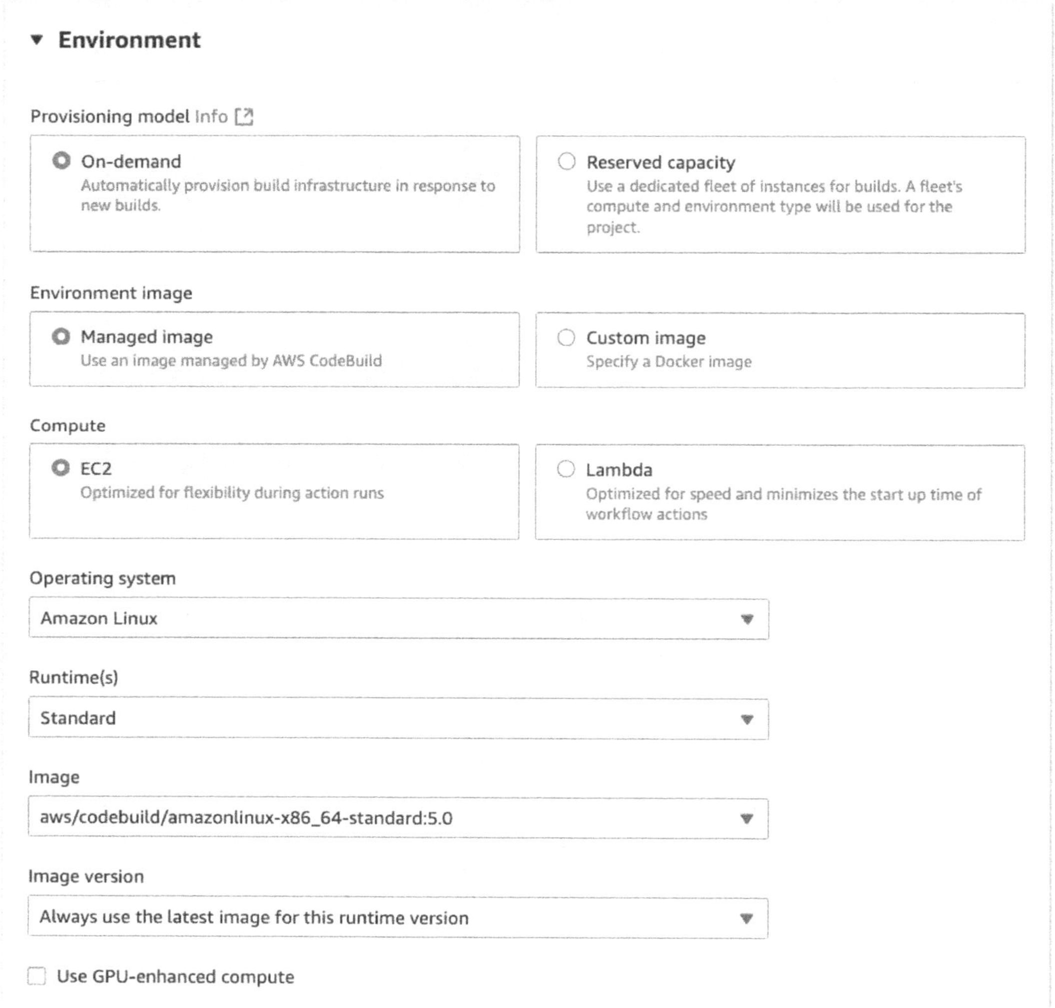

▼ **Environment**

Provisioning model Info ↗

● On-demand	○ Reserved capacity
Automatically provision build infrastructure in response to new builds.	Use a dedicated fleet of instances for builds. A fleet's compute and environment type will be used for the project.

Environment image

● Managed image	○ Custom image
Use an image managed by AWS CodeBuild	Specify a Docker image

Compute

● EC2	○ Lambda
Optimized for flexibility during action runs	Optimized for speed and minimizes the start up time of workflow actions

Operating system

Amazon Linux ▼

Runtime(s)

Standard ▼

Image

aws/codebuild/amazonlinux-x86_64-standard:5.0 ▼

Image version

Always use the latest image for this runtime version ▼

☐ Use GPU-enhanced compute

Figure 13.13 – The compute and instance configuration of our environment setup in CodeBuild

11. CodeBuild will need AWS credentials when running our code. These will be the credentials that are also used to run our Terraform commands. To do so, we need to provide a service role. Select **New service role**. CodeBuild will automatically create a new name for the role based on how you named the project.

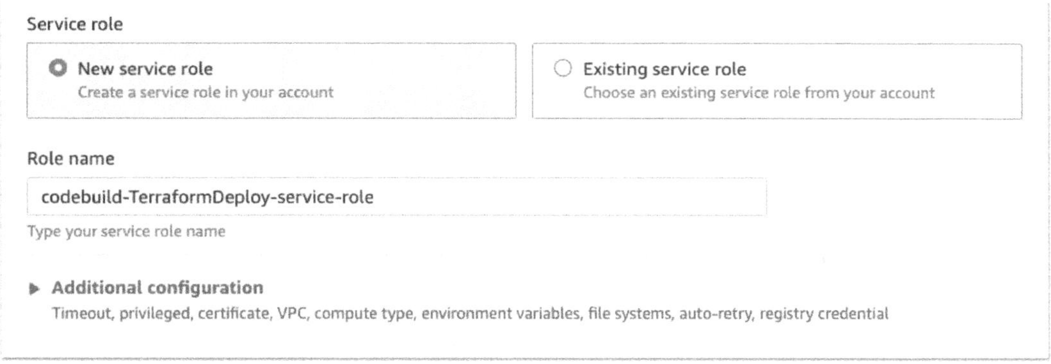

Figure 13.14 – The definition of our service role that will be used to run our Terraform code

12. Next, we need to define the steps that will be carried out when running this project. We'll explain the buildspec format more later in this chapter. For now, select **Use a buildspec file** and leave the **Buildspec name - optional** field empty as we'll use the default name of buildspec.yml.

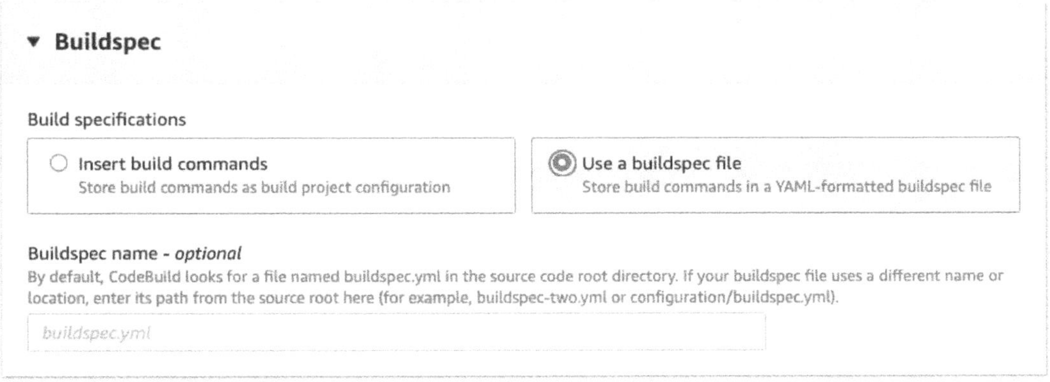

Figure 13.15 – Buildspec configuration

13. Finally, we need to configure the artifacts and logs. Artifacts are the result of our build jobs, such as test coverage reports or the results from unit tests. We don't have these artifacts in our current project, so we'll choose **No artifacts** as the type. For logs, we'll stream all the logs from our build jobs to CloudWatch Logs into its own log group. CodeBuild should already pre-populate the group name for you based on the project name, as shown in the following screenshot:

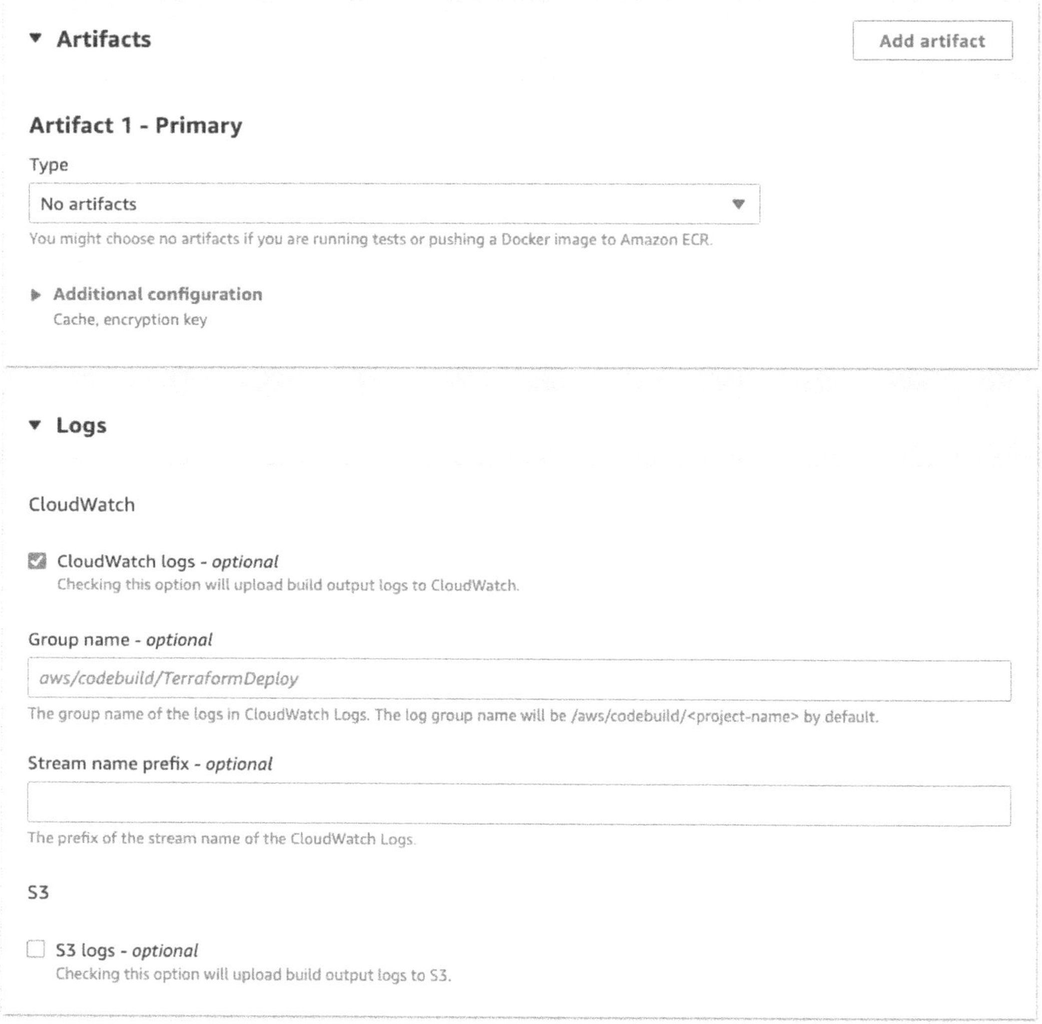

▼ **Artifacts**   Add artifact

Artifact 1 - Primary

Type

No artifacts   ▼

You might choose no artifacts if you are running tests or pushing a Docker image to Amazon ECR.

▶ **Additional configuration**
  Cache, encryption key

▼ **Logs**

CloudWatch

☑ CloudWatch logs - *optional*
  Checking this option will upload build output logs to CloudWatch.

Group name - *optional*

aws/codebuild/TerraformDeploy

The group name of the logs in CloudWatch Logs. The log group name will be /aws/codebuild/<project-name> by default.

Stream name prefix - *optional*

The prefix of the stream name of the CloudWatch Logs.

S3

☐ S3 logs - *optional*
  Checking this option will upload build output logs to S3.

Figure 13.16 – Artifacts and logs for our CodeBuild project

14. Click **Create build project** to create a new build project and be redirected to the overview page for this build project.

With the configuration of our build project done, it is time to push some resources and see the work in action. To do this, we'll need to first introduce the previously mentioned `buildspec` file. A `buildspec` file defines the different phases of a build and which commands should be run there. You can think of it like a script where each command is run one after another. We can store this file in our repository and CodeBuild will read it upon every execution of the project. So, let's create a `buildspec` file and Terraform scripts to run.

To do this, follow these steps:

1. Open up the repository you previously cloned to your computer in a text editor of your choice (such as Visual Studio Code), and create a new file called `buildspec.yml`.

2. In the `buildspec.yml` file, we'll first specify the version of the buildspec standard we want to use – version 0.2, in this case:

    ```
    version: 0.2
    ```

3. Next, we define a list of phases. The first phase, the `install` phase, is where we can set up any custom software we need to run our commands. In our case, this custom software is Terraform. The following code will use `wget` to download the 1.10.3 version of Terraform for Linux to the machine, unzip the file, and then move it to the `bin` folder so that it can be used later. To verify that everything works, we then run a `terraform --version` command. You can visit `https://developer.hashicorp.com/terraform/install` to find the latest version of Terraform and change the following URL accordingly:

    ```
    phases:
      install:
        commands:
          - wget -O terraform.zip https://releases.hashicorp.com/
    terraform/1.10.3/terraform_1.10.3_linux_amd64.zip
          - unzip terraform.zip
          - mv terraform /usr/local/bin/
          - terraform --version
    ```

    > **Additional information**
    >
    > The project will fail if any of the commands return an error code. So, if something goes wrong with the Terraform installation shown earlier, this phase will exit with an error code due to the `terraform --version` command exiting with an error code.

4. In the next stage, the `pre_build` stage, we'll initialize Terraform and also run validation on our Terraform files to check that they are syntactically correct:

    ```
    pre_build:
      commands:
        - terraform init
        - terraform validate
    ```

5. Now, we come to the `build` command. This section will run `terraform plan` to generate a new plan. If the push was on our `main` branch, it will also run `terraform apply` on the previously created plan:

```
build:
    commands:
        - terraform plan -out=out.tfplan
        - if [ $CODEBUILD_WEBHOOK_EVENT = "PUSH" ] && [
$CODEBUILD_WEBHOOK_HEAD_REF = "refs/heads/main" ]; then
terraform apply -auto-approve out.tfplan; fi
```

6. With our `buildspec` done, it is time for us to write the Terraform code that will be run by the project. For this example, we'll use very simple Terraform code that just creates a new S3 bucket. However, we need to use our new S3/DynamoDB backend for the state file, so let's first set this up. Create a new file called `backend.tf`.

7. In the `backend.tf` file, configure Terraform to use the S3 backend. Remember to change the name of your bucket and DynamoDB table, as well as the Region, to the one you used when setting up this infrastructure previously:

```
terraform {
  backend "s3" {
    bucket         = "<insert your state bucket name>"
    key            = "terraform.tfstate"
    region         = "eu-central-1"
    dynamodb_table = "<insert your DDB table name>"
  }
}
```

8. Next, we can configure our providers. A more detailed explanation of what is happening here can be found in *Chapter 1, Setting Up the AWS Environment*:

```
terraform {
  required_providers {
    aws = {
      source  = "hashicorp/aws"
      version = "~> 5.0"
    }
  }
}
provider "aws" {
  region = "eu-central-1"
}
```

9. Finally, we can create a file called `main.tf`. In `main.tf`, we'll define all the resources that we want to create with this pipeline. In this simple example, we'll only use it to create a new S3 bucket. To do so, add the following code to the file:

```
resource "aws_s3_bucket" "pipeline_bucket" {
    bucket = "<insert a new unique bucket name>"
}
```

10. Your directory should now look like this:

```
└── Infra-Demo/
    ├── .gitignore
    ├── backend.tf
    ├── buildspec.yml
    ├── main.tf
    └── provider.tf
```

11. We'll now add these changes to our Git commit, commit them, and then push the changes to our GitHub repository. First, add all the files to our commit using the following command. You need to run this in the directory of your Git repository:

```
git add .
```

12. Next, commit it:

```
git commit -m "Initial version of infra"
```

13. Then, we can push it:

```
git push --set-upstream origin main
```

With our changes committed, our pipeline will now start to run. Navigate back to the AWS console and, in your build project under **Build history**, you should see a new build run with a status of **Pending**. The following figure shows the details of the build. As you can see, the **Phase details** tab shows you the names of the different phases that we defined in the `buildspec` file (such as **INSTALL**, **PRE_BUILD**, **BUILD**, etc.) as well as their status.

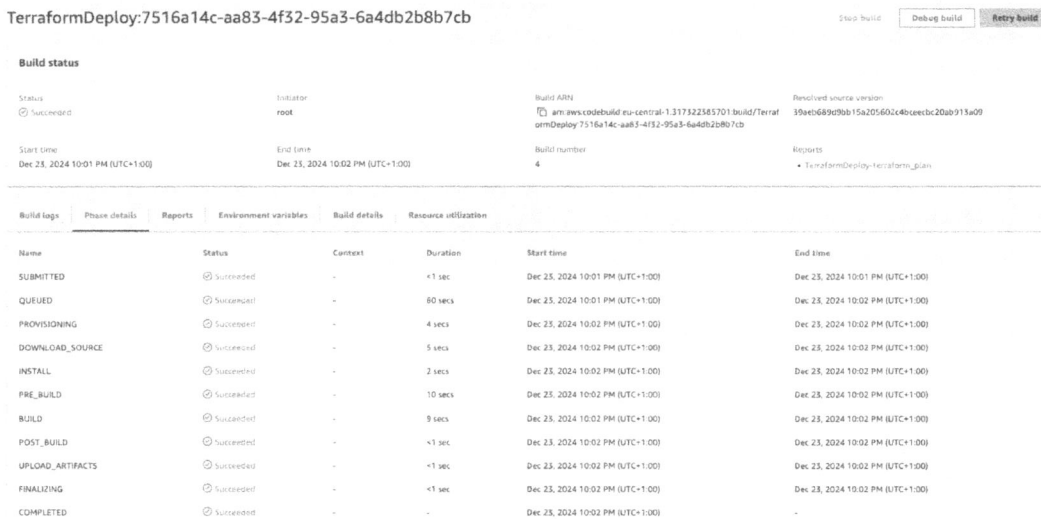

TerraformDeploy:7516a14c-aa83-4f32-95a3-6a4db2b8b7cb

Figure 13.17 – Build overview

Build logs will show you the output of each of the stages. And if we navigate to S3, we can verify that the bucket we specified was indeed created.

With this, we have successfully connected GitHub with AWS and created a continuous deployment of our infrastructure.

Summary

In this chapter, we have covered the basics of CI/CD before creating an actual CI/CD project for provisioning infrastructure on AWS. We saw how we can connect AWS to have access to repositories in our GitHub account and how we can then use CodeBuild to run a set of steps every time the source code in the repository changes.

In the next chapter, we'll see how we can scale IaC across an organization by building reusable modules that can then be deployed via CI/CD pipelines.

Get This Book's PDF Version and Exclusive Extras

UNLOCK NOW

Scan the QR code (or go to `packtpub.com/unlock`). Search for this book by name, confirm the edition, and then follow the steps on the page.

Note: Keep your invoice handly. Purchase made directly from packt don't require one.

14

Building Reusable Infrastructure-as-Code Components

Throughout the previous chapters, we have seen how **Infrastructure as Code (IaC)** can be leveraged to build up the infrastructure we want to deploy in our AWS account in a reproducible manner.

Especially when you are operating multiple workloads within your account, you'll have common patterns that are shared across the workloads. Maybe each workload should have the same general VPC setup, or you want a standardized configuration for your S3 buckets and their integration into the CloudFront CDN. We could copy and paste the IaC code between different workloads; however, this makes it hard to track where pieces of infrastructure came from (are they custom or provided by a component?), and if we want to update a shared configuration, it becomes even more difficult, since for every workload where the code was copied and pasted, we would need to update it manually.

This is where IaC components come into play. Both CDK and Terraform allow us to package a set of resources into reusable components that can be shared across teams. Besides reducing the time it takes to write infrastructure – since, for example, every DevOps engineer in every workload team doesn't have to re-implement the same standardized VPC based on an architecture sketch, we can also ensure consistency between different workloads.

This standardization makes it easier for engineers to pick up work in different teams since they already know the underlying standards that have been used for these basic components.

In essence, your IaC components can become a codification of your enterprise architecture and other architectural best practices.

In this chapter, we're going to cover the following main topics:

- A short introduction to reusable IaC components
- Writing and using modules in Terraform

- Writing and using constructs in CDK

Technical requirements

Before following this section, please create an AWS account for yourself. You can sign up at `aws. amazon.com`. You should also have:

- A basic understanding of AWS – for example, what a service is – will be beneficial.
- A basic understanding of Python will help with the programming-based sections of this chapter.
- A basic understanding of Terraform will be beneficial
- A basic understanding of the Linux command line will help you follow along with this chapter.

You'll also need the following software installed on your system:

- Python version 3.8 or later
- Node.js version 14.15.0 or later

Both of these version requirements are as at the time of writing, in January 2025. You can check the following links for the required versions:

- For Python: `https://boto3.amazonaws.com/v1/documentation/api/latest/ guide/quickstart.html#install-or-update-python`
- For Node.js: `https://docs.aws.amazon.com/cdk/v2/guide/getting_started. html#getting_started_prerequisites`

All scripts from this section can be found at the following GitHub link:

`https://github.com/PacktPublishing/AWS-for-System-Administrators- Second-Edition`

The CiA video for this chapter can be found at `https://packt.link/0kfIX`

An introduction to reusable components

Before we can get started with writing modules in Terraform or constructs in CDK, we need to think about what a reusable component is from a conceptual point of view. A component is a reusable set of pieces of infrastructure resources (such as an EC2 instance) that are deployed together to provide some infrastructure to a workload. A component itself usually does not host a workload. It provides the infrastructure that your workload will run on.

When designing these components, it is best to analyze the architecture of your workloads and how they are built up. What commonalities do they share in terms of the infrastructure components (such as EC2 instances or S3 buckets) and their configuration? Do they all run in a VPC that is always configured with a private and public subnet per Availability Zone? Do you have a classic three-tier architecture with a load balancer in front of a set of EC2 instances that use a database provided by RDS in the background? Do you have to configure your logging in a certain way because of compliance requirements?

These common pieces of infrastructure would be prime candidates to put into a component that can be shared among all workloads. Finding the right size for your component is tricky. If you make the scope of your component too small, you'll end up just writing thin abstractions over existing resources.

Think about the Terraform code that configures an EC2 instance. If all your module is doing is configuring an EC2 instance by passing through all the variables from the module to the resource, it doesn't add any value to have the component. This doesn't mean that a component must have multiple resources. If your component configures your EC2 instance in a standardized way, sets up common logging, configures sensible default security groups, enforces a standardized naming schema, and configures other security defaults, then it makes sense to put this into a component.

The Terraform documentation from HashiCorp has a good litmus test to see whether what you are designing should be a component/module or not:

If you have trouble finding a name for your module that isn't the same as the main resource type inside it, that may be a sign that your module is not creating any new abstraction and so the module is adding unnecessary complexity.

Source: `https://developer.hashicorp.com/terraform/language/modules/develop`

However, the other extreme, where your component is too wide in scope, can also be disadvantageous. Think about a component that just deploys a whole landing zone plus a workload into your AWS account. It sets up an account structure, configures and peers VPCs, deploys database services, configures logging, deploys instances, sets up auto scaling, defines custom metrics, and configures backup. This starts to sound like your entire workload, doesn't it? The downside of having huge components that configure many different areas of a workload is that you lose flexibility. What if workload B does not need all the configured auto scaling? What if you don't want backups enabled for a testing environment but there is no way to disable it in the component?

Components should serve as building blocks for your eventual workload infrastructure. Besides the naming test from the HashiCorp quote earlier, you can think about whether all the pieces of infrastructure in your component serve the same purpose for the workload that should run on it. Configuring a standardized RDS cluster and defining the logging and backup strategy for it is a perfect use case for a component. If that component would then also configure EC2 instances, that would not fit the scope of the component.

When defining which parts of an infrastructure to put into a component, here are some best practices and guidelines:

- Analyze your workloads and identify common patterns such as the network configuration or the configuration of database clusters. These are examples of pieces of infrastructure that could be standardized for all the workloads via IaC components.

- Identify any infrastructure that always must be deployed in a certain standardized way – often for compliance purposes. If you are following an enterprise architecture or a different set of standards, this could be a source of such components. Here, it makes sense to provide components that already follow the best practices or requirements.

- Make your components small enough to be usable as building blocks for your workload infrastructure. You can always compose multiple components into the infrastructure required for your workload instead of putting all of it into one static and difficult-to-change component.

- Make your components big enough to be an abstraction. A good check is the naming test from HashiCorp – if you are having trouble coming up with a name for your resource that is different from the main resource, it probably isn't enough of an abstraction to warrant a component.

So, let's next have a look at an example of a component and how we can implement this in Terraform.

Building reusable components in Terraform

In this chapter, we'll implement a standardized VPC module that will deploy a VPC with a public and private subnet in three different availability zones. In Terraform, these components are called **modules** and will be used by our Terraform code.

> **Additional information**
>
> We have discussed the technical details of VPCs in a previous chapter and won't be repeating them here. Please see *Chapter 3, Creating a Data Center in the Cloud Using a VPC*, for a more detailed explanation of the concepts of VPCs and how we can implement them in IaC.

The following diagram shows the high-level architecture that our component will build out.

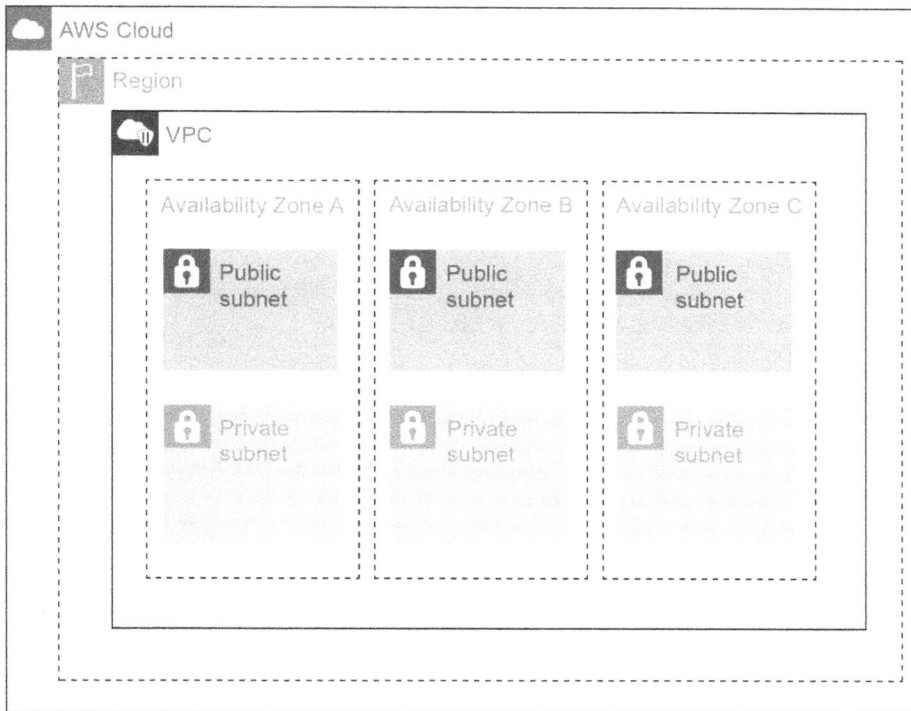

Figure 14.1 – The high-level architecture of the standard VPC that we will build in the Terraform module

To get started, we'll need to create a directory structure for our Terraform code that is going to use the module and the module code itself. Create a new directory called vpc_example and create the following directory structure:

```
.
└── vpc_example/
    └── modules/
        └── standard_vpc
```

The vpc_example folder will contain our high-level Terraform script, from which we'll call our module. The standard_vpc folder in the modules subfolder will contain the code for our actual module.

While the naming convention for modules isn't enforced, HashiCorp recommends a standardized way of naming the files within a module. A module should contain the following files:

- A `main.tf` file, which contains all the resource creation that the module has.
- A `variables.tf` file, which contains all the variables that our module offers. These are the inputs that a user will be able to pass into your module so they should contain variables for all the inputs required from the user.
- An `outputs.tf` file, which contains the outputs of your module. Typically, you would expose anything that the user of your module would need. In the case of a VPC, this could be the ARN of the VPC or the ARNs of the public subnets since these will be needed by other parts of the Terraform script to, for example, create an instance in them.

You can find more details on the recommended structure in this documentation: `https://developer.hashicorp.com/terraform/language/modules/develop/structure`

For our VPC module, let's get started with creating the `variables.tf` file in `vpc_example/modules/standard_vpc/variables.tf`:

1. Open a code editor such as Visual Studio Code and create the `variables.tf` file under `vpc_example/modules/standard_vpc/`.
2. In it, we'll define four variables. The CIDR range of the VPC, the CIDR ranges of the public and private subnets, and the region to which we want to deploy this module.
3. Let's start with the variable for the VPC CIDR range. We define this variable with the name `vpc_cidr` and give it a default of `10.0.0.0/16`:

```
variable "vpc_cidr" {
  description = "VPC CIDR block"
  type        = string
  default     = "10.0.0.0/16"
}
```

4. Similarly, we define the three CIDR ranges for our public subnets. Since we need three CIDR ranges (one for each Availability Zone), the type of our variable will be a list of strings instead of just a simple string. We also provide defaults. Make sure to define your defaults such that they map with the VPC CIDR range:

```
variable "public_subnet_cidrs" {
  description = "public subnets CIDR"
  type        = list(string)
  default     = ["10.0.1.0/24", "10.0.2.0/24", "10.0.3.0/24"]
}
```

5. We can then define the private CIDR ranges in the same way:

```
variable "private_subnet_cidrs" {
  description = "private subnets CIDR"
  type        = list(string)
  default     = ["10.0.11.0/24", "10.0.12.0/24", "10.0.13.0/24"]
}
```

6. We need a variable for the AWS region to which this VPC should be deployed:

```
variable "region" {
  description = "AWS region"
  type        = string
}
```

7. We also want to add a standardized naming convention to our VPCs. Each VPC should have the name {project}-{region}-VPC for easier identification. To achieve this, we'll also pass in a variable called "project" that will contain the project name:

```
variable "project" {
  description = "Name of the project"
  type        = string
}
```

With the inputs of our module defined in the variables.tf file, we can next define the actual creation of our resources in main.tf.

8. Open up a code editor of your choice (such as Visual Studio Code) and create a file called main.tf in the vpc_example/modules/standard_vpc folder.

9. The first resource we'll be creating is the VPC resource from AWS itself. We pass the CIDR block from our variables into the VPC and then define the desired naming convention inside of the tags. We also pass a tag that identifies that this resource has been created with our standard_vpc module. This isn't a requirement but can help identify how resources were created.

```
resource "aws_vpc" "main" {
  cidr_block          = var.vpc_cidr
  enable_dns_hostnames = true
  enable_dns_support   = true
  tags = {
    Name        = "${var.project}-${var.region}-VPC"
    TF_Module   = "standard_vpc"
  }
}
```

10. Since we have public subnets, we'll next need to create an **Internet Gateway** (**IGW**) that is associated with our previously created VPC (via the vpc_id property). We add the same tagging structure with the name referencing our project as well as TF_Module here:

```
resource "aws_internet_gateway" "main" {
  vpc_id = aws_vpc.main.id
  tags = {
    Name        = "${var.project}-${var.region}-IGW"
    TF_Module   = "standard_vpc"
  }
}
```

11. With our IGW created, we can now get started with creating our subnets. We'll start with the public subnets. But before we can create subnets, we need to find the names of the availability zones in this region. Since we want this module to be generally applicable, we can't hardcode the names. We'll instead use a data source in Terraform that gives us the available resources in the region we are deploying resources into.

```
data "aws_availability_zones" "available" {
  state = "available"
}
```

12. We can now create our three public subnets. By using the count argument, we can let Terraform create three instances of this resource. We associate them with the previously created VPC and use the CIDR blocks that were passed in as a variable. Since these CIDR blocks are a list of strings, we can use count.index to access a different CIDR for each of the three iterations. We do the same with the Availability Zone. Since we have a public subnet, we'll map a public IP address on launch and do a tagging following the naming convention of the other resources:

```
resource "aws_subnet" "public" {
  count                   = 3
  vpc_id                  = aws_vpc.main.id
  cidr_block              = var.public_subnet_cidrs[count.index]
  availability_zone       = data.aws_availability_zones.
available.names[count.index]
  map_public_ip_on_launch = true
  tags = {
    Name        = "${var.project}-${var.region}-public-subnet-
${count.index + 1}"
  }
}
```

13. As we saw in *Chapter 3, Creating a Data Center in the Cloud Using a VPC*, what differentiates a public from a private subnet is the fact that a public subnet has a route to the IGW. We'll now create a route table that will be associated with the public subnet that contains a route to the previously created IGW. In this example, we create a single route entry that sends all traffic for "0.0.0.0/0" to the IGW that was created:

```
resource "aws_route_table" "public" {
  vpc_id = aws_vpc.main.id
  route {
    cidr_block = "0.0.0.0/0"
    gateway_id = aws_internet_gateway.main.id
  }
  tags = {
    Name        = "${var.project}-${var.region}-public-route-
table "
  }
}
```

14. We now need to associate the previously created public route table with our public subnet. This is done via a route table association:

```
resource "aws_route_table_association" "public" {
  count            = 3
  subnet_id        = aws_subnet.public[count.index].id
  route_table_id   = aws_route_table.public.id
}
```

Additional information

List resources in Terraform are zero-indexed. This means that the count variable we use in the preceding goes from 0 to n - 1 (in our example, the indexes would be 0, 1, and 2). This is why, in the name tag, we increment the count by 1 (count.index + 1) so that we have -public-subnet-1, public-subnet-2, and -public-subnet-3 as the suffixes instead of public-subnet-0.

15. Similar to how we have created our public subnets, we can create our private subnets and associate them with a private route table. Contrary to the public route table, this private route table does not contain a route to the IGW.

```
# Create Private Subnets
resource "aws_subnet" "private" {
  count             = 3
  vpc_id            = aws_vpc.main.id
  cidr_block        = var.private_subnet_cidrs[count.index]
  availability_zone = data.aws_availability_zones.available.
```

```
    names[count.index]
      tags = {
        Name           = "${var.project}-${var.region}-private-subnet-
    ${count.index + 1}"
      }
    }
    # Create Private Route Tables
    resource "aws_route_table" "private" {
      count  = 3
      vpc_id = aws_vpc.main.id
      tags = {
        Name           = "${var.project}-${var.region}-private-route-
    table-${count.index + 1}"
      }
    }
    # Connect private route table to private subnets
    resource "aws_route_table_association" "private" {
      count          = 3
      subnet_id      = aws_subnet.private[count.index].id
      route_table_id = aws_route_table.private[count.index].id
    }
```

With our inputs and infrastructure defined, we only need to create the outputs that we want our module to expose. We'll expose three outputs. The ARN of our VPC, the IDs of our public subnets, and the IDs of our private subnets. These could then, for example, be used by Terraform code using our module to schedule web server instances in.

1. Open up a code editor of your choice (such as Visual Studio Code) and create a file called outputs.tf in vpc_example/modules/standard_vpc.

2. We first define an output for our VPC by linking the value back to our previously created resource of type aws_vpc:

    ```
    output "vpc_id" {
      description = "VPC ID"
      value       = aws_vpc.main.id
    }
    ```

3. Similarly, we do the same for our public and private subnet IDs. We use the [*] syntax to return all resources of type aws_subnet that were named private or public:

    ```
    output "public_subnet_ids" {
      description = "IDs of the public subnets"
      value       = aws_subnet.public[*].id
    }
    output "private_subnet_ids" {
    ```

```
      description = "IDs of the private subnets"
      value       = aws_subnet.private[*].id
    }
```

With our module defined, it is time to write the Terraform code that will use the module. To do this, we define another Terraform file called `main.tf`. This file will be in the `vpc_example` directory, and in it, we'll consume the `standard_vpc` Terraform module we have just created.

1. Open up a code editor of your choice (such as Visual Studio Code) and create a file called `main.tf` in the `vpc_example/` folder. After this, your directory structure should look like this:

    ```
    .
    └── vpc_example/
        ├── main.tf
        └── modules/
            └── standard_vpc/
                ├── main.tf
                ├── variables.tf
                └── outputs.tf
    ```

2. In it, we'll first have to create the Terraform and provider configuration. See *Chapter 1, Setting Up the AWS Environment*, for a more detailed explanation of what is being done here:

    ```
    terraform {
      required_providers {
        aws = {
          source  = "hashicorp/aws"
          version = "~> 5.0"
        }
      }
      required_version = ">= 1.2.0"
    }
    provider "aws" {
      region = "eu-central-1"
    }
    ```

3. With the provider defined, it is time to use our module. To do this, we use the `module` block. The first argument, the source, defines where to find the module we want to use. In this case, we'll pass the directory path to our `standard_vpc` module folder:

    ```
    module "vpc" {
      source = "./modules/standard_vpc"
    ```

4. Next, we define all the variables of our module. We'll call our project `test-project` and we pass the same region we used for creating our provider (`eu-central-1` in this example). This means that our VPC will have the name `test-project-eu-central-1-VPC`:

```
project = "test-project"
region  = "eu-central-1"
```

5. We then define the 7 CIDR ranges. First, the overall CIDR range of the VPC and then the three CIDR ranges for our public and private subnets respectively:

```
vpc_cidr = "10.10.0.0/16"
public_subnet_cidrs = [
  "10.10.1.0/24",
  "10.10.2.0/24",
  "10.10.3.0/24"
]
private_subnet_cidrs = [
  "10.20.11.0/24",
  "10.20.12.0/24",
  "10.20.13.0/24"
]
}
```

6. With this, we can run our Terraform script. Open a console. We'll first have to initialize our Terraform directory. This will create the state file, download the provider, and load the module from our subdirectory. To do this, run the following:

```
terraform init
```

7. Next, we can apply the changes with `apply` and run the following command:

```
terraform apply
```

Once Terraform has finished provisioning your infrastructure, you can open up the AWS console in the region you have selected in the provider (and module) and see your newly created standardized VPC.

Don't forget to run `terraform destroy` to delete all the infrastructure we have just created.

Building reusable components in CDK

We have now seen how we can deploy a component using modules in Terraform. In this section, we'll explore how we can do the same with CDK.

In *Chapter 1*, *Setting Up the AWS Environment*, we discussed how CDK can be used to generate CloudFormation code from a programming language such as Python. Before starting, let's quickly revisit the level system when we talk about constructs in CDK.

In CDK, resources such as an S3 Bucket or an EC2 instance are defined by constructs. These constructs are separated into three different levels:

- L1 constructs are low-level constructs that track the underlying CloudFormation resource. They are usually prefixed with `Cfn` and they map one-to-one to a resource in CloudFormation. So, the CloudFormation resource of an S3 bucket, as defined at `https://docs.aws.amazon.com/AWSCloudFormation/latest/UserGuide/aws-resource-s3-bucket.html`, maps one-to-one to a resource in CDK called `CfnBucket` (which you can find here: `https://docs.aws.amazon.com/cdk/api/v2/docs/aws-cdk-lib.aws_s3.CfnBucket.html`).

- L2 constructs are curated higher-level constructs that also model a single resource such as a bucket. In contrast to the L1 constructs, which track a CloudFormation resource one-to-one, the L2 constructs offer a higher level of abstraction and convenience functions for the developer while still mapping to one resource (such as an S3 bucket). As an example of such convenience functions, in our L2 construct of the S3 bucket, we have a function called `grantRead(role)`, which will generate the required IAM policies to grant the passed `role` object the rights to read this bucket.

- L3 constructs represent entire components that are made up of multiple different resources.

We'll model our VPC as an L3 construct in which we'll use L2 constructs to create the required resources.

Before we can create our L3 construct, we'll first need to create a new CDK project. We have already seen an explanation of this in *Chapter 1*, *Setting Up the AWS Environment*, so the following steps will be only briefly explained. For a more detailed explanation, please have a look at *Chapter 1* again.

1. Create a new directory in which our CDK project will be contained. In this example, we'll use the name `cdk_vpc_example`. Open up a terminal and type the following command:

   ```
   mkdir cdk_vpc_example
   ```

> **Additional information**
>
> Note that the name of the folder of a CDK project also defines the project name. So, if you choose to change the name of your folder, you'll have to adapt the name of the stack and the paths as well.

2. Navigate into the directory by using the `cd` command:

   ```
   cd cdk_vpc_example
   ```

3. Inside the directory, create a new CDK project using the CDK CLI. We'll be using Python as our language of choice for this example, but the concept is the same for all other languages, such as Java, Typescript, and Go, that CDK supports:

```
cdk init app --language python
```

4. CDK has created a new virtual environment for us that we'll need to activate:

```
# On Unix operating systems (like Mac OS X or Linux)
source .venv/bin/activate
# On Windows systems
.venv/bin/activate.bat
```

5. Next, install the dependencies for our CDK project:

```
python3 -m pip install -r requirements.txt
```

With the CDK project created, our virtual environment activated, and the required packages installed, we can now get started with creating our VPC component. Throughout this example, you'll see both L1 and L2 constructs being used to create our resources. Besides showing you how to use them in tandem, we resort back to the L1 constructs if properties aren't available in the more abstract L2 construct for that resource.

1. To get started, we'll need to create a new file called `standard_vpc.py` in the `cdk_vpc_example` folder. Open a code editor (such as Visual Studio Code) and create a new file called `standard_vpc.py` in the `cdk_vpc_example/cdk_vpc_example/` folder. The folder should already contain a file called `cdk_vpc_example_stack.py`, so the directory structure looks like this:

```
.
└── cdk_vpc_example/
    └── cdk_vpc_example/
        ├── __init__.py
        ├── cdk_vpc_example_stack.py
        └── standard_vpc.py
```

Inside the `standard_vpc.py` file, we'll define our new construct. We'll first have to import a few libraries. Our class will inherit from the parent `Construct` class of CDK, so we'll need to import this as well as the `ec2` package, `Tags`, and `Stack`. The `ec2` package contains all our L1 and L2 resources related to VPCs that we'll need.

2. We'll be using type hints when defining our construct, so we'll also import the type hint classes for `List` and `Optional` (properties that can have a value or None) from the Python library's `typing` package:

```
from constructs import Construct
from aws_cdk import (
```

```
    aws_ec2 as ec2,
    Tags,
    Stack
)
from typing import List, Optional
```

3. Next, we create our class. We'll call it `StandardVpc` and it'll inherit from `Construct`:

```
class StandardVpc(Construct):
```

4. When writing CDK code, we can leverage standard concepts of our programming language such as constructors. So, we'll use the constructor to define all the variables that need to be passed into this construct.

   The scope is of type `Construct` and will later be our stack. This tells CDK which CloudFormation stack our resources will be associated to.

   The `construct_id` is a string to identify our construct and auto-generate names.

   We then pass the same variables we have already seen in Terraform, the project name, `vpc_cidr`, as well as the public and private subnets. Notice that we don't have to pass the region since we can extract that from the stack:

```
def __init__(
    self,
    scope: Construct,
    construct_id: str,
    project_name: str,
    vpc_cidr: str = "10.0.0.0/16",
    public_subnet_cidrs: Optional[List[str]] = None,
    private_subnet_cidrs: Optional[List[str]] = None,
    **kwargs
) -> None:
```

5. We first need to call the construct's super constructor:

```
        super().__init__(scope, construct_id, **kwargs)
```

6. Next, we store the project name as a property of our Python class:

```
        self.project_name = project_name
```

7. We'll also set some default for our public and private subnets (similar to the default value in our Terraform variables) if none are passed into the constructor:

```
        self.public_subnet_cidrs = public_subnet_cidrs
        if not self.public_subnet_cidrs:
            self.public_subnet_cidrs = [
```

```
            "10.0.1.0/24", "10.0.2.0/24", "10.0.3.0/24"
        ]
    self.private_subnet_cidrs = private_subnet_cidrs
    if not self.private_subnet_cidrs:
        self.private_subnet_cidrs = [
        "10.0.11.0/24", "10.0.12.0/24", "10.0.13.0/24"
    ]
```

8. Every CloudFormation stack, which is what the CDK code ultimately gets translated into, contains information about the region in which it is deployed. So, we can access that region information and store it as a property of our class:

    ```
    self.region = Stack.of(self).region
    ```

9. With this, we are ready to create the resources for our architecture. We start by creating the VPC itself using the ec2.Vpc L2 construct. We pass vpc_name as the naming convention, {project_name}-{region}-vpc, and define our IP range using the ip_addresses property. We can use the ec2.IpAddress.cidr helper class to turn our string into the proper CIDR object. Since our VPC will be deployed into a maximum of three AZs, we define this using the max_azs property.

    Notably, we'll leave the subnet configuration as an empty list since we'll create our subnets ourselves and then associate them with the VPC:

    ```
    # Create the VPC
    self.vpc = ec2.Vpc(
        self,
        "StandardVPC",
        vpc_name=f"{self.project_name}-{self.region}-vpc",
        ip_addresses=ec2.IpAddresses.cidr(vpc_cidr),
        max_azs=3,
        subnet_configuration=[],
        enable_dns_hostnames=True,
        enable_dns_support=True,
    )
    ```

10. With the VPC created, we can go ahead and create a new subnet resource for each of the public CIDR ranges that were passed into our construct. We create a new list that will contain our L2 ec2.Subnet constructs, called public_subnets, and then iterate over all provided public CIDR ranges.

    For each of the subnets, we'll set cidr_block, a different Availability Zone from the VPC, and set the public IP mapping to true since this is a public subnet.

    Finally, we add our naming convention to the subnet using a tag and then add it to our list of public subnets:

```
            # Create public subnets
            self.public_subnets = []
            for i, cidr in enumerate(self.public_subnet_cidrs):
                subnet = ec2.Subnet(
                    self,
                    f"PublicSubnet{i+1}",
                    vpc_id=self.vpc.vpc_id,
                    availability_zone=self.vpc.availability_
zones[i],
                    cidr_block=cidr,
                    map_public_ip_on_launch=True,
                )
                self.public_subnets.append(subnet)
                Tags.of(subnet).add(
                    "Name", f"{self.project_name}-{self.region}-
public-subnet-{i+1}"
                )
```

Additional information

The enumerate() function in Python takes an iterable, such as a list, as an argument and returns a list of tuples where the first item in the returned tuple is the index and the second is the element.

So, enumerate() called on a list such as l = ["one", "two", "three"] returns a list (technically an iterator) of [(0, "one"), (1, "two"), (2, "three")].

---

11. We'll next create our internet gateway and associate it with our VPC. Here, we are using the L1 constructs of the internet gateway and the internet gateway association, as indicated by the Cfn prefix.

We use the tags to set our standardized naming convention, and for VPCGatewayAttachment, we pass the VPC ID from the previously defined L2 VPC construct:

```
    self.igw = ec2.CfnInternetGateway(
            self,
            "InternetGateway",
            tags=[{"key": "Name", "value": f"{self.project_
name}-{self.region}-igw"}]
        )
        ec2.CfnVPCGatewayAttachment(
            self,
            "IGWAttachment",
            vpc_id=self.vpc.vpc_id,
            internet_gateway_id=self.igw.ref
        )
```

12. With the IGW created (and attached to our VPC), we can create the public route table that will route all its traffic to the IGW. We once again use the CfnRouteTable L1 construct to create a route table that follows our naming convention using the Name tag:

```
# Create public route table
self.public_route_table = ec2.CfnRouteTable(
    self,
    "PublicRouteTable",
    vpc_id=self.vpc.vpc_id,
    tags=[{"key": "Name", "value": f"{self.project_
name}-{self.region}-public-rt"}]
)
```

13. We then create a CfnRoute resource that has a destination of "0.0.0.0/0" and sends that traffic to our previously created IGW (as indicated by the gateway_id=self.igw. ref argument). We associate this with our previously created route table via the route_table_id property:

```
ec2.CfnRoute(
    self,
    "PublicRoute",
    route_table_id=self.public_route_table.ref,
    destination_cidr_block="0.0.0.0/0",
    gateway_id=self.igw.ref
)
```

14. Now we need to loop over each of our previously created subnets and create a route table association. We'll use the enumerate function again to get the index that we can then use in properly naming our associations:

```
# Associate public subnets with public route table
for i, subnet in enumerate(self.public_subnets):
    ec2.CfnSubnetRouteTableAssociation(
        self,
        f"PublicSubnetRouteTableAssociation{i+1}",
        subnet_id=subnet.subnet_id,
        route_table_id=self.public_route_table.ref
    )
```

15. With the public subnets done and associated, we can follow the same pattern for our private subnets. We first create a list that will contain all our private subnet constructs and then iterate over all the private CIDR ranges that were provided:

```
# Create private subnets
self.private_subnets = []
for i, cidr in enumerate(self.private_subnet_cidrs):
```

```
            subnet = ec2.Subnet(
                self,
                f"PrivateSubnet{i+1}",
                vpc_id=self.vpc.vpc_id,
                availability_zone=self.vpc.availability_
    zones[i],
                cidr_block=cidr,
                map_public_ip_on_launch=False,
            )
            self.private_subnets.append(subnet)
            Tags.of(subnet).add(
                "Name", f"{self.project_name}-{self.region}-
    private-subnet-{i+1}"
            )
```

16. Next, create a private route table for our private subnets:

```
        # Create private route tables
        self.private_route_tables = []
        for i in range(3):
            route_table = ec2.CfnRouteTable(
                self,
                f"PrivateRouteTable{i+1}",
                vpc_id=self.vpc.vpc_id,
                tags=[{
                    "key": "Name",
                    "value": f"{self.project_name}-{self.
    region}-private-rt-{i+1}"
                }]
            )
            self.private_route_tables.append(route_table)
```

17. And finally, iterate over the list of private subnets and associate them with the private route tables:

```
        # Associate private subnets with private route tables
        for i, subnet in enumerate(self.private_subnets):
            ec2.CfnSubnetRouteTableAssociation(
                self,
                f"PrivateSubnetRouteTableAssociation{i+1}",
                subnet_id=subnet.subnet_id,
                route_table_id=self.private_route_tables[i].ref
            )
```

With our construct done, we can now use it inside of our stack to create a new VPC.

1. Open the cdk_vpc_example_stack.py file in the cdk_vpc_example/cdk_vpc_ example/ folder.

2. The CdkVpcExampleStack class, inheriting from Stack, defines the underlying CloudFormation stack. In addition to the standard imports, we'll need to import our newly created custom construct. Your imports should look like the following. Notice how we have added the import for our StandardVpc class at the bottom:

```python
from aws_cdk import (
    # Duration,
    Stack,
    # aws_sqs as sqs,
)
from constructs import Construct
from cdk_vpc_example.standard_vpc import StandardVpc
```

3. Inside our stack, we can now create a new instance of StandardVpc by creating a new Python object. Notice how we pass the values, such as the project name or the CIDR ranges of the VPC and the public and private subnets, as arguments to the constructor of our custom construct:

```python
class CdkVpcExampleStack(Stack):
    def __init__(self, scope: Construct, construct_id: str,
**kwargs) -> None:
        super().__init__(scope, construct_id, **kwargs)
        # The code that defines your stack goes here
        vpc = StandardVpc(self, "standard_vpc",
                          project_name="test-cdk-project",
                          vpc_cidr="10.30.0.0/16",
                          public_subnet_cidrs=[
                              "10.30.1.0/24",
                              "10.30.2.0/24",
                              "10.30.3.0/24"
                          ],
                          private_subnet_cidrs=[
                              "10.50.1.0/24",
                              "10.50.2.0/24",
                              "10.50.3.0/24"
                          ])
```

4. With our stack done, we can run the deploy command. This will generate the required CloudFormation code from our CDK code and then create a new CloudFormation stack for us. To do this, open a terminal and run the following command:

```
cdk deploy
```

Once the deployment is done, open up your AWS console in the region to which you deployed the new stack and you should see a new VPC that follows the configuration we defined in our CDK application.

Don't forget to use `cdk destroy` to delete all the resources.

Summary

In this chapter, we saw how we can create reusable infrastructure components. We first introduced some ideas on how to define the boundaries of your components and then saw practical examples of how these infrastructure components can be implemented as modules in Terraform and as L3 constructs in CDK.

Infrastructure components are a great asset when we want our infrastructure to adhere to a defined standard. However, nothing prevents a DevOps engineer from manually changing the configuration of a resource deployed by one of our components in the AWS console. In the next chapter, we'll see how we can use config rules and SCPs to monitor for or prevent unwanted configurations in our AWS environment.

## 15

Ensuring Compliance Using AWS Config and SCPs

So far, we have only dealt with a single AWS account and a single user to which we attached the rights to carry out API operations via IAM policies. However, we quite often have the use case for more than one AWS account. Think about a typical development project. Here, we'd usually want to have a separate account for production and testing and maybe even a third for development.

As the number of accounts grows, it makes sense to ensure that even the admins of these accounts can't do everything in the account. We want to enforce certain guardrails and define upper limits for what kind of API actions can be allowed by IAM policies. This is done by applying **Service Control Policies** – or **SCPs** for short. SCPs are a powerful concept to prevent even admin users from carrying out certain API actions.

But sometimes, we don't want to outright deny an action or configuration but just want to be informed about it. This is where AWS Config – a service to continuously monitor the configuration of the resources in your AWS account – comes into play.

In this chapter, we're going to cover the following main topics:

- An introduction to SCPs
- Writing an SCP
- An introduction to AWS Config
- Writing your own AWS Config rule using Guard

Technical requirements

Before following this section, please create an AWS account for yourself. You can sign up at aws. amazon.com. A basic understanding of AWS – for example, what a service is – will be beneficial.

All scripts from this section can be found at the following GitHub link:

`https://github.com/PacktPublishing/AWS-for-System-Administrators-Second-Edition`

The CiA video for this chapter can be found at `https://packt.link/DpFUI`

An introduction to SCPs

SCPs are used to define an upper limit of rights that can be granted to a principal (such as an IAM role or IAM user) via an IAM policy. It is important to understand that an SCP itself – even though it looks like an IAM policy – does not grant any access. So, just because there is an SCP that defines that an API action is allowed, the principal still needs an attached IAM policy.

In other words, an SCP defines the maximum rights that are allowed to be carried out. You can use SCPs to restrict/block certain API actions. For example, you could have an SCP that blocks an entire service from being used. If you wanted to block the usage of S3, you could do this in an SCP by denying `s3:*` API operations.

But just because no SCP denies the usage of a service/an API operation does not mean that every principal (such as an IAM role or IAM user) is authorized to then do it. You'd still need an IAM policy that allows your principal – for example, your IAM role – to execute said API call.

Consider the following examples – we'll assume you want to execute the `s3:PutObject` API action from an IAM role:

- If you have *an* IAM policy that allows `s3:PutObject` to be executed and *no* SCP blocking it, the request will be allowed

- If you have *no* IAM policy that allows `s3:PutObject` and *no* SCP blocking it, the request will not be allowed because no IAM policy allows you to execute it – despite it not being blocked by an SCP

- If you have *an* IAM policy that allows `s3:PutObject` to be executed and *an* SCP blocking it, the request will be blocked. SCPs supersede IAM policies

You can find more information about the evaluation logic of the different kinds of policies in this documentation: `https://docs.aws.amazon.com/IAM/latest/UserGuide/reference_policies_evaluation-logic_policy-eval-basics.html`

SCPs use the same JSON-based syntax to define them as IAM policies, covered in *Chapter 2*.

Setting up an AWS organization

Since SCPs act on an organization level, we'll need to create an organization to which we can then attach SCPs. We'll go a lot deeper into organizations in the next chapter, but let's start with a small primer on what organizations are.

In AWS, organizations allow you to manage and create multiple accounts that should be handled together. Organizations allow you to – through SCPs – enforce rules across all the accounts that are part of the organization. Think about a large enterprise where hundreds of teams are using AWS to deploy their solutions. If every team would just sign up with their own credit card and an arbitrary e-mail address – as private people using AWS might do – it would be difficult to even keep track of all the accounts that are in use. By using an organization, you have one central place where AWS accounts are created and mechanisms to ensure that only certain features of AWS are used.

Before setting up our organization, let's introduce a few key terms:

- An account is an AWS account. Within organizations, there are two types of accounts. *Member accounts* are part of your organization. The *management account* is the root account of your organization. In it, the organization itself is set up. The management account retains control over the organization itself. Protecting the root user of a management account is of vital importance and we'll elaborate on best practices in the next chapter.

- Accounts in an organization can be associated with an **Organizational Unit** – commonly abbreviated to **OU**. When we create SCPs, we then have to attach them to an OU where they take effect on all accounts in that OU.

Let's set up a simple AWS organization that we can use to demonstrate SCPs. We'll then add to this organization in the next chapter.

Follow these steps to create the organization. Pay particular attention that you are logged into the correct account:

1. Open the AWS Console and search for AWS Organizations. AWS Organizations is a global service so there is no region selection.

2. On the service page – shown in the following screenshot, you'll see a **Create an organization** button. Click on it to create the organization.

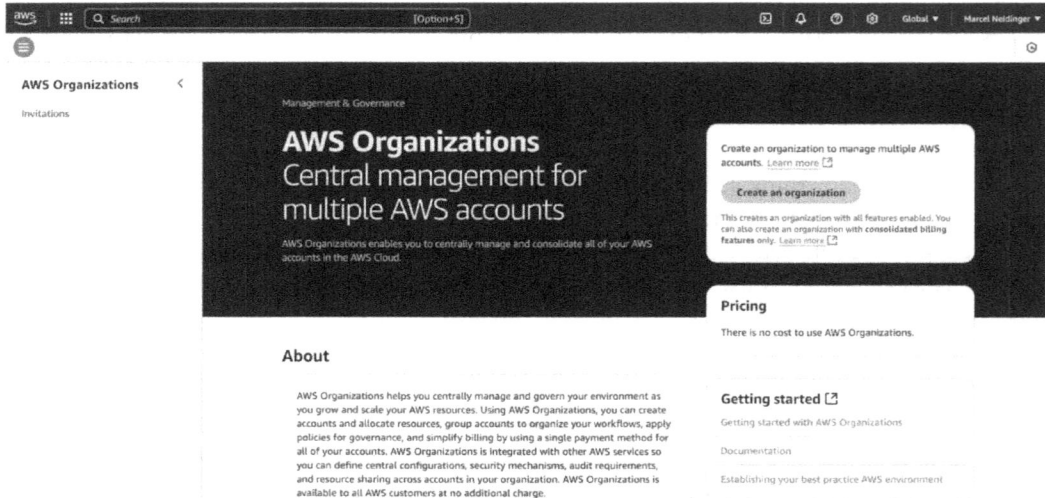

Figure 15.1 – Creation of our first organization

3. You might have to click a verification link in an email sent to the email address that is connected to this AWS account.

4. After the organization has been created, you'll see the overview page – shown in the following screenshot, which shows you an overview of the OUs and accounts associated with this organization. By default, there is a **Root** OU and the account from which we have created the org is joined. Notice the **management account** flag that is next to its name. We'll want to create a new OU underneath the root OU. To do so, select the checkmark on the root OU and – in the **Actions** menu – select **Create new** as shown in the following screenshot:

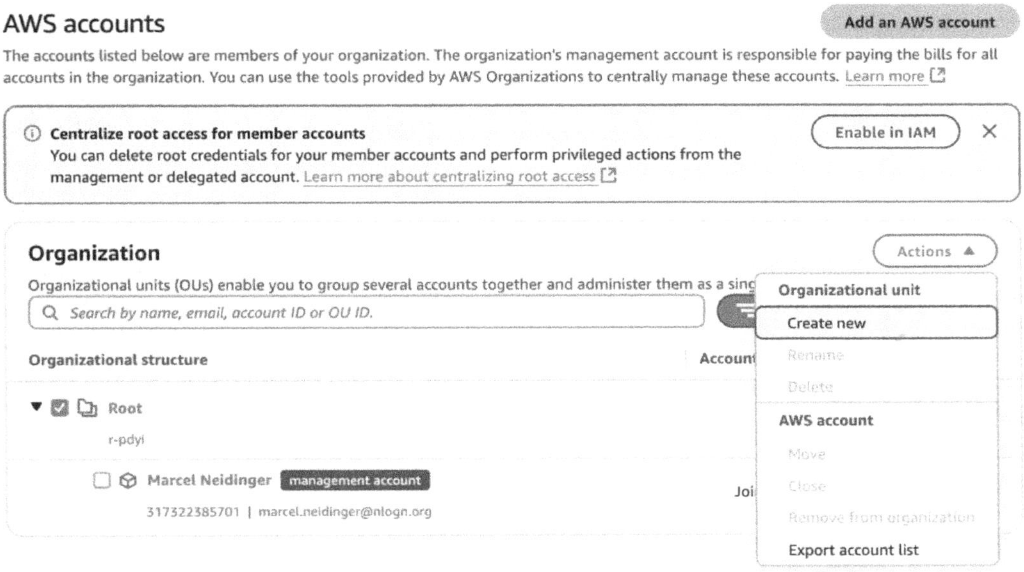
AWS accounts
Add an AWS account
The accounts listed below are members of your organization. The organization's management account is responsible for paying the bills for all accounts in the organization. You can use the tools provided by AWS Organizations to centrally manage these accounts. Learn more
Centralize root access for member accounts
You can delete root credentials for your member accounts and perform privileged actions from the management or delegated account. Learn more about centralizing root access
Enable in IAM
Organization
Actions
Organizational units (OUs) enable you to group several accounts together and administer them as a sinc
Search by name, email, account ID or OU ID.
Organizational structure
Account
Root
r-pdyi
Marcel Neidinger
management account
317322385701 | marcel.neidinger@nlogn.org
Joi
Organizational unit
Create new
Rename
Delete
AWS account
Move
Close
Remove from organization
Export account list

Figure 15.2 – Overview of our AWS organization and creation of a new OU

5. Each OU has a name, which we need to define in the dialog. In the **Organizational unit name** field, type the desired name. For this example, we'll be creating an OU with the name `Sandbox`. Click **Create organizational unit** after typing the name.

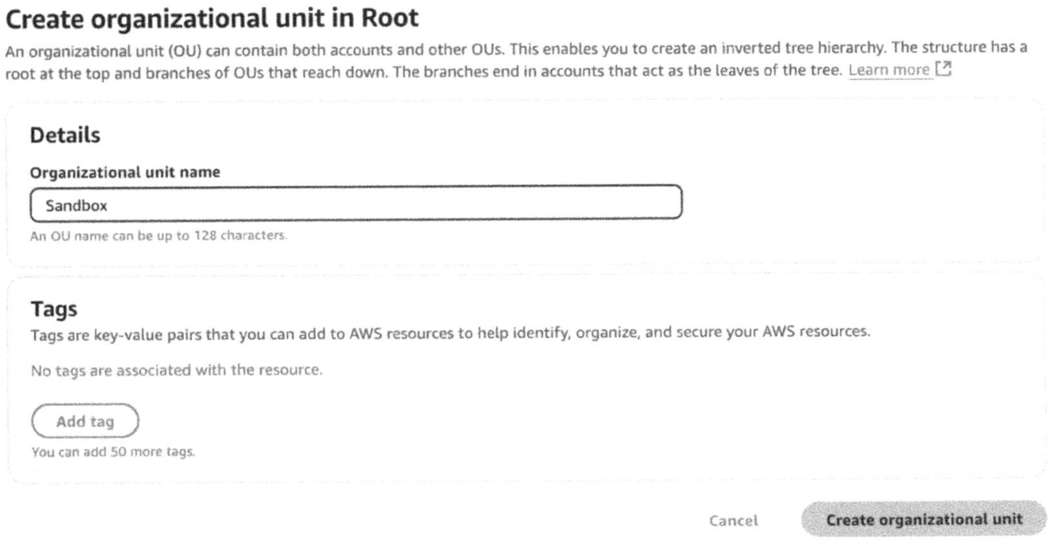
Create organizational unit in Root
An organizational unit (OU) can contain both accounts and other OUs. This enables you to create an inverted tree hierarchy. The structure has a root at the top and branches of OUs that reach down. The branches end in accounts that act as the leaves of the tree. Learn more
Details
Organizational unit name
Sandbox
An OU name can be up to 128 characters.
Tags
Tags are key-value pairs that you can add to AWS resources to help identify, organize, and secure your AWS resources.
No tags are associated with the resource.
Add tag
You can add 50 more tags.
Cancel
Create organizational unit

Figure 15.3 – Dialog to create a new OU in our organization

6. With our OU created, we can now create a new account. Back in the overview page, at the top right, there is a button called **Add an AWS account**. On the dialog shown in the following screenshot, you are given the choice of either creating a new AWS account or inviting an existing account to your organization. For this example, we'll create a new testing account. Select **Create an AWS account** and fill in the details.

For the AWS account name, we'll choose `Testing` in this example. The account will also need an associated email address. The IAM role name is the name of the role – by default, with admin privileges – that will be created in the member account. We'll assume this role from the management account to manage resources in our member account. It is the mechanism for cross-account access.

After filling in the details, click **Create AWS account** to get a new account created.

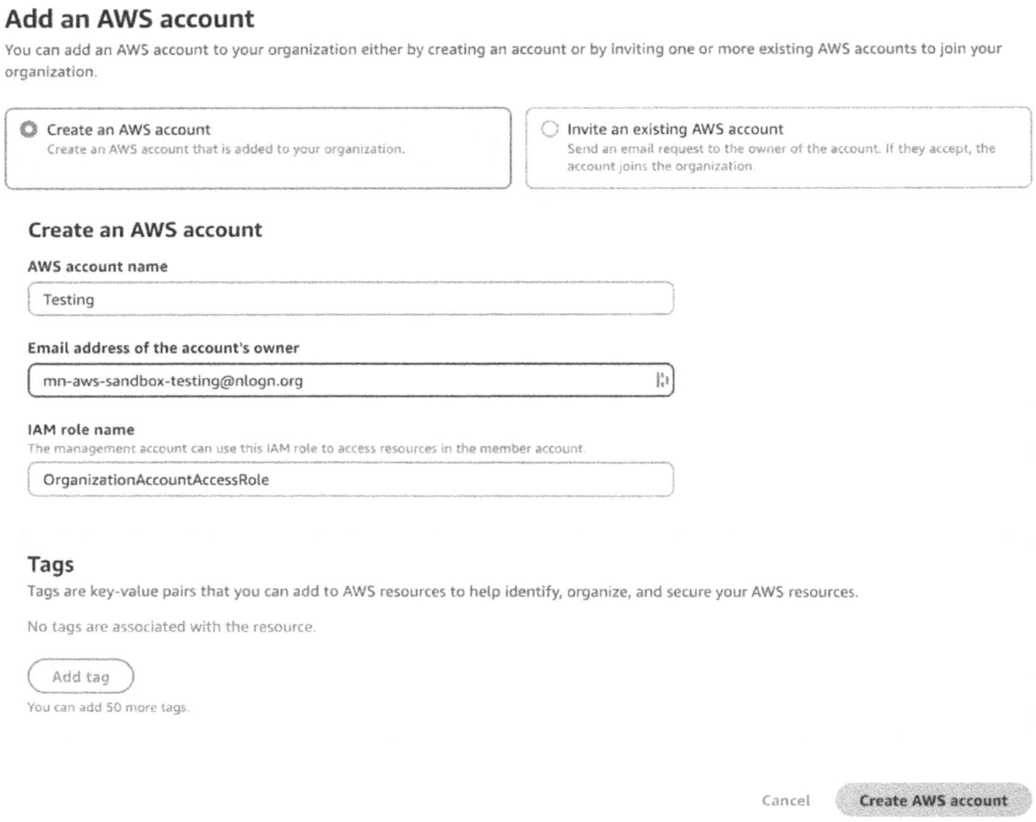

Add an AWS account

You can add an AWS account to your organization either by creating an account or by inviting one or more existing AWS accounts to join your organization.

⦿ Create an AWS account	◯ Invite an existing AWS account
Create an AWS account that is added to your organization.	Send an email request to the owner of the account. If they accept, the account joins the organization.

Create an AWS account

AWS account name

Testing

Email address of the account's owner

mn-aws-sandbox-testing@nlogn.org

IAM role name
The management account can use this IAM role to access resources in the member account.

OrganizationAccountAccessRole

Tags

Tags are key-value pairs that you can add to AWS resources to help identify, organize, and secure your AWS resources.

No tags are associated with the resource.

(Add tag)

You can add 50 more tags.

Cancel   **Create AWS account**

Figure 15.4 – Adding a new AWS account to our org

7. We now have a new AWS account – but this account is currently not associated with our **Sandbox** OU. To associate the account, select it in the overview – as shown in the following screenshot – and, under **Actions**, select **Move**.

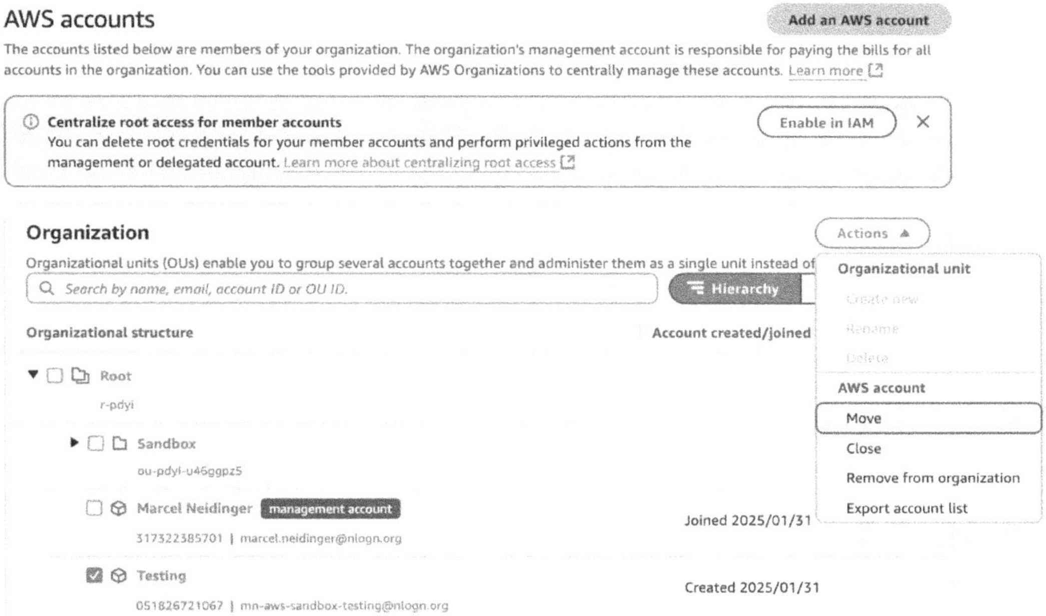

AWS accounts

Add an AWS account

The accounts listed below are members of your organization. The organization's management account is responsible for paying the bills for all accounts in the organization. You can use the tools provided by AWS Organizations to centrally manage these accounts. Learn more ↗

ⓘ **Centralize root access for member accounts**
You can delete root credentials for your member accounts and perform privileged actions from the management or delegated account. Learn more about centralizing root access ↗

Enable in IAM   ✕

Organization

Actions ▲

Organizational units (OUs) enable you to group several accounts together and administer them as a single unit instead of

Organizational unit

Q Search by name, email, account ID or OU ID.

≡ Hierarchy

Create new

Rename

Delete

Organizational structure

Account created/joined

AWS account

▼ ☐ 🗋 Root
  r-pdyi

Move

Close

▶ ☐ 🗋 Sandbox
  ou-pdyi-u46ggpz5

Remove from organization

Export account list

☐ ⊕ Marcel Neidinger management account
  317322385701 | marcel.neidinger@nlogn.org

Joined 2025/01/31

☑ ⊕ Testing
  051826721067 | mn-aws-sandbox-testing@nlogn.org

Created 2025/01/31

Figure 15.5 – Action to move an account to a different OU

8. Copy the account number of the **Testing** account (the number ending in **1067** in this example) as we'll need it in the next section.

9.   Select the OU you want to move this account into – in this example, our previously created **Sandbox** OU – and click **Move AWS account**.

Move AWS account 'Testing'

When you move an AWS account from one organization unit (OU) to another, it changes the policies that apply to the account. This can change the permissions for the account and how supported AWS services can interact with the account. Learn more [↗]

AWS account to be moved

Account name ▲	Account ID ▽	Email ▽
Testing	051826721067	mn-aws-sandbox-testing@nlogn.org

Destination

Select root or organizational unit that account should be moved to.

Organizational structure

▼ ○ 🗁 Root
    r-pdyi

▶ ◉ 🗀 Sandbox
    ou-pdyi-u46ggpz5

Cancel   **Move AWS account**

Figure 15.6 – Selection of the OU we want to move our account to

We now have created a new AWS account and associated it with a new OU. You might be wondering how we can connect to the newly created account – since we never entered a password. Let's explore how this is done next.

Logging into the AWS console of our new account by assuming a role

Accessing the account is done by assuming an IAM role. We created that role when creating the account. Before attaching an SCP to our OU, let's log in to the AWS console of our newly created member account. We'll see how to set up programmatic access in the next chapter.

Note

As of January 2025, AWS has rolled out a new feature that allows signing into multiple AWS console sessions at the same time. This chapter assumes that you have activated this feature.

Check this link in the documentation for more information on multi-session support: https://docs.aws.amazon.com/awsconsolehelpdocs/latest/gsg/multisession.html

---

To access the AWS account, follow these steps:

1. Log in to your management account and click on the account ID at the top right. A dialog, as shown in the following screenshot, will appear. Click on the little arrow next to **Add session** to reveal the **Switch role** option. *Note that you can't use your root user to switch roles into a different account.*

2. You'll be taken to a dialog where you have to define the account ID and IAM role name you want to assume. You can see the dialog in the following screenshot:

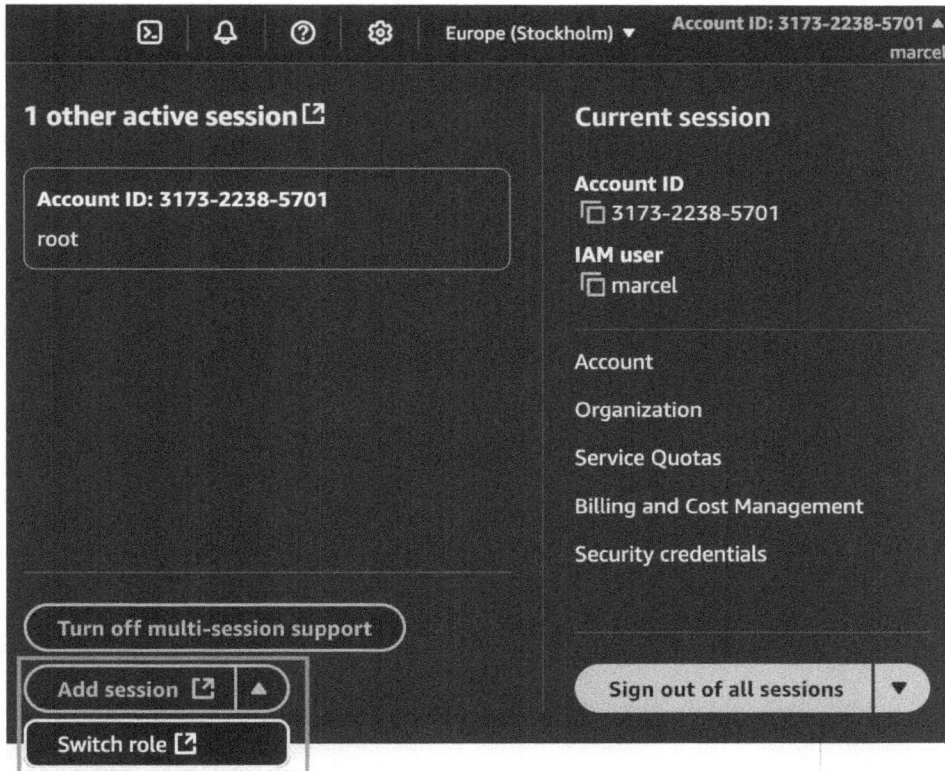

Figure 15.7 – Dialog to switch the role to another account

The **Account ID** is the 12-digit account ID of our member account that you copied in step 8 of the previous set of instructions. **IAM role name** is the name of the role you want to assume. Use the org's default admin role here. The default name is **OrganizationAccountAccessRole** and you defined it in step 8 when creating the new AWS account. You can define **Display name**, which will be shown in the **Switch Role** dialog, but this is optional. Once you have put in the role and account ID, click **Switch Role**.

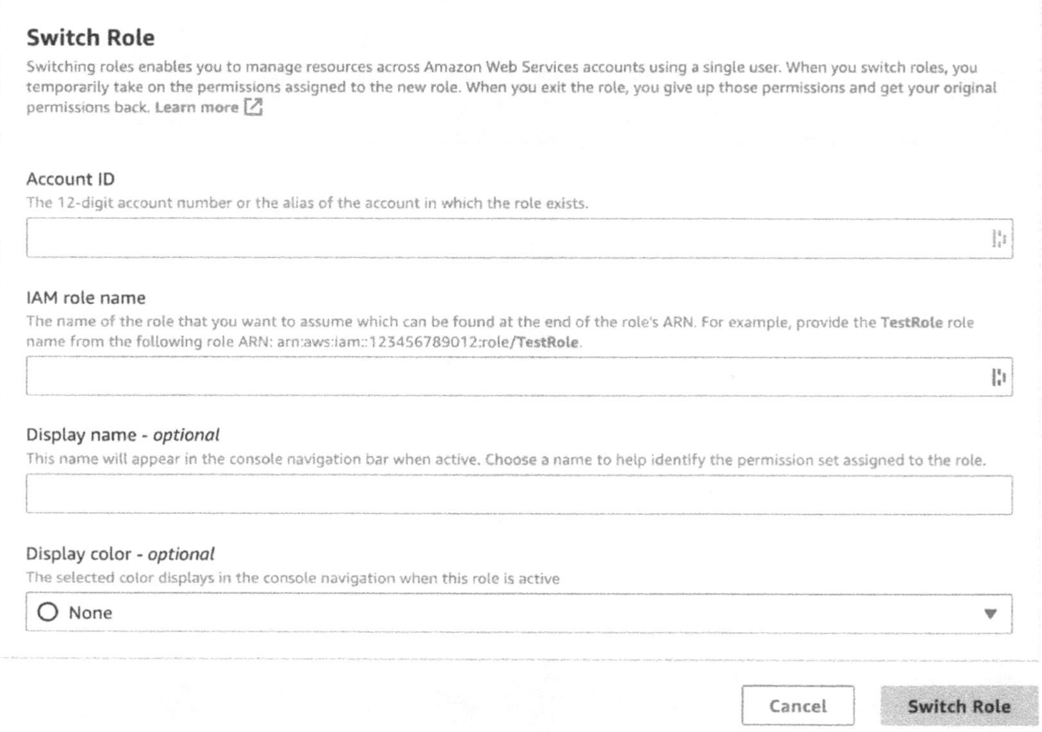

Switch Role

Switching roles enables you to manage resources across Amazon Web Services accounts using a single user. When you switch roles, you temporarily take on the permissions assigned to the new role. When you exit the role, you give up those permissions and get your original permissions back. **Learn more** [↗]

Account ID

The 12-digit account number or the alias of the account in which the role exists.

[   ] |¦|

IAM role name

The name of the role that you want to assume which can be found at the end of the role's ARN. For example, provide the **TestRole** role name from the following role ARN: arn:aws:iam::123456789012:role/**TestRole**.

[   ] |¦|

Display name - *optional*

This name will appear in the console navigation bar when active. Choose a name to help identify the permission set assigned to the role.

[   ]

Display color - *optional*

The selected color displays in the console navigation when this role is active

[○ None   ▼]

[Cancel]   [**Switch Role**]

Figure 15.8 – The dialog to set the role and account we want to switch into

Additional information

You can use the switch role dialog not only to switch to a role in a different account but also in the same AWS account. This can be particularly useful to troubleshoot permission issues.

3. After clicking the **Switch Role** button, you'll be taken to the AWS console of your new account. In the following screenshot, notice how – at the top right – you have a different AWS account ID from the ID of your management account. You can see that we are logged into the account ending in **1067** with the federated user **OrganizationAccountAccessRole/marcel**. The first part is the role that we have just assumed and the second part is the name of the IAM user that was used in this example to switch the role. You can also see that I have two other sessions open, one for the root user and one for the IAM user marcel. These sessions are logged into the management account. You should have at least one active session – with the IAM user you logged in to your management account.

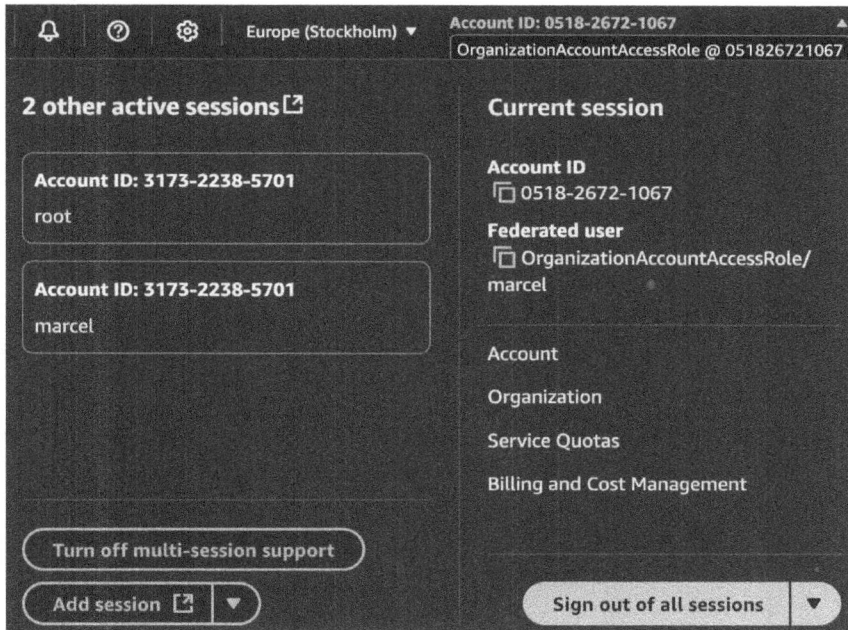

Figure 15.9 – Overview of the user sessions

We can now easily access our **Testing** account, which is part of our **Sandbox** OU. But so far, we haven't imposed any restrictions via SCPs on this account. That's what we'll do now.

Enabling SCPs and creating a new policy

In order to create SCPs, we need to log back in to our management account. Either log in to your AWS console with the IAM user of your management account or use one of the "active sessions" in the menu (shown in *Figure 15.9*) to go back to your management account.

By default, SCPs are not enabled when creating a new org.

Follow these steps to enable SCPs and create your first policy:

1. Open the AWS Organizations service by searching for it.
2. In the left navigation pane, click on **Policies**. You'll see a list of all the available policy types – also shown in the following screenshot. We'll discuss each of them in detail in the next chapter. For now, we are only interested in the SCPs.

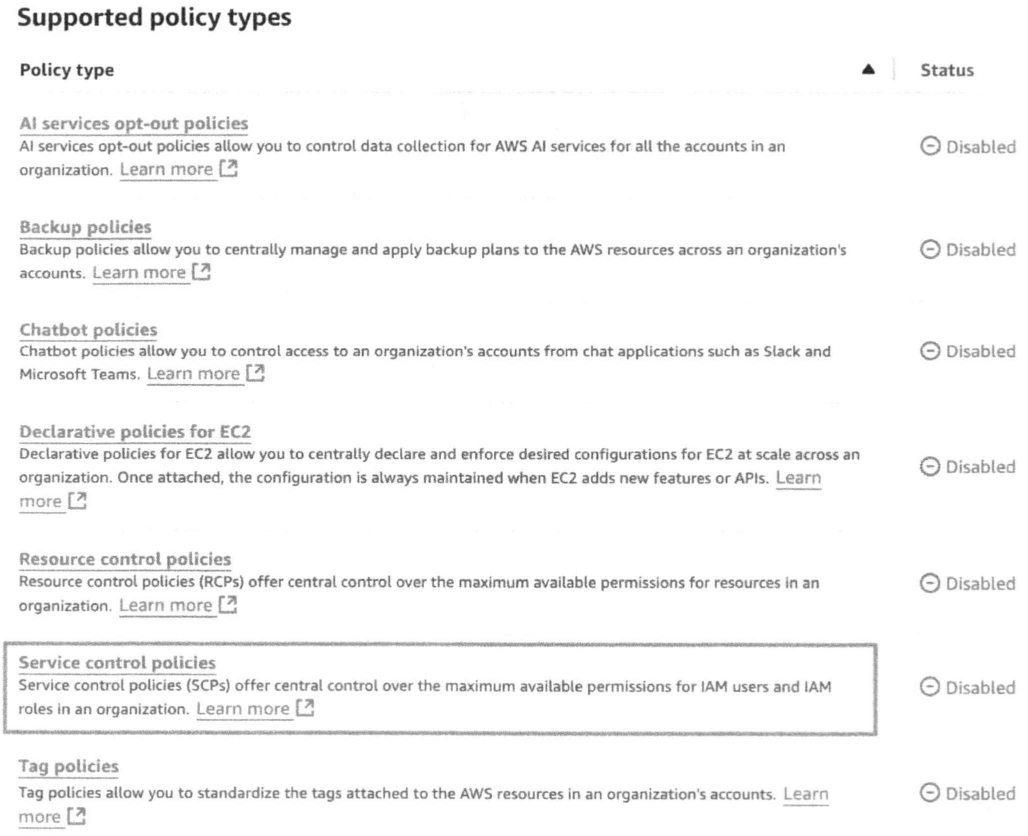

Supported policy types

Policy type ▲	Status
AI services opt-out policies AI services opt-out policies allow you to control data collection for AWS AI services for all the accounts in an organization. Learn more [↗]	⊖ Disabled
Backup policies Backup policies allow you to centrally manage and apply backup plans to the AWS resources across an organization's accounts. Learn more [↗]	⊖ Disabled
Chatbot policies Chatbot policies allow you to control access to an organization's accounts from chat applications such as Slack and Microsoft Teams. Learn more [↗]	⊖ Disabled
Declarative policies for EC2 Declarative policies for EC2 allow you to centrally declare and enforce desired configurations for EC2 at scale across an organization. Once attached, the configuration is always maintained when EC2 adds new features or APIs. Learn more [↗]	⊖ Disabled
Resource control policies Resource control policies (RCPs) offer central control over the maximum available permissions for resources in an organization. Learn more [↗]	⊖ Disabled
Service control policies Service control policies (SCPs) offer central control over the maximum available permissions for IAM users and IAM roles in an organization. Learn more [↗]	⊖ Disabled
Tag policies Tag policies allow you to standardize the tags attached to the AWS resources in an organization's accounts. Learn more [↗]	⊖ Disabled

Figure 15.10 – Overview of all available policy types with the SCPs highlighted

3. You'll be taken to a dialog that allows you to enable SCPs by clicking the **Enable service control policies** button as shown in the following screenshot:

Service control policies

Service control policies (SCPs) offer central control over the maximum available permissions for IAM users and IAM roles in an organization. Learn more [↗]

> **Enable service control policies**

Figure 15.11 – The button to enable SCPs for our org

4. With SCPs created, you'll be taken to an overview page of all the SCPs that are currently active for this org, as shown in the following screenshot. By default, there is only one SCP, the **FullAWSAccess** AWS managed SCP that is attached to the root. This SCP simply allows access to all available AWS services.

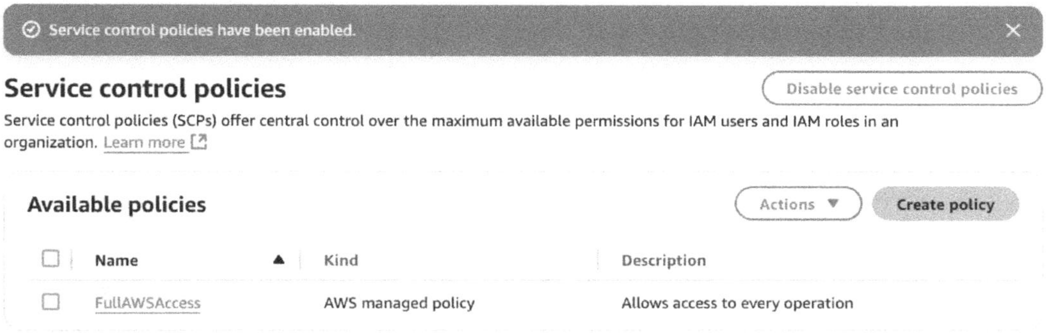

> ⊘ Service control policies have been enabled.   ✕
>
> ## Service control policies   (Disable service control policies)
>
> Service control policies (SCPs) offer central control over the maximum available permissions for IAM users and IAM roles in an organization. Learn more [↗]
>
> **Available policies**   (Actions ▼)   (**Create policy**)
>
> | ☐ | Name | ▲ | Kind | Description |
> |---|---|---|---|---|
> | ☐ | FullAWSAccess | | AWS managed policy | Allows access to every operation |

Figure 15.12 – Overview of active SCPs

We are now ready to create our new SCP. For this walk-through, we'll create an SCP that allows the creation of EC2 instances only in a few selected regions. This is a very common use case for SCPs since many companies have restrictions on where their infrastructure can be deployed. These restrictions can come from regulatory requirements or can be set by the enterprise architecture. By only allowing a few select regions in which the `ec2:StartInstance` operation can be called, we can efficiently enforce this rule and prevent our workload teams from accidentally running workloads in one of the disallowed regions.

To create this new policy, follow these steps:

1. Click on the **Create policy** button at the top right.

2. You'll be taken to the dialog to create a new SCP. At the top – as shown in the following screenshot – you'll have to give your SCP a name. For this example, we'll use `Sandbox-EU-Only`. The name of your policy should be descriptive. Here, we are including the name of the OU that this will be applied to (**Sandbox**) and a description that *EU only* is allowed. In the policy description, we then expand that this policy will allow the starting of EC2 instances only in `eu-west-1` and `eu-central-1`.

Create new service control policy

A service control policy (SCP) specifies the maximum permissions that can be used by users and roles in your organization's accounts. An SCP doesn't grant permissions. You must still use IAM permission policies or resource policies to grant permissions. Learn more 🗗

Details

Policy name

Sandbox-EU-Only

A policy name can be up to 128 characters and can include the following characters: a-z, A-Z, 0-9, and .,*=@_-

Policy description - *optional*

Only allow starting of instances in eu-west-1 and eu-central-1

A description can have up to 512 characters and can include the following characters: a-z, A-Z, 0-9, and .,*=@_-

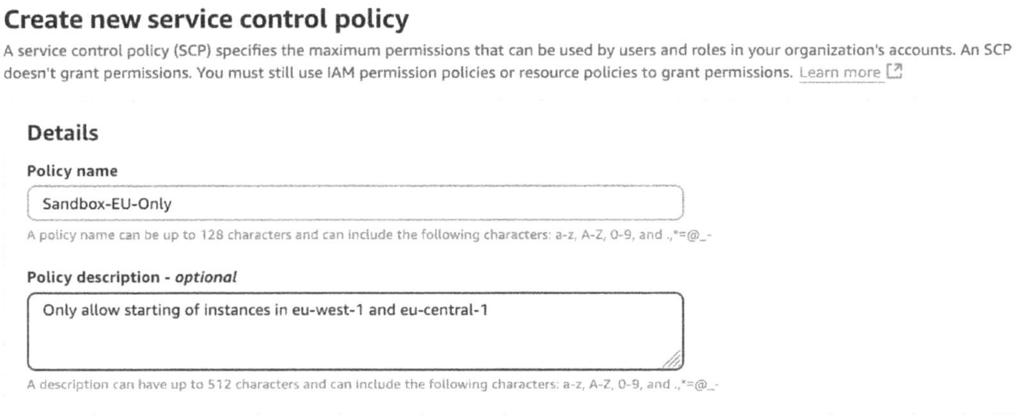

Figure 15.13 – Dialog to create the new policy

3. Below the naming details of your policy is the editor to create your new policy. SCPs use the same JSON syntax as IAM policies. We'll go through the parts of the policy step by step.

4. We first define the version of our policy language. This is the same as with our IAM policies, so `"2012-10-17"`:

```
{
    "Version": "2012-10-17",
```

5. Next, we define the list of statements that we want to use. Similar to IAM policies, statements define the API actions (such as `ec2:StartInstance`) and the effect (allow or deny). We start by giving a descriptive `Sid` (or statement ID) for our first statement – `NoEC2OutsideEurope` for this example:

```
"Statement": [
  {
    "Sid": "NoEC2OutsideEurope",
```

6. Next, the effect. By default, we want to deny any IAM policy from granting these permissions. So, we use `"Deny"` as the effect:

```
    "Effect": "Deny",
```

7. Next, our list of actions that we want to deny. We use the two explicit `ec2:RunInstance` and `ec2:StartInstances` EC2 API actions as well as the `ec2:StartInstance*` wildcard to capture all API actions as well as future ones that might be added:

```
"Action": [
  "ec2:RunInstances",
  "ec2:StartInstances",
  "ec2:StartInstance*"
],
```

8. We need to now scope the resources to which we want to apply this SCP. For this example, we want this SCP to apply to all instances in all accounts in this OU. This is why we use the wildcard for the instance ID and the region and account number in the ARN:

```
"Resource": [
  "arn:aws:ec2:*:*:instance/*"
],
```

9. So far, we have written an SCP that would deny any IAM user/role, regardless of their attached IAM policies, from using the `ec2:RunInstances` API action. This is a great way to block certain undesired API actions or (by using a wildcard such as `ec2:*`) to block entire services.

10. In our example, however, we want to allow these API actions in a defined set of regions (namely `eu-west-1` and `eu-central-1`). To implement this, we use a condition:

```
"Condition": {
```

11. The operator of our condition will be `"StringNotLike"` and the `"aws:RequestedRegion"` property. This means that any request that isn't in the defined list will get the preceding deny applied. Only if the request is for `eu-west-1` or `eu-central-1` (and the user/role has an IAM policy with the correct access rights attached) will the deny not apply.

```
"StringNotLike": {
  "aws:RequestedRegion": [
    "eu-west-1",
    "eu-central-1"
  ]
}
}
}
]
}
```

It is important to remember that SCPs do not grant any permissions. They define an upper bound of what permissions can be granted to a principal (such as an IAM role or IAM user) via an IAM policy.

We now have our SCP created – however, it does not currently apply to any of our OUs. To change this, we need to attach it to an OU. Follow these steps to do this:

1. On the overview page of your SCPs, select the newly created **Sandbox-EU-Only** policy and – as shown in the following screenshot – select **Attach policy**.

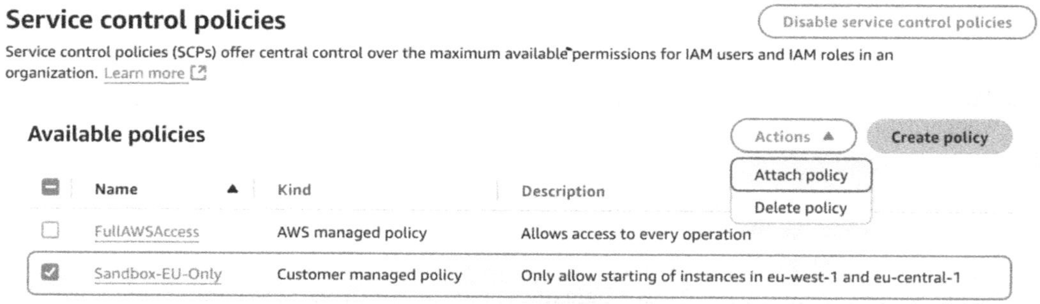

Service control policies

Service control policies (SCPs) offer central control over the maximum available permissions for IAM users and IAM roles in an organization. Learn more

Available policies

	Name ▲	Kind	Description
☐	FullAWSAccess	AWS managed policy	Allows access to every operation
☑	Sandbox-EU-Only	Customer managed policy	Only allow starting of instances in eu-west-1 and eu-central-1

Actions ▲   Create policy

Attach policy
Delete policy

Figure 15.14 – Action to attach an SCP to an OU

2. In the dialog (shown in the following screenshot), select the OU you want to attach the SCP to. In this example, select **Sandbox** and click **Attach policy**.

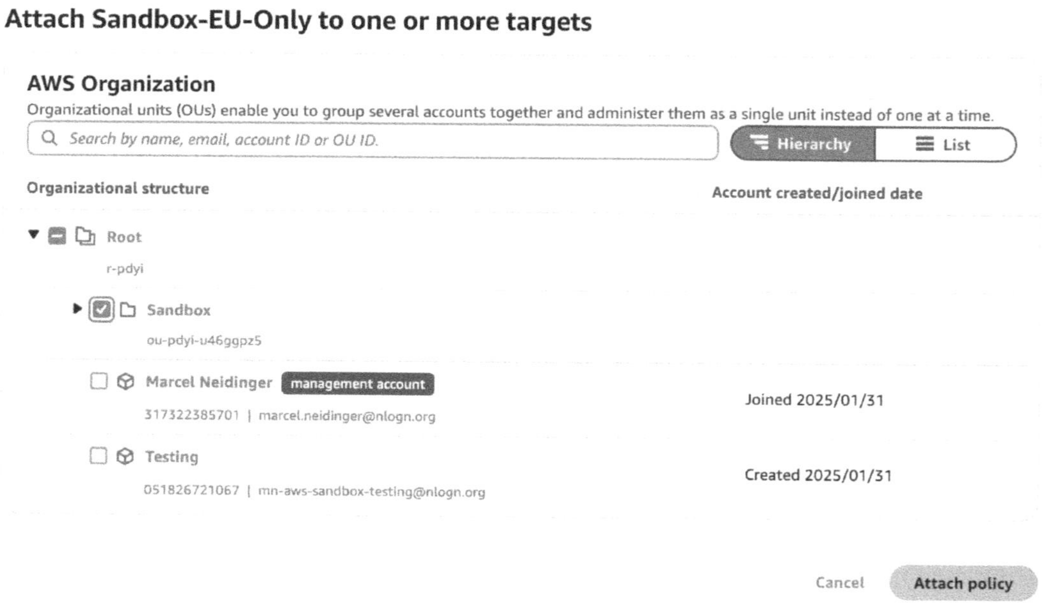

Attach Sandbox-EU-Only to one or more targets

AWS Organization

Organizational units (OUs) enable you to group several accounts together and administer them as a single unit instead of one at a time.

Q Search by name, email, account ID or OU ID.   Hierarchy | List

Organizational structure	Account created/joined date
▼ ☐ Root	
r-pdyi	
▶ ☑ Sandbox	
ou-pdyi-u46ggpz5	
☐ Marcel Neidinger [management account]	Joined 2025/01/31
317322385701 | marcel.neidinger@nlogn.org	
☐ Testing	Created 2025/01/31
051826721067 | mn-aws-sandbox-testing@nlogn.org	

Cancel   **Attach policy**

Figure 15.15 – Attaching the policy to our OU

We can now verify that the SCP is really in effect. Use the switch session feature to log back into the **Testing** account that is under the **Sandbox** OU.

Then follow these steps to verify that your SCP is in effect:

1. Open up a new session on the **Testing** account.

2. Navigate to the IAM service to confirm the access rights of the IAM role. Within IAM, under **Roles** in the left-hand navigation, select **Roles** and find **OrganizationAccountAccessRole**. As shown in the following screenshot, that role has the AWS-managed **AdministratorAccess** policy attached to it. So, just from the IAM permissions, this role is allowed to do everything.

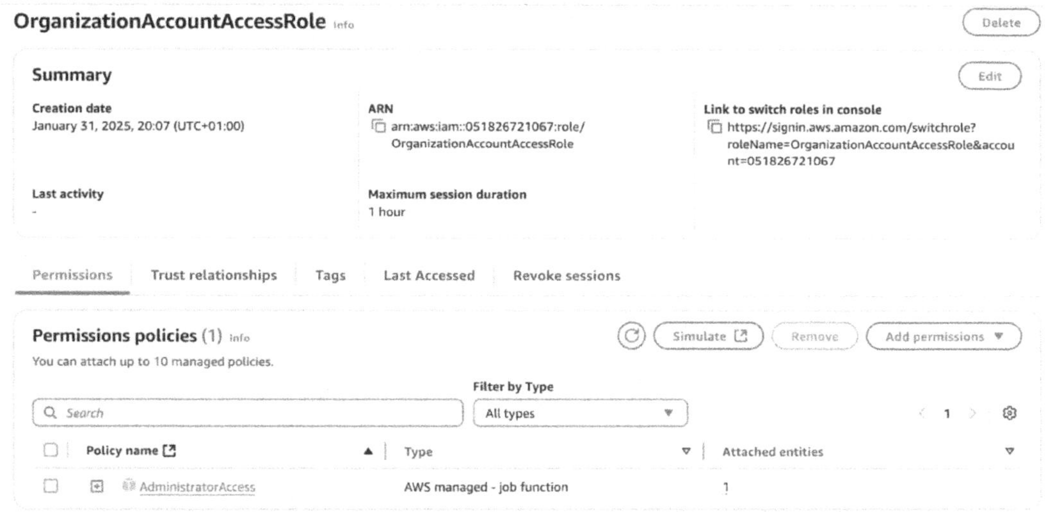

Figure 15.16 – Overview of our IAM role showing the attached IAM
policies that grant administrative access to the AWS account

To see our SCP in action, navigate to the EC2 service and then switch your region to any region that wasn't part of the list of allowed regions in the SCP. In this example, I am trying to create an EC2 instance in the `eu-north-1` (Stockholm) region. Consult the *Setting up EC2 instances* section in *Chapter 4*, on scalable compute with EC2 for a more detailed guide on how to launch an instance.

3. Trying to create an instance in the Stockholm region will result in the error that can be seen in the following screenshot. As you can see, the error indicates that it can't complete the `ec2:RunInstances` API operation due to an explicit deny in an SCP.

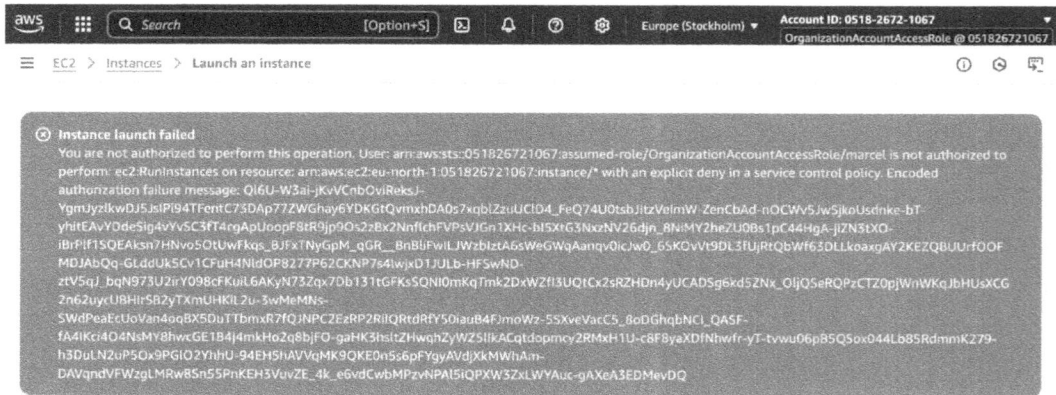

Figure 15.17 – Launch error due to the SCP blocking the API operation in the Stockholm region

You can verify that the SCP only denies the API actions in the regions by repeating the same process in the `eu-central-1` (Frankfurt) or `eu-west-1` (Ireland) regions.

We have now seen how we can use SCPs to explicitly deny API actions. But what if we just want to be able to detect any non-compliant resources? This is what AWS Config and its config rules can be used for.

Using AWS Config to detect non-compliant resources

In the previous section, we saw how we can explicitly deny API actions on an org level using SCPs. However, there might be cases where we do not want to deny API actions. Instead, we want to be alert when a resource has a certain configuration value, such as an instance that is being launched in a non-standard region. After all, there could be good reasons for that instance to be launched in a region.

This detection of non-compliant configuration of resources is what AWS Config can be used for. Config is a service that allows you to scan existing and newly created resources for configuration changes. It then applies a set of rules to it and marks any resource that doesn't comply with our rules as *non-compliant*. This is a very powerful mechanism to soft-enforce compliance by alerting but not losing the agility that the cloud offers.

Config does this by using the concept of a recorder that listens for configuration changes within your account (or accounts in your organization). It then writes these changes to a central location, usually an S3 bucket, and runs the rule checks against them.

> **Note**
>
> Follow these steps in the management account or detach the SCP from the `Sandbox` OU. Otherwise, the SCP will block you from seeing the Config rule in action since no non-compliant instance can be launched due to the SCP blocking it.

Before we can get started, we need to enable AWS Config. Follow these steps to do this:

1. Log in to your management account with a user that has admin permissions.

2. Search for the **Config** service.

3. When first opening the service page, you'll be greeted with a **1-click setup** button for AWS Config, as shown in the following screenshot:

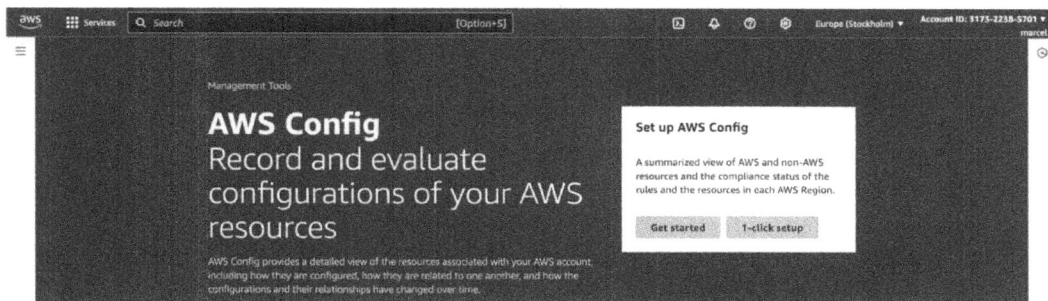

Figure 15.18 – 1-click setup for Config

4. During the one-click setup, the configuration dialog will be preset with the AWS-provided sensible defaults. As you can see in the following screenshot, you'll be taken directly to the **Review** part of the configuration dialog.

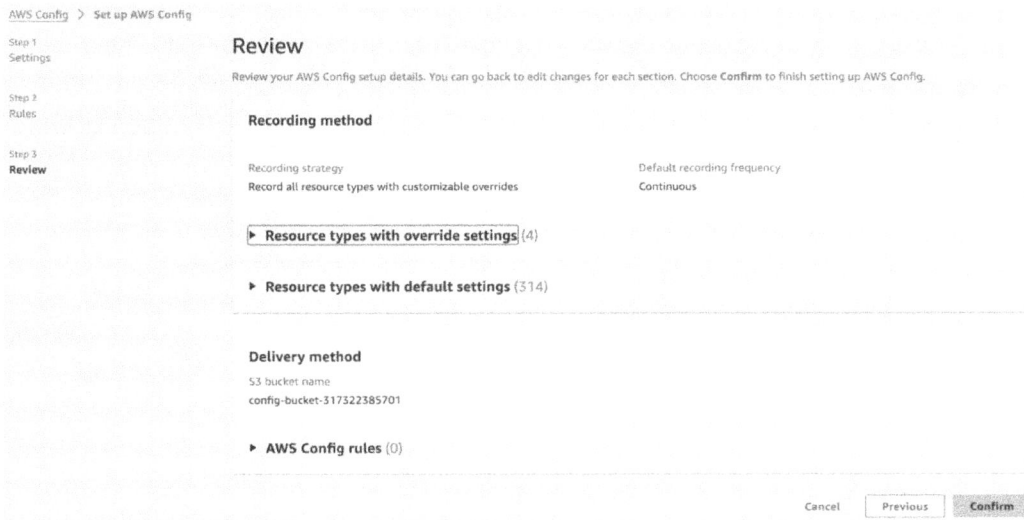

Figure 15.19 – One-click configuration review

5. The default settings exclude four resource types, the IAM role, IAM user, IAM Group, and IAM Policy from being recorded. The data is written to an S3 bucket and configuration changes are captured continuously.

6. By clicking the **Confirm** button, Config will create an IAM role with the required privileges, as well as a new S3 bucket (in your account), to which the data is saved. By default, config will keep the records for 7 years.

With config configured, we are taken to the dashboard. Here, we find an overview of the compliance status of the resources in our account. The following screenshot shows this overview.

Compliance status

Rules

⚠ 0 Noncompliant rule(s)
⊘ 0 Compliant rule(s)

Resources

⚠ 0 Noncompliant resource(s)
⊘ 0 Compliant resource(s)

Figure 15.20 – Compliance status of our rules and resources

Compliance is shown both in terms of rules and resources. The number of non-compliant rules indicates how many rules have at least one resource that isn't compliant, while the number of non-compliant resources indicates how many resources are violating at least one compliance rule.

Creating our own Config rule to detect instances in other regions

We now want to create a config rule that allows us to detect if a resource isn't deployed in our two allowed regions, `eu-central-1` and `eu-west-1`.

Config supports three types of rules:

- **AWS managed rules** are pre-configured rules provided by AWS. At the time of writing, there are 498 AWS managed rules with use cases spanning from ensuring that the AWS access key was rotated within a maximum number of days to checking that all ALBs redirect their HTTP traffic to HTTPS.

- **Custom Lambda rules** use a Lambda function to run the checks. With a Lambda rule, you can run any kind of API calls (including calls to third-party systems such as an external IT inventory management tool) to validate the compliance of your resource.

- **Guard rules** use the Guard language to specify rule criteria. The example in this chapter will use a Guard rule.

To create the new rule, follow these steps:

1. In the left-hand navigation of Config, select **Rules**.

2. On the **Rules** overview page – as shown in the following screenshot – select **Add rule** at the top right.

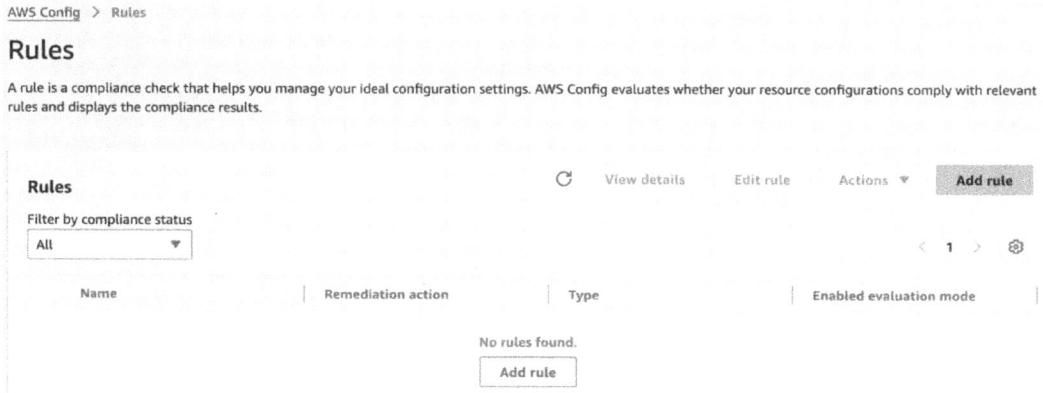

AWS Config > Rules

Rules

A rule is a compliance check that helps you manage your ideal configuration settings. AWS Config evaluates whether your resource configurations comply with relevant rules and displays the compliance results.

Rules			C View details	Edit rule	Actions ▼	**Add rule**

Filter by compliance status

All ▼

< 1 > ⚙

Name	Remediation action	Type	Enabled evaluation mode

No rules found.

Add rule

Figure 15.21 – Empty set of rules in Config

3. We first need to specify the rule type. Select **Create custom rule using Guard** and click **Next**.

Specify rule type

Add rules to help you manage the ideal configuration settings of your AWS resources. You can add any of the following predefined, customizable AWS Config Managed rules, or you can create your own AWS Config Custom rule using AWS Lambda functions or Guard Custom policy.

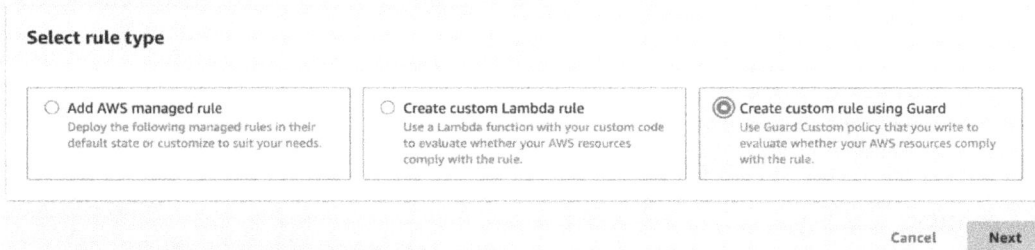

Select rule type

○ **Add AWS managed rule**	○ **Create custom Lambda rule**	◉ **Create custom rule using Guard**
Deploy the following managed rules in their default state or customize to suit your needs.	Use a Lambda function with your custom code to evaluate whether your AWS resources comply with the rule.	Use Guard Custom policy that you write to evaluate whether your AWS resources comply with the rule.

Cancel   Next

Figure 15.22 – Selection of the type of rule we want to create

4. We first need to define a name for our rule. In the **Details** section shown in the following screenshot, type the name of your rule. In this example, we'll use `no-ec2-outside-europe` and the Guard runtime version `guard-2.x.x`, which is the latest guard runtime. We'll also enable debug logs. This is especially helpful when developing config rules.

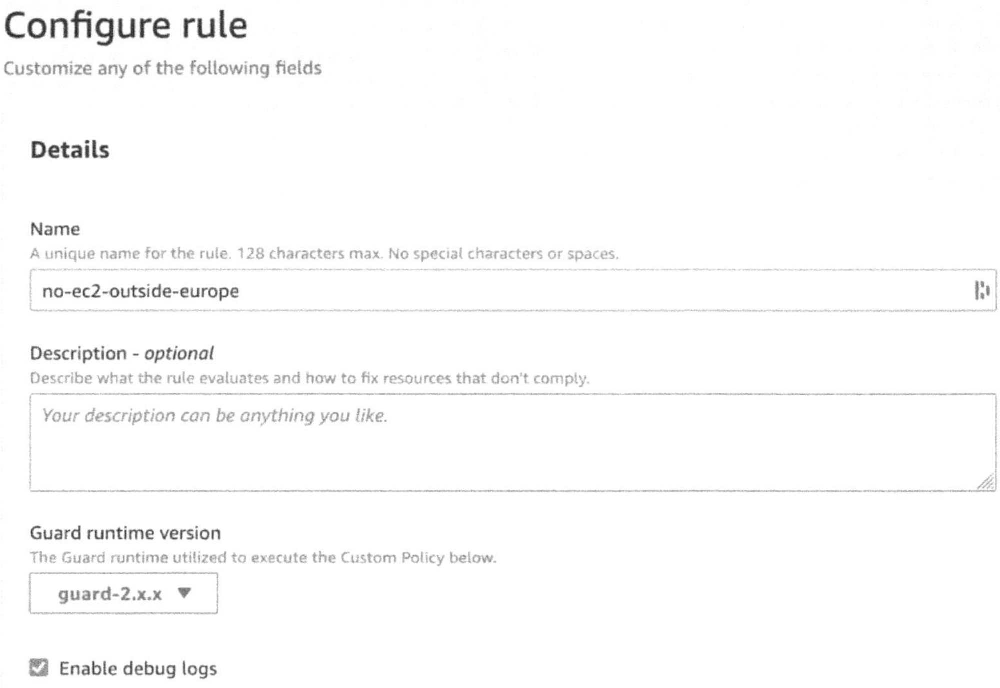

Configure rule

Customize any of the following fields

Details

Name

A unique name for the rule. 128 characters max. No special characters or spaces.

```
no-ec2-outside-europe
```

Description - *optional*

Describe what the rule evaluates and how to fix resources that don't comply.

```
Your description can be anything you like.
```

Guard runtime version

The Guard runtime utilized to execute the Custom Policy below.

```
guard-2.x.x  ▼
```

☑ Enable debug logs

Figure 15.23 – Details of our new Guard rule

5. The editor in the **Rule content** section allows us to specify our guard rule content. We'll go over each line of the guard rule in the following step.

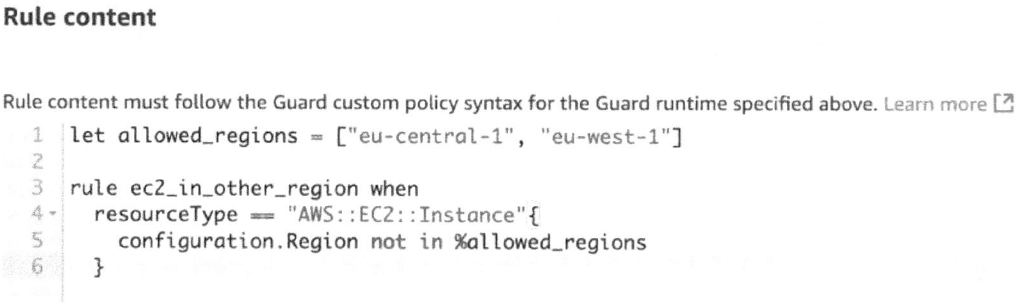

Rule content

Rule content must follow the Guard custom policy syntax for the Guard runtime specified above. Learn more ☑

```
1   let allowed_regions = ["eu-central-1", "eu-west-1"]
2
3   rule ec2_in_other_region when
4 -   resourceType == "AWS::EC2::Instance"{
5       configuration.Region not in %allowed_regions
6   }
```

Figure 15.24 – Content of our rule

6. In the rule, we first define a list variable that will contain the regions we want to allow an instance to be in. Variables have a name and are defined using the `let` keyword:

```
let allowed_regions = ["eu-central-1", "eu-west-1"]
```

7. We then define the name of our rule:

```
rule ec2_in_other_region when
```

Next comes the rule body. We first need to define to which type of resources we want this rule to apply. The name of the resource is the same as the name of that resource in CloudFormation. For EC2 instances, this is the `"AWS::EC2::Instance"` resource type. By using the curly brackets to scope the block, we can define that the following checks should only apply to resources of the selected type. This check is also called a **clause**. Clauses are either true or false and the following block is only run if the clause evaluates to true:

```
resourceType == "AWS::EC2::Instance"{
```

8. We can access the configuration of the instance – all variables that would also be available in CloudFormation – using the `configuration` variable. We can use the dot operator to access the properties, such as the `Region` property in this example, and then use it in a clause. This clause checks that the region is not in the allowed regions. We can reference previously defined variables using the variable name with the percentage sign before it.

The following clause is true if the region is not in the allowed regions list:

```
configuration.Region not in %allowed_regions
}
```

9. A resource is in violation of the rule if the clause evaluates to true.

> **Additional notes**
>
> You can find the list of available operators in Guard at this link: `https://docs.aws.amazon.com/cfn-guard/latest/ug/writing-rules.html`

10. With the rule defined, we can next decide on the evaluation mode. Our new rule can either be evaluated pro-actively (before a resource is provisioned) or in a detective mode. Here, all previously provisioned resources will also be evaluated. This is a great way to programmatically check for violations of a policy.

We can also define where we want to apply this rule. In the rule, we are already scoping to EC2 instances. Since our rule only applies to resources of the EC2 instance type, we can use **Resources** scoping. Select **AWS resources** as the resource category and, under **Resource type**, search for **AWS EC2 Instance** and select it.

In addition to applying the rule to all changes or only for a certain subset of resource types, we can also apply the rule based on tags using the **Tags** scope of change.

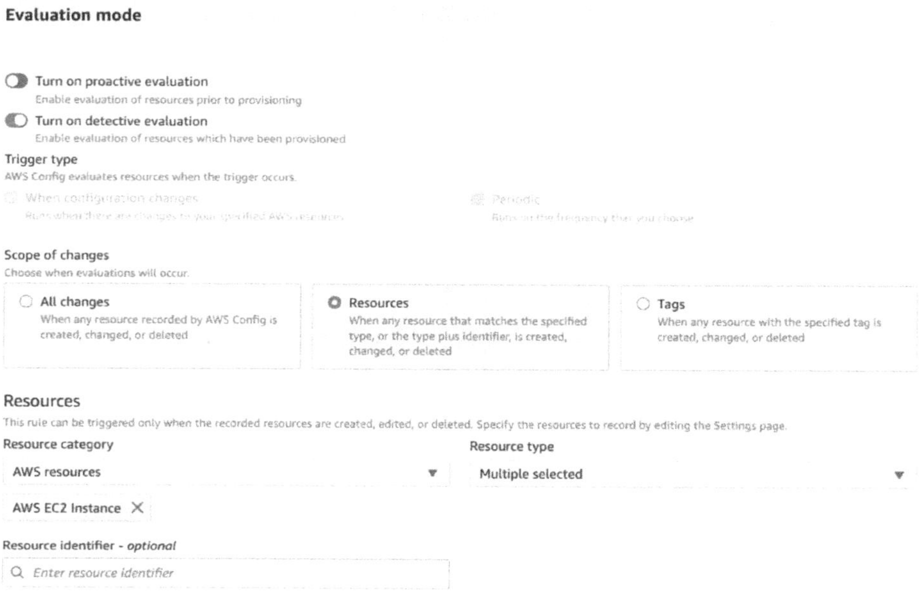

Evaluation mode

○ **Turn on proactive evaluation**
Enable evaluation of resources prior to provisioning

◉ **Turn on detective evaluation**
Enable evaluation of resources which have been provisioned

Trigger type
AWS Config evaluates resources when the trigger occurs.

○ When configuration changes
Runs when there are changes to your specified AWS resources

○ Periodic
Runs at the frequency that you choose

Scope of changes
Choose when evaluations will occur.

○ All changes	◉ Resources	○ Tags
When any resource recorded by AWS Config is created, changed, or deleted	When any resource that matches the specified type, or the type plus identifier, is created, changed, or deleted	When any resource with the specified tag is created, changed, or deleted

Resources
This rule can be triggered only when the recorded resources are created, edited, or deleted. Specify the resources to record by editing the Settings page.

Resource category	Resource type
AWS resources ▼	Multiple selected ▼

AWS EC2 Instance ✕

Resource identifier - *optional*

🔍 *Enter resource identifier*

Figure 15.25 – Configuration of the evaluation mode

11. Below the evaluation mode definitions, we can define parameters and rule tags. Parameters allow us to define attributes that we can then use inside of our rule content. We'll leave them empty.

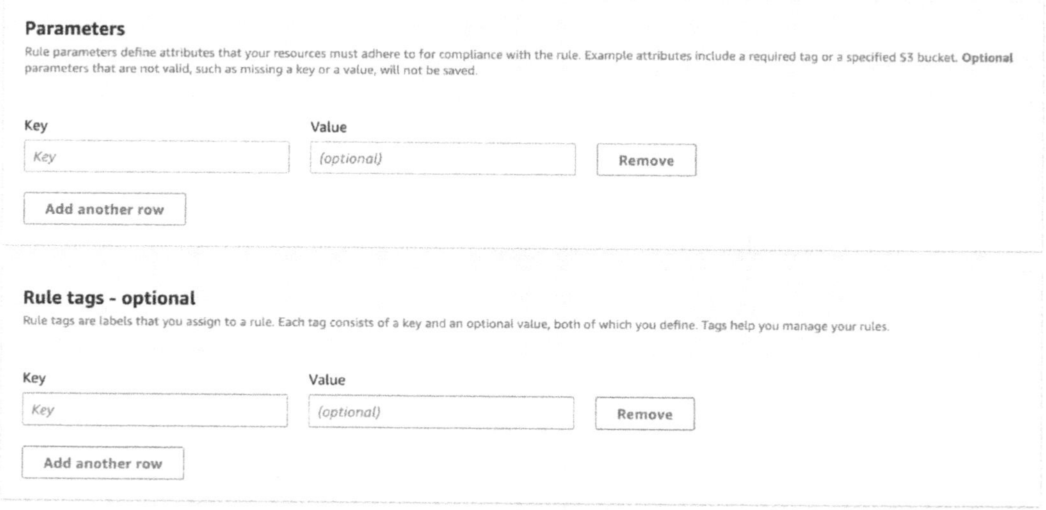

Parameters
Rule parameters define attributes that your resources must adhere to for compliance with the rule. Example attributes include a required tag or a specified S3 bucket. **Optional** parameters that are not valid, such as missing a key or a value, will not be saved.

Key	Value	
Key	(optional)	Remove

Add another row

Rule tags - optional
Rule tags are labels that you assign to a rule. Each tag consists of a key and an optional value, both of which you define. Tags help you manage your rules.

Key	Value	
Key	(optional)	Remove

Add another row

Figure 15.26 – Parameters for our config rule

12. Click **Next** and review the content of the new config rule. Then click **Save** to create it. You'll be taken back to the overview of rules where there is now one entry – a custom rule called `no-ec2-outside-europe`.

With the rule defined, we now need to trigger non-compliance to validate that it works. To do this, follow these steps:

1. Open the EC2 service, navigate to a region that isn't part of the allowed list of resources, and create a new EC2 instance. Refer to the *Setting up EC2 instances* section in *Chapter 4*, on scalable compute with EC2, for a more detailed guide on how to launch an instance.

2. In comparison to the SCP, Config won't prevent you from creating the instance so it should start successfully.

3. Navigate back to the rules in Config. It can take a few minutes for the new resource to be picked up by Config.

4. Once the resource has been picked up, it will show up in the list of non-compliant resources – as shown in the following screenshot:

no-ec2-outside-europe

Actions ▼

Rule details

Edit

Description	Enabled evaluation mode	Detective evaluation trigger type
	• DETECTIVE	• Oversized configuration changes
Config rule ARN		• Configuration changes
arn:aws:config:eu-north-1:317322385701:config-rule/config-rule-lqu5qg	Last successful detective evaluation	
	⊘ January 31, 2025 11:30 PM	Scope of changes
		All changes

Resources in scope

View details   Remediate   ⟳

Noncompliant ▼

⟨ 1 ⟩ ⚙

ID	Type	Status	Annotation
i-06ae6bd1ef0d14b1e	EC2 Instance	-	Attempting to retrieve array index or key from map at path = /

Figure 15.27 – Rule details and the list of non-compliant resources

We have successfully created a config rule to monitor for EC2 instances that are created outside of the list of allowed regions.

Config rules and SCPs can also be used in tandem. Especially if you are thinking about establishing a new SCP, you could write a config rule to flag all resources that would be blocked by the new SCP. You can then inform the resource owners to warn them that they need to change their resources before enforcing compliance using an SCP.

Summary

In this chapter, we saw two different approaches to ensuring compliance in our AWS account. We saw how we can use SCPs to enforce that certain API operations – such as the creation of EC2 instances outside of a set of allowed regions – can't be carried out. We then saw how we can use AWS Config to create custom rules that monitor resources in our AWS account and flag them when they violate our specified rules.

In the next chapter, we'll expand on our organization setup and will see how we can apply Config rules across our organization.

Join the CloudPro Newsletter with 44000+ Subscribers

Want to know what's happening in cloud computing, DevOps, IT administration, networking, and more? Scan the QR code to subscribe to **CloudPro**, our weekly newsletter for 44,000+ tech professionals who want to stay informed and ahead of the curve.

`https://packt.link/cloudpro`

16
Operating in a Multi-Account Environment

When dealing with an AWS environment, it is often useful to think of an account as a container into which workloads and infrastructure are deployed. In theory, we can put all our resources into one account. However, this will quickly lead to problems with separation. Imagine you have your development and production all in one account. Which of the databases was the production one again? And which resource can be deleted without any side effects for our production workload?

It thus makes sense to operate multiple AWS accounts that are dedicated to aspects of your cloud infrastructure. Depending on the size of your organization, you might want to have a dedicated account just for backups, one where you store audit logs and multiple accounts for a workload – one for each stage.

To make these kinds of setups easier to build, AWS provides us with a few tools. To manage our accounts, we have the previously introduced AWS Organizations, and to share resources between the accounts, we can use AWS **Resource Access Manager** (or **RAM** for short).

In this chapter, we'll explore how these two services can be used together to lay the foundations of a multi-account setup.

In this chapter, we're going to cover the following main topics:

- An introduction to designing AWS organization structures
- Sharing resources within an organization using RAM
- Setting up cross-account access via IAM

Throughout this chapter, we'll consider best practices to follow when operating in a multi-account setup.

Technical requirements

Before following along with the examples in this chapter, please create an AWS account for yourself. You can sign up at aws.amazon.com. A basic understanding of AWS – for example, what a service is – will be beneficial.

A basic understanding of IaC tools such as Terraform will be beneficial. Follow the instructions in *Chapter 1* to set up Terraform on your local machine.

All scripts from this section can be found on the following GitHub page:

https://github.com/PacktPublishing/AWS-for-System-Administrators-Second-Edition

The CiA video for this chapter can be found at https://packt.link/Php5g

If you haven't completed the previous chapter, please set up the AWS organization as described there.

Designing AWS organizations

In the previous chapter, we saw how to create a basic AWS organization to which we could add a new AWS account. We then used **Organizational Units (OUs)** to apply **Service Control Policies (SCPs)** to restrict what the newly created accounts could do within AWS.

In this chapter, we will revisit the previously seen organization and expand it.

> **Additional information**
>
> This chapter follows the best practices recommended by AWS in their documentation. You can find a full list of best practices under this link: https://docs.aws.amazon.com/organizations/latest/userguide/orgs_best-practices.html.

The first decision we have to take when designing our organization is how we want to group our accounts. This is done via OUs. Purely based on the name, you might be tempted to simply reproduce the corporate structure into the cloud environment.

The following diagram shows the corporate structure of a made-up company:

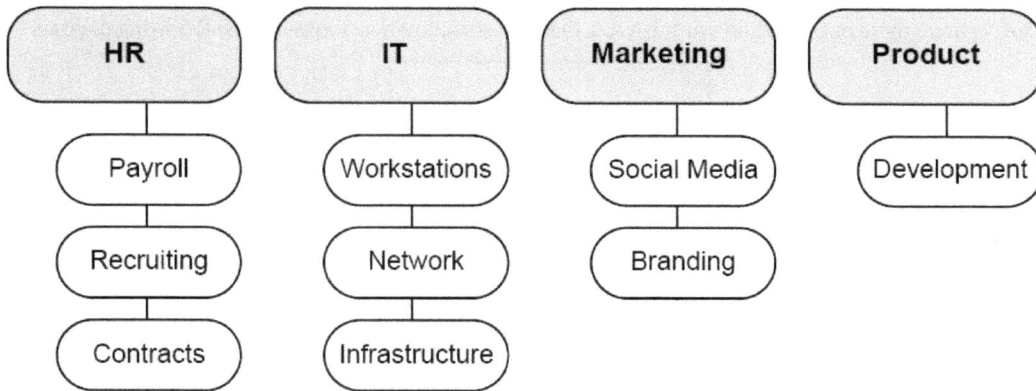

Figure 16.1 – Corporate structure of our made-up company

We might be tempted to now reproduce this exactly into our OU structure. This means we'd have an OU for workloads from HR, one for workloads from IT, and so on.

However, this is not recommended. As we saw in the previous chapter, SCPs are applied to OUs and thus define the boundaries of what an account within an OU can do. Let's take two workloads as an example: a payroll application that is needed by HR to handle employee payslips and a ticketing solution that is used by the workstations group within IT to handle support requests. Both of them use EC2 instances for compute and RDS for their databases.

When being run in AWS, do these two workloads require different boundaries when it comes to AWS API actions? Or would we end up reproducing the same SCPs across the HR and IT OUs?

> **Best practice**
> This is why AWS advises us as a best practice to "*Group workloads based on business purpose and not reporting structure*" (see https://docs.aws.amazon.com/organizations/latest/userguide/orgs_best-practices.html).

So, instead of grouping our OUs by our company structure, we introduce a workload OU, which will house all of our workloads. When building a workload, we typically have at least two environments: a production environment, which handles all our production traffic, and a development or testing environment, which is used for the next iteration of the product. Based on your software development processes, you might also have more environments, such as integration or testing.

We can separate these out into different sub-OUs. Our OU structure now looks like the following diagram.

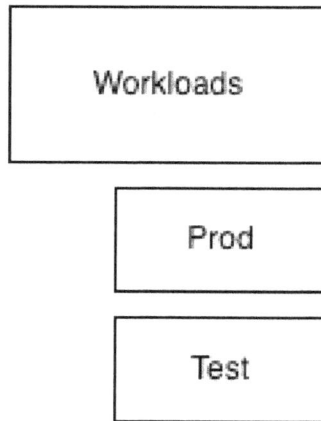

Figure 16.2 – Child OUs, prod and test, for our workloads parent OU

Before continuing, let's implement this structure in Terraform.

> **Important**
>
> Remember that you need to run this Terraform script in the account that owns the AWS organization.
>
> This walk-through assumes that you have set up your organization in the previous chapter. If not, follow the instructions there first.

Creating an OU in Terraform

To create a new OU in Terraform, follow these steps:

1. Create a new folder called `org_setup` using the `mkdir` command and navigate into it using the `cd` command:

    ```
    mkdir org_setup
    cd org_setup
    ```

2. Inside, create a new file called `org_setup.tf` and open it in a text editor such as Notepad++ or Visual Studio Code:

    ```
    touch org_setup.tf
    ```

3. We start by defining the Terraform configuration, such as the AWS provider needed as well as the AWS Region we want to use. Since organizations are a global feature, you can use any Region you want here:

```
terraform {
  required_providers {
    aws = {
      source  = "hashicorp/aws"
      version = "~> 5.8"
    }
  }
}

provider "aws" {
  region = "eu-central-1"
}
```

4. Any organization starts with a root OU, and all of our OUs will need to reside under this root OU. Since we haven't created the organization itself using Terraform, we can use the `aws_organizations_organization` data source to retrieve the organization of this account. Remember that an account can only be a member of one organization, so we have a one-to-one mapping here:

```
data "aws_organizations_organization" "org" {}
```

5. With this, we are ready to create the workloads OU. For this, we use the `aws_organizations_organizational_unit` Terraform resource. We only need to provide a name and the parent OU. In this case, the parent of our newly created workloads OU will be the root OU:

```
resource "aws_organizations_organizational_unit" "workloads" {
  name      = "workloads"
  parent_id = data.aws_organizations_organization.org.roots[0].
id
}
```

6. Using the same pattern, we now create a `prod` and `test` OU underneath the workloads OU:

```
resource "aws_organizations_organizational_unit" "prod" {
  name      = "prod"
  parent_id = aws_organizations_organizational_unit.workloads.id
}

resource "aws_organizations_organizational_unit" "test" {
  name      = "test"
  parent_id = aws_organizations_organizational_unit.workloads.id
}
```

7. AWS accounts can be associated with an OU. In the previous chapter, we saw how to create an account within an OU using the GUI. We can also do this using the `terraform aws_organizations_account` resource.

8. Create a new file called `accounts.tf` in which we'll create our accounts for this org. Open it in a text editor such as Visual Studio Code.

9. Create a new account using the `aws_organizations_account` resource.

    We provide the name of the account in the `name` property and the email that is associated with the account. This needs to be a unique and valid email. Two accounts, even within the same AWS organization, can't share the same email:

    ```
    resource "aws_organizations_account" "test_account" {
      name    = "test-acc"
      email   = "<insert unique mail>"
    ```

10. We now need to associate this account with an OU. We'll assign it to the test OU by passing the `parent_id` property:

    ```
    parent_id = aws_organizations_organizational_unit.test.id
    ```

11. Since Terraform can manage the entire life cycle of a resource, this also includes the deletion of an account. We usually don't want to close the account when `terraform destroy` is called since accidentally deleting an account can result in large data loss and downtime. We thus set the `close_on_deletion` property to `false`. If you want to delete accounts via Terraform, for example, because you are just experimenting with multi-account setups, set this property to `true`:

    ```
    close_on_deletion = false
    }
    ```

12. With this, we can now run Terraform to create our new OUs. First, initiate the Terraform working directory. This will download the provider and create a local state file:

    ```
    terraform init
    ```

13. Next, apply the changes using `terraform apply`. This should only take a couple of seconds:

    ```
    terraform apply
    ```

After the Terraform script has successfully run, we can view our new OUs and account in the AWS console. Open up the Organizations page. The following screenshot shows the new OUs as well as the created account:

Organizational structure

▼ ☐ ⌂ Root
      r-pdyi

   ► ☐ ☐ Sandbox
         ou-pdyi-u46ggpz5

   ▼ ☐ ☐ workloads
         ou-pdyi-8619dj7f

      ► ☐ ☐ prod
            ou-pdyi-jlkc4qt3

      ▼ ☐ ☐ test
            ou-pdyi-vu8a1m2x

         ☐ ⬢ test-acc
           976193241037 | mn+workloads-test-acc@nlogn.org

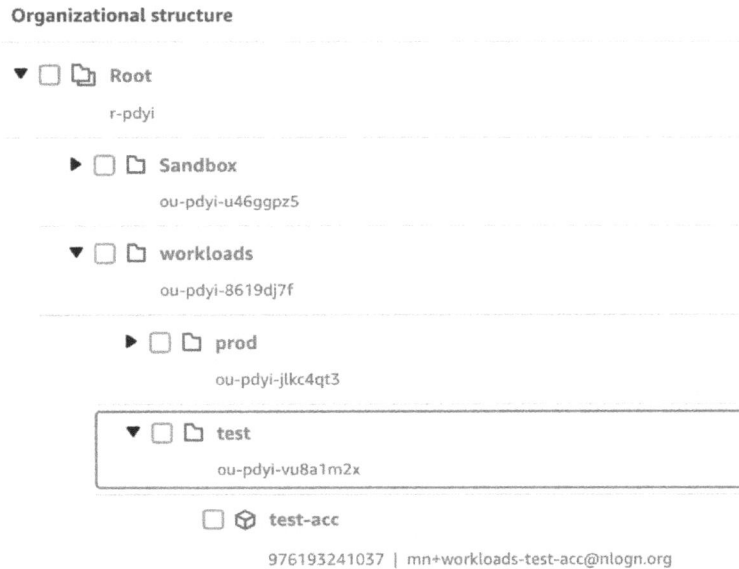

Figure 16.3 – Implementation of our workloads OU with sub-OUs for prod and test

Besides workloads, the AWS infrastructure usually also includes some resources that are more on the infrastructure side than specific to a workload. Examples of these kinds of resources are domains in Route 53 or network connectivity to on-premises, via either a VPN or Direct Connect. AWS calls these *foundational* OUs. Another example of foundational OUs is *security*. The account that owns the config rules we discussed in *Chapter 16* or the account that owns the S3 bucket into which audit logs are copied are examples of an account that resides under this OU.

AWS itself defines foundational OUs as "*OUs that contain accounts, workloads, and other AWS resources that provide common security and infrastructure capabilities to secure and support your overall AWS environment.*" The following figure shows our OUs after adding the foundational OUs:

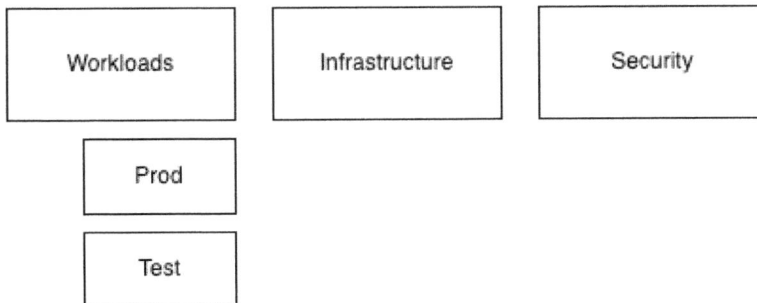

Workloads	Infrastructure	Security

Prod

Test

Figure 16.4 – The OU structure after adding infrastructure and security

Additional information

The exact setup of your OUs highly depends on the size of your operation. Keep in mind that accounts can be shifted between OUs, so you can start with a smaller setup and then expand your OUs as the infrastructure in the cloud expands.

Remember that different SCPs could apply to different OUs. So, a workload that works fine in an account while being under *OU A* might no longer work under *OU B* due to differing restrictions.

With our workloads OU, we'll want to be restrictive. A classic example of an SCP – and one we have seen in the previous figure – is the restriction of the accounts in an OU to one or a few defined AWS Regions.

However, we sometimes want to allow the exploration of services that might not be available in our designated Regions. Or we may want to force experimentation outside of the workload accounts. This is where sandbox OUs, OUs for accounts meant for experimentation outside of hosting any workload or infrastructure, come into the picture.

Including a previously created OU in Terraform

We have previously created a sandbox OU, so let's see how we can import a previously created OU into our Terraform stack so that we can later reference it. To do this, follow these steps:

1. Open the previously created `org_setup.tf` file in a code editor such as Visual Studio Code.

2. We'll use a data source to find the previously created OU. The data source is called `aws_organizations_account` and takes two required arguments: the parent ID, in our case, this is the root organization, and the name of the OU; in our case, this is `Sandbox`:

    ```
    data "aws_organizations_organizational_unit" "sandbox" {
      parent_id = data.aws_organizations_organization.org.roots[0].id
      name      = "Sandbox"
    }
    ```

3. In addition, we'll also create the two infrastructure and security OUs:

    ```
    resource "aws_organizations_organizational_unit" "security" {
      name      = "security"
      parent_id = aws_organizations_organizational_unit.workloads.id
    }

    resource "aws_organizations_organizational_unit" "infrastructure" {
      name      = "infrastructure"
      parent_id = aws_organizations_organizational_unit.workloads.id
    }
    ```

4. Run `terraform apply` to apply the new changes:

```
terraform apply
```

With this, we now have the OU structure shown in the following figure, which can be accessed from Terraform:

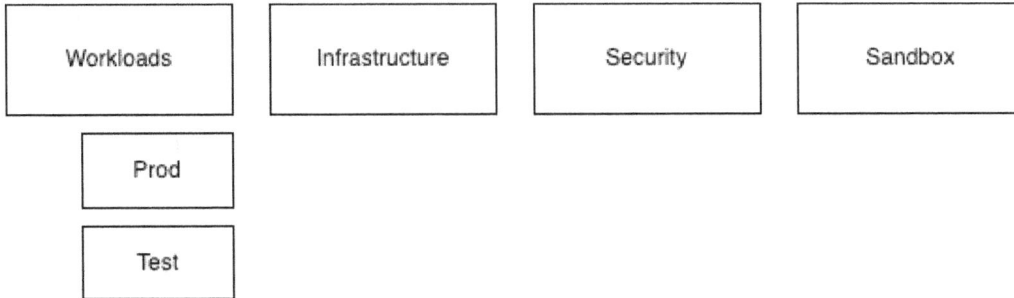

Figure 16.5 – OU structure with infrastructure, security, and the
data source for the previously created sandbox OU

Before moving on, let's use Terraform to attach an SCP to an OU. We'll use the SCP example from the previous chapter, which only allows EC2 instances to be created in the `eu-central-1` (Frankfurt) and `eu-west-1` (Ireland) Regions.

Attaching an SCP to an OU with Terraform

Follow these steps to attach a new SCP:

1. Create a new file called `scp.tf` in the `org_setup` folder and open it with a code editor such as Visual Studio Code.

2. We first need to define a new SCP. The resource for this is called `aws_organizations_policy`. We'll need to pass a name, a description, and the `jsonencoded` policy that we want to apply. For a more detailed explanation of how this policy works, please see the explanation in the previous chapter:

```
resource "aws_organizations_policy" "ec2_region_on_allowed" {
  name = "ec2-region-restriction"
  description = "Restricts EC2 instance launch to allowed
regions"
  content = jsonencode({
    Version = "2012-10-17"
    Statement = [
      {
        Sid = "DenyEC2LaunchOutsideAllowedRegions"
```

```
            Effect = "Deny"
            Action = [
              "ec2:RunInstances",
              "ec2:StartInstances",
              "ec2:StartInstance*"
            ]
            Resource = "*"
            Condition = {
              StringNotEquals = {
                "aws:RequestedRegion" = [
                  "eu-central-1",
                  "eu-west-1"
                ]
              }
            }
          }
        ]
      })
    }
```

3. With our SCP defined, we now need to attach it to our workloads OU. The `aws_organizations_policy_attachment` resource takes two arguments: the ID of the policy that we want to attach and the ID of the OU to which we want to attach the policy. We can reference both from the resources since both are managed via Terraform:

```
resource "aws_organizations_policy_attachment" "ec2_region_only_
allowed_to_workloads" {
  policy_id = aws_organizations_policy.ec2_region_on_allowed.id
  target_id = aws_organizations_organizational_unit.workloads.id
}
```

4. After applying the changes, we can see the new policy attached to our workloads OU:

```
terraform apply
```

The details page, as shown in the following figure, of our newly created SCP in the AWS console shows the Region restriction being applied to our workloads OU.

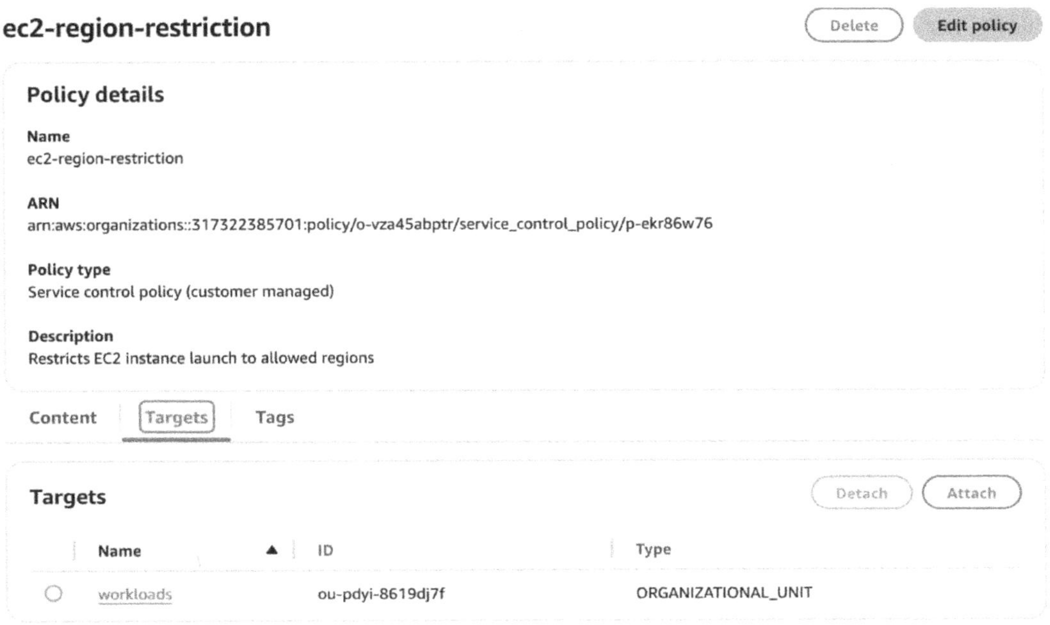

ec2-region-restriction

<button>Delete</button> <button>Edit policy</button>

Policy details

Name
ec2-region-restriction

ARN
arn:aws:organizations::317322385701:policy/o-vza45abptr/service_control_policy/p-ekr86w76

Policy type
Service control policy (customer managed)

Description
Restricts EC2 instance launch to allowed regions

Content | Targets | Tags

Targets

<button>Detach</button> <button>Attach</button>

	Name	▲	ID	Type
○	workloads		ou-pdyi-8619dj7f	ORGANIZATIONAL_UNIT

Figure 16.6 – Details page of our newly created policy showing the targets, including the workloads OU

With our restrictions – via the SCP – applied to the workloads OU, we now cover infrastructure-related accounts, as well as workloads, and we have an OU for experimentation in the sandbox OU. But what about accounts that require exceptions? This could be accounts that were created before the current organizational structure was imposed, accounts that come from an acquisition, or simply workloads that require some sort of exception in order to run. To allow this, we can establish an exceptions OU that these accounts can be moved to.

Adding the exceptions OU

Let's create this in Terraform using the previously shown resources:

1. Open the previously created `org_setup.tf` file in a code editor such as Visual Studio Code.

2. Add the Terraform resources for the exceptions OU:

    ```
    resource "aws_organizations_organizational_unit" "exceptions" {
      name      = "exceptions"
      parent_id = aws_organizations_organizational_unit.workloads.id
    }
    ```

3. Apply the changes using Terraform:

    ```
    terraform apply
    ```

With this, our organization now looks like the following figure.

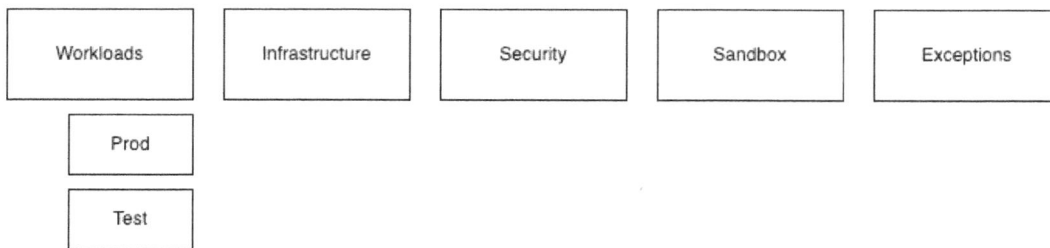

Figure 16.7 – Final org layout including the exceptions OU

With this, we have created an organization layout that follows the best practices from AWS, and we have seen how we can add accounts, OUs, and SCPs within Terraform. Next, we want to share resources between accounts.

Sharing resources within an organization using Resource Access Manager

One downside of spreading resources across multiple accounts is that we need to find a way to share resources that are used by multiple accounts simultaneously.

A classic example of such a resource is the concept of a shared VPC. In a shared VPC, the VPC (or subnets of the VPC) is shared out to multiple different accounts. These accounts can then place their resources, such as EC2 instances or lambdas, into the shared service VPC.

The main benefit of such an approach is the easy network communication between instances deployed in the different accounts. We'll use AWS RAM to share the subnets of a VPC, created in our management account, to all accounts in the dev sub-OU of our workloads OU.

> **Additional information**
> Whether or not a shared VPC is the right approach for you is an architectural decision. You can find more details about the pros and cons of a shared VPC in this blog post: https://aws.amazon.com/blogs/networking-and-content-delivery/vpc-sharing-key-considerations-and-best-practices/.

Before we get started, here are two key concepts of RAM:

- RAM deals with resources. It does not support all resources, however, so you'll need to verify that the resource of the service you want to share out is supported by RAM. The following documentation page contains the up-to-date list: https://docs.aws.amazon.com/ram/latest/userguide/shareable.html.

- The resources are then shared within a **resource share**. This resource share defines the resource that will be shared as well as the sharing account and the consumer.

- Within the resource share, we also define **managed permissions** that define what actions can be taken by the consuming account on a shared resource.

Enabling organizational resource sharing in RAM

One benefit of using organizations is that, in RAM, we don't have to enumerate all accounts that we want to share a resource with. Instead of having to create individual RAM sharing for every single account, we can simply share a resource with an OU.

We first need to create a resource we can share. For this example, we'll create a new VPC in the `eu-central-1` (Frankfurt) Region. Within this VPC, there are three subnets that will then be shared out to our OU.

> **Note**
>
> For brevity, this example only contains three private subnets. The structure would be the same for a VPC that also includes public subnets.

Sharing subnets in our VPC via Terraform

To first create the VPC that will be shared, follow these steps:

1. Create a new file called `vpc.tf` inside the `org_setup` folder and open it with a text editor such as Visual Studio Code.

2. Inside, we'll create a new VPC with a private subnet in each AZ. For a more detailed explanation of the different components of a VPC, consult *Chapter 3*:

```
# Get available AZs
data "aws_availability_zones" "available" {
  state = "available"
}

# Create VPC
resource "aws_vpc" "main" {
  cidr_block          = "10.0.0.0/16"
  enable_dns_support  = true
  enable_dns_hostnames = true
}

# Create private subnets
resource "aws_subnet" "private" {
```

```
  count              = length(data.aws_availability_zones.
available.names)
  vpc_id             = aws_vpc.main.id
  cidr_block         = "10.0.${count.index + 1}.0/24"
  availability_zone = data.aws_availability_zones.available.
names[count.index]
}

# Create route table for private subnets
resource "aws_route_table" "private" {
  vpc_id = aws_vpc.main.id

  tags = {
    Name = "private-rt"
  }
}

# Associate private subnets with private route table
resource "aws_route_table_association" "private" {
  count           = length(aws_subnet.private)
  subnet_id       = aws_subnet.private[count.index].id
  route_table_id = aws_route_table.private.id
}
```

Now that the resources we intend to share have been created in our AWS account, we can continue with the RAM setup and start sharing them.

Enabling resource sharing inside organizations

Before we can use our new VPC inside of a share, we'll need to enable RAM sharing to organizations. To do this, follow these steps:

1. Open the AWS console and navigate to the **Resource Access Manager** service page.

2. Open the **Settings** page in the left-hand navigation, as shown in the following screenshot:

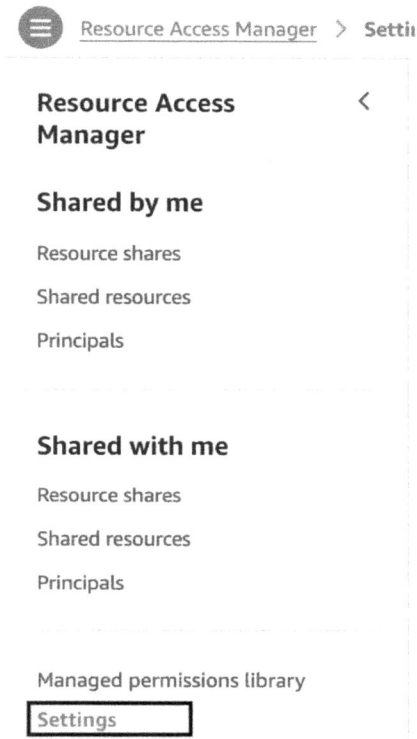

Figure 16.8 – Settings in the left-hand navbar

3.   Check the **Enable sharing with AWS Organizations** checkbox and click **Save settings** on the lower right, as shown in the following screenshot:

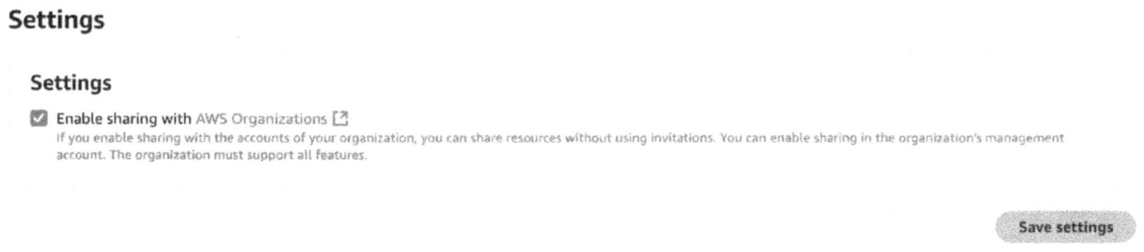

Settings

Settings

☑ **Enable sharing with** AWS Organizations 🔗
if you enable sharing with the accounts of your organization, you can share resources without using invitations. You can enable sharing in the organization's management account. The organization must support all features.

Save settings

Figure 16.9 – Enable sharing with AWS Organizations

With resource sharing enabled, we can now turn back to the Terraform code and create the share itself.

Sharing resources with Terraform

To do this, follow these steps:

1. Create a new `shares.tf` file inside the `org_setup` folder and open it in a text editor of your choice, such as Visual Studio Code or Notepad++.

2. We'll first create the resource share itself using the `aws_ram_resource_share` resource. We need to give the share a name that will also be visible inside the AWS console:

    ```
    resource "aws_ram_resource_share" "subnet_share" {
      name                       = "private-subnets-share"
    ```

3. We don't want anyone outside of our organization to be able to receive this resource share. Hence, we set the `allow_external_principals` flag to `false`:

    ```
    allow_external_principals = false
    ```

4. We can also tag our resource share, in this example, with a `Name` tag:

    ```
    tags = {
      Name = "private-subnets-share"
    }
    }
    ```

5. With the resource share created, the next step is to create an association between the resource we want to share and the resource share we have just created. This is done via the `aws_ram_resource_association` resource in Terraform:

    ```
    resource "aws_ram_resource_association" "subnet_share" {
    ```

6. We need to create such an association for each of our subnets, so we use the `count` attribute on the length of our previously created subnet list and use the counter to iterate over all of the previously created subnets:

    ```
    count        = length(aws_subnet.private)
    resource_arn = aws_subnet.private[count.index].arn
    ```

7. We also need to define which resource share we want to attach this resource to:

    ```
    resource_share_arn = aws_ram_resource_share.subnet_share.arn
    }
    ```

8. With our resource associated with our resource share, we now need to associate the resource share with our OU. We do this via the `aws_ram_principal_association` Terraform resource.

9. Here, we only need to pass the principal, the test OU that is managed by Terraform, and the resource share ARN that we have just created:

```
resource "aws_ram_principal_association" "ou_share" {
  principal            = aws_organizations_organizational_unit.
test.arn
  resource_share_arn = aws_ram_resource_share.subnet_share.arn
}
```

10. With this, we can now apply these changes:

```
terraform apply
```

After the Terraform update has successfully run through, we can navigate to the RAM service in the AWS console to verify that the resource has been shared. Navigate to the RAM service, and on the left navigation pane, select **Resource shares** under **Shared by me**.

In the overview, you'll see all the shares from your account. The details page, also shown in the following screenshot, indicates the shared resources – in this case, our subnets.

private-subnets-share (a02c5446-9321-431c-a891-b5974f884e76)   (Modify)   (Delete)

Details and information relating to this resource share.

Summary

Name	Owner	Created on	Status
private-subnets-share	317322385701	2025/02/12	⊘ Active

ID	ARN	Allow external principals	
a02c5446-9321-431c-a891-b5974f884e76	arn:aws:ram:eu-central-1:317322385701:resource-share/a02c5446-9321-431c-a891-b5974f884e76	No	

Shared resources (3)   (Disassociate)

Q Filter by text   ‹ 1 › ⚙

	Resource ID	Resource type	Status
☐	subnet-014b76c379e205a8a ↗	ec2:Subnet	⊘ Associated
☐	subnet-0d8214dcf308c9be3 ↗	ec2:Subnet	⊘ Associated
☐	subnet-06d9f37d9d4adc2cc ↗	ec2:Subnet	⊘ Associated

Figure 16.10 – Resource share details page showing the shared subnets

We can also verify that the resources have been shared by logging in to the account we previously created inside the dev OU.

Additional information

See the *Logging in to the AWS console of our new account by assuming a role* subsection in the previous chapter for a step-by-step guide on how to open up a new session in the dev account.

Inside the account, we can first navigate to the RAM console and see that we have received the resource share. Notice the differing account IDs of the owner and the account currently logged in in the following screenshot:

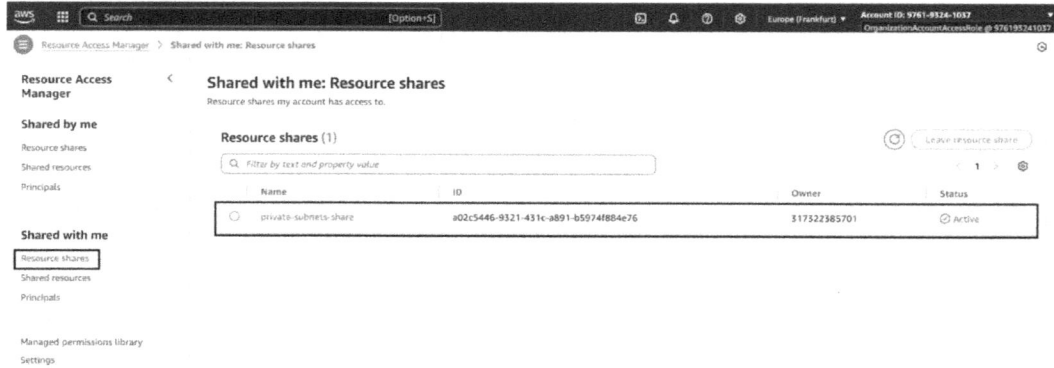

Figure 16.11 – Resource share in an account that is part of our target OU

We can also verify that we see the VPC (and its subnets). This is done by navigating to the VPC service. The overview – shown in the following screenshot – indicates the VPC that the subnets are part of. The **(shared)** text under the differing owner ID indicates that this is a VPC that was shared out to this account.

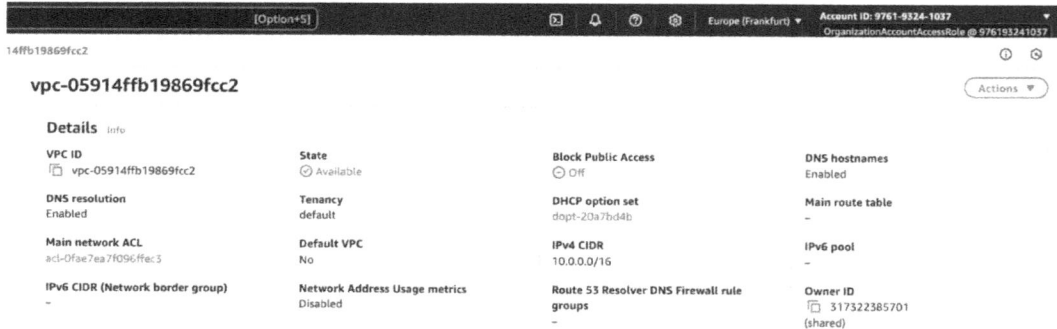

Figure 16.12 – Details page of our shared VPC

This shows how we can share a VPC within an organization. But what about use cases where we don't want to roll out an entire organization? In the next chapter, we'll see how RAM works with sharing just between accounts.

Cross-account sharing for use cases with small amounts of AWS accounts

We have seen how we can share resources within an organization, but we also want to see how the same can be achieved with RAM but without organizations.

In the previous chapter, we initially had to enable RAM sharing within the organization. The step that this automated away is the acceptance of a RAM share. The consumer account does not (unless you are part of the same organization and resource sharing is enabled) automatically accept an incoming RAM share.

In this chapter, we'll walk through the Terraform code that creates a resource share, as well as how to automate the acceptance of the resource share.

The first steps remain the same. We also need to create a resource share and associate our subnets with that resource share through an association, as shown in the following code snippet:

```
resource "aws_ram_resource_share" "subnet_share" {
  provider               = aws.source
  name                   = "private-subnets-share"
  allow_external_principals = true

  tags = {
    Name = "private-subnets-share"
  }
}


# Share private subnets
resource "aws_ram_resource_association" "subnet_share" {
  provider           = aws.source
  count              = length(aws_subnet.private)
  resource_arn       = aws_subnet.private[count.index].arn
  resource_share_arn = aws_ram_resource_share.subnet_share.arn
}
```

The difference now lies in the principal association. We can start by defining a local variable that contains a list of all the accounts we want to share our resource with:

```
locals {
  target_account_ids = [
    "<add your account ids here>",
  ]
}
```

We can then iterate over all of these and create a new principal association for each:

```
resource "aws_ram_principal_association" "account_share" {
  provider            = aws.source
  for_each            = toset(local.target_account_ids)
  principal           = each.value
  resource_share_arn  = aws_ram_resource_share.subnet_share.arn
}
```

In the preceding example, we use the built-in `toset()` function to remove any potential duplicates since the same resource share can only be associated with a principal once. The `for_each` argument defines the set we want to iterate over and we can access the value in each iteration, in this case, the account ID we want to create the principal association for, via the `each.value` variable.

On the account that owns the resource, this is all we need to do. But on the consumer side, we also need to accept the incoming resource share. We could do this manually in the AWS console, but the Terraform provider also offers the `aws_ram_resource_share_accepter` Terraform resource.

This resource allows us to programmatically accept incoming shares. We first define the ARN of the incoming share:

```
resource "aws_ram_resource_share_accepter" "subnet_share_accepter" {
  share_arn            = aws_ram_resource_share.subnet_share.arn
```

Next, we don't want to accept all incoming shares but only the ones we are expecting. Since we are not part of an org, we have no concept of "trustworthy" AWS accounts. We thus use the life cycle block to define a pre-condition – in this case, that the name of the share is `private-subnet-share`:

```
  # Important: only accept shares that match our expected pattern
  lifecycle {
    precondition {
      condition    = aws_ram_resource_share.subnet_share.name ==
"private-subnets-share"
      error_message = "Share name does not match expected pattern"
    }
  }
}
```

Instead of relying on the name, we could also verify the account ID of the provider account:

```
lifecycle {
    precondition {
      condition    = split(":", aws_ram_resource_share.subnet_share.
arn)[4] == "<insert account id of sharing account>"
      error_message = "Share is not from the expected AWS account"
    }
  }
```

With this, you have seen how you can do resource sharing without using AWS organizations. This is a reasonable method to use when sharing between only a few accounts, but as soon as you introduce more than a few accounts, it is advisable to look into setting them up via organizations and then sharing with OUs, as described previously.

Summary

In this chapter, we discussed the overall layout of an AWS organization, including some best practices to follow. We then saw how organizations – including OUs, sub-OUs, and AWS accounts – can be programmatically created using Terraform.

The chapter concluded with a guide on using AWS RAM – both within an organization and without an organization – to share resources between AWS accounts. In the next chapter, we will combine everything we have learned, not just in this chapter but throughout the entire book, to set up an application from end to end.

Get This Book's PDF Version and Exclusive Extras

UNLOCK NOW

Scan the QR code (or go to `packtpub.com/unlock`). Search for this book by name, confirm the edition, and then follow the steps on the page.

Note: Keep your invoice handly. Purchase made directly from packt don't require one.

17

End-to-End Deployment of an Application

In the previous chapters of this book, you have been introduced to many different services that all fit together as building blocks for modern applications. You have seen how EC2 – together with auto-scaling and a load balancer – can be used to provide scalable compute. We have also covered organizational aspects such as multi-account setups with AWS Organizations and how we can use pipelines to deploy infrastructure based on pushes to a GitHub repository.

In this chapter, we'll tie all the learnings together into a worked example of how we can deploy an application into AWS. We'll leverage the tools and techniques explored throughout this book in the process.

In this chapter, we're going to cover the following main topics:

- Setting up an AWS Organization including Single Sign-On
- Building a CI/CD pipeline that automatically deploys our Terraform to different accounts
- Deploying and updating the sample application

Technical requirements

Before following this section, please create an AWS account for yourself. You can sign up at aws. amazon.com. A basic understanding of AWS – for example, what a service is – will be beneficial.

A basic understanding of Python will help with the programming-based sections of this chapter.

A basic understanding of IaC tools such as Terraform will be beneficial. You can find more information about Terraform in *Chapter 1*.

A basic understanding of the Linux command line will help you to follow along with this chapter. You'll also need the following software installed on your system:

- Python version 3.8 or later
- Node.js version 14.15.0 or later

Both of these version requirements are at the time of writing in May 2024. You can check the following links for the required versions:

- For Python: `https://boto3.amazonaws.com/v1/documentation/api/latest/guide/quickstart.html#install-or-update-python`
- For Node.js: `https://docs.aws.amazon.com/cdk/v2/guide/getting_started.html#getting_started_prerequisites`

All scripts from this section can be found at the following GitHub link:

`https://github.com/PacktPublishing/AWS-for-System-Administrators-Second-Edition`

The CiA video for this chapter can be found at `https://packt.link/dYGOT`

What we will build in this chapter

The solution we'll be building throughout this chapter is a simple web application that offers an API for a click counter that stores its values inside of a Postgres database. While – from a software development perspective – this isn't a big application, it does cover many of the major infrastructure and deployment and automation aspects.

> **Note**
>
> Throughout this chapter, we'll make use of tools and techniques explored throughout this book. Wherever we are using knowledge previously covered in a chapter, there'll be a note where you can find more detailed information.
>
> Please note that the explanations will only cover new content, and this chapter won't cover aspects that we have previously covered.
>
> It is thus advisable that you have read the previous chapters or are willing to jump back in case something is unclear.

The following figure shows the application architecture that we'll deploy:

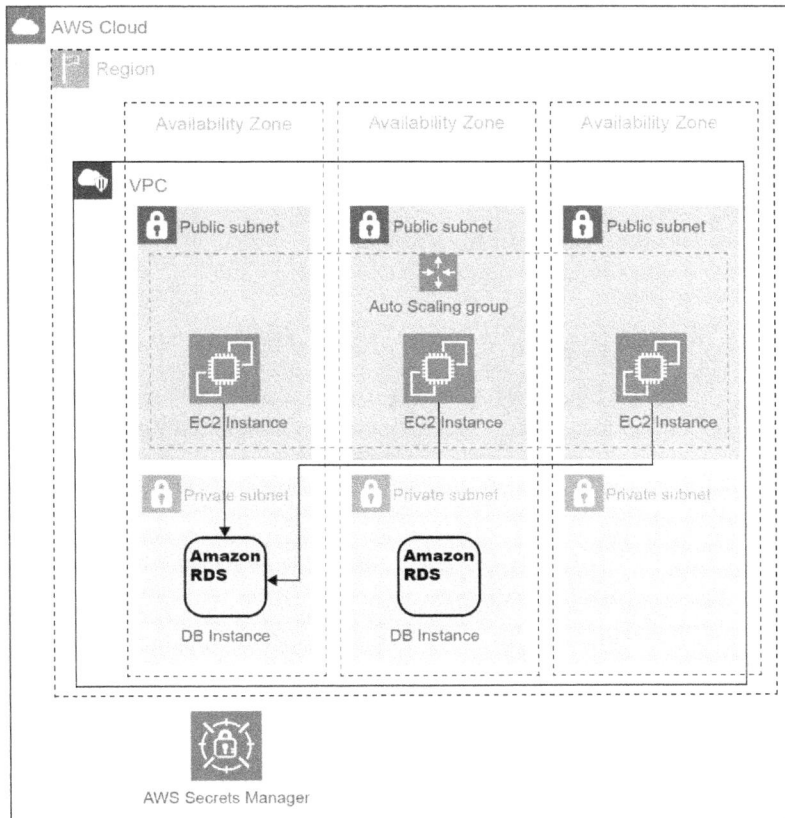

Figure 17.1 – Application architecture

For our compute, we'll leverage EC2 instances inside of an Auto Scaling group. To improve resiliency, these instances are spread across three different Availability Zones and a load balancer is used to send traffic between them.

For keeping our counter values, we'll use an Aurora Postgres deployment with two instances running inside the private subnet of our application. All secrets and configurations are handled through AWS Secrets Manager.

Instead of just deploying this application into one AWS account, we'll implement a simple organizational structure with three different accounts:

- The **production** account will contain the productive (i.e., user-facing) version of our infrastructure and application.

- The **staging** account will be used to test changes to our application.

- The **deployment** account is used to orchestrate the deployment. The pipeline used for deployment will reside inside of this account.

The source code for our application, as well as the code for the infrastructure, resides in a GitHub repository with two branches. Pushing changes to the *main* branch will update the production account while changes to the *staging* branch will update the staging environment.

Additional information

We'll be reusing the repository and code from *Chapter 14*.

Implementing Single Sign-On (SSO) with AWS Identity Center

So far in this book, we have used IAM users with long-lived credentials whenever we logged into our AWS account. Their ease of use makes them ideal for playing around and testing things. However, for production workloads, AWS itself recommends – in its best practices – using temporary credentials from an identity provider instead of the long-lived credentials provided by an IAM user.

Additional information

Long-lived credentials are credentials that don't have an expiry time. Once obtained, they are valid for a long time or indefinitely. This makes the authentication process very easy but also prone to error. For example, a common issue with this is that developers commit their credentials into (possibly public) Git repositories and thus leak long-lived credentials.

This is why we want to use short-lived credentials. In case a user accidentally submits these credentials into a version control system or they are compromised in a different way, they only retain a limited validity.

You can read more about this recommendation in *Security best practices in IAM* from AWS here: `https://docs.aws.amazon.com/IAM/latest/UserGuide/best-practices.html`

In this section, we'll set up IAM Identity Center to manage the human users (such as your developers or DevOps engineers) that have access to the different AWS accounts. IAM Identity Center – formerly known as AWS SSO – allows you to define users, user groups, and their access levels for different accounts within an AWS Organization.

AWS Identity Center comes with its own user management (which we'll use in this chapter), but you can also connect it to external identity providers such as Active Directory. This allows you to have only one company-wide inventory of users.

Setting up Identity Center using Terraform

Let's start by using Terraform to enable AWS Identity Center for our organization, and see how we can manage users, user groups, and their permissions within an account covered by the organization.

For more information on AWS Organizations, please reference *Chapter 16, Operating in a Multi-Account Environment.*

> **Attention**
>
> This walk-through assumes that you have set up an organization as shown in *Chapter 16, Operating in a Multi-Account Environment.* Before proceeding, please walk through the steps in that chapter.

We'll first need to enable AWS Identity Center in the AWS Console. To do this, follow these steps:

1. Open the AWS Console in the root account of your organization and select your preferred region (for example, **eu-central-1**).

2. In the search bar, search for `Identity Center` and navigate to the Identity Center service.

3. If you haven't yet enabled AWS Identity Center, you'll be greeted with a button to **Enable** IAM Identity Center, as shown in the following screenshot:

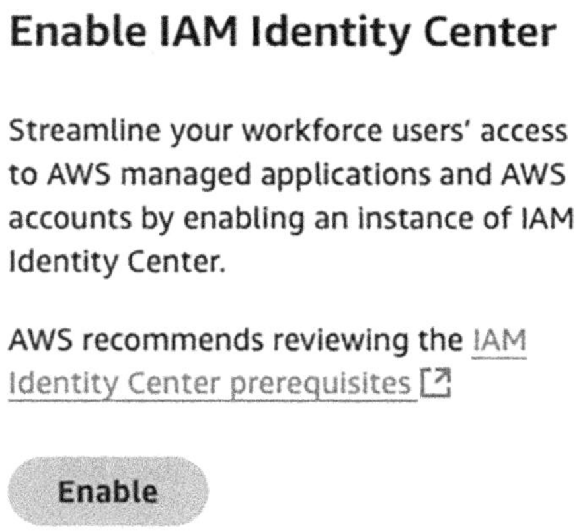

Enable IAM Identity Center

Streamline your workforce users' access to AWS managed applications and AWS accounts by enabling an instance of IAM Identity Center.

AWS recommends reviewing the IAM Identity Center prerequisites [↗]

Enable

Figure 17.2 – Enabling IAM Identity Center in the AWS Management Console

With Identity Center enabled, we can now use it from within Terraform.

To create the Terraform scripts required for this, follow these steps:

1. Create a new folder called `click_project` – this will be the project folder for this entire project. Inside the `click_project` folder, create a folder called `infrastructure`, which will contain all the infrastructure scripts. Again, inside of the `infrastructure` folder, create a folder called `organization`. This will contain the Terraform scripts used for the initial account setup. This includes the AWS organization itself, as well as the **Organizational Units (OUs)** that we'll create beneath it. We discussed AWS Organizations and OUs in detail in the previous chapter:

    ```
    mkdir -p click_project && \
    mkdir -p click_project/infrastructure && \
    mkdir -p click_project/infrastructure/organization && \
    cd click_project/infrastructure/organization
    ```

2. Inside the `organization` folder, create a new file called `main.tf` and open it in a code editor such as Visual Studio Code.

3. We'll start by defining the information for the `aws` provider:

    ```
    terraform {
      required_providers {
        aws = {
          source  = "hashicorp/aws"
          version = "~> 5.0"
        }
      }
      required_version = ">= 1.2.0"
    }
    provider "aws" {
      region = "eu-central-1"  # Change to your preferred region
    }
    ```

4. With Identity Center enabled, we can use the `aws_ssoadmin_instances` data source to access its properties, such as the identity store ID or the ARN of our Identity Center instance, from our code:

    ```
    # Enable AWS IAM Identity Center
    data "aws_ssoadmin_instances" "identity_center" {}
    ```

5. Next, we create a new user – inside of the default user directory that comes with Identity Center:

    ```
    # Configure Identity Center to use the built-in identity store
    (internal directory)
    resource "aws_identitystore_user" "example_user" {
      identity_store_id = tolist(data.aws_ssoadmin_instances.
    identity_center.identity_store_ids)[0]
    ```

6. We need to assign a display name, username, and properties such as the `name` and `emails` that are associated with this user:

```
display_name = "Marcel Neidinger"
user_name    = "mn-dev@nlogn.org"

name {
  given_name  = "Marcel"
  family_name = "Neidinger"
}

emails {
  value   = "mn-dev@nlogn.org"
  primary = true
}
}
```

7. Next, we can create a centrally managed permission set. This is the IAM policy that will be assigned to a group of users. In this example, we'll create a permission set for our admin users. We also define that the credentials obtained from this permission group will be valid for 12 hours. Having different validity periods – for example, allowing longer credentials for read-only accounts – can make it more convenient to use this setup since our users don't have to constantly reauthenticate:

```
# Create a permission set (defines a set of permissions that can
be assigned to users)
resource "aws_ssoadmin_permission_set" "admin" {
  name             = "AdministratorAccess"
  description      = "Administrator access permission set"
  instance_arn     = tolist(data.aws_ssoadmin_instances.
identity_center.arns)[0]
  session_duration = "PT12H"  # 12-hour session
}
```

8. With the permission set defined, we can now attach a policy to give the permission set actual permissions. In this example, we'll attach the Amazon managed `AdministratorAccess` policy that we previously also attached to our IAM users:

```
# Attach AWS managed policy to the permission set
resource "aws_ssoadmin_managed_policy_attachment" "admin_policy"
{
  instance_arn        = tolist(data.aws_ssoadmin_instances.
identity_center.arns)[0]
  managed_policy_arn = "arn:aws:iam::aws:policy/
AdministratorAccess"
  permission_set_arn = aws_ssoadmin_permission_set.admin.arn
}
```

9. Instead of assigning a permission set to an individual user in Identity Center, we'll use a user group – in this case, called `admin_group`. Users added to this group will gain the assigned permissions within the assigned accounts:

```
# Create a group in the internal directory
resource "aws_identitystore_group" "admin_group" {
  display_name     = "Administrators"
  description      = "Group for administrators"
  identity_store_id = tolist(data.aws_ssoadmin_instances.
identity_center.identity_store_ids)[0]
}
```

10. Finally, assign the user to the group:

```
# Add the user to the group
resource "aws_identitystore_group_membership" "admin_membership"
{
  identity_store_id = tolist(data.aws_ssoadmin_instances.
identity_center.identity_store_ids)[0]
  group_id          = aws_identitystore_group.admin_group.group_
id
  member_id         = aws_identitystore_user.example_user.user_
id
}
```

With Identity Center activated and users created, we'll next create three AWS accounts. For this, we'll create a new OU called `Environments` and then create the three AWS accounts underneath it. Refer to *Chapter 16* for more detailed information on the specific Terraform commands.

1. At the bottom of the `main.tf` file, add the following resources. First, we use a data resource to get the current AWS organization:

```
data "aws_organizations_organization" "current" {}
```

2. Next, we create the OU:

```
resource "aws_organizations_organizational_unit" "environments"
{
  name      = "Environments"
  parent_id = data.aws_organizations_organization.current.
roots[0].id  # Use data resource instead of variable
}
```

3. Finally, create the three different accounts within the OU. Please reference the previous chapter for a more detailed explanation of the different attributes in this Terraform script:

```
resource "aws_organizations_account" "deploy" {
  name            = "Deploy"
```

```
    email             = "<insert unique mail>"
    role_name         = "OrganizationAccountAccessRole"  # Default
role for cross-account access
    parent_id         = aws_organizations_organizational_unit.
environments.id

      # Prevent account from being destroyed when using Terraform
      # Remove this for the initial creation, then uncomment for
subsequent runs

    }
# Staging account
resource "aws_organizations_account" "staging" {
    name              = "Staging"
    email             = "<insert unique mail>"
    role_name         = "OrganizationAccountAccessRole"
    parent_id         = aws_organizations_organizational_unit.
environments.id

    }
# Production account
resource "aws_organizations_account" "production" {
    name              = "Production"
    email             = "<insert unique mail>"
    role_name         = "OrganizationAccountAccessRole"
    parent_id         = aws_organizations_organizational_unit.
environments.id
    }
```

4. With our accounts created, we can now assign the previously created account to our admin group. This will grant users in that group the permissions defined by the previously created (and referenced) permission set. We define this permission set via the `permission_set_arn` property and reference the principal we want to assign this account to. In our example, this is the previously created group (referenced via the `principal_id` property), and `principal_type` will need to be set to GROUP:

```
resource "aws_ssoadmin_account_assignment" "deploy_account_
assignment" {
    instance_arn        = tolist(data.aws_ssoadmin_instances.
identity_center.arns)[0]
    permission_set_arn = aws_ssoadmin_permission_set.admin.arn

    principal_id       = aws_identitystore_group.admin_group.group_id
    principal_type = "GROUP"
```

5. We also need a target, in this case of type (specified via the `target_type` property) `AWS_ACCOUNT`, and we pass the account ID from our newly created deployment AWS account:

```
target_id   = aws_organizations_account.deploy.id
target_type = "AWS_ACCOUNT"
}
```

6. We repeat this with our staging account:

```
resource "aws_ssoadmin_account_assignment" "staging_account_
assignment" {
  instance_arn       = tolist(data.aws_ssoadmin_instances.
identity_center.arns)[0]
  permission_set_arn = aws_ssoadmin_permission_set.admin.arn

  principal_id   = aws_identitystore_group.admin_group.group_id
  principal_type = "GROUP"

  target_id   = aws_organizations_account.staging.id
  target_type = "AWS_ACCOUNT"
}
```

7. With our basic structure defined, let's deploy this to AWS and then see how we can log into one of these accounts. To make it easier for us to find the relevant resources, we'll introduce two outputs. One that contains the AWS account ID of the staging account and one that contains the login URL for our Identity Center instance:

```
output "staging_account_id" {
    value = aws_organizations_account.staging.id
    description = "Account ID of the staging account"
}
output "identity_center_user_portal" {
  value       = "https://${substr(tolist(data.aws_ssoadmin_
instances.identity_center.identity_store_ids)[0], 0, 10)}.
awsapps.com/start"
  description = "The URL of the AWS IAM Identity Center user
portal"
}
```

8. Initiate the Terraform workspace:

```
terraform init
```

9. Then deploy the entire infrastructure using `terraform apply`:

    ```
    terraform apply
    ```

Navigate to the Identity Center URL that is shown in the output from Terraform. You'll be asked for a username and password. Since this is the first time you are logging into this new account, use the **Forgot password** flow to reset your password. After setting a new password, you'll be asked to create an MFA device (for example, via the Google Authenticator app). Follow the steps to add multi-factor authentication to this user account.

With this initial setup concluded, you'll be redirected to an overview page (shown in the following screenshot) that contains all the accounts and their roles that you have access to.

Figure 17.3 – Access portal with our two accounts we have access to

Besides using the login portal to get into the graphical interface, we can also use the SSO login to authenticate the CLI. To do this, follow these steps:

> **Note**
> This setup assumes that you have installed the AWS CLI as shown in the first chapter.

1. Open up a terminal and initiate the SSO configuration:

    ```
    aws configure sso
    ```

2. You'll be prompted for some information that is based on your deployment. For **SSO session name (recommended)**, use a name for your SSO configuration – for example, `click-sso`.

3. The **SSO start URL** is the URL from your Terraform output that you previously used to reset the password.

4. For **SSO region**, select the region you used for your SSO instance – for example, `eu-central-1`.

5. Leave the default for the **SSO registration scopes** and hit *Enter*.

```
SSO session name (Recommended): click-sso
SSO start URL [None]: https://d-99676c6091.awsapps.com/start
SSO region [None]: eu-central-1
SSO registration scopes [sso:account:access]:
Attempting to automatically open the SSO authorization page in your default browser.
If the browser does not open or you wish to use a different device to authorize this request, open the following URL:
```

Figure 17.4 – Sample input for the local SSO configuration

This will redirect you to the browser, where you'll be asked to authorize the AWS CLI to interact with your SSO instance. On the authorization screen, click **Allow access**.

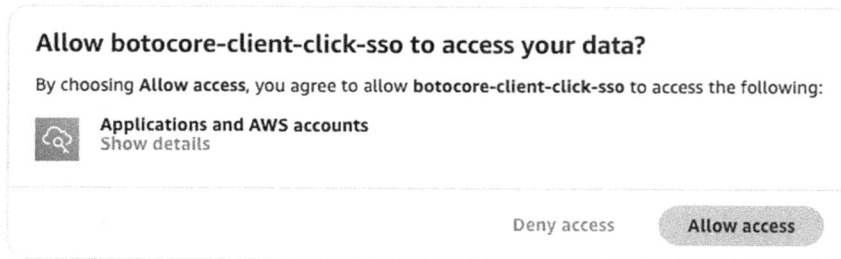

aws

Allow botocore-client-click-sso to access your data?

By choosing **Allow access**, you agree to allow **botocore-client-click-sso** to access the following:

Applications and AWS accounts
Show details

Deny access   **Allow access**

Figure 17.5 – The authorization screen for the AWS CLI

Back on the CLI, you'll be presented with the two different accounts – as shown in the following screenshot – that you have access to.

```
There are 2 AWS accounts available to you.
 Staging, mn-click_button-staging@nlogn.org (518103494808)
 Deploy, mn-click_button-deploy@nlogn.org (855289842796)
```

Figure 17.6 – The list of accounts you have access to

Select the *deploy* account and hit *Enter* to accept the CLI default client region and CLI default output format. For the CLI profile name – as shown in the following screenshot – use an easy-to-remember profile name such as `click-deploy-Admin`.

```
There are 2 AWS accounts available to you.
Using the account ID 855289842796
The only role available to you is: AdministratorAccess
Using the role name "AdministratorAccess"
CLI default client Region [eu-central-1]:
CLI default output format [None]: json
CLI profile name [AdministratorAccess-855289842796]: click-deploy-Admin
```

Figure 17.7 – Profile configuration for our SSO-based account login

We can now use the profile flag, when interacting with the AWS CLI, to specify which profile (and thus which role in which account) to use. Try this out by running the following command:

```
aws sts get-caller-identity -profile click-deploy-Admin
```

Your output should look something like this and show that the CLI command was run under the assumed role of `AdministratorAccess` with your SSO user (`mn-dev@nlogn.org` in this example):

```
{
    "UserId": "AROA4OIZ7JRWNEHW7TTSL:mn-dev@nlogn.org",
    "Account": "855289842796",
    "Arn": "arn:aws:sts::855289842796:assumed-role/AWSReservedSSO_
AdministratorAccess_e275eb5961bac439/mn-dev@nlogn.org"
}
```

Setting up the pipeline

In this section, we'll set up our pipeline – but before we can do this, we'll need to create an IAM role that allows our deployment account to assume it (cross-account access). We'll then use that role and its attached policy to give the pipeline – running in the deployment account – enough rights to run Terraform.

Before we do this, let's see how we can also modify the existing account assignment and include the production account in the list of accounts our SSO user has access to. To do this, we'll need to modify the `main.tf` file in `infrastructure/organization/`.

Add the following account assignment to also let the production account be managed by members of the admin group:

```
resource "aws_ssoadmin_account_assignment" "prod_account_assignment" {
  instance_arn       = tolist(data.aws_ssoadmin_instances.identity_
center.arns)[0]
  permission_set_arn = aws_ssoadmin_permission_set.admin.arn

  principal_id   = aws_identitystore_group.admin_group.group_id
  principal_type = "GROUP"
```

```
        target_id   =  aws_organizations_account.production.id
        target_type = "AWS_ACCOUNT"
}
```

After running `terraform apply`, you should now have access to all three accounts – as shown in the following screenshot:

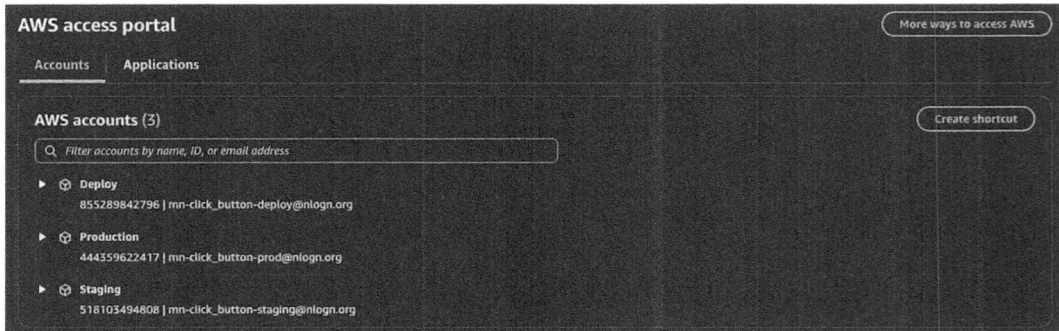

Figure 17.8 – Access to all three AWS accounts in the admin portal

You can now use the admin portal to log into the different accounts and create a IAM role called `TerraformDeploymentRole` in the staging and production accounts. The policy to attach can be found in the GitHub repository for this chapter named `cross_account_role.json`.

> **Requirement**
>
> This section assumes that you have successfully set up a GitHub connection and a CodeBuild project in your deployment account. Follow the instructions in *Chapter 13*, under the *Connecting Your GitHub Account* section, to complete this task.

With the role in the two target accounts created, we now need to modify the role that our CodeBuild project is using and attach an additional policy that allows it to assume these roles in the staging and production accounts.

To do this, open the IAM console in your deployment account and identify the CodeBuild role. To this role, attach an inline policy (for example, `CrossAccountAccessRole`) with the following content:

```
{
    "Version": "2012-10-17",
    "Statement": [
        {
            "Effect": "Allow",
            "Action": [
```

```
            "sts:AssumeRole"
        ],
        "Resource": [
            "arn:aws:iam::<ID of your staging account>:role/
TerraformDeploymentRole",
            "arn:aws:iam::<id of your production account>:role/
TerraformDeploymentRole"
        ]
    }
    ]
}
```

> **Requirement**
>
> The following section assumes that you have cloned your application repository locally, as described in *Chapter 14*.

Next, we'll need to modify our `buildspec.yaml` file. Recall that this file defines the steps that our CodeBuild project will run through upon every step. The basic flow is the following:

1. Identify which environment to deploy to based on the branch we are pushing to.

2. Define the credentials (via the assumed role) based on what environment we are deploying to.

3. Run `terraform apply`.

In the `buildspec.yaml` file, this process then looks like this:

1. Open up the `buildspec.yaml` file in your cloned repository from *Chapter 14* and replace it with the instructions from the following steps.

2. In the environment, we define our PROD and STAGING account IDs and also the role that we'll assume in these accounts:

    ```yaml
    version: 0.2
    env:
      variables:
        PROD_ACCOUNT_ID: "YOUR_PROD_ACCOUNT_ID" # Replace with your
    production account ID
        STAGING_ACCOUNT_ID: "YOUR_STAGING_ACCOUNT_ID" # Replace with
    your staging account ID
        ROLE_NAME: "TerraformDeploymentRole"
    ```

3. The install phase is almost the same as in the previous chapter – the only difference is that we are also installing jq. We'll use jq later on to extract specific values from a JSON-encoded dictionary:

```
phases:
  install:
    commands:
      - echo "Installing Terraform version ${TF_VERSION}"
      - wget -O terraform.zip https://releases.hashicorp.com/
terraform/1.10.3/terraform_${TF_VERSION}_linux_amd64.zip
      - unzip terraform.zip
      - mv terraform /usr/local/bin/
      - terraform --version
      - apt-get update && apt-get install -y jq
```

4. Next, we determine which branch the build was triggered from. We first check that the trigger was indeed a push and then read the CODEBUILD_WEBHOOK_HEAD_REF environment variable, which contains the branch reference. If it is the main branch, we set the target to production and set the target account ID to the previously defined PROD_ACCOUNT_ID:

```
  pre_build:
    commands:
      - |
        if [ "$CODEBUILD_WEBHOOK_EVENT" = "PUSH" ]; then
          if [ "$CODEBUILD_WEBHOOK_HEAD_REF" = "refs/heads/main"
]; then
            export TARGET_ACCOUNT_ID=$PROD_ACCOUNT_ID
            export ENVIRONMENT="production"
```

5. If it is the staging branch, we set the target accordingly, and for all other branches, we do not do any deployment and end the pipeline execution:

```
          elif [ "$CODEBUILD_WEBHOOK_HEAD_REF" = "refs/heads/
staging" ]; then
            export TARGET_ACCOUNT_ID=$STAGING_ACCOUNT_ID
            export ENVIRONMENT="staging"
          else
            echo "Branch ${CODEBUILD_WEBHOOK_HEAD_REF} is not
configured for deployment"
            exit 0
          fi
```

6. Next, we assume the cross-account role (i.e., the Terraform role in the respective PROD or STAGING account):

```
          echo "Assuming role for ${ENVIRONMENT} account"
          CREDENTIALS=$(aws sts assume-role --role-arn
arn:aws:iam::${TARGET_ACCOUNT_ID}:role/${ROLE_NAME} --role-
session-name TerraformDeploySession)
```

7. Based on the output from STS, we can set the (short-lived) AWS credentials inside of this CodeBuild worker:

```
# Set AWS credentials for this session
export AWS_ACCESS_KEY_ID=$(echo $CREDENTIALS | jq -r
'.Credentials.AccessKeyId')
export AWS_SECRET_ACCESS_KEY=$(echo $CREDENTIALS | jq
-r '.Credentials.SecretAccessKey')
export AWS_SESSION_TOKEN=$(echo $CREDENTIALS | jq -r
'.Credentials.SessionToken')

echo "Successfully assumed role for ${ENVIRONMENT}
account"
else
echo "Not a webhook push event - skipping deployment"
exit 0
fi
```

8. Next, we initialize `terraform` and validate the build plan:

```
# Initialize Terraform with the target environment
- terraform init
- terraform validate
```

9. To then build the project, we'll run Terraform in our staging and production environments:

```
build:
  commands:
    - echo "Planning Terraform changes for ${ENVIRONMENT}
environment"
    - terraform plan -out=out.tfplan

    # Only apply changes on push events to configured branches
    - |
    if [ "$CODEBUILD_WEBHOOK_EVENT" = "PUSH" ]; then
        if [ "$CODEBUILD_WEBHOOK_HEAD_REF" = "refs/heads/main"
] || [ "$CODEBUILD_WEBHOOK_HEAD_REF" = "refs/heads/staging" ];
then
            echo "Applying Terraform changes to ${ENVIRONMENT}
environment"
            terraform apply -auto-approve out.tfplan
        fi
    else
        echo "Not a webhook push event - skipping apply"
    fi
```

10. And finally, we store artifacts such as the generated Terraform plan:

```
reports:
  terraform_plan:
    files:
      - out.tfplan
    base-directory: .
    file-format: TerraformPlan
artifacts:
  files:
    - out.tfplan
    - terraform.tfstate
    - '**/*'
```

Now, to deploy the infrastructure, replace the `main.tf` and `backend.tf` file with the samples provided at this GitHub link: `https://github.com/PacktPublishing/AWS-for-System-Administrators-Second-Edition/blob/main/ch17/sample_application/`.

The `main.tf` file simply creates the infrastructure seen in our sample architecture using EC2 and other components we already know.

For the backend, there is one slight variation. We use an account-specific S3 bucket to host our Terraform state.

With the three files (`main.tf`, `backend.tf`, and `buildspec.yaml`) changed locally, it is time to commit them to GitHub.

After pushing the new code, you should see a deployment running in your CodeBuild project, as well as the infrastructure being deployed in your production account.

Summary

In this chapter, you have seen multiple concepts that were previously covered in the book interlinked together. In addition, the chapter introduced AWS Identity Center as the preferred method for managing user credentials and how the concepts of Identity Center – together with Organizations – can be used to deploy well-defined access to your AWS accounts.

In this book, we have covered several of the key aspects of operating and automating applications within AWS.

Thank you for reading this book and I hope you have picked up some valuable learnings along the way. How do you proceed from here? Here are a few ideas:

- Read through the AWS Whitepapers to expand your knowledge of best practices – you can find the library here: `https://aws.amazon.com/whitepapers/`

- Have a look at the other books on AWS available from Packt: `https://www.packtpub.com/en-us/search?q=aws&country=us&language=en`
- Build hands-on projects – if you need inspiration, check out *AWS Cloud Projects* by *Ivo Pinto* and *Pedro Santos*: `https://www.packtpub.com/en-us/product/aws-cloud-projects-9781835889282`.

I wish you all the best on your cloud journey!

Get This Book's PDF Version and Exclusive Extras

UNLOCK NOW

Scan the QR code (or go to `packtpub.com/unlock`). Search for this book by name, confirm the edition, and then follow the steps on the page.

Note: Keep your invoice handly. Purchase made directly from packt don't require one.

Stay Sharp in Cloud and DevOps – Join 44,000+ Subscribers of CloudPro

CloudPro is a weekly newsletter for cloud professionals who want to stay current on the fast-evolving world of cloud computing, DevOps, and infrastructure engineering.

Every issue delivers focused, high-signal content on topics like:

- AWS, GCP & multi-cloud architecture
- Containers, Kubernetes & orchestration
- Infrastructure as Code (IaC) with Terraform, Pulumi, etc.
- Platform engineering & automation workflows
- Observability, performance tuning, and reliability best practices

Whether you're a cloud engineer, SRE, DevOps practitioner, or platform lead, CloudPro helps you stay on top of what matters, without the noise.

Scan the QR code to join for free and get weekly insights straight to your inbox:

https://packt.link/cloudpro

18
Unlock Your Exclusive Benefits

Your copy of this book includes the following exclusive benefit:

- ☁ Next-gen Packt Reader
- 📄 DRM-free PDF/ePub downloads

Follow the guide below to unlock them. The process takes only a few minutes and needs to be completed once.

Unlock this Book's Free Benefits in 3 Easy Steps

Step 1

Keep your purchase invoice ready for *Step 3*. If you have a physical copy, scan it using your phone and save it as a PDF, JPG, or PNG.

For more help on finding your invoice, visit `https://www.packtpub.com/unlock-benefits/help`.

> **Note**
>
> If you bought this book directly from Packt, no invoice is required. After *Step 2*, you can access your exclusive content right away.

Step 2

Scan the QR code or go to packtpub.com/unlock.

On the page that opens (similar to *Figure 18.1* on desktop), search for this book by name and select the correct edition.

Figure 18.1: Packt unlock landing page on desktop

Step 3

After selecting your book, sign in to your Packt account or create one for free. Then upload your invoice (PDF, PNG, or JPG, up to 10 MB). Follow the on-screen instructions to finish the process.

Need help?

If you get stuck and need help, visit
`https://www.packtpub.com/unlock-benefits/help`
for a detailed FAQ on how to find your invoices and more. This QR code will take you to the help page.

> **Note**
>
> If you are still facing issues, reach out to `customercare@packt.com`.

Index

‹packt›

Subscribe to our online digital library for full access to over 7,000 books and videos, as well as industry leading tools to help you plan your personal development and advance your career. For more information, please visit our website.

Why subscribe?

- Spend less time learning and more time coding with practical eBooks and Videos from over 4,000 industry professionals

- Improve your learning with Skill Plans built especially for you

- Get a free eBook or video every month

- Fully searchable for easy access to vital information

- Copy and paste, print, and bookmark content

Did you know that Packt offers eBook versions of every book published, with PDF and ePub files available? You can upgrade to the eBook version at packtpub.com and as a print book customer, you are entitled to a discount on the eBook copy. Get in touch with us at customercare@packtpub.com for more details.

At www.packtpub.com, you can also read a collection of free technical articles, sign up for a range of free newsletters, and receive exclusive discounts and offers on Packt books and eBooks.

Other Books You May Enjoy

If you enjoyed this book, you may be interested in these other books by Packt:

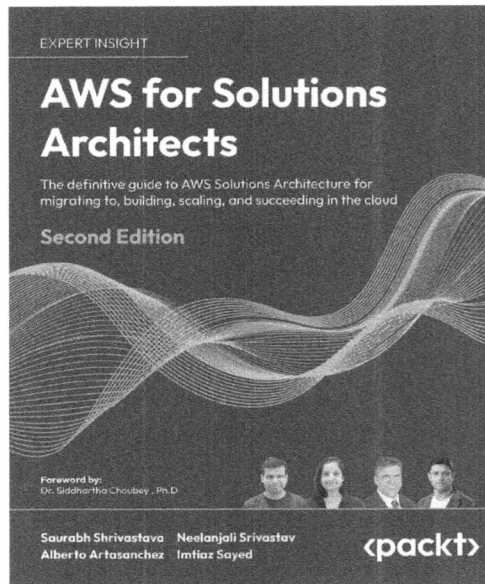

AWS for Solutions Architects – Second Edition

Saurabh Shrivastava, Neelanjali Srivastav, Alberto Artasanchez, Imtiaz Sayed

ISBN: 978-1-80323-895-1

- Optimize your Cloud Workload using the AWS Well-Architected Framework
- Learn methods to migrate your workload using the AWS Cloud Adoption Framework
- Apply cloud automation at various layers of application workload to increase efficiency
- Build a landing zone in AWS and hybrid cloud setups with deep networking techniques
- Select reference architectures for business scenarios, like data lakes, containers, and serverless apps
- Apply emerging technologies in your architecture, including AI/ML, IoT and blockchain

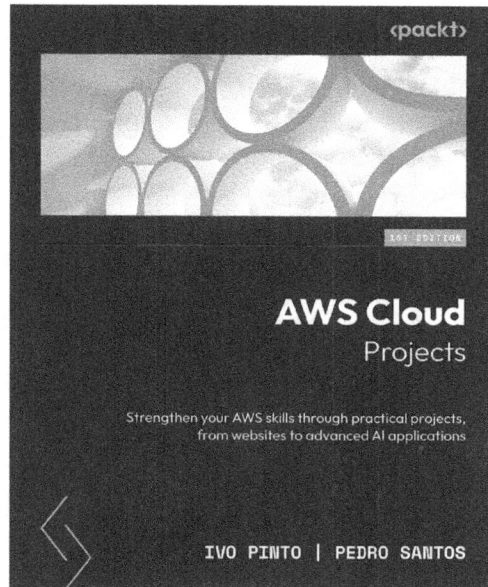

AWS Cloud Projects

Ivo Pinto, Pedro Santos

ISBN: 978-1-83588-928-2

- Develop a professional CV website while learning AWS fundamentals

- Build a recipe-sharing application using AWS's serverless toolkit

- Leverage AWS AI services to create a photo friendliness analyzer for professional profiles

- Implement a CI/CD pipeline to automate content translation across languages

- Develop an AI-powered Q&A chatbot using Amazon Lex and cutting-edge LLMs

- Build a business intelligence application to analyze website clickstream data and understand user behavior with AWS

Packt is searching for authors like you

If you're interested in becoming an author for Packt, please visit `authors.packtpub.com` and apply today. We have worked with thousands of developers and tech professionals, just like you, to help them share their insight with the global tech community. You can make a general application, apply for a specific hot topic that we are recruiting an author for, or submit your own idea.

Share Your Thoughts

Now you've finished *AWS for System Administrators, Second Edition* we'd love to hear your thoughts! Scan the QR code below to go straight to the Amazon review page for this book and share your feedback or leave a review on the site that you purchased it from.

`https://packt.link/r/1835463665`

Your review is important to us and the tech community and will help us make sure we're delivering excellent quality content.